THE
DYNAMICS
OF
LEGISLATION

Charles R. Wise

THE
DYNAMICS
OF
LEGISLATION

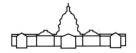

*Leadership and Policy Change
in the Congressional Process*

KF
4945
.W57
1991
West

Jossey-Bass Publishers

San Francisco • Oxford • 1991

THE DYNAMICS OF LEGISLATION
Leadership and Policy Change in the Congressional Process
by Charles R. Wise

Copyright © 1991 by: Jossey-Bass Inc., Publishers
350 Sansome Street
San Francisco, California 94104
&
Jossey-Bass Limited
Headington Hill Hall
Oxford OX3 0BW

Library of Congress Cataloging-in-Publication Data

Wise, Charles R.
 The dynamics of legislation : leadership and policy change in the
congressional process / Charles R. Wise.
  p. cm. — (The Jossey-Bass public administration series)
 Includes bibliographical references and index.
 ISBN 1-55542-335-3
 1. Legislation—United States. 2. Criminal law—United States.
3. United States. Congress. I. Title. II. Series.
 KF4945.W57 1991
 328.73'0778—dc20   90-23576
                                                              CIP

Manufactured in the United States of America

The paper in this book meets the guidelines for
permanence and durability of the Committee on
Production Guidelines for Book Longevity of
the Council on Library Resources.

JACKET DESIGN BY VICTOR ICHIOKA

FIRST EDITION

Code 9138

The Jossey-Bass
Public Administration Series

Contents

Preface

On June 19, 1986, Len Bias, a former University of Maryland basketball All-American, appeared at a press conference following his selection as the first-round draft choice of the world champion Boston Celtics. Two days later, he was found dead in a University of Maryland dormitory room. The autopsy revealed that he had died of an overdose of cocaine. This event and the resulting media coverage symbolized the drug crisis for large segments of the American public. Six months later, Ronald Reagan signed H.R. 5484, the Anti-Drug Abuse Act of 1986, and ever since, Congress has passed one crime bill after another to deal with the crisis.

This incident raises the issue of whether major legislative policy change occurs in America only in response to perceived crisis; that is, do freak galvanizing events followed by frantic legislative activity result in occasional legislative achievements?

Numerous commentators have argued that the answer is yes: Congress lags behind and responds only to a crisis, and the fundamental process of policy-making is neglected. Others have pointed to a tendency for Congressional representatives to concentrate on narrow bills of constituency interest that deliver federal largesse to their districts but result in piecemeal and unresponsive national policies. Many have expressed doubt in recent years that it is possible to enact large-scale public interest legislation or, for that matter, to get much through Congress at all. There is concern that the legislative system has been hamstrung by partisan division, the rise of narrow interest groups, and the decline of leadership influence. As a result, some have argued that the normal state of Congress is deadlock, with an occasional perceived crisis liberating some bill.

The purpose of *The Dynamics of Legislation* is to address the question of whether it is possible to pass large-scale public interest legislation through the Congress of the United States, and, if so, how such passage is achieved.

The position taken and developed is that it is possible — but that it requires both an understanding of the dynamics of the legislative process and skillful policy leadership by various participants. This book covers basic issues and processes of legislative policy-making and discusses the roles that the participants — legislators, executive branch officials, courts, interest group supporters, the media, and citizens — play in the process. It also examines the barriers to passing legislation and the factors that can help overcome them.

The book's approach is to focus first on the issues and elements of legislative policy-making and then to examine how the dynamics of legislation work in action. The vehicle for this examination is a discussion of attempts to pass bills that seek to reform federal criminal laws. The focus is not on facets of Congress as an institution per se. The research on particular aspects of Congress as an institution is vast and no attempt to replicate it here is intended. Instead, the aim is to explain how the strategies and actions of legislative participants, operating within the governmental and political context, interact to produce legislative outcomes. This perspective was taken because by examining the dynamics of the legislative process one can develop an understanding of how policies are made and of the possibilities for passing large-scale public interest legislation. As such, there is no expectation that this treatment will constitute the definitive statement on the dynamics of legislation in Congress. It may be argued that each policy area, indeed each bill, confronts its own set of legislative dynamics. Nonetheless, it is useful to examine both the parameters of legislative dynamics and how they operate, even within the context of one policy area, in order to understand more fully the interactive manner in which the consideration of legislation occurs. Legislating is not so much a mechanistic process that occurs within a defined structure as it is a political and social dynamic within a particular governmental context — a context that itself is altered in response to changes in the wider political and social milieu.

Audience

A variety of people will benefit from a greater understanding of the dynamics of legislation. Those who are concerned about the vitality of the system and who evaluate reform proposals need to consider the problems and the proposed remedies within the context of how Congress operates. A wide range of people beyond representatives and senators are actually engaged in the legislative process. In the executive branch, not only legislative liaison officers, but line executives, managers, and all of their staffs are heavily engaged. In addition, many managers and professional staff from the private sector are involved with issues management. Attorneys and other professionals who work with the law can benefit from understanding the context of legal history. Finally, citizens who want their government to change its policies or its processes can acquire a greater understanding of the factors in the legislative process that affect policy change.

Overview of the Contents

Chapter One covers both popular and professional charges that Congress can no longer work, especially in an era of divided government. It analyzes these arguments and presents counter arguments for why Congress can pass policies in the public interest. The chapter then presents a perspective for understanding and assessing the legislative process.

Chapter Two provides an overview of how Congress has changed in the last two decades and what those changes mean for the possibilities of enacting large-scale policy. The formal leadership, committees and subcommittees, norms, and staff of Congress are analyzed, as well as the media, interest groups, the President, the Cabinet, and elections.

Chapter Three covers how public opinion influences leaders in government and how it can initiate policy debate and action. The chapter discusses how public dissatisfaction with the level of crime in the 1960s was translated into an electoral issue and then into the appointment of a commission to reform federal criminal laws.

Chapter Four discusses the dynamics of how issues become transformed into bills that can receive serious consideration in Congress. It illustrates the process by relating how the proposal to overhaul federal criminal law was placed on the Senate agenda.

Chapter Five discusses factors in the legislative process that produce conflict and how forces opposed to certain legislation mobilize conflict to block it. The chapter illustrates the dynamics of conflict by discussing how opponents of a major federal criminal law reform bill maneuvered to stall it.

Chapter Six discusses the necessity for building a consensus to support a bill and the strategies and tactics a bill's supporters use in trying to achieve a consensus. It illustrates the process by discussing how proponents of a major federal criminal law reform bill accommodated change in an attempt to build a winning coalition.

Chapter Seven discusses the effects of political change, such as major electoral shifts that result in large turnovers of elected officials. It demonstrates how new issues can buffet the processing of legislation that has been under development for some time. The chapter illustrates these dynamics by discussing how both the election of Ronald Reagan and the Republicans gaining control of the Senate were followed by a shift of issue emphasis in Congress that necessitated a shift in direction for criminal law reformers.

Chapter Eight discusses strategies and tactics that legislative proponents use to gather and coordinate the support of allies behind a single legislative vehicle sufficient to sustain movement. It illustrates the process by describing how a leadership group was constructed for a major federal crime bill and how they put together their coalition.

Chapter Nine discusses how the decision is made to use partisan pressure in support of a bill and how a bill's supporters mobilize legislative leaders and the President to put the heat of public opinion on opponents. The potential impact of elections is analyzed as well. This process is illustrated by relating the efforts of proponents of the Comprehensive Crime Control Act.

Chapter Ten describes how a bill gets to the floor under difficult circumstances. Gaining the opportunity for final consideration on the floor of a house of Congress means looking for a path through the jungle of legislation and procedure that crowd the legislative calendar, especially at the end of a session. The chapter discusses the barriers proponents of a single bill face and what strategies they use to grab an opportunity for floor consideration when it presents itself. The situation is illustrated by relating how proponents of the Comprehensive Crime Control Act successfully achieved floor consideration and final passage.

Chapter Eleven discusses the process whereby executive branch leaders and administrators implement and consolidate newly won legislative gains. It also describes how a major policy breakthrough leads to future legislative successes by discussing how other major criminal law bills were passed in the 1980s.

The conclusion recaps the arguments for and against Congress in light of what has been revealed by the preceding chapters. It also relates how other legislative successes reveal a similar dynamic, which suggests that the system works, if not reliably and dependably.

With respect to the legislation explored, readers should understand that the federal criminal reform bills are the vehicle, not the object, of the study. This book does not attempt an exhaustive treatment of the reform of federal criminal laws. The particulars of the proposals and the issues involved in those proposals are truly encyclopedic. A thorough treatment of all the extremely complex and significant issues involved in criminal law reform attempts would replay the hundreds of meetings and reargue the thousands of debates within Congress, the executive branch, and the judicial branch. It would be pretentious even to claim that the essence of all these debates has been captured here. Instead, I selected the provisions and issues that best illustrate the legislative dynamics of the federal government as it has evolved to this point. Various people privy to meetings and events I could not cover or of which I was unaware will no doubt be able to discern mistakes on my part or point to issues and events that they feel deserved treatment. Some material has been omitted in order to simplify the reporting of years of legislative developments and make the narrative less unwieldy.

Acknowledgments

I am indebted to many people in and out of government who have supplied documents, information, suggestions, insights, leads, and contacts for this volume. So many have been helpful that I can mention only a few. While none is responsible for the contents, I wish to express my appreciation to Roger Adams, Philip Brady, G. Robert Blakey, Cary Copeland, Thomas Donally, Donna Enos, Kenneth Feinberg, Ronald L. Gainer, Mark Gittenstein, Scott Green, Hayden Gregory, Jeffrey Harris, Kevin Holzclaw, Vinton D. Lide, Robert McConnell, Lillian McEwen, Patrick McGuigan, Paul McNulty, John F. Nash, Jr., Ed O'Connell, Deborah K. Owen, Roger Pauley, William R. Pitts, Jr., Randall R. Rader, James Range, Jay Stephens, and Kathy Zebrowski. Special thanks and appreciation must go to Paul Summit, whom everyone I talked to regards as the consummate professional. His materials and guidance were indispensable. Thanks also to anonymous reviewers and to editor Alan Shrader at Jossey-Bass, who supplied helpful comments on an earlier version of this manuscript.

Bloomington, Indiana   Charles R. Wise
January 1991

The Author

Charles R. Wise is associate professor of public affairs at Indiana University, Bloomington. He received his B.A. degree (1967) from Arizona State University in political science and his M.A. (1970) and Ph.D. (1972) degrees from Indiana University in political science.

Wise's research has focused on legislative process, public law, and policy analysis. From 1977 to 1983 he was managing editor of the *Public Administration Review.* In 1985 he received the William E. Mosher award for the best scholarly article published in the *Public Administration Review.* Wise's books include *Clients Evaluate Authority: The View from the Other Side* (1976) and (with H. G. Frederickson) *Public Administration and Public Policy* (1977).

Wise served with the Office of Legislative and Intergovernmental Affairs, United States Department of Justice, from 1982 to 1984. He is the current chairman of the Section on Public Law of the American Society for Public Administration.

THE
DYNAMICS
OF
LEGISLATION

• 1 •

Can Congress Legislate to Meet Today's Challenges?

The United States Congress does many things. It oversees the executive branch and investigates wrongdoing, it calls attention to new public problems, it debates public issues and vents the public spleen over topics of the day, and its members act as problem solvers and go-betweens for constituents who are having difficulties with the government bureaucracy. However many things Congress does, there is broad general agreement that the chief congressional function is lawmaking, and that Congress should carry out that function so that laws are responsive to the views and needs of a majority and should do so in a way that allows the full range of significant views to be heard (Sinclair, 1990).

In recent years, serious doubt has been expressed that Congress has been fulfilling its central function to meet public needs, and that it will meet the challenges of a rapidly changing world. As the 101st Congress was about to convene, *Congressional Quarterly* echoed these misgivings: "Congress enters the 1990s when it returns Jan. 23, but whether this passage signifies a new legislative era will hinge on whether members can snap the deadlocks that stalled action on major problems in the 1980s. . . . Such stalemates are the product of a glacial policy-

1

making process that surely will be tested in what seems like the dawn of a new epoch in world affairs. . . . But it is not clear whether Congress' crisis management style is up to the challenges posed by the breathtaking changes in Eastern Europe, the Soviet Union and Panama" (Hook, Jan. 6, 1990, p. 9).

An oft-heard charge today is that Congress is incapable of meeting the challenges facing the nation. A cover story in *Business Week* entitled "Congress: It Doesn't Work. Let's Fix It" levies a typical indictment: "The U.S. Congress now works about as well — and as cleanly — as a Polish steel mill. It huffs and puffs, and it belches fire. But Congress produces very little of tangible value. . . . This once proud institution is paralyzed by cynicism and a corrupting quest for campaign dollars. Partisan sniping and issue ducking are so pervasive that basic congressional functions — such as approving the budget and appropriating funds — have become too much to manage. . . . Political action committees (PACs) representing powerful special interests increasingly dominate congressional elections, driving members into a frenzied money chase that leaves little time for problem solving" (April 16, 1990, p. 55).

The American public, too, in recent years seems to share a low opinion of Congress. Gallup polls between 1973 and 1985 asked citizens to indicate on a list of American institutions how much confidence they had in each. The percentage that replied "a great deal" or "quite a lot" for Congress varied between a high of 42 percent in 1973 to a low of 28 percent in 1983, ending with 39 percent in 1985. In 1985 Congress was fourth out of six, trailing the Church (66 percent), the Supreme Court (56 percent), and the public schools (48 percent) (Lipset and Schneider, 1987, p. 57). Harris and NORC surveys asked about confidence in leaders of ten institutions. An analysis of responses from 1966 to 1981 showed that the average expressing a "great deal of confidence" varied from medicine (50.3 percent) to organized labor (15.3 percent). Congressional leaders occupied the next-to-last position (18.8 percent), just behind the executive branch (20.5 percent) (p. 69).

This despondency about the capacity of Congress continues during a remarkable period in history. Given the developments in Eastern Europe, the Soviet Union, and Latin America, at perhaps no other time have so many countries been engaged in establishing or rejuvenating representative legislative institutions. However, historian James McGregor Burns advises the leaders of these countries to look elsewhere for political models. In arguing that we face the need to make the same kinds of changes that Eastern European leaders do, Burns (1990) charges: "Our system of checks and balances, with the resulting fragmentation of power, frustrates leadership, saps efficiency, and erodes responsibility."

Lloyd Cutler (1987), counsel to former President Carter, lays the problem of recent administrations and congresses in deadlocking over domestic and foreign policy on divided government—one party controlling the presidency, and the other Congress. He observes that divided government is a recent phenomenon, from Truman through Reagan (now Bush) and traces its origins to well-meaning reforms like the primary system, which has boosted the role of media campaigns and decreased the value of political parties. Cutler quotes Woodrow Wilson as declaring that divided government is arrested government that is not functioning, one whose very energies are stayed and postponed.

And yet, at times even divided government seems to enact legislation hurriedly. In the 1980s many leaders in local communities, law enforcement, and agencies were increasingly alarmed about the growing use of cocaine. Yet to many, it did not seem to be much of a priority in Congress. However, on June 19, 1986, Len Bias, a University of Maryland basketball star who had been drafted by the Boston Celtics, was found dead from an overdose of cocaine. This event was widely reported in the media and caught widespread public attention. Within days, new antidrug bills were introduced in Congress, and by October, Congress had enacted a large Anti-Drug Act. Some thought Congress had acted hastily.

An observer might ask, Can this be the same institution at work? On the one hand, Congress drags out legislation interminably on many critical policy issues. On the other hand, one basketball player dies, and a major crime bill is drafted and sails through Congress in a matter of weeks.

The answer is that it is, of course, the same institution, but to understand it, one needs to understand the dynamics by which it operates. This is more than the formal rules and processes, and more than conditions such as divided government, although these are important, too. This volume seeks to discuss those dynamics and the barriers and factors that influence them to produce significant legislation—large-scale legislation—that addresses the demands of the public. More will be said about these terms below.

The perspective here is that a greater understanding of the dynamics of the legislative process as it operates in the United States Congress can be achieved by examining it in action—in the course of developing and processing an actual large-scale legislative package in a significant area of public policy. The public policy area chosen for this examination is criminal law— specifically, the reform of federal criminal law. Federal crime legislation has proceeded at a time of both increasing crime on a national scale and increasingly public concern over it. This book seeks to show how Congress has responded to these phenomena as a method of describing the dynamics of the legislative process. It is hoped, thereby, that the reader will have a more detailed and informed basis for judging whether the congressional legislative process is adequate to the task of addressing public demands.

Adequacy of the Legislative Process — A Continuing Question

Actually, doubt about the viability of the structure of representative government in the United States has existed for some time. During the deliberations over the drafting of the Constitution of the United States, the participants in the process observed a pact of secrecy until the document was finished and the agreement over the governmental structure was sealed. Numerous citizens in Philadelphia were bursting with curiosity as to what the assembled representatives were doing. Upon emerging from the final deliberations, Benjamin Franklin was approached by one such citizen, who asked, "Well, Mr. Franklin, what kind of government have you given us?," to which Franklin replied, "A republic, if you can keep it."

Thus, even at the founding of our structure of government, those most intimately involved with the nature and workings of government were not completely sure that the structure to which they had agreed would be up to the challenges facing the nation. This very uncertainty has remained with us throughout the course of the history of the United States. It is built into the fabric of our political culture and sets America quite apart from other political cultures. The British routinely proclaim, "There will always be an England." The Americans refer to the United States as the "Grand Experiment."

This is not to postulate that the United States is in a perpetual state of hand-wringing over its governmental processes. The significance of the concern by those in government, in academia, and among the citizenry ebbs and flows with events. The expansion of the country beyond the original thirteen states, the Civil War, the Industrial Revolution, the introduction of America as a world power, the urban riots and the student protests of the sixties, and now the drug epidemic and the technological and international transformation of the U.S. economy have all resulted in periods of doubt and sharp questioning. The concern has been whether popular government in general, and the constitutional structure agreed to at the end of the eighteenth century in particular, would prove equal to the latest challenge, or whether, like the German Weimar Republic or the French First through Fifth republics, would simply collapse. Alexis de Tocqueville, in the course of analyzing American government, observed, "The history of the world affords no instance of a great power retaining the form of republican government for a long series of years" (Heffner, 1956, p. 82). The issue of the viability of representative government has taken on new urgency with the collapse of Communist dictatorships in Eastern European countries and the initiation of efforts by their populations to introduce representative legislatures. The ability of these legislatures to cope with large-scale policy issues will be tested rapidly with immense consequences for their societies.

Short of worrying about collapse in the United States (a seemingly remote possibility), numerous observers have wondered if the United States is doing as well as it should. At the close of World War II, Thomas Finletter (1945) asked in his book, *Can Representative Government Do the Job?*, "Will the old methods of government, which were designed for the less ambitious policies of the nineteenth century, be able to carry out these new responsibilities?" (p. 2). Finletter, like many others, was concerned: "For if the representative form is unable to achieve what the people want, it may be repudiated and some other kind of government be substituted for it. And if representative government does fall, it will pull down with it the political freedoms" (p. 3). His fundamental concern was no doubt influenced by observing the collapse of democratic governments in Europe.

Others, while less worried about imminent collapse, have nonetheless concluded that the policies produced by the national government are unresponsive to the public's needs. James Sundquist (1986), in reviewing the legislative difficulties experienced in the passage of social security, unemployment compensation, Medicare, and civil rights laws, argues that if these legislative measures are deemed necessary and useful now, they would have been useful earlier, "and the delays — the laggardness — that are a consequence of America's constitutional structure have been the nation's loss" (p. 6).

There are, then, really two predominant concerns that observers have expressed over time about the structure and functioning of American government: whether it preserves popular control and its essential freedoms, and whether it produces public policies that are responsive to public needs. The first concern has been a major preoccupation of political science since its inception. It is the central focus of Charles S. Hyneman's *Popular Government in America,* in which he defines popular government as "a political system in which the people have effective means for expressing expectations and preferences and for inducing compliance with their demands" (1968, p. 4). As Hyneman points out, the answer to the question is embedded in a whole host of factors among which the structure and functioning of formal government is only one, let alone the legislative process subset. So, why focus on the legislative process? Hyneman contends: "A representative assembly is the principal institution in the decisional apparatus of any democratic government. There appears to be no exception to this rule in countries with a large population. In all such countries, where government has proved responsive to demands arising from all parts of the population, the basic policies of the government are made in a representative assembly" (p. 139).

While one cannot settle the issue conclusively by examining the legislative process, understanding that process plays a central role in forming a judgment concerning whether popular control sufficiently exists. I am aware of no democratic theorist who believes that the appointed officials and civil servants operating through the administrative process will be able to make up for a fundamentally flawed representative assembly.

Also, even so avowed a proponent of presidential power as Richard Neustadt affirms that the essential power of the president is the power to persuade, particularly because the structure of our government limits the president's power to command. Neustadt elucidates that the power to persuade is the power to bargain, and the chief parties with whom the president is bargaining are members of Congress. The president cannot move without Congress and vice versa. "Their formal powers are so intertwined that neither will accomplish very much, for very long without the acquiescence of the other" (Neustadt, 1980, p. 29). Likewise, Hargrove and Nelson's examination (1984) of presidents from Wilson to Reagan led them to conclude: "In sum all presidents some of the time find themselves . . . needing programmatic support from Congress but lacking the large majority there that would make such support relatively easy to come by" (p. 215). Thus, the powers of the president are intertwined with, not independent of, those of Congress.

Following Hyneman, the position taken here is that the question of whether the nature of the legislative process functions adequately to preserve popular control and to be judged democratic cannot be answered yes or no. The issue is rather, Does the process possess enough of the qualities of popular control to suit one's notions of responsiveness and democracy? In order to address this issue, it is necessary to examine the nature of public problems, the demands of the public with respect to those problems, the policies that are proposed to respond to those demands, and how the legislative process treats those policies. This also ultimately involves an evaluation of the quality of public policy produced. How can one appraise that? Kelman (1987) suggests two criteria: (1) a significant level of public spirit in the system, and (2) a reasonable ability to create the organizational capacity necessary to produce final government actions that resemble earlier political choices. The first leaves room for self-interested partisans advocating their positions, but it also postulates a marketplace of ideas in which there is deliberation and learning by the participants. The second criterion refers to the capacity of the system to produce policy that validates basic choices citizens believe they have made through the political process. This latter is related to the issue of whether the process is representative enough to maintain popular control of the political system.

As with the issue of popular control, observers with divergent perspectives will have to judge the results in various policy areas in order to discern whether good public policy is produced. However, the position here is that judgments are best made by viewing the dynamics of the legislative process as it produces large-scale public policy change. The challenge for the legislative process today is to deal with the complex national and international challenges facing the country.

Large-Scale Public Interest Policy-Making

Congress is a highly complex and decentralized set of shifting alliances and forums that considers a myriad of policies at any given time. The decentralized nature of the legislative process fosters a preference by congressional members to legislate in the area in which their committee, and preferably their subcommittee, has control. This leads to an emphasis on smaller individual bills and thus incremental and more easily controlled changes for which representatives have greater confidence of obtaining agreement from their colleagues.

Thus, the normal order of things does not presumably encourage large-scale policy change. Political scientists have long recognized the effects of interest group bargaining in leading to incremental changes in existing policies. Schulman's summary (1980) of a major trend in political science describes policy as the outcome of pluralist bargaining processes producing many small disaggregated policies: "Basically a process of bargaining and adjustment, it is characterized by fluid objectives supported by shifting political coalitions. Public policy goods are apportioned piecemeal — in line with prevailing distributions of power or publicized need. Conventional public policy is transacted in this manner largely because conventional policy objectives are, in essence, highly *divisible* — that is, they may be easily disaggregated *while still maintaining coherent form*. Divisible outputs, in other words, may be readily enlarged or contracted, differentially apportioned among specialized constituencies" (p. 7). Thus, grant programs, tariffs, and even regulatory policies can be divided in such a way that there is something in each for the contending and cooperating parties active in the particular policy arena. The result is "the piecemeal apportionment of public goods in line with the prevailing distribution of organized power" (Schulman, 1980, p. 9).

Such policy-making facilitates, and in turn is facilitated by, decision making focused at the margins of public policy in line with the shifting coalition of interests. Lindblom (1979) argues that this mode is actually preferable as a way of achieving policy change because, in not provoking significant power groups, change is more likely to proceed, whereas large changes will provoke these groups and result in deadlock. From this perspective, legislators, bureaucrats, and interest groups are engaged in a continuous process of bargaining, and legislative enactments merely confirm the latest bargain struck.

Comprehensive policy goals in such a system are irrelevant. Putting together the winning coalition of parties that allows them to achieve their individual goals is the task and results in successful legislation.

Critics have charged that a mere accumulation of incremental changes is not expected to yield the equivalent of a contextual or fundamental decision, because the incremental model provides no guidelines for the accumulation. Therefore, it is likely to be random or scattered (Etzioni, 1986; Starkie, 1984). They also charge that the incremental approach — and therefore its disciples, the incrementalists — favors conserving the status quo because it is blind to opportunities for radical departures or major reforms (Dror, 1969).

Incremental policy-making through pluralistic bargaining processes has been shown to work well for those aspects of policy that can be aggregated or disaggregated in various combinations, such as money for water projects or additional personnel for regional installations, at least from the perspective of the beneficiaries. It describes fairly accurately policy-making for significant sectors of U.S. policy. The recognition of iron triangles or subgovernments, described below, in which different tripartite coalitions of committee congressmen, bureaucrats, and interest group leaders (for example, House Public Works Committee–Army Corps of Engineers–inland water industry) bargain with each other and determine policy outcomes, has often been relied upon to describe how many policies have been made.

There are two major difficulties with this mode of policy-making — one normative and one analytical. Both have implications for those trying to decide whether or not to try to achieve large-scale policy change through the legislative process.

The normative issue focuses on whether the public interest is well served or not. One position in this regard is simply that there is no overarching public interest within these various policy areas contending in the legislative arena. The public interest is simply the accumulation of the various individual interests. People holding this view argue that self-interest drives all participants in the policy process, including congressional representatives, who, in pursuing their interest in reelection, represent the predominant self-interests of the proximate players — the interest groups — that help them. Critics observe that this leaves out policy integration. They complain that logrolling leaves large gaps that hinder the achievement of national objectives. For example, pluralist bargaining among various transportation interests leads to heavy subsidies for trucking and barge interests that are not available to railroads, with the result that we have a declining railroad system and a transportation system that is poorly integrated across modes. Critics also offer that incrementalism leads participants to shorten their perspectives, which squeezes out creativity and thus tends to reinforce the status quo (Adams, 1979).

Others have criticized incrementalism both as a method of policy-making and as a mode of analysis for understanding policy on grounds that it works in both arenas only for a certain class of policies. That is, incremental policy-making works best for those policies that can be more easily disaggregated and for which shares can be allocated to participants; for example, water projects or agricultural subsidies. Such a requirement of divisibility facilitates short-term decision making directed toward the allocation of "shares" at the margins to participants. Nevertheless, as Schulman (1980) argues: "Caught up in divisibility and incremental outlooks, we have gained little insight into the politics surrounding the pursuit of objectives of a very different order. We have ignored the significance of large-scale phenomena" (pp. 17–18).

The distinction between large-scale public interest policy and small-scale special-interest policy is not a clear one. They undeniably blend into each other. The space program is an example of a large-scale policy directed toward public interest objectives of scientific advancement and national prestige. Nonetheless, it certainly has its distributive benefits, as President Johnson clearly understood when he located the Manned Space Flight Control Center in Houston rather than at the launching site in Florida.

Some distinguishing characteristics of large-scale policies are:

- indivisibility
- impact on large numbers of citizens
- directed toward alleviation of major social problems, the development of new technologies, or the attainment of collectivized aspirations
- intense and diverse ramifications throughout the political system

Indivisibility refers to the "wholeness" of the outputs or the resources required for their pursuit. It is the dimension that is at the heart of the "publicness" of policies. Ostrom and Ostrom (1977) define public goods as those that are jointly used and infeasible to exclude from anyone deriving their benefits.

The other dimensions are not discrete but are rather continuous criteria. That is, for example, it is possible to describe policies as affecting smaller or larger numbers of citizens (from agricultural subsidies for rice growers to social security); as being directed toward social problems affecting fewer or more segments of society (from aid to the maritime industry to the National Labor Act); and as having light to intense ramifications throughout the political system (from allocations within the National Endowment for the Humanities to the Civil Rights Act of 1964).

The idea is, the further policies are arrayed along the continuation of indivisibility, impact on citizens, major social significance, and ramifications throughout the political system, the less useful are incremental modes of policy-making in achieving such policies. Maass (1983), as a proponent of the public interest basis of legislation, for example, rejects partisan mutual adjustment for policy-making at the national level as being both far from realistic and not satisfying the requirements of democratic government. He points to issues such as ratification of the Panama Canal treaties, which did not involve in any important way the aggregation and reconciliation of particular interests. Other such issues are the use of governmental funds to finance abortions, and the ethics and standards of conduct of government officials. From this perspective, large-scale public interest policy change *ought to be* possible through the legislative process. The question then becomes, How likely is it actually to be achieved?

There is not one readily identifiable factor that points to the answer. Overall, we know that the chances of any given bill of any kind are against passage. For example, in the 99th Congress, (1985–86) 2,954 bills and resolutions were introduced in the Senate and 5,743 in the House. This includes innocuous resolutions celebrating National Rose Week. Even so, a total of 664 became law — 11.1 percent of those introduced in the House and 22.5 percent in the Senate. Over time, the chances of a bill's being passed have declined. In the 80th Congress (1947–48), the ratio of bills passed to bills introduced in the House was .228; in the 100th (1987–88), it was .169. The comparable ratio for the Senate was in the 80th, .524, and in the 100th, .301 (Ornstein, Mann, and Malbin, 1990).

But what are the chances of passing a large-scale policy change? Surely, they are less than for passage of a simple modification of some program. But how much less? There is not a precise way to determine this. However, it should be pointed out that several serious observers of the governmental process have questioned whether significant large-scale policy change is achievable through the legislative process anymore. Several have leveled serious charges that what Congress and the president are doing is merely going through the motions, and that the process of legislating has been dispossessed of any significant meaning in terms of bringing about large-scale changes that the public really needs. The persistence of multibillion-dollar budget deficits, environmental problems, and widespread homelessness are cited as evidence that the legislative process is not responding.

Just one such charge is that the Congress has delegated so much power and authority to the administrative agencies that real policy determination is done in the administrative process, not in the legislative one (Woll, 1977). A broader charge, and one with a number of subelements, is that the institutional processes of our government have been so hamstrung that they are incapable of responding to the demands placed on them, and the legislative process has become so bogged down as a result that it is incapable of addressing major public priorities.

If this is the case, the response by people seriously interested in effecting real policy changes may well be to decide to avoid the legislative process and turn to other avenues — the courts or the executive branch. Alternatively, they may simply give up.

Is the Legislative System Broken?

At least one element of the argument of system breakdown traces the problem to the constitutional structure of our government and asserts that the assumptions on which our government is based have been superseded by changes in our society. The question posed is, Can a structure that was created two hundred years ago following a colonial revolution meet the needs of a far different people and nation today?

A chief target of criticism is the separation of powers. Critics argue that concerns over preventing tyranny in the infantile republic of 1787 may then have properly led to a dispersal of power regardless of costs in efficiency and decisiveness. However, the growth over two centuries in the responsibilities of government in an interdependent world, it is argued, demands harmony and decisiveness in governmental decision making (Dillon, 1985). The conclusion reached is that the separation of powers does not provide a framework to facilitate such decision making but, together with some other features and developments, inhibits significant needed policy change. As Sundquist (1981) puts it, "Even more important, the national interest can be gravely disserved by the stalemates that occur while the branches are locked in contest" (p. 462).

Cutler (1985) argues that the natural inclination of Congress and the president to disagree has been exacerbated in modern times by the tendency for the presidency and at least one house of the Congress to be in the hands of different parties. He points out that in the twenty Congresses elected after 1945, party government (one party controlling both) has prevailed during only two. He asserts that "party government does not assure creative and effective government, but divided government comes close to assuring stagnant and ineffective government" (p. 101). Olezsek (1989) states that divided government has contributed to heightened partisanship, and the trend toward confrontation politics (even partisan civil war) is particularly evident in the House, where the rules emphasize majority rule and where Republicans have been in the minority for nearly four decades. He observes that Republicans are bitter at what they perceive as majority party abuses, such as distorted committee memberships and staffing ratios, partisan scheduling of measures, "gag" rules that restrict floor amendments, and proxy voting in committees. With the presidency in the hands of the

Republicans in recent years and Congress in the hands of the Democrats, some sense a new partisan overlay in the constitutional separation of powers. Republicans in the minority in Congress have come to support an expansion of presidential power, and the Democrats have come to support expansion of congressional power (Olezsek, 1989). Sundquist (1988–89) argues that an increasingly rigid partisanship seems to be characterizing the relationship between Congress and the presidency.

Sundquist, following his review of the political leadership and policy integration capabilities of Congress, is also pessimistic that the current system can produce meaningful policies. He concludes that: the capacity to produce a comprehensive and integrated program remains missing in Congress; the independent work of the committees and subcommittees cannot be integrated without instrumentalities for that purpose; and the conceptual and practical obstacles to creating such instrumentalities appear insuperable (Sundquist, 1981). In a later work, Sundquist (1986) opines that the effect of all this is deleterious for the timely passage of important policies and damaging to the country. Mezey (1989a) concurs and argues that the system cannot deliver coherent and effective public policy and is likely to produce stalemate — "meaning that neither the executive nor the Congress is capable of acting on its own and each is capable of stopping the other from acting" (p. 125).

Thus, the root of the inability of the process to produce significant policies, according to several observers, lies in the composition of American government itself. James MacGregor Burns in his classic, *The Deadlock of Democracy,* outlines the consequences of these defects he considers paramount:

1.   We have been captured by that model, which requires us to await a wide consensus before acting, while we have neglected, except furtively and sporadically, the Jeffersonian strategy of strong leadership, majority rule, party responsibility, and competitive elections.
2.   Our four-party system requires coalition government, which is notoriously unable to generate strong and steady political power.

3. Hence, as a nation we have lost control of our politics.
4. We lack popular control of the policy-making process.
5. Our government lacks unity and teamwork or, when it exists, it is often the integration of drift.
6. We oscillate fecklessly between deadlock and rush of action.
7. We can choose bold and creative leaders without giving them the means to make their leadership effective.
8. We cannot define our national purpose and mobilize our strength to move vigorously against the problems that beset us at home and abroad, or to exploit the enormous possibilities of urban man and world man in the last third of the twentieth century [Burns, 1963, pp. 323–325].

A statement for the Committee on the Constitutional System (1985), prepared by a group headed by James Sundquist, embraces Burns's viewpoint: "That is the dilemma of the American Constitutional System. The checks and balances inspired by the eighteenth century have led repeatedly, in the twentieth century, to governmental stalemate and deadlock, to indecision and inaction in the face of urgent problems. For the most part, rash and arbitrary actions have been deterred. But this benefit has been gained at a growing cost. Except in times of great crisis, the government is now unable to act in a timely manner — or at all" (p. 69). Therefore, according to this view, prospective initiators of large-scale policy change would be well advised either to lower their sights and go after smaller increments, or to await basic structural change.

The Legislative System Works —
Public Interest Policy Is Possible

There are other observers who do not believe either that the legislative process is incapable of producing public interest policies or that policy-making is controlled by interest group and policymaker bargaining. Maass (1983) claims that models of policy-making based on interest group theory are insufficient or misleading and give insufficient emphasis to leadership or accountability in government. He asserts that instead of conducting a political process that simply aggregates and reconciles narrow group or individual interests, government conducts a process of deliberation and discussion that results in decisions based on broader community interests, and it designs and implements programs in accordance with these decisions. Kelman (1987) makes the related argument that public spiritedness, and thus effective policy-making, does live in Congress. He cites numerous features of Congress that promote public spirit:

1. Many voters do not necessarily prefer that their representatives simply "vote the district" but expect them to exercise their own best judgment.
2. The growth of congressional staff has increased the presence of people who are interested in issues and are making an impact on policy.
3. Committee members focusing on a narrow view do not enjoy the unconditional deference of the body as a whole but must pay attention to whether their proposals are acceptable to a wider range of congressional concerns.
4. Competing pressures of constituents and lobbyists can create room for members to exercise independent judgment.
5. Concern about the regard of their congressional colleagues encourages members to become well informed on issues and able to argue on the merits in order to gain respect.

Kelman (1987), like Maass, finds the narrow-interest explanation of policy-making wanting: "As a general rule, however, the more important a policy is, the less important is the role of self-interest in determining that policy. Self-interest does a great job explaining the location of a new federal building in Missoula. When all is said and done, it falls down with regard to the major policy upheavals of the past decades" (p. 250).

With respect to the claimed deleterious effects of divided government on the quality and timeliness of public policy, Olezsek (1989) observes for the recent period: "Yet for all the laments that some have about divided government, it produced a large number of policy successes. Significant, if not landmark, legislation passed in such areas as tax, health, welfare, immigra-

tion reform, trade, deficit reduction, and defense. . . . Other
post-World War II Presidents who faced Congresses controlled
by the opposition party — Truman, Eisenhower, and Nixon, for
example — also achieved major successes, such as the Marshall
Plan, civil rights legislation, and the normalization of relations
with China" (p. 32).

From these perspectives, large-scale policy-making is certainly possible within the dynamics of the legislative process.
It is, however, by no means certain or easy. There have been
a number of proposals to make policy-making easier, of course.
Pfiffner (1989), in reviewing proposals offered to reduce the perceived conflict in divided government — such as changing the
War Powers resolution, changing the recision process, and continuing the use of the informal legislative veto — concludes that
they would refine the checks and balances system "a bit," but
observes: "These proposals also recognize that there is no me-
chanical fix. There is no substitute for leadership, trust, and
comity. If the political will does not exist, automatic mechanisms or procedural reforms cannot force accommodation" (p. 24).
As former Secretary of State George Schultz put it: "We have
this very difficult task of having a separation of powers that
means we have to learn how to share power. Sharing power is
harder, and we need to work at it harder than we do. But that's
the only way" (Smith, 1988, p. 726). Is the system up to the
challenge of producing policies that fulfill the promise of representative government, or is the legislative process so cumber-
some that the actual enactment of an important large-scale policy
is a fluke?

Understanding and Assessing the Legislative Process

Which view is correct — the system is broken or the system
works? In order to address that question it is necessary to understand the major elements of the legislative process as well
as legislative dynamics. A complete answer would require the
analysis of the processing of hundreds of bills in diverse policy
areas through several sessions of Congress.

Politics being what it is, even following through a dozen major bills would involve hundreds of different actors, employing scores of strategies, using many different tactics and legislative maneuvers. Such an undertaking is beyond the scope of one study. Nonetheless, it is possible to identify from past research major elements to look for in the processing of legislation and then see how they interact in the processing of legislation in one large-scale public policy area. In this way, the major barriers to passing such large-scale legislation can be revealed and, in addition, the factors that influence its movement within the legislative process can be viewed as they confront such barriers. By examining in detail how such elements combine to determine the fate of particular bills, one can come to understand the dynamics of the legislative process.

The policy area that will be the subject of the examination here is criminal law legislation, as it has been considered by the United States Congress. Protecting citizens from harm, both foreign and domestic, has long been considered a basic function of government. While there may be an abundance of debate over the relative priorities of government, few would dispute that a government having laws that do not serve to produce a society in which citizens and their property are protected from criminal activity is failing in one of its fundamental purposes.

However, even though basic, the issues involved in criminal law are neither simple nor easily resolved in the legislative process. In perhaps no other area of public policy are so many diverse values at issue in determining what a government of laws is really to mean. In fact, criminal law is not an easily isolated area of public policy but one that is threaded through the very fabric of most areas of public policy.

When Congress decides that dumping hazardous waste in rivers, refusing to hire someone because of his or her race, or sniffing cocaine are illegal acts and subject to criminal penalties, it is not only rearranging the policy landscape in areas of environmental, employment, and public health policy but it is also rearranging the system of criminal laws for the nation. In addition, few other areas of public policy carry with them so many ramifications for society. Citizens want a system of criminal laws that is capable of protecting their persons and property but also of fulfilling other collective purposes, whether they are the preservation of pristine landscapes or habitable cities. At the same time, citizens want a system of criminal laws that preserves and even expands individual freedom. They want criminal laws that are fair, equitable, and just, without a full understanding of how these are to be realized in terms of any particular act. Finally, citizens want criminal laws that adjust to the times, to advances in technology and knowledge, and to changes in public demands and understanding.

Such desires are not easily met in an increasingly diverse and interdependent world where transportation and communication changes have produced capabilities for criminal activity on an international scale. Even though government is much bigger and is involved in more areas of individuals' lives than ever before, people have become increasingly restive about the persistent question of why they have to endure so much violent crime in a free society. This restiveness has brought escalating pressure on the federal government for a greater national response. Thus, criminal law reform as a policy area may be one of the most germane to examining how the legislative process addresses large-scale public policy issues.

Before turning to the area of federal criminal legislation in particular, it is first necessary to examine the major elements that make up the dynamics of the legislative process. A casual observer of the operation of Congress may see only the formal process — the actual meetings at which decisions are announced but not necessarily made — or a jumble of seemingly unrelated (and unproductive) activity. Given that in highly complex and interdependent institutions, everything is connected to everything else, it is fairly easy to become confused by trying to take it all in at once. Therefore, the approach here is first to identify some of the main barriers and factors that influence the dynamics of legislation, and then to examine their interactions within the context of actual legislating in the policy area of federal criminal law reform.

• 2 •

Policy Change and
the Legislative
Process

The previous chapter discussed a possible role for large-scale public policy legislation. The perspective was that there are instances where the public needs a more comprehensive statement or redirection of policy, and not merely an incremental change in policy. From time to time, proponents of such change will offer a "comprehensive bill." At that point, participants in the policy process will consider the very legitimate question, What are the chances of passing it through the legislative process?

Policy Change and the Legislative Process

Large-scale policy change through the legislative process is not achieved readily. Out of the thousands of bills Congress considers each session, many have negligible effects on the country and others bring noticeable but still incremental change. As Wright, Rieselbach, and Dodd (1986) observe: "Major policy change, departures that chart genuinely new directions of governmental action in new areas, is rare" (p. vii). The fact is that the opponents of policy change are in a better position to block and thus protect the status quo than are the proponents of change to push bills through Congress that bring about new directions. Thus, according to Herzberg (1986): "Although Congress was established in the Constitution as a legislature that makes de-

21

cisions by simple majority rule, its decision making process today is quite complex so that legislation faces a number of potential veto points in each chamber" (p. 201). The following table
shows points of delay or defeat in the House.

Points at Which Delay or Defeat May Occur in the House

Delay	*Defeat*
Committee inaction in refer- ring to a subcommittee	Committee inaction
	Negative vote in committee
Subcommittee inaction (pro- longed hearings; refusal to report)	Subcommittee inaction
	Negative vote in subcommittee
Committee inaction (pro- longed hearings; refusal to report)	Rules Committee inaction
Rules Committee inaction (refusal to schedule hear- ings; prolonged hearings; refusal to report)	Negative vote in Rules Committee
	Defeat of rule on the floor
	Motion to strike enacting clause
Slowness in scheduling the bill	Motion to recommit
Floor action (demanding full requirements of the rules) reading of the journal repeated quorum calls refusing unanimous consent to dispense with further proceed- ings under the call of the roll prolonging debate various points of order	Final passage

Source: Froman, L.A., Jr., 1967, p.18.

As mentioned earlier, some argue that the multiplicity
of veto points, along with other factors, has made comprehen-

sive policy change impossible. Actually, the undertaking of more comprehensive policy development through the legislative process is possible, but the factors that permit this to occur are different now than in the past because of changes that have taken place in the congressional milieu and the national policy agenda. One of the key factors is effective policy leadership exercised by a number of players in both the legislative and executive branches. Policy leadership is necessary to overcome the existing complex of barriers that advantage those who would block policy change and permit only incremental changes, if any.

But, how is policy leadership exercised effectively to bring about significant policy change? The fact is that there is little systematic research evidence that combines all the relevant factors. As previously noted, there has been some research on how party officials seek to lead, and research on congressional committees has provided insight into some of the influence relationships there. However, as Rieselbach (1986) concludes from his survey of this research: "Such studies of committees and parties are promising but partial beginnings in the quest to comprehend leadership strategies, tactics, and effectiveness. They highlight the pervasive question of leadership and our general ignorance of the specific ways leaders deal with followers" (p. 266). The leadership question involves a number of subsidiary questions — for example, what strategies and tactics do leaders employ, and what conditions facilitate follower support? Rieselbach concludes: "Policymaking and policy change, in sum, involve complex issues of leadership which constitute a challenging research agenda for students of Congress" (p. 267).

In order to understand why proponents of legislation employ the strategies and tactics they do, it is first necessary to understand something about the congressional context. In particular, it is useful to understand the major acting elements, the constraints and barriers, and the factors that influence the movement of bills within the legislative dynamics of Congress. In this chapter, these considerations will be discussed in overall terms. There is an inherent conceptual problem in that it is difficult to examine all the interactions that occur with respect to all the different bills at once, even within a given session of Congress.

The best that can be done is to examine legislative activity and observe the interactions within the context of a single legislative area. That is the approach in the following chapters. Specifically, how the elements interact within the context of consideration of federal criminal law legislation will be explored. But first, the major elements will be discussed.

Party Leadership — Tasks and Limitations

Party organization and, concomitantly, party leaders of both houses of Congress are two of the most recognizable features of the dynamics of legislation. While it is difficult to specify the impact either will have on a particular piece of legislation, members pay some attention to party guidance. The allegiance is so ephemeral, however, that it is impossible to make predictions concerning whether the role of the formal party leaders will be significant or not with respect to any given bill. Davidson (1981) observes that "congressional leadership may seem a contradiction in terms" and quotes former Majority Leader Mike Mansfield as stating, "You don't organize chaos" (p. 136).

Nonetheless, the formal party leadership in each house has some role in processing legislation, particularly when it is beyond the committee stage and is ready for consideration by the entire body. Each house of Congress has a different leadership structure that is, in part, a function of the size of the two bodies. The House, with its larger membership, relies on a more complex leadership structure, with the Speaker, majority leader, majority whip organization, and Rules Committee functioning for the majority, and the minority leader and minority whip organization functioning for the minority. The Senate, with its smaller membership, relies on a smaller leadership contingent, with the majority floor leader and majority whip, and the minority floor leader and minority whip.

The Senate majority floor leader has five somewhat overlapping tasks: (1) managing party organizational machinery, (2) supervising the scheduling of legislation, (3) implementing the flow of the Senate's business, (4) enhancing the electoral opportunities of colleagues, and (5) contributing to policy innovation (Peabody, 1981). The policy innovation role is the least well defined. Senators see themselves as equals and act accordingly. The leader's role in policy is seen by many as assisting in scheduling and providing procedural advice. Others wish for a more active leadership role in policy development. Of course, procedural control has policy implications, in that much of the procedural maneuvering is over facilitating or restricting passage of specific policies. Nonetheless, formal leaders have a choice of which aspects to emphasize. Schick (1978) argues that the factors making the Senate an even more decentralized and open body have made it even more difficult to move anything, and thus formal leaders have become more and more absorbed in the procedural aspects of Senate work and less in substantive concerns.

In sum, the floor leader operates in a context of conflicting role demands and varying expectations by his colleagues within an environment that has enhanced the opportunities for individual action as opposed to collective action that can be managed by the leadership. It is thus not surprising that, as Mackaman (1981) puts it: "Different floor leaders inevitably emphasize some facets of their job, delegate others, and ignore still others, but each has to balance complex and competing demands inside the Senate within the broader context of key external relationships" (p. 6).

The situation is similar in the House. The rules changes of the 1970s, such as the subcommittee bill of rights, removed from the committee chairmen the power to appoint subcommittees and gave it to the majority caucus on the committees. They also guaranteed bill referral to subcommittees as well as adequate budget and staff.

Loomis (1981) points to the enhanced position of subcommittees as a barrier to effective policy leadership by House party leaders: "To the extent that the resources provided by the subcommittees and even personal office staffs allow diligent experts the chance to obtain hearings, offer amendments, and participate widely in the legislative process, these members are likely to act more as obstacles to than as allies of the leadership" (p. 175). The positive effects of strengthening subcommittees were the bringing of more members into the policy process, the opening up of the possibility of policy innovation by a wider range of members, and probably increased legislative expertise in the House (Dodd and Oppenheimer, 1989). Deering and Smith (1985) find that "on balance, independent subcommittees have made the job of central party leaders more difficult by extending and multiplying the lines of communication for leaders and by increasing the number of effective participants placing demands on them" (p. 207). Relatedly, Sinclair's (1989) analysis shows that the House leadership, in coping with a more decentralized power situation, has employed four major strategies: (1) providing services and favors to members; (2) involving as many House Democrats as possible in the coalition-building process, for example, employing task forces for high majority interest policies; (3) using the rules for floor consideration of bills to structure members' choices at the floor stage; and (4) influencing public opinion through the media.

Those holding the formal leadership posts face significant restraints in taking the substantive policy lead on legislation. The altered House environment provides more power to individual members to express themselves, with the concomitant result of making it more difficult for congressional leaders to integrate the policy-making efforts of their members. Even when the Democrats controlled the presidency and both the Senate and the House, efforts of the formal House leadership were frequently frustrated. During 1979–80 the leadership regularly lost votes on energy, budget, and foreign policy issues. Speaker O'Neill complained, "I've got a lot of friends out there who won't even give me a vote to adjourn" (*CQ Almanac,* 1986, p. 30).

Jones (1981), in reviewing such reforms as those that provided for more staff and information-gathering capabilities, more membership control over selection of committee chairperson, and the strengthening of the subcommittees in the House, finds that the principal aim was to promote individual expression, not policy integration. Peters (1990), in his extensive examination of the evolution and functioning of Speakers of the House, points to the increasingly autonomous power structure of the House and concludes: "Modern Speakers will be forced to operate in an inchoate environment. The House is a more fluid body today than at any time since the Civil War" (pp. 294–295).

Some of the rules changes in the House have the potential to strengthen the hand of formal leaders: (1) the requirement that the committee chairpersons and chairpersons of the appropriations subcommittees win majority caucus approval; (2) the rule giving the Speaker the right to nominate Democratic members of the Rules Committee subject only to the ratification of the majority caucus; (3) the assignment of members to committees by the new Steering and Policy Committee which the Speaker chairs; and (4) new multiple referral rules. These latter rules provide for the assignment of more bills to more than one committee and give the Speaker authority to set a deadline for reporting (Sinclair, 1990). Further, with multiple referred bills, the Speaker's possibilities for coordinating and integrating increase if the House is to function, and they make committee chairs more reliant on leadership assistance to get bills they want to the floor so they can pass (Sinclair, 1989).

The Speaker's influence on the Rules Committee has also helped him to have more influence on managing the floor (Dodd and Oppenheimer, 1989). The responsibility of the Rules Committee, through which bills must pass before consideration on the House floor, is to limit or bar amendments and set the conditions for debate, including time limits. This responsibility carries with it significant power to block legislation as well as affect its content. In the 1980s, the Rules Committee has employed special rules written by a handful of Rules Committee Democrats, often under the personal direction of the Speaker, particularly for "key vote" measures of high majority caucus and leadership interest. These rules have been more restrictive and have limited greatly the opportunities for rank-and-file members to offer their own amendments on the floor (Bach and Smith, 1988).

The net effect of House rules changes seems to be that both formal majority party leaders and rank-and-file members have gained influence at the expense of committee chairpersons, and on balance individual rank-and-file members have gained influence in relation to formal leaders. Sinclair (1990) contends that where the balance is at any point in time depends on other political variables. One of these is how much emphasis members put on policy outputs compared to other values. And, as Dodd and Oppenheimer (1989) observed about the future of then Speaker Wright: "The point is that the future for Speaker Wright and the Democratic Leadership is contingent on not only the skills and goals of the leadership but also electoral politics and organizational dynamics within the House and on the fiscal and political environment of the nation at large" (p. 60).

The leadership styles of formal leaders as well as the political environment influence the policy approach of particular leaders. Speaker O'Neill normally deferred to his committee chairpersons until bills neared the floor stage. O'Neill related, "I don't know the depth of every piece of legislation that goes on around here. The important stuff, I understand it" (Ehrenhalt, 1986b, p. 2133). However, the O'Neill-Wright team often used control of the rules to structure policy choices on the floor. O'Neill also did favors for members and practiced the politics of inclusion (Sinclair, 1989). On occasion, O'Neill, responding to major political challenges, used the politics of inclusion to push a major policy initiative. For example, at the end of the Carter administration, he salvaged the faltering administration energy initiative by forming an energy task force that involved numerous members in order to circumvent the hard lines that had formed in the regular committees on energy.

Jim Wright's speakership was characterized by his individual policy activism. "Wright was the first speaker in the recent period to use the power of the office systematically to pass his own legislative agenda" (Peters, 1990, pp. 267–268). Wright did not wait for the committees to percolate legislation to the top. "Wright effectively used House rules and his own partisan majority to set and pursue an aggressive legislative agenda, often ignoring and sometimes exploiting the outrage voiced by House Minority republicans. While legislation passed, one side effect of Wright's strong and assertive leadership was sharply heightened partisan conflict, exacerbated by frayed tempers and personal clashes" (Ornstein, 1990, p. 24). Complaints often came from members of his own party, some calling Wright the "Lone

Ranger." They also complained that he was not consulting them enough prior to taking off on policy initiatives (Hook, May 27, 1989). Wright was known as strong-willed, impetuous, and willing to play procedural hardball with opponents (Hook, Sept. 30, 1989).

The style of Speaker Thomas Foley appears to be a return to normalcy. Foley is known as more conciliatory than Wright, but he was a strong supporter of the 1970s rules changes. He made it clear at the start to committee chairpersons that he expected them to be accountable to the majority and pursue policies acceptable to the Democratic rank-and-file. Foley is more of a consensus builder even with the Republican minority and emphasizes bringing members on board before acting (Cohen, 1989). Foley was a committee chairman and has expressed his recognition of the difficulties under which chairmen labor. Majority Whip Gray, also a former committee chairman, said early on that the leadership would not likely be inclined to become more deeply involved in committees' affairs (Cohen, 1989). Majority Leader Gephardt predicted the leadership approach would be "from the bottom up." "We've had huge turnover in the last ten years and they are not the kind of people who came here to take orders" (Hook, June 10, 1989, p. 1377).

The question some House Democrats raise about the Foley team is whether the cautious and conciliatory leadership approach can establish control over the legislative and political agenda in order to cast legislation in terms favorable to Democrats (Hook, Sept. 30, 1989). After Foley agreed not to present President Bush's budget for consideration on the House floor, depriving Democratic candidates of a chance to hammer their opponents in the fall for voting for a spending plan that contained deep cuts for popular domestic programs, Representative Barbara Boxer (D-Calif.) said: "We lost an opportunity to graphically show which party has its act together. You have to articulate the differences and allow the body to work so they are clearly shown" (Kenworthy, June 18–24, 1990, p. 14). Another Democrat complained: "People are asking themselves, are they [the leadership] at all capable of playing hardball. What they don't appreciate is that Republicans get out of bed every day and come to work figuring out how to eat our lunch. This is about winning and losing" (Kenworthy, 1990, p. 14). In June 1990, even though a simple majority in the House voted for a constitutional amendment to allow a federal law prohibiting flag burning, Foley did lead the charge that denied President Bush and the Republicans the votes needed to achieve the constitutional majority. Foley seemed more comfortable, however, in negotiating with the administration and assisting the arrangement of coalitions necessary to pass bills on rights for the disabled and on clean air. Foley observed about his role within a divided government: "I keep having people say to me, 'you ought to be the constant daily scourge of George Bush,' that I ought to get up in the morning and figure out what I can say or do to embarrass the president or obstruct the president or whatever. That's not my concept of the job. . . . There are issues on which you have to take a stand even if you fail, but for the most part I would rather have a successful and important achievement in cooperation with the executive branch than just have a political issue" (Kenworthy, 1990, p. 14).

The Senate, of course, has always been a bastion of individualism, with perhaps the ability to mount a filibuster and the requirement of sixty votes to shut off debate as the premier emblem of the right of even a single senator to hold up progress on legislation. Other possibilities that individual senators can use to delay and possibly kill legislation include: generous opportunities for amending bills at different stages; repeated votes on budget or other items; repeated quorum calls; and requesting the floor leader to place a "hold" on legislation which, according to senatorial courtesy, delays its floor consideration. The Senate majority leader has long been the key to supervising the scheduling of legislation and keeping the flow of the Senate's business going. Perhaps the most effective as floor leader was Lyndon Johnson who, even though he found himself working with closely divided Senates, was able consistently to fashion majorities to move legislation. However, conditions have changed, as borne out by former Majority Leader Robert Byrd: "I could not run the Senate as Johnson did. . . . Johnson could not lead this Senate [the 96th]. These are different times. He had cohesive blocs, he had the southern senators. When Johnson was majority leader, both senators from Texas were Democrats; both senators from Virginia, from South Carolina, and so on. Now you have a lot of Republican senators from the south. The members are younger now; they tend to be more independent. We are living in different times now" (Peabody, 1981, p. 72).

The impact of this increased independence on the ability of the leadership to lead should not be underestimated. As Peabody (1981) has observed: "More than most institutions, Senate leaders are dependent on what their followers will tolerate, and the Senate of the 1960s and 1970s has been characterized by greal individual autonomy, perhaps as great as at any time since the late nineteenth century" (p. 164). In the 1980s, however, the insistence on individual senator autonomy became even more pronounced. Increasingly, numerous senators came to worry that the individualism had gotten out of hand to the detriment of the Senate. As Ehrenhalt (1983) reports: "It is seen from within as a place where there is little time to think, close personal relationships are rare, and individual rights, not community feeling, is the most precious commodity" (p. 2175).

The difficulties for the formal Senate leadership in moving the business of the Senate at all, let alone moving their colleagues in any particular policy direction, are enormous. It would be hard from observing the process to claim that the leadership is setting directions. According to Davidson (1989b): "The contemporary Senate, with its widely dispersed prerogatives, requires a more restrained leadership, one that relies not on forceful commandeering but on fairness, camaraderie, and accommodation" (p. 303).

Whereas Johnson was an aggressive leader, Mike Mansfield (D-Mont.) conducted a long career as majority leader with a permissive style and one that respected the policy activism of individual senators. He observed early in his term that there had been a dispersal of responsibility: "I'm not the leader, really. They don't do what I tell them. I do what they tell me. How can I know everything that's going on? The brains are in the committees" (*New York Times,* July 17, 1961, p. 11). Robert Byrd, who assumed the majority leader post in 1977, was also service-oriented but devoted more time to floor procedures and scheduling matters (Davidson, 1989b). On his second tour as majority leader in 1987, Byrd used more centralized control of scheduling to try to move legislation, scheduling no votes on Mondays but trying to keep the Senate floor proceedings going through Fridays. Later he put the Senate on a schedule of three full weeks in session and one week out of session, so that members could go to their districts (Davidson, 1989b).

Howard Baker's low-key style was to network individual senators, sometimes including Democrats, to get them to agree to move something. His approach was to meet endlessly with Republican members, singly and in groups, letting them talk and argue until they would finally agree to proceed, even if only out of sympathy for his plight in getting them to move. Robert Dole, who followed Baker, was more hard-nosed, aggressive, and partisan, and would gather groups of Republican senators in his office, sometimes for hours, to mold a partisan majority on issues. He then would push them to agree on strategy and substance (Ornstein, 1990). He did this, for example, on the 1985 deficit reduction package and the 1986 drug bill. Byrd and Dole were not always successful, however, and strong-willed senators like Jesse Helms (R-N.C.) fairly often wrecked the Senate agenda over policy disputes.

George Mitchell was chosen for majority leader with the television age very much in the minds of Democratic senators. Even though junior to his rivals, Mitchell had demonstrated his media skills during the Iran-Contra hearings, and he has continued to use those skills during televised Senate proceedings and on network news shows to articulate majority positions on issues. Inside the Senate, Mitchell early adopted an accommodating and consensus-oriented style which some veterans compared to that of Howard Baker. On policy, he has tended to let the initiative rest with his committee chairpersons (Hook, September 9, 1989). However, on at least one complex bill, the Clean Air Act amendments, when Mitchell concluded that the Environment and Public Works Committee bill did not have the votes to overcome a filibuster, he negotiated a compromise with the White House himself, and then lobbied senators on a direct personal basis to overcome amendments offered by Democrats that would have broken the deal and provoked a veto (Hook, April 7, 1990 p. 1046).

In both the House and Senate, a number of variables, including the political environment, size of majority and minority, degree of member disposition to cooperate on policy, and leader's style and capabilities, influence the leader's success in leading. Some formal leaders are more aggressive in policy terms and more successful in constructing coalitions behind bills than others. The internal environment and rules largely preserve much room for individual member action. Under normal circumstances, the best that the formal leaders can do is serve the members in order to encourage cooperation and seek to assist in building coalitions to keep the business of the body moving. On occasion, the formal leaders may choose to serve as policy leaders, but this will not be the normal pattern.

Committees and Subcommittees — Decentralization, Participation, and Fragmentation

Of course, the overall leadership of the two chambers is only part of the story. Long-time observers of Congress dating back to Woodrow Wilson have characterized legislative policy-making as "committee government." The committee system has long responded to institutional needs of the two houses of Congress — namely, the need to process a growing flow of legislation on diverse topics in settings with a large number of people. The division of labor met the need for increased expertise and specialization. " The committee system is a means of bringing expertise and attention to bear on congressional tasks in a more concerted fashion than the free enterprise of scattered members could ever accomplish" (Price, 1985, p. 169). For a long period of our history, this functional treatment of issues was integrated by strong party leaders, particularly the House Speaker.

Formal committee leadership consists of committee chairs and ranking minority members chosen by their party caucuses, and subcommittee chairs and ranking members chosen by the committee party caucuses. Seniority still plays a large role in who is selected, but chairs have to pay more attention to the policy dispositions of their members now or risk being ousted. There is variation in the influence relationships between committee and subcommittee chairs—from committees where the chairperson is the chief contact point for all committee activity, to committees with strong chairs but relatively autonomous subcommittees, to committees with complete subcommittee autonomy (Hammond, 1990). Sometimes the committee or subcommittee chair will be the main force behind a policy, but other times the initiative will come from some other member of the committee.

Following the 1910 revolt against Speaker Cannon, the committees in the House became more autonomous when seniority, rather than appointment by the Speaker, became the basis for committee assignments and chairmanships. As Davidson (1981) points out, committee autonomy in both houses arose from such factors as rising workloads in the chambers, members' careerism, rigid adherence to seniority in the selection of committee leaders, and the long-term erosion of partisan loyalties. The pinnacle of committee influence occurred between the years 1937 and 1971, when committee chairs seemed to dominate. In moving policy, these chairpersons spoke for intracommitte majorities and they facilitated the political and career goals of these majorities (Davidson, 1981).

However, as discussed earlier, consequential changes in congressional rules and practices have fundamentally altered the integrating function of committees as centers of policy-making. Taken together, these changes have led congressional observers to substitute "subcommittee government" for "committee government" in describing Congress. "As a general proposition, the influence of full committees has declined in comparison with other elements in the process" (Davidson, 1981, p. 114). There are some differences in subcommittee dominance between the House and Senate. In the first place, the Senate is more likely to conduct hearings and markups on bills without prior subcommittee action, which seldom happens in the House. Within committees, Hall's (1989) analysis shows that House subcommittee leaders were more likely to be the principal actors in markups where legislation is amended than were Senate sub-committee leaders, but in both houses, subcommittee leaders were more likely to be the principal actors than other members. Changes in both houses have created more subcommittees and guaranteed wider dispersal of chairmanships, widely dispersing leadership. The effect of these changes is to fragment policy-making activity and to make policy integration more difficult. The increase in the power and autonomy of the subcommittee chairs has come, to some extent, at the expense of the committee chairs and, it has been observed, at the expense of the ability of Congress to move legislation. "In addition, it is important to recognize that subcommittee chairs are not true substitutes for the once dominant full committee chairs in the decision making process of the House. On major issues, subcommittee chairs are in no position to guarantee party leaders that certain legislation will be reported to the floor in a particular form at a particular time" (Deering and Smith, 1985, p. 207). "Decentralization helped to create less cohesive committees, increased the chances committee disputes would spill onto the floor, and contributed to the declining deference to committee recommendations" (Smith, 1989, pp. 333–334). As Representative Steny Hoyer (D-Md.) lamented, "We've decentralized so much authority, it's difficult to come to grips with some of our problems" (Hook, Jan. 6, 1990, p. 11). In short, the capacity to provide for policy integration, at least at the committee level, has been dissipated among a profusion of subcommittees which by themselves are able to offer members a platform for discussing policy but not a pipeline for moving it (Price, 1985).

The Role of Staff

A related development contributing mightily to the growing de-centralization of Congress is the tremendous growth of congressional staff resources that have been made available to members. As a result of the "Johnson Rule" in the Senate, which guaranteed senators at least one good committee assignment, most majority senators were able to become subcommittee chairs as well, each with his or her own staff. Similarly, in the House, because of the "Subcommittee Bill of Rights," which gave sub-committee chairs more autonomy, most committee staff increases occurred at the subcommittee level. Overall, between 1950 and 1979, committee staff increased 366 percent in the Senate and 796 percent in the House. From 1979 to 1987, House commit-tee staff increased a more modest 5.3 percent and Senate com-mittee staff declined 14 percent (Ornstein, Mann, and Malbin, 1989, p. 130). The result was a shift away from nonpartisan professional staffs serving a whole committee to a proliferation of staffs working for individual subcommittee chairs (Malbin, 1981).

Personal staffs have also grown, further contributing to the capacity of the individual congressman to "go it alone." From 1947 to 1987, personal staffs increased 590 percent in the Senate and 426 percent in the House (Ornstein, Mann, and Malbin, 1989, p. 132). Hammond (1978) describes how staffs have not only grown but have also become more professionalized and dis-tributed among more members. Thus, vastly larger staffs have augmented the policy capability of members and contributed to the increasing autonomy of subcommittees in both chambers.

An important effect of these changes in the size and na-ture of staff is to make the individual congressman less depen-dent on the executive branch, the legislative leadership, or com-mittee chairs for information, analysis, or publicizing activities when it comes to considering and promoting legislative ideas. As such, these centers of leadership have less to hold over the-heads of individual members.

In addition, staff proliferation has added not merely more hands to aid in legislative work; it has added a whole new set of "players" who see their role as much more than sifting others' ideas and explaining options to members. A growing number of staffs have become what Price has termed "entrepreneurial" staffs who actively look for new ideas for their bosses. As Mal-bin (1981) notes: "Senators and Representatives believe their interests with the electorate are advanced if they can claim credit for authoring important bills or amendments or instigating well-publicized hearings" (p. 155). All of this has noticeably added to the volume of congressional activity, but it vastly complicates the process while emphasizing the credit-claiming activities of individual representatives.

It also has been said to lead to a deterioration in the deliberative process required to develop and move good legislation. A chief casualty is believed to be the simple process whereby representatives talk over legislative proposals with each other. According to Senator David Boren (D-Okla.): "Very often, I will call a senator on an issue, and he won't know anything about it. He'll ask me to get someone on my staff to call someone on his staff" (Ehrenhalt, 1982, p. 2156). What is lost is direct communication among members with the concomitant decrease in the ability of members to get a feel or sense of their colleagues' reactions to the various arguments. According to Malbin (1981), this has substantially contributed to a growing inability of members to deliberate over policy.

In addition, staff have become key players in the process itself—an occurrence not lost on interest groups and particularly their representatives, as well as agency administrators. Bureaucrats and lobbyists know that often it is more important to obtain the opportunity to present their views and information to the chief committee staff person or a senator's administrative assistant than in a brief session on the run with a senator or representative. The staff member very often is the one who will be the last to brief the committee chairperson or the senator before the vote occurs on the substance of the bill or on an amendment. With staff playing such key roles, the number of people in the process is more diffused and points of influence more scattered.

Congressional Norms—Do the Ties Still Bind?

For a considerable period of time, cohesion felt necessary to move policy in both houses was promoted by a cluster of practices and norms that provided guides and incentives for members' behavior. The prevailing belief was that adherence to such rules of the game resulted not only in greater respect by other members but also greater effectiveness in achieving the passage of legislation. Such norms fulfilling these functions were found to include:

- *Cordiality.* Undergirding many of the other norms was an understanding that with so many members representing so many diverse interests, and so many diverse and potentially contentious policy issues to be dealt with, a continuing reliance on courtesy to other members was essential to moving policy through the two houses to completion.
- *Reciprocity.* With each bill required to go through so many stages where different members have influence, it was felt to be imperative that members of Congress put emphasis on helping each other or nothing would move. This required an approach to legislating that stressed bargaining, logrolling, and compromise.
- *Seniority.* For approximately fifty years, seniority was rather consistently applied as a means of selecting committee and subcommittee chairs, determining the rankings of members on committees, and determining choice of committee assignments. Seniority was felt to have the virtue of being less susceptible to transitory, and thus disruptive, political manipulation, and therefore provided for a type of equal treatment. Everyone could aspire to a power position, provided he or she continued to be reelected and lived long enough. Seniority lent support to the maintenance of smooth working relationships in Congress by avoiding disruptive and potentially destructive struggles for selecting committee chairs, thus promoting harmony among members. It also provided incentives for members to return to Congress, specialize on committees, concentrate on doing good committee work, and develop policy specialties. The process benefited by having genuine "policy experts" on hand to whom other members could refer in deliberations but also were largely expected to defer in debate. Admittedly, numerous observers pointed to a number of negative consequences in terms of what

kinds of external interests were overrepresented and underrepresented.

- *Apprenticeship.* A corollary of seniority was the idea that early in a member's career, he or she should concentrate on learning the rules of the body, keep a low profile (not speak much in debate), pay serious attention to committee work, and defer to the senior members of his or her party on major policy issues. In the words of the immortal House Speaker Sam Rayburn, "To get along, go along." After a time, when policy expertise had been developed in committee, and the member had gained the confidence of the leaders, he or she could step out and assert more influence. This norm buttressed the ability of committee chairs and senior members to move legislation. It was not uncommon through the forties, fifties, and early sixties to witness major bills moving through both houses of Congress with hardly any changes on the floor at all.

- *Legislative work.* Members were expected to spend their time on legislative duties in committee and on the floor and not sacrifice those duties for grandstanding before the media. Members expected to gain influence by being patient and doing their share of the work, and eventually they would be recognized by their colleagues.

- *Specialization.* Members were expected to specialize in one or perhaps a few legislative areas, primarily coinciding with subcommittee assignments. In this way, they developed in-depth expertise and could over time know their subject so well that other members would respect their views. Also, given the vast array of subjects with which Congress has to deal, this fosters a division of labor that makes sure the work is covered.

Taken together, such norms appeared to facilitate the passage of large-scale complex legislation. However, during the 1960s and 1970s, the same pressures that led to the overhaul of formal rules governing committee and subcommittee procedures also resulted in a significant lessening of adherence to these norms. In short, during this period, a large number of new and younger members entered the House and Senate who were not only willing to speak out on the floor and in the media but were also numerous enough to force changes in the rules that significantly decentralized power in both houses, creating stronger and independent subunits (Cooper and West, 1981).

These changes also led to a greater fragmentation among members and seemingly a reduction in the overall level of member expertise in subcommittees (Malbin, 1981). As a result, greater policy individualism and a lessened willingness to "go along" received greater emphasis by more members. Apprenticeship has all but disappeared. Seniority, for example, did not disappear, but it lost its singularity. The caucuses in the House gained more control over the appointment of chairpersons, for exmple. At the same time, junior members deemphasized the desirability of deferring to the senior members. While specialization still exists, it has lessened. Sinclair's (1986) study shows that senators offer more floor amendments and offer more amendments to bills from committees on which they do not serve, and that overall, "specialization has declined; more and more senators have become generalists" (p. 895). Members have other ways to gain influence.

Senators are now more likely to develop national policy agendas on many topics, which is facilitated not only by multiple committee memberships but also by increased use of the national media. Certain House members, too, have adopted ideological and policy agendas and have pursued those. With respect to concentration on legislative work, while there is still the expectation that members will do their share, there is much more involvement in media activity. Numerous senators and representatives make a great effort to get on major news shows and do spots for back home outlets for election and legislative purposes. Some of this is done to pave the way for a chance at the White House or just to become a national celebrity (Ornstein, Peabody, and Rohde, 1989). Some of it is a way of pushing issues and policies. Representative Thomas Downey (D-N.Y.) observed: "If you want to reach your colleagues, sometimes the best way is to let them see you on TV or read your name in the paper. If you say something pithy or clever, you can find your-self on the national news in a matter of hours. . . . News management by members through the electronic media is a more viable option than it ever was" (Ehrenhalt, Sept. 13, 1986a, p. 2134).

The lessening or, in some cases, elimination of the norms, make Congress a less orderly and predictable institution and make integrating the activities of members to produce significant legislation more difficult. Stanga and Farnsworth (1978) observe, after examining the decline of seniority in the House, that there is likely to be an increase in "position taking"—pronouncing and holding to a policy position regardless of prospects for legislating it—rather than a move to a system dominated by responsible political parties or a return to the old pattern of governance through expert, subject-matter standing committees. They point out that subcommittee chairs (which are now widely dispersed) provide a good forum for position taking. With respect to the Senate, the overall effect of the changes in informal norms has been to make it a more open institution in which the ability to affect policy is less dependent upon a senator's formal position or seniority (Ornstein, Peabody, and Rohde, 1989).

Elections—A Preoccupation

Astute observers of Congress have contended that in order to understand the behavior of congressional representatives, one must examine the electoral environment within which members operate. Most observers have concluded that, in recent years, members have become increasingly preoccupied with electoral aspects of their work and this has led them to emphasize certain modes of behavior other than legislating on national issues.

One can trace the seeds of an electoral focus to a fairly recent increase in the turnover in membership of both houses. Starting at the beginning of the 1970s, turnover increased markedly. By 1981, the proportion of House members who had served six years or less was about 47 percent, a marked change from the 34 percent in only 1971. It has since decreased again to 28 percent in 1989 (Ornstein, Mann, and Malbin, 1989, pp. 17–18). Similarly, the number of senators serving six years or less went from twenty-seven in 1971 to fifty-five in 1981 to forty-three in 1989. When one considers that many newcomers were elected during a period in which political party organizations declined markedly in their ability to influence elections, it is not surprising to find them less naturally beholden to party leaders when they arrived in Congress. The direct primary has meant that congressional candidates have increasingly developed their own electoral organizations separate from (and sometimes in opposition to) local party organizations. Although in recent House elections the effect of party has declined and the effect of incumbency has increased, as Mann (1981) points out, House incumbents do not *feel* more secure or independent of their constituencies: "Their advantage is seen as soft, based not upon enduring party loyalties but rather on voter evaluations that are thin and highly personalized. Feelings can sour, opposition groups in the district can mobilize, serious challengers can surface, suddenly rendering a safe incumbent vulnerable" (p. 43). The Senate has experienced considerable turnover as well, owing to both retirement and electoral defeat. Thus, while the insecurities of House members may be largely a matter of perception, those of senators increasingly have a foundation in observing their colleagues' electoral defeats.

The result has been characterized as an increased feeling of obligation of members that they must tend to their districts — a stress on "home style" (Fenno, 1978). The focus in such an approach is not on overall national policy but on constituent service and projects of local interest. It also means traveling home more often, deploying staff in home district offices where they constitute the core of a continuous campaign staff, and devoting increasing amounts of personal time to constituent concerns rather than national policy-making. In the words of former Senator Gaylord Nelson:

> Some days I had somebody from the state in my office every 15 minutes. Seventy-five percent of my time, or maybe 80 percent, was spent on non-legislative matters. . . . The floor is being used as an instrument for political campaigning far more

than it ever has before. People seem to expect that [Ehrenhalt, 1982, p. 2177].

or Senator Dale Bumpers:

The Founding Fathers gave senators six-year terms so they could be statesmen for at least four years and not respond to every whim and caprice. Now a senator in his first year knows any vote could beat him five years later. So senators behave like House members. They are running constantly [Ehrenhalt, 1982, p. 2177].

As pointed out earlier, House members increasingly focus on the district. Why? Because constituency service, rather than policy agreement, seems to be a factor in the increase in incumbents among House members (Fiorna, 1977). Little wonder increasingly vulnerable senators would choose to act like House members, especially when it is considered that many served there before coming to the Senate. As Mann (1981) points out, this localization of political forces provides the electoral base for increasingly individualized behavior. As a result, the attention of members is easily diverted from national issues. "As far as elections are concerned, senators and representatives are in business for themselves. From the initial decision to seek the nomination and the rigors of the first primary and general election campaigns all the way to eventual retirement or defeat, they are political entrepreneurs, in their states and districts, seizing opportunities, generating resources, responding to pressures, shaping the image that voters react to on election day" (p. 53).

Congressmen's focus on their districts is not misplaced in terms of maximizing reelection chances. Mann's analysis shows that, increasingly, congressmen are responsible for their own margins of victory or defeat, and the electoral constraints they face are defined in their own districts. Mann (1978) finds that the public is more aware of congressional candidates than previously believed, and independent voting is on the rise. As a result: "If voters choose the preferred candidate in congressional elections instead of automatically voting their party or bowing to the incumbent, then congressmen have little basis for judging themselves invulnerable. . . . Voters are sufficiently discriminating to make congressmen wary of the possible public reaction to their actions in office" (p. 103). Congressmen, regardless of past victory, still try to anticipate future electoral reactions. Kingdon's study (1973) found that congressmen anticipate possible campaign occurrences and take them into account as they vote. They have in mind that a given vote can be used as a campaign talking point for or against them. So many things can happen in a campaign that could damage or ruin a carefully built career that congressmen act to hedge against uncertainty.

And what is the impact of this electoral focus on policy-making? Arnold's study (1981) finds that one result is that when congressmen are focusing on legislative activity, it is to secure local benefits for their constituency, without the mediating effects of parties. Instead, he finds that most coalitions that produce legislation are assembled ad hoc, one program at a time; congressmen's support is contingent upon receiving satisfactory shares of benefits for their districts. Mayhew's study (1974) finds that another result is representatives who are posturers and advertisers rather than responsible policymakers. Kingdon's study (1973) showed that even when congressmen took unpopular votes on principle, they assessed the electoral reaction and, if it was perceived as negative, often adapted their behavior in subsequent votes. Thus, the reactions of congressmen, whether focusing on localized benefits, position taking, or voting on national issues, are all influenced by their anticipation of reactions in the electoral environment.

The Media

Some of the impacts of the media on congressional behavior have been discussed earlier, and there is little doubt that congressmen pay attention to what is covered in the media. One of the reasons for this is that the media play an important agenda-setting function in elections — particularly on what issues are considered important in elections (Weaver, Graber, McCombs, and Eyal, 1981). In addition to influencing what issues people talk about, the prominence of issues can have an important effect on public opinion, especially the strength of opinion (Weaver, 1984; Iyengar and Kinder, 1987). Also, by emphasizing certain issues and not others, the press can influence the criteria that people use for evaluating candidates in their campaigns (McCombs and Weaver, forthcoming). Thus, members of Congress follow, to some extent, the issues that the media are covering and try to anticipate how they will play out in both legislative and electoral contexts. In addition, as will be discussed below, the issues that the media chooses to emphasize with respect to particular large-scale legislation go a long way in characterizing that legislation and setting the agenda for it.

Media coverage of Congress is also greater in recent years, and congressmen's interest in being involved in media activity has increased. Floor proceedings of both the House and Senate are now televised, and more local media are covering what their congressmen are doing. Perhaps the biggest change in the behavior of members of Congress is a result of the expansion of the coverage of the news media, and particularly the electronic media. Between 1960 and 1976, the number of correspondents holding credentials to cover Congress from radio and television increased 175 percent (*Congressional Directory,* 1960–1976). In addition, policy battles between the president and Congress are being increasingly covered in the media. Former Majority Whip Tony Coelho (D-Calif.) has noted: "Ten years ago, nobody paid any attention to us. The Reagan years have forced the House in the spotlight. The question is whether we can go back anymore. I don't think the press is going to let the House go back to where it was. It's a goldfish bowl" (Ehrenhalt, 1986a, p. 2132).

However, the bigger change may have occurred as a corollary of the large turnover of congressmen in the 1970s. Robinson's study (1981) found that, compared with the class of 1958, the class of 1978 was three times more likely to make heavy use of the congressional recording studio, to find the House television system "very useful," and to have relied "a lot" on television in the last election. There is little doubt that the media have given newer members more visibility than ever. Robinson finds that the new media mix in congressional politics encourages and promotes people who are telegenic and possibly egocentric, and thus produces a Congress that is focused on higher office and is less likely to behave as a group than as a disjointed collection of individuals. Veteran Representative Henry Hyde of Illinois comments on the media orientation of representatives: "You've got a bunch of verbalizers who have a smattering of the jargon and who have natural media ability. A lot of them have been touched by the aphrodisiac of seeing their name in the papers or going on the evening news. It's a heady experience for them" (CQ Almanac, 1986, p. 32).

Considering that, taken together, the electoral arena and the media environment encourage and reward individualistic position taking, the incentives to focus on longer-term national policy legislation that is difficult to pass would seem to be scant. However, congressmen must remain uncertain about whether or when a particular legislative initiative will be coupled with events in the political stream and take on electoral significance. Thus, while many congressmen may not devote themselves to long-term projects, they may not be able to ignore the products of those who do.

Interest Groups — Growing Participation

So, if longer-term national policy is not the natural focus of such congressmen, what is? What does preoccupy their attention when it comes to policy-making? In recent years, observers have more and more expressed the view that it is the special interests that have become more dominant. In the words of Representative Romano Mazzoli (D-Ky.): "People feel like it's big money, big business, big labor, the lobbyists who are represented, that little by little the playing field has been tilted" (Alston, 1990, p. 2026). But why this claim of a special-interest focus if not dominance? The factor to which numerous observers point is the concurrence of the character of Congress described earlier and the electoral environment that congressmen must continually confront. In short, campaigning is at once more expensive and more hazardous. It is more hazardous because as interest groups have proliferated to cover practically every area of government activity (Wooton, 1985), they have become not only more organized and cohesive but also more sophisticated in their approach to monitoring and influencing the activities of congressional representatives, and seemingly more single-minded in their orientations.

This concurrence is particularly claimed to be strengthened by the expanded role of special-focus groups in financing political campaigns. The Federal Election Campaign Act of 1974 limited political action committees (PACs) to $5,000 per candidate per election, but it placed no limit on overall contributions by a PAC per election. Between the end of 1974 and the end of 1982, the number of PACs registered with the Federal Election Commission increased 554 percent from 608 to 3,371, and campaign contributions from them to federal candidates in 1982 were $42.7 million, a nearly three and a half-fold increase (Schlozman and Tierney, 1986, p. 222). For the six-year period 1983–88, receipts from PACs for senators ranged from zero for only three senators to over $2 million for four (*Congressional Quarterly*, Apr. 28, 1990). The ostensible negative impact on congressional policy-making is described by Senator Robert Dole (R-Kans.): "When these political-action committees give money, they expect something in return other than good government. It is making it more difficult to legislate. We may reach a point where if everybody is buying something with PAC money, we can't get anything done" (Hunt, 1982, p. 13). We know that some policy-making is getting done, however. The question is, what kind and how do the interest groups participate? Concomitantly, how do the congressmen respond?

Political scientists have produced a considerable body of research that examines the workings of Congress in several policy areas. In studying the relationships among congressmen, administrators in federal agencies, and interest-group representatives, some have come to describe these relationships as "iron triangles" or "subgovernments," and have traced their development and change, as well as how they have come to predominate in several policy areas. The triangle of participants consists of agency career bureaucrats building programs, congressional sub-committees with program control and constituent largesse to protect, and interest groups with special interests to be served. Ripley (1983) argues that subgovernments exist and play a key role in subcommittee dominance in Congress.

One of the key characteristics of such subgovernments is said to be their functional autonomy, which is the ability of the participants to formulate and implement policies within the tri-angle or subgovernment, with scant attention from other ac-tors, let alone the public at large. This means that the key policy determinations made within functionally autonomous iron tri-angles provide little opportunity for nonmember political ac-tors, such as the president, party leaders, or other congressmen, to participate. Instead, members of the relevant committee or subcommittee (and particularly the members' staffs), along with the responsible agency administrators, work out policy accom-modations with administrators and interest-group representa-tives that will be satisfactory to them and will preserve a stable relationship among them. Policies are the product of a bargain-ing process. The process is sometimes referred to as partisan mutual adjustment—the aggregation and reconciliation of the particular interests that assert themselves. The point of depar-ture is the self-interests of the parties.

In such a system, interest groups have natural points of access to influence policy because they are in constant interac-tion with the administrators and congressmen who are making it. There are significant incentives for congressmen as well. Con-gressmen tend to get on committees and subcommittees that will allow them to aid their districts and help them with reelec-tion—that is, western senators to Interior, rural to Agriculture. Therefore, congressmen tend to gain influence within those sub-governments that have direct relevance to their districts and thus enhance their reelection chances. This tends to strengthen their desire to keep serious policy decisions within the subgovernment, hence reinforcing the influence of the subcommittees. This flow of power toward subcommittees, in turn, adds to the decentrali-zation of the political process.

This is fine from the perspective of the subcommittee

member as long as the subject of policy-making is distributive policy, such as the construction of new federal facilities or the configuration of the formula in a grant program under the exclusive jurisdiction of the committee. However, it increases the difficulty of harmonizing competing priorities. In addition, larger crosscutting policies — for example, immigration reform — are more likely to be referred to multiple committees and subcommittees, making it more unlikely that a single subgovernment can dominate and, in fact, making it more difficult to get action on a single bill at all. Competing interests have more opportunity to hold out longer. As Cohen (1979) observed in the *National Journal:* "Many Democrats . . . are nostalgic for the days — less than a decade past — when heads of committees could bring major bills to the floor with the support of their committees and frighten away all potential challengers" (p. 1330). It is well to be careful in extending the subgovernment explanation for congressional policy-making too far. Ripley and Franklin (1987), in examining different types of issues, show how the degree of subgovernment dominance varies among them. Chubb (1983) found they continued to thrive in energy policy-making, but Wilson (1980) could find little evidence to support such influence in the regulatory areas he examined. Heclo (1977) argues that if we look "for closed triangles of control, we tend to miss the fairly open networks of people that increasingly impinge upon government" (p. 88). Heclo suggests that more issue areas involve issue networks that are more loose and through which people move in and out. Others refer to these as policy communities. With the boundaries much less tight than in subgovernments, new coalitions of participants form as issues develop.

Berry (1988) argues that in understanding how an issue network or policy community operates, it makes a difference whether legislators are preeminently concerned with reelection or highly concerned with other goals, too. Those preoccupied with reelection are going to be less interested in the nuts and bolts of policy formulation. Those highly interested in good public policy, whether because of ideology or personal interest, are more willing to devote considerable time to long-term evolution of legislation and to choose issues to work on with an eye toward doing more than maximizing credit. This can have an effect of increasing real influence within policy communities because such efforts are also important to other actors, such as interest groups. It can also have positive electoral effects because the reputation of being a workhorse rather than a show horse is helpful at election time. Berry cites the work of Sam Nunn (D-Ga.) on defense policy as a case in point.

The Executive Branch — The President

The dynamics of legislation cannot be understood simply by analyzing the workings of Congress. This is because the process is one that involves the actions of participants in both Congress and the executive branch.

The Constitution does not assign any powers to an executive branch, but rather to the president. The powers and duties of the executive branch derive from the powers of the president. The Constitution specifies a limited role for the president in the legislative realm in Article 2: (1) to inform Congress from time to time on the state of the union; (2) to recommend necessary and expedient legislation; (3) to summon Congress into special session and adjourn it if the two houses cannot agree on adjournment; and (4) to exercise a qualified veto.

The separation of powers envisioned in our constitutional scheme notwithstanding, in operation our system is, as Fisher (1987) extensively documents, one of shared powers, and the legislative process is a central example of this. As Fisher states: "The process of government requires constant interaction between executive and legislative leaders. Congress and the President can seldom afford to spin in separate orbits. Among the fundamental duties of the executive branch, since 1789, has been to structure itself for a continuing dialogue with Congress regarding legislation, appointments, and other matters that demand close consultation and cooperation" (p. 38). This interactive process has carried the presidential, and thus the executive branch, roles beyond consultation. Members of the executive branch are key players in the legislative process. It begins with the president. As Edwards and Wayne (1985) point out: "Presidents today have a central role in the legislative process. They are expected to formulate and promote policies. They are expected to coordinate them within the executive branch, to introduce them to Congress, and to mobilize support for them on Capitol Hill and, increasingly, with the general public" (p. 311).

As noted earlier, critics of divided government have bemoaned the ability of a president to "form a government" based on a party program. Others have decried the lack of party discipline and strong constituency ties as causing problems for formal leaders within Congress in formulating a program. However, Riggs (1988) claims that these factors also make legislators available for mobilization by the president. Mezey (1989b) observes that in presidential systems with stronger political parties, control of the Congress by a party different from the president's would always lead to deadlock, but in the United States, opposition legislators can be induced to support the president's position through ideological considerations or through favors from the executive that can benefit constituents. Consequently, Seligman and Covington (1989) argue that the consensus-type coalitions that parties once approximated have given way to interest-based conglomerate electoral coalitions, which make it more likely that presidents must govern through issue-specific, exclusive coalitions. They postulate that beginning with the nominating process, presidential candidates build a coalition and continue to construct coalitions essential to election and, once in office, to effective governance. Presidents are enabled to do this in government in the absence of strong supporting parties because the emergence of a large, internally differentiated presidential establishment has strengthened presidents' ability to achieve policy goals and lessened their dependence on other political actors (Seligman and Covington, 1989). Presidents, even ones whose party controls neither house of Congress, have significant levers to use in coalition building if they enjoy sufficient public popularity and are skillful. For example, during the 101st Congress, President Bush had a perfect record of fifteen vetoes that Congress failed to override. Bush's record has helped him use the veto as a bargaining tool to pressure Congress to fashion legislation more to his liking (Cook, 1990).

While executive branch participation in the dynamics of legislation begins with the president, it does not end there. In many cases of executive–congressional legislative interaction, the president is either not informed or not involved. There is really an extensive web of potential legislative actors within the executive branch. It is possible only to begin to identify them by organizational location and/or title, in that formal legislative duties are not as significant as informal ones that develop within the context of the policy process. Nonetheless, even the categories demonstrate some of the scope of the legislative actors within the presidential establishment, and thus of potential policy leaders. They include: (1) White House staff — the president's principal assistants and their deputies; (2) White House Office of Congressional Relations staff; (3) Office of Management and Budget (OMB) — principal officers and legislative clearance staff; (4) department and agency political appointees — secretaries, deputy secretaries, assistant secretaries; (5) departmental and agency legislative liaison officials — assistant secretary for legislative affairs; and (6) department, agency, and bureau civil servants.

One of the most visible elements of the presidential legislative establishment is the Office of Congressional Relations. Since the Eisenhower administration, every president has used it to orchestrate presidential legislative initiatives with Congress — some more successfully than others. It represents the institutional adaptation to the president's need to build congressional coalitions. Its functions include lobbying, intelligence gathering, representation, and interdepartmental coordination. This last refers to the responsibility to oversee the congressional liaison units within the various departments and agencies (Seligman and Covington, 1989). Coordination of the legislative efforts of the departments is important to sustain complex and far-flung presidential legislative initiatives. The Legislative Reference division of OMB is also crucial in keeping track of the hundreds of bills and coordinating departmental bills, testimony, and legislative policy statements to try to ensure that they are in keeping with the president's policy objectives. Departments and agencies operate extensive legislative liaison activities with respect to matters that range from their budgets, to perfecting legislation for existing authorities and programs, to major policy initiatives. Congress, its members collectively and individually, its committees and subcommittees, and its staff offices and agencies, is in the center of the external relationships toward which bureau chiefs and their staffs direct major parts of their total efforts. In fact, bureau chiefs pay more attention to Congress than to any other external or internal actor (Kaufman, 1981).

In actuality, executive branch congressional relations typically proceed at several levels at once, with the above actors interacting with congressional actors with respect to everything from simple information exchange to complex tactical maneuvering on complex legislation. As Ripley and Franklin (1987) point out: "Regardless of party control there are also instances in which the executive branch and the congressional committee are clearly in disagreement on some policy but close technical cooperation between staff members continues unimpaired" (p. 42).

The notion that the president initiates legislation and that the Congress merely reacts has been refuted by a number of studies (Moe and Teel, 1970; Chamberlain, 1946, Polsby, 1969). The fact is that sometimes some element of the executive branch is more in the lead in initiating legislation, and sometimes some element of Congress is in the lead. Regardless of where initiation takes place, the dynamics of legislation inevitably involve modes of interaction between elements of both branches.

This is not to say that there are not important differences in the approach to legislative action among different administrations. The differences are significant. For one thing, presidents have different styles in their approach to Congress. They differ in their amount of accessibility, level of involvement, and degree of personal interaction. According to these criteria, Wayne's (1978) examination of five presidents concluded: "Johnson and Ford's styles were the most responsive to the exigencies of Congress; Nixon's was the least. Johnson and Ford were the most reachable; Kennedy and Eisenhower less so; Nixon the most remote" (p. 166).

For another thing, while the White House congressional

liaison organization has become institutionalized, there are significant differences in skill and effectiveness observable between administrations, and indeed among departments and agencies. Several observers have reported considerable differences in the legislative effectiveness between the Carter and Reagan administrations. The contrast between the Carter and Reagan administrations' legislative liaison operations in particular was stark.

Carter selected Frank Moore, who had been his legislative liaison with the Georgia legislature when Carter was governor. Moore had no previous congressional experience, and executive-legislative relations, despite conditions where the same party controlled both branches of government for the first time in a great while, proceeded to a breakdown. Complaints from the congressional membership to the leadership ranged from matters of individual treatment, such as missed meetings and unreturned phone calls, to inadequate consultation on legislative priorities and presidential appointments. In addition, the departments and agencies were seemingly running their own legislative programs with little guidance from the White House. Carter allowed the cabinet secretaries to choose their own legislative liaison heads and let cabinet members deal directly with Congress with little White House control. In addition, while the Kennedy, Johnson, Nixon, and Ford administrations organized their liaison operations according to the major blocks within the Senate and the House that took care of the interests of the members, the Carter operation was initially organized according to policy areas, an arrangement which then had to be dumped within the first six months. Jones (1984b) pointed out the reason for the jettisoning of the "new" system: "Unfortunately, this system did not work. It was out of kilter with the multiple issue demands on individual members of Congress. The office never recovered from this initial mistake" (p. 121).

In contrast, President Reagan appointed Max Friedersdorf, who had served both the Nixon and Ford administrations in congressional relations, to serve as head of White House congressional relations, and he had assistants with substantial congressional experience. Also, the Reagan administration, in contrast to Carter's, took coordination of departmental legislative activities very seriously right from the start. The White House had a Legislative Strategy Group consisting of White House staff who decided tactics, and direction and guidance to the departments was coordinated by White House Chief of Staff James Baker and his aides. A system of Cabinet Councils organized by policy areas provided for airing of major policy proposals before concerned departmental political officials and White House aides. The OMB clearance process for legislative proposals and testimony was systematically enforced. The White House congressional liaison staff was organized once again according to the blocks of Congress. Bush followed Reagan's practice of hiring experience and appointed Frederick McClure, a former Senate aide and then lobbyist for the Reagan White House, as head of the Office of Congressional Relations and appointed other experienced congressional aides and lobbyists to staff the office (Hook, Jan. 14, 1989).

Carter's problems with Congress began early and colored the rest of his administration. The proposed deletion of nineteen water projects from his 1978 fiscal year budget proposal was announced in the first month of his administration and was seemingly done to indicate that this president was not only in charge but also emphasized a different set of issues — economy and environmental protection. Carter lost on the projects and created important enemies among his own party in Congress. As Bert Lance, Carter's budget director lamented: "We alienated a large portion of Congress: those who had projects and those who had hopes of having projects: 100 percent alienation. It was not a good decision in my judgment, but the President felt very strongly about it" (Pfiffner, 1988, p. 147).

In contrast, the Reagan administration experienced early legislative victories involving both the budget and taxes, even though the Democrats had a majority in the House. To be sure, Reagan's popularity and Republican control of the Senate were large factors in these successes, but Carter was also popular, at least at the beginning, and his party controlled both houses of Congress. The president's approach and actions can make the difference. Pfiffner (1988) concludes his review of the Reagan performance: "How did President Reagan achieve virtually all of his legislative goals during his first eight months in office? He included members of Congress in his preelection and pre-inaugural activities. After his election he dropped most of his anti-Washington rhetoric and assiduously courted Congress, emphasizing his respect for the institution. Once in office he moved quickly to take advantage of his 'mandate' from the voters and to create momentum with early victories. He strictly limited his legislative agenda to his budget and tax initiatives, to the neglect of other priorities. Finally, he became personally involved with the lobbying for his program and spent a significant proportion of his time on his legislative agenda" (p. 155).

It was not all merely adept tactics that explained Reagan's legislative success. The Reagan legislative program was policy driven. Newland's (1984) review of Reagan's policy apparatus in the first term concluded, "To reiterate, in the Reagan presidency, the long-term Reagan agenda persistently defines policy" (p. 149). The president constructed a White House staff apparatus that kept an eye on his agenda and, at the same time, coordinated the effort of his administration to propose, enact, and implement that agenda. Not that there were not reverses. His "new Federalism" legislation went nowhere. Nonetheless, the successes were unmistakably significant and fit with President Reagan's policy agenda. As Jones (1984a) put it, "Reagan has been successful in managing the context for congressional choice" (p. 286). The conclusion that approach, organization, and skill in legislative activity — in short, mastering the dynamics of legislation — is critical to presidential legislative success seems inescapable. Also, to achieve large-scale legislative success requires presidential policy leadership, which means focusing on a large-scale policy priority, such as the budget and tax package, as opposed to squandering presidential efforts on water projects, at least initially. As will be seen below, Reagan had his own fight with Congress over water projects but handled it much more successfully.

President Bush had a mixed record with Congress in his first two years in office. On the one hand, the Democratic-dominated Congress failed to override all fifteen of his vetoes, and his proposal to rewrite the Clean Air Act transformed the environmental debate in Congress, which had stalled legislative action on the Act for over ten years, and forced the key congressional players to sit down and deal (Hager, June 17, 1989). His agreement with the Senate leadership over a compromise omnibus bill won him twelve successive victories in opposing "deal busting" amendments (Gettinger, October 13, 1990). There would have been no passage of the massive overhaul of the Clean Air Act without Bush (Pytte, October 27, 1990).

On the other hand, Bush's overall success rate on contested votes was lower in his first year (62.6 percent) than any of the last eight presidents except Gerald Ford (58.2 percent). His second year was even worse (43.6 percent) and was the lowest of the last eight presidents. Bush's success rate was better in the Senate (73 percent the first year, 61 percent the second year), where the Republican deficit was smaller, 55–45, than in the house, 260–175. Bush had a smaller proportion of his party in Congress than did Reagan. In Reagan's first term, Republicans controlled 192 seats in the House compared to 175 for Bush's first term. In addition, in Reagan's first term, the Republicans enjoyed a 53–46 majority as opposed to a 45–55 minority in Bush's first term. A president's leverage to achieve the substantive policies he desires in negotiation is affected by the proportion of seats in Congress his party controls.

Bush's biggest defeat came on the budget-tax package that resulted from the months-long budget summit negotiations involving the House and Senate leadership and administration officials (chief of staff John Sununu and budget director Richard Darman). A majority of Bush's own party deserted him in the House, with Minority Whip Newt Gingrich (R-Georgia) leading dissident Republicans in opposing both the first package, which was defeated, and the second one, which passed. Bush's television appeal for public support for the first deal with the Democratic leadership was too little and too late. If the policy gets too far away from the rank and file, skillful negotiation with the leadership is not enough in this era of a decentralized and fragmented Congress. The rank and file will not necessarily support a president unless a president has or builds sufficient public support for the particular policy. Mitchell Daniels, a political director in the Reagan White House, put it this way: "The reaction against the so-called government-by-entertainment of the Reagan years is a healthy one, but I do think you can pay a price if you so consciously disregard the formation of public opinion that you leave yourself naked to your enemies. For good motives, the Bush White House may have been too studiedly indifferent to aggressively getting their story out" (Dowd, October 21, 1990, p. E-1). The Bush administration's inattention to getting the story out on the budget-tax package may have in large part been due to a preoccupation with managing the nation's foreign and defense policies and rallying support for those in the face of a confrontation with Iraq following its conquest of Kuwait.

Even though presidents are expected to have and pursue a legislative program, this activity cannot receive nearly the attention that presidents could profitably devote to it. Presidents and the other officials of the executive branch face multiple demands and thus have a number of options concerning which functions to emphasize in their jobs.

Presidents are called upon to perform several roles, including those as Chief of State, Administrative Chief, Party Chief, Public Leader, Chief Diplomat, Commander in Chief of the Armed Forces, as well as legislative policymaker (Koenig, 1968). Reagan has probably added the role of Chief Communicator, that is, chief commentator on what is on the minds of the public and enunciator of what the government is doing or ought to do about it. Different presidents have emphasized different roles, and their choice has been influenced both by the political environment of their presidencies and their personal orientations. Nixon, for example, emphasized the foreign policymaking role of the president and, in facing a Congress dominated by the opposing party, deemphasized new legislative initiatives.

The president's legislative leadership role is, in reality, of rather recent vintage in our history. Most trace the beginning to the presidency of Theodore Roosevelt and continuing with that of Woodrow Wilson. Their successors—Harding, Coolidge, and Hoover—downplayed the president's legislative policy-making role. The president's modern legislative leadership position is credited to the enlargement of that role by Franklin Roosevelt in his enactment of the New Deal legislation. Roosevelt's performance, in many ways, has conditioned contemporary expectations that presidents will take the lead in proposing a legislative program. Eisenhower was criticized, for example, for not submitting a legislative program in his first year. As one member of the House Foreign Affairs Committee told an administration official: "Don't expect us to start from scratch on what you people want. That's not the way we do things here. You draft the bills and we work them over" (Edwards and Wayne, 1985, pp. 236–237). However, as Wayne (1978) observes, "While all presidents have proposed legislative programs, they have not placed equal emphasis on the development and enactment of new policy initiatives" (p. 20).

Presidents have policy goals, which they may choose to pursue not through legislation but through executive orders or other administrative actions. Executive orders do not require presidents to secure the approval of Congress to make policy, and consequently presidents may prefer to issue them in order to act more autonomously in policy-making. Nixon, in particular, undertook numerous environmental policy initiatives in the form of executive orders to respond to the demands of the environmental crisis, as did Carter. Since Franklin Roosevelt's institutionalization of the assumption that presidents can use executive orders for policy-making and not just for administration, presidents have been active in issuing them in defense, foreign trade, economic management, natural resources, and social welfare/civil rights (King and Ragsdale, 1988). Nixon also tried to bypass Congress to scale back the social programs of the Johnson administration through budget impoundment and other administrative actions (Nathan, 1975). However, there are clearly limits on what presidents can do in the form of independent executive actions, and Congress has sometimes reacted to such actions, passing legislation restricting them, as Congress did in the Congressional Budget Reform Act when it curtailed the president's use of budgetary impoundment. Sooner or later, presidents must come to grips with their legislative leadership responsibility. Their leadership skills can make an important difference in the success or failure of large-scale legislative efforts.

The Executive Branch—Cabinet and Departments

As mentioned earlier, the president is not the only policy actor in the executive branch, and even when he is active in a particular policy area, he does not act alone but in concert with other members of his administration and the civil service. The president is particularly dependent upon his political appointees in the departments and agencies for policy advice and support activities. Even with an expanded role for the White House staff, the intricacies of complex large-scale policies demand that issues, alternatives, and priorities be extensively analyzed and their complexities revealed as much as possible if the president's proposals are to be expected to stand up to the scrutiny they will receive in the legislative process. The departments have both the numbers of personnel and range of expertise to vet the substance and political reactions of the numerous potentially affected groups. Presidents have learned the hard way that policies pursued by White House staff alone can cause serious unanticipated embarrassment, as the Reagan administration's Iran-Contra affair demonstrates. Increasingly, concern has been raised about the drift toward centralization of power in the White House staff. New presidents often profess allegiance to cabinet government and then proceed to ignore the cabinet as a policy-making body. John Ehrlichman claims that presidents begin their terms with strong cabinets and end them with strong White House staffs (Pfiffner, 1988). There is a tendency for the president, and particularly his staff, to view the cabinet members as unresponsive and slow in response to presidential initiatives—"having gone native"—and thus some presidents countenance greater policy development leadership by the White House staff. President Johnson, after his landslide election victory, felt the need to move fast and encouraged his staff to draft much of the Great Society's social programs. The risk of unanticipated problems due to inadequate information in such large-scale initiatives is correspondingly greater. As one Johnson assistant later put it: "If

you shouldn't fire a pistol with a blindfold on, you shouldn't propose a major program without some basic knowledge of what
will happen. The Great Society was crippled by unanticipated
consequences. We were driving at night without our headlights
on" (Light, 1982, p. 20).

In order to anticipate consequences, programmatic and
political, presidents can look to the heads of their departments
for policy advice, though they need not necessarily follow it.
This is only the tip of the iceberg, however. The other political
appointees, such as the under secretaries and assistant secretaries, are continuously engaged with White House staff and
with members of Congress in policy deliberations as well. The
initiative, or lack thereof, by the president's complement of political appointees in legislative policy-making can make a significant difference in the success of his legislative program. Political appointees, like presidents, also vary in their degree of
aptitude for, and interest in, legislative policy leadership.

Cabinet secretaries, like presidents, have multiple demands on them and make choices concerning what to emphasize in their jobs. Departments are really not integrated hierar-
chies but collections of bureaus and agencies that the cabinet
officer must win over, at least to some extent, if he or she is
to have any hope of obtaining their notice, let alone their cooperation. Operational management of the Washington headquarters
of these subdivisions can be fully occupying. However, as many
a department head has learned, preoccupation with internal
departmental operations can carry a high cost. Michael Blumenthal, Carter's Secretary of the Treasury, observed shortly after
leaving the post of chief executive of Bendix Corporation for
Treasury, "Businessmen don't understand that what matters in
government is what you appear to do . . . so if you appear to
have influence, that counts" ("Carter's Harried Businessmen,"
1978, p. 80). That is, if you are not perceived by other policymakers in both the executive and congressional branches as effective in dealing with political issues as well as operational ones,
then they will not supply the cooperation necessary for the department head to obtain the resources — budget, personnel, executive orders, regulatory changes, legislative changes — that will

allow him to demonstrate to his subordinates that he has successfully defended the interests of the agency and thus gain their cooperation. Blumenthal himself suffered from an external appearance problem in that he appeared not to be a major policy spokesman on economic policy with access to the president. He was undermined by opponents on the White House staff and was dismissed along with some others during Carter's infamous "Saturday Massacre."

The requisite appearance of effectiveness is conveyed in significant part by the press, and thus the department head, to a considerable extent, ignores the function of chief press spokesman for his department at his peril. Departments also typically have extensive field operations with which lines of communication and cooperation must be established and maintained. Congressional relations occupies a large amount of time, but much of this is involved with budget matters and congressional oversight activities (Bartlett and Jones, 1974). All of these demands compete with each other and with any significant policy initiatives that a department head may seek to push legislatively.

Added to these demands are the very real limitations on the opportunity for departmental officials to pursue complex legislative policy objectives. The average political appointee is in office about twenty-two months, and because the secretaries, under secretaries, and assistant secretaries come and go sporadically, there is seldom the same political team in place for very long that is capable of sustaining long-term legislative effort (Heclo, 1977). Given the obstacles in the legislative process, it would not be surprising if cabinet officers and their fellow political appointees steered clear of the legislative process as much as possible, other than responding to congressional requests.

There are, nevertheless, countervailing forces that encourage participation in legislative policy-making. A main force is the relationship of departmental appointees to the president. According to Seidman and Gilmour (1986), "As far as the president is concerned, a Cabinet member's primary responsibility is to mobilize support both within and outside Congress for presidential measures and to act as legislative tactician" (p. 82). A large part of this is to mobilize friendly interest groups in sup-

port of the president's initiatives (Pfiffner, 1988). Political appointees need to do this if they are to retain White House support. The White House staff always suspects that the political
appointees have been co-opted by the "bureaucrats." However,
the political appointee is literally caught in the middle. If he
does not gain presidential support, he will be unlikely to be able
to defend the department and deliver the resources that gain
him legitimacy and cooperation from his subordinates. He also
must be seen as a strong advocate of the priorities of his department, which sometimes runs against presidential wishes. "He
must act in the president's best interests while at the same time
convincing his career subordinates that he is sticking up for them"
(Pfiffner, 1988, p. 43).

Departmental policy and presidential policy are not necessarily at odds, however, In the first place, presidential policy
is not static. Presidents typically do not enter office with full-
blown legislative programs in hand. Even such policy-oriented
presidents as Reagan had fairly fully developed policies in only
a few areas — budget, taxes, and defense. In addition, the White
House staff, as enlarged as it has become, simply does not have
the capability to generate all the policy ideas. As one of Carter's
assistants said: "We are dealing with a system that places a
premium on bureaucratic initiatives. The executive branch has
all the advantages . . . the information, the manpower, the congressional support, and the expertise. Instead of fighting the
bureaucracy, the President should get some kind of control. But
only God knows how" (Light, 1982, p. 92). Therefore, there
is an opportunity for political appointees to aid the president
in developing those policies that fit with his basic political philosophy and approach. Some portion of these will become presidential legislative initiatives. The federal government is simply too
large and the number of policy areas too vast to expect that the
president or even the White House staff will always be the driver
behind major legislative policy proposals. Instead, the expectation must be that the president's department heads, acting as
the president's policy advisors, will utilize their staffs to come
up with policy proposals in their areas that further the president's
basic political program.

Unfortunately, it does not always work this way. One of the reasons is conflict between the White House staff and the departmental political appointees. Cronin's (1975) interviews of eighty White House aides in the 1970s found that considerable conflict in White House departmental exchanges was felt by 66 percent, with 25 percent feeling moderate conflict. The problem is that as the president and his staff see departmental officials responding sluggishly to White House budget-cutting ideas or legislative strategies that may promote other interests at the expense of theirs, they may perceive these officials as weak and reject their advice in policy matters (Cronin, 1975). Therefore, just as departmental officials vary in their interest and capacity to engage in policy leadership on legislative initiatives, presidents and their staffs vary in their capacity and willingness to use departmental officials as sources of policy advice and legislative allies. They have alternative sources of ideas that can be used either along with or as substitutes for policy proposals from the executive branch. These include Congress, events outside Washington, public opinion polls, parties, interest groups, the media, and various staffs of the executive office of the president (Light, 1982).

In sum, there are forces that both encourage and inhibit policy leadership on the part of executive branch officials. The degree to which they will become involved in legislative policy leadership is dependent upon both the interaction of these forces and the individual choices of roles and strategies the participants make.

Policy Leadership— Opportunity, Need, and Characteristics

In the field of legislative leadership so far, the focus has tended to be on individuals in formal leadership positions. Peabody's (1984) extensive review of legislative leadership concludes that most of the leadership studies examined one or more incumbents of a single formal leadership position (such as speaker or floor leader) in a single country's legislative institution, usually over a limited time. These are helpful, if somewhat limited, in achieving insight into the bringing about of policy change. Previously, the formal leadership of Congress and the constraints within which such leaders operate were discussed. Peabody further discusses a key distinction — that between formal and informal leadership — with Lyndon Johnson as Senate Majority Leader and Richard Russell as mainly behind-the-scenes leader in the 1950s being a famous example. As he observes, formal and informal leadership are frequently fused in practice, but there is no guarantee that this will occur. Smith's analysis (1990) shows that only about one-third of the cases of policy leadership stem directly from senator's duties as formal party or committee leaders. Institutional context is important, but so are personal orientations and skills.

What is required to understand the contribution of leadership to enacting large-scale legislation, then, is analysis of the activities of legislative leadership that combines the various factors involved in the dynamics of the process. The reforms that diluted the formal leadership and opened up the legislative process at the same time created considerably more opportunities for policy entrepreneurship among members. That is, it became easier for members to raise and debate policy issues in their areas of interest. However, concomitantly, it became more complicated to actually move policies to final passage, in that other policy entrepreneurs were similarly unconstrained in raising what they wanted.

A few analysts have come to observe the emergence of a congressional style exhibited by some members who choose to emphasize policy entrepreneurship and have described these as policy entrepreneurs. Kingdon (1984) defines them as "advocates who are willing to invest their resources — time, energy, reputation, money — to promote a position in return for anticipated future gain in the form of material, purposive, or solidary benefits" (p. 188). The objective is to "promote a position." Uslaner (1978) describes this orientation: "Policy entrepreneurs . . . are concerned with the formulation of policy, but see themselves as active participants in every stage of policy development. They are egocentric in wanting to be the leading congressional spokesmen on a particular, even if narrow, policy area. They are willing to cooperate with other members, particularly those of their party, but not to repudiate the personal satisfaction and recognition that comes with effective control of the policy area" (p. 106).

Loomis (1985) notes that the structural changes in Congress, combined with new interest by the media in Washington policy formulation, created opportunities for a number of congressmen to establish themselves as articulate and attractive spokespersons on issues. Once having established themselves as such, they are often asked to comment on a range of related issues. As a result, he avers, issues have become significant in themselves and as opportunities for attention and advancement. Loomis found that "in interview after interview members and staff aides emphasized the legislative significance of obtaining publicity" (p. 12). Increasingly, the method for doing this is to speak out on policy issues. Relatedly, he found that members emphasized the importance of affecting the policy agenda, of moving public opinion, and of formulating the questions that the institution should be considering.

Such emphases, however, do not, as a natural matter of course, include policy enactment — achieving passage of comprehensive legislation. Instead, the focus is on what Loomis (1985) calls contributing meaningfully to the policy debate. As Representative Richard Gephardt (D-Mo.) put it, "The satisfaction is more with ideas and concepts than with a bill" (Cohen, 1983, p. 2063). Thus, policy entrepreneurs provide a reservoir of members interested in policy. What is needed from here is the activation of a subset of them to serve as leaders to secure the enactment of policy and not merely to act as issue promoters.

In the post-reform House, the formal leadership is dependent upon including as many members as possible in the process and giving them a stake in it (Sinclair, 1981). Out of this, the leadership hopes to build some kind of winning coalition. For that hope to be realized, the formal leadership, if it is involved, is dependent on tying in with a smaller subset of the policy entrepreneurs who can serve as effective leaders to secure the cooperation of others and to work with the formal leadership to guide the legislation to enactment. The formal leadership is unlikely to be the initiator of the policy or of the action on it. It will be more reactive. Policy leaders among the membership are likely to be self-activating. Such policy leaders will push policies as far as they can with the resources at their disposal. Concurrently, the formal leaders will seek to identify policy issues, and policy entrepreneurs associated with those issues, as possible candidates for their efforts in assisting coalition building, as they emerge.

There is no degree of certainty in these endeavors. The dynamics of the legislative process have become much more unpredictable and subject to numerous forces internal and external to the legislative body. The legislation, if it progresses at all, is likely to proceed in spurts followed by backtracking. Several sessions of Congress may be required, during which the legislation may undergo substantial or minor alteration. Thus, policy leaders are needed to sustain focus and movement through the episodic fits and starts to which the legislation will be subject.

This is particularly true of complex large-scale legislation. Such legislation, by its very nature, is likely to engage the interests and thus the activity of various legislators, many of whom will be triggered by outside groups and will not be friendly to passage. Policy leadership is necessary to guide the legislation through the myriad blocking tactics of the opposition and to engage in strategic reformulation, when necessary, to move it to passage.

Therefore, policy leaders need to be policy entrepreneurs, but they need to be something more. They need to raise and debate issues. However, their goal is to move beyond policy expression to policy enactment. Their objective is not only to transform the policy debate but also to pass significant large-scale legislation that transforms government's substantive approach, and, it is hoped, the way government impacts the society and the populace. Policy leadership is a collective type of leadership. It takes several such leaders positioned at strategic points in the branches of government to effect large-scale policy change. Policy leadership is an inter-branch phenomenon. It takes policy leadership in both branches and at different levels — elected officials, political appointees, and staff — sustained over time to enact large-scale public interest policy. Policy leadership is not necessarily all-encompassing. That is, a single policy leader need not perform all the leadership functions from the gestation period of a piece of legislation through final passage in order to be effective as a policy leader. He or she also need not always play the policy leadership role exclusively. Congressmen, for example, have a choice among a number of different roles (as do officials of the executive branch, as discussed earlier). Some congressmen put greater stress on one or two roles to the virtual exclusion of others; other congressmen attempt to balance the roles.

Some members stress constituent representation, and either push for bills that provide direct benefits to their particular districts, or concentrate on constituent casework, or both. Other congressmen devote themselves to the work of their committees. Their focus often is to carve out an area of expertise and exercise their skill within the committee, whether that involves committee oversight, legislation, or publicizing issues. Still others are closely aligned with particular interest groups and attempt to foster the priorities of such groups. Some are devoted to election activity, either on behalf of themselves or their political party. A portion stress electioneering because they are new and vulnerable to electoral challenge or they represent districts where their party is weak — marginal districts. Another portion stress electioneering because they have ambitions for higher party positions in the formal leadership, and helping colleagues get elected is one way to build credits for support for such positions. Some congressmen are interested in higher office — usually a Senate seat for House members, and the presidency for senators. Finally, some stress enacting policy out of a commitment to an idea, ideology, sense of national concern, or a combination of these and other factors. Policy leaders have to stress this last role, at least for a time, in order to see their legislation move to final passage.

The dynamics of legislation most often take different twists and turns, and various requirements for action may need to be fulfilled at these different junctures. Kingdon (1984) describes the process of one stage of policy development, agenda setting — that is, the placing and framing of policy problems on the political agenda. As he points out, a complex combination of factors is generally responsible for the movement of a given item into agenda prominence and thus a variety of resources is needed. Some actors bring to the policy process their political popularity, others their expertise, others their pragmatic sense of the possible, others their ability to attract attention. The key is for actors in both the legislative and executive branches to use their particular talent in pursuit of policy adoption according to the requirements of the dynamics of the legislative process, and to subordinate, at least for a time, other roles.

The dynamics of legislation may require a certain entrepreneurship and popularizing in order to get a comprehensive piece of legislation onto the political agenda. It may require the concerted use of expertise to develop policy approaches that are workable and acceptable to other participants in the process and in the wider political environment. It may require the brokering of conflicting positions on parts of the comprehensive package. It may require the articulation of various rationales for the policies contained in the comprehensive package so that different interests are attracted to support it, and opponents, if not mollified, are less motivated to devote maximum resources in opposition. Sometimes, it may require the articulation of the political ramifications, even partisan implications, to overcome political obstacles, which in themselves are either partisan or idcological in nature.

Thus, policy leadership exercised within the dynamics of the legislative process is a multifaceted phenomenon engaging several participants who play either single or multiple roles according to their resources, and according to the dynamics of the particular legislative process involved in a given effort. It is a blending of substantive and political imperatives tailored to the dynamics of the legislative process. It is exercised by different actors who attempt to coordinate their efforts, at least in a loose fashion, as they simultaneously seek to fulfill the requirements associated with their positions, as well as with their personal objectives.

As has been discussed earlier, participants in government, whether in the legislative or executive branches, have a number of different roles from which to choose. Thus, at any given time, participants in the legislative process—both potential allies and potential opponents—will be governed by different motives. The question is how to successfully motivate participants to stress their possible policy-making roles in a cooperative fashion. This is where leadership is crucial. Participants move in and out of such policy collectivities associated with different legislative initiatives. Policy leadership is a form of interactive leadership in which the leaders motivate each other and other types of political leaders as well. Thus, they alternate as leaders and followers. In comprehensive policy-making, this willingness to pick up the followership role with respect to some subsets of the overall legislative package in order to assert the lead on others is critical. If all participants insisted on being in the lead on all aspects of a comprehensive package, or if the process depended upon a preeminent policy leader, then the task of policy adoption would be problematic. Either the single leader would become overwhelmed by the complexity of the package and the need to respond to multiple requests and challenges affecting different parts, or strident conflict, as different leaders thrust themselves forward, would ensue. Indeed, these circumstances sometimes do arise, and policy defeat is the result.

To understand large-scale policy change, it is necessary to examine the factors involved in policy leadership not just singly, but in interaction with each other. If there is a consensus about any aspect of leadership, it is that it involves an interactive process. As Tucker (1981) observes, "Leadership is a process of human interaction in which individuals exert, or attempt to exert a determining influence upon others" (p. 11). This is not to say that it is purely an exchange relationship between individuals. The activity of leaders—in this case, policy leaders—is qualitatively distinct and significant in enabling complex legislation to proceed to enactment. Nonetheless, that activity is best revealed and understood when viewed in interaction within the dynamics of the legislative process.

The passage of legislation that has substantially reformed federal criminal law is an example of the triumph of policy leadership in action. It is typical of large-scale policy initiatives in that its substantive and political evolution proceeded through several Congresses and different presidencies and involved efforts of numerous policy leaders in Congress and the executive branch. The following chapters describe the efforts of policy leaders through those sessions. The dynamics involved illustrate what has come to be required to pass large-scale public interest legislation.

• 3 •

Policy Initiation:
From Public Opinion
to Congressional
Attention

The legislative process in Congress is not linear. There are no well-defined stages or steps to provide recognizable points of demarcation. Members of Congress and their staffs are constantly discussing and acting upon problems, policies, and proposals in various forms and stages of development in various overlapping policy areas. It is taken as axiomatic by long-term staffers that there are few "blank-slate" issues. A favorite saying is that there are no new proposals, merely recycled ones, newly discovered by the uninitiated. There is a certain degree of truth to this, in that government is constantly bombarded with problems and proposals in all policy areas, and the needs and demands of the public usually do not suddenly explode from periodic revolutionary wrenching in American society.

While there certainly have been critical historical events and forces that have converged to produce important political and policy changes, such as the Depression of the 1930s and World War II, policy change in the United States has generally been more evolutionary than revolutionary. Thus, participants in government are accustomed to issues that rise and decline, combining and recombining with other issues as the political winds shift in the country and in Washington.

Translating Public Opinion into Policy Initiatives

At some point, as a result of their testing of the political winds in the country and in Washington, policymakers periodically can get serious about initiating a major change. Although no one announces that "now is the time for serious policy initiation," such a conceptual category can help would-be policymakers to understand the requirements of the dynamics of legislation and to bring into focus how the efforts of the participants in the legislative process fit together to produce policy change.

Policy initiation refers to the dynamic whereby participants in the policy process seriously begin to formulate a legislative solution to a perceived public problem The words "seriously begin to formulate" are used because bills are introduced all the time for various purposes, several of which have little to do with any expectation by the introducer that actual changes in the law will take place. For example, because of constituent or interest group requests congressmen regularly sponsor bills that they have little or an unknown degree of intention of supporting in later stages of the process. They also introduce legislation merely to signify sympathy or concern with the interests of those affected, with no expectation of passage but because of election implications. Sometimes they introduce legislation to encourage or force some administrator or group of administrators to take some executive action in the implementation of an existing policy or program favorable to some interest they support. In many of these cases, the sponsors go very little beyond throwing the bill in the hopper and making an introductory speech. They expend little time or political capital in efforts to get other legislators to take notice and move the bill further. This may be legislative introduction, but it is not policy initiation.

One requirement for policy initiation is to achieve sufficient recognition by legislative policymakers that a problem requiring government attention exists and that it is susceptible to legislative treatment. In short, the problem must be brought into the government as government's problem, and it must be perceived as something that has a chance of being formulated into law that could achieve passage. This does not mean that no alternative has been proposed anywhere before. For some policies, alternatives may have been proposed by someone well before the need for a solution is widely recognized, while for others, the recognition of the need and the invention of the solution occur together (Polsby, 1984). It simply means that there will not be serious initiation in the legislative process unless legislators recognize that a problem suitable for legislative solution exists.

Numerous problems never cross this threshold for various reasons. For example, even though broad-based public opinion polls showed support for more stringent forms of gun control during the 1970s and 1980s, most legislators declined to make gun control a central crime control issue in crime legislation because of the intense and well-organized activities of groups such as the National Rifle Association. Crime reform advocates knew that inclusion of a gun control provision in any criminal law reform bill would doom that bill. Gun control legislation was unlikely to pass, so serious legislative initiatives were not pursued very far.

For a problem to receive attention from governmental actors, it must first be perceived and defined as a problem. In the process of getting the problem to government, perception is important, and people who perceive certain events as being unsatisfactory and seek redress bring into sharp relief the social effects of events (Anderson, 1990). This can serve to define a problem as a policy problem.

How a predominant perception or a predominant contending perception of a social problem comes to be formed in the minds of policy makers will greatly influence both the priority they place on formulating a legislative solution and what approach they will embrace.

Questions such as the following will be asked: (1) Is this problem susceptible to legislative treatment or is it best treated by administrative, judicial, or symbolic action? (2) Is there public political significance to this problem? Is there a wide or narrow constituency clamoring for a solution? If wide or narrow, are they nonetheless cohesive, active, and influential politically, either in the electoral or legislative arenas? and (3) Where does this problem fit within priorities of other significant political actors? Is it likely to be a priority of the president, the leadership of the House or Senate, or influential committee chairs, and so on.

Depending on how the problem comes to be perceived as a result of the political process, a range of alternative policy directions will be defined as appropriate for consideration, and others will be defined as inappropriate. As will be demonstrated in this chapter, the debate over whether there was a "crime problem"—and if so, whether it resulted from poverty and discrimination requiring social justice approaches, or from deviant behavior encouraged by weak government and requiring stronger law enforcement approaches—played a critical role in structuring the federal legislative approach to crime control.

Governmental actors do not often come to perceive that a problem is a policy problem through individual inspiration. Rather, public policies emerge in response to policy demands, or to those claims for action or inaction on some public issue made by other actors—private citizens, group representatives, or other public officials—upon government officials and agencies (Anderson, 1990). However, the linkage between public opinion, public policy demands, and public policies is complex, and there is considerable debate in political science over whether sufficient linkage exists to conclude that public opinion has significant impact and that democratic control over policy can be said to exist (see Luttbeg, 1981). Nonetheless, as Converse (1987) concludes: "Surely those studies capable of examining potential congruence between popular will and personal predilection contrasted across candidates competing for representative roles tend to show that winners display much higher congruence with their districts than losers do. Here the causal mechanism producing a legislature of winners rather than losers is incontrovertible in a democracy: it is popular selection at the polls" (pp. 522–523). The whole consultation process is a delicate process of mutual adjustment and accommodation between the revealed opinion of constituents and a legislator's own convictions. Congruence between a legislator's own disposition and constituent's views does vary from time to time and issue to issue (Converse, 1987).

The fact that a significant segment of the public perceives a policy problem and makes policy demands to resolve it is insufficient to start policy initiation. The policy problem and accompanying demands must be made into an issue. "An issue arises when a public with a problem seeks or demands governmental action, and there is public disagreement over the best solution to the problem (Eyestone, 1978, p. 3).

Actually, there is no reliable route for policy problems to be translated into policy issues. Policy issues may be generated in any one of at least four ways: (1) manufactured by one or more contending parties who perceive an unfavorable bias in the distribution of public resources; (2) generated by individuals or groups doing what they believe is in the public interest; (3) initiated through an unanticipated triggering event; and (4) manufactured by a group or individual for personal gain, such as being elected to political office (Cobb and Elder, 1983).

With respect to the first way that policy issues are generated, President Johnson manufactured the "war on poverty," which resulted in the initiation of the Great Society legislation, because he and his allies perceived an unfavorable distribution of resources in regard to the poor. In his memoirs, Johnson (1971) acknowledged that most citizens were unaware of how extensive poverty was in the United States, and he discussed how he set out to "rally the nation" to the issue. Senator John McClellan's successful efforts to make membership in an organized crime syndicate illegal would fall into the second group. As an example of the third group, the death of University of Maryland basketball star Len Bias from a cocaine overdose reverberated with a base of public opinion that had built up over two decades and triggered the rapid introduction of the 1986 Anti-Drug bill. However, this base of public demand had its roots in a much earlier period. The base was initiated as a result of efforts that fall into the last category. The linkage between public opinion and federal crime legislation found its start in the electoral arena in which candidates, in an attempt to get elected, explicated the burgeoning public unease over crime as an issue. Republican candidates over several elections articulated the crime problem as a national issue demanding a policy response from the federal government.

The articulation of policy demands is not enough. Policy formulation — the development of a plan or method for acting on the problem — also must occur if the legislative wheels are to be engaged and the legislative process set in motion. Jones (1984a) offers several initial realities that would-be policy initiators confront:

1. Formulation need not be limited to one set of actors. Thus, there may well be two or more formulation groups producing competing (or complementary) proposals.
2. Formulation may proceed without a clear defintion of the problem, or without formulators ever having much contact with the affected groups.
3. There is no necessary coincidence between formulation and particular institutions, though it is a frequent activity of bureaucratic agencies.
4. Formulation and reformulation may occur over a long period of time without ever building support for one proposal.
5. There are several appeal points for those who lose in the formulation process at any one level.
6. The process itself never has neutral effects. Somebody wins and somebody loses. [p. 78]

As will be demonstrated, the formulation of crime legislation confronted several of these realities.

There is considerable variation in the circumstances surrounding policy initiation. Some policies move quickly from initiation to enactment; other take years. Some are shaped largely by experts; others involve politicians early. Some are accompanied by wide agreement that a need exists; for others the agreement is narrower. Some are highly salient to the public right from the beginning; others are not so salient until the decision stage. Some generate great political conflict; others generate only a little. Some policies require sophisticated research; others are improvised (Polsby, 1984).

The formulation of a policy proposal will not necessarily mean that it will be processed within Congress. A multitude of problems, issues, and proposals are being pushed at policymakers all the time by various interest groups and associations. In addition, representatives and senators gather intelligence about perceived problems and issues affecting their districts and states through their campaign activities, frequent visits to their districts, the liaison with constituents provided by their district offices, and mail and phone calls directly from constituents. Also, congressmen are supplied with public opinion polls and formal analyses of issues prepared by committee staffs, by research agencies of Congress, such as the Congressional Research Service or the General Accounting Office, and by operational bureaus and research staffs of the executive branch (Jones, 1982).

These sources may serve to convince a member of Congress that the public is ready to have Congress address an issue through legislation, but they will not prove to such a member that the government is ready. Problems and issues have to achieve a priority with the participants in the policy-making process in Washington before they will receive serious attention, and members of Congress know this. They look for signals from other proximate policymakers — the president and his key advisors, the cabinet secretaries, the leadership of the parties in both houses of Congress, informal leaders with significant followings — that out of all the problems clamoring for attention, some problem is emerging on their political radarscopes and will receive consideration for policy treatment if serious legislation is formulated. What is needed is a broad problem that has achieved critical political mass among both the public and the proximate policymakers in Washington, which suggests that legislation could move.

Out of all this, policymakers form a perception that some problem is ripe for large-scale policy change and requires a comprehensive legislative solution. Crime is such a problem envelope, encompassing everything from street muggings to riots to international drug deals.

The Crime Problem and Policy Initiation

How crime has come to be perceived as a national problem has had much to do with its relatively new designation as being considered, in part, a federal government responsibility, at least in providing a leadership role.

Although, in the presidential election of 1988, the candidates of both parties continuously pronounced their solutions to the federal government's responsibility to combat crime, particularly when drug-related, crime has in fact only fairly recently in our history come to be defined as a national issue. Legislating about crime, as well as actual crime control, has always been overwhelmingly a state and local responsibility, and our decentralized and disaggregated approach is unique among Western countries. Increasingly, however, it has come to be defined as more of a national responsibility. The operative term is, as discussed earlier, defined not discovered. Issues considered ripe for the initiation of policy change do not exist until they are identified and framed for government action. Crime is such an issue.

Public demand for increased crime control has increased over time and has a basis in the actual crime situation in the country. American levels of violent crime in general, and murder in particular, are greater than those of any other industrialized nation (United Nations, 1987). Without going into all the nuances of all the different crime statistics (see Bureau of Justice Statistics, 1983), it is nonetheless apparent that at least some serious crimes increased in the 1960s and 1970s. For example, murder, which had decreased in the 1940s and 1950s, increased in the 1960s and 1970s, with the homicide rate rising from 4.5 per 100,000 people in 1963 to a peak of 10.7 in 1980, which was the highest this century (Niemi, Mueller, and Smith, 1989, p. 131). In addition, the percentage of people who were afraid to walk alone at night in their own neighborhoods rose from 34 percent in 1965, for which we have the first poll data, to a high of 48 percent in January 1982 (p. 135). As a result, there was a noticeable increase in the salience of crime as a public issue, with more people, beginning in 1960, indicating that crime was the nation's most important problem (Stinchcombe and others, 1980, p. 24). Concomitantly, the public became more punitive in its attitude toward criminals. For example, the percentage of people in polls who said that courts are "not harsh enough" on criminals increased from 48 percent in 1965 to 79 percent in 1975 to 84 percent in 1985 (Niemi, Mueller, and Smith, 1989, p. 136).

While public punitiveness was increasing, actual punishment was decreasing. The incarceration rate per capita, as well as the number of persons in prison, declined during the 1960s (Bureau of Justice Statistics, 1983, p. 81). In addition, the average serious crime arrest resulted in about .116 years of sentence served in prison in 1970, which decreased to .089 years in 1976 (Stinchcombe and others, 1980, p. 33). As serious crime was increasing and people were becoming more concerned about it and demanding tougher action, governments were actually carrying out a more lenient policy. This mismatch was ripe for making a national political issue.

The public perception of crime and the politicians' discernment of that public perception would come to be a key factor in getting the problem to government, and also in providing and sustaining support for policy initiation.

The 1960s were not the first time crime had been addressed at the national level. National meetings to discuss possible solutions to prison reform, juvenile crime, and overcrowded courts had been held as early as 1870 in Cincinnati, and in 1925 the National Crime Commission was organized in New York City and included Franklin D. Roosevelt and Chief Justice Charles Evans Hughes as members (Cronin, Cronin, and Milovic, 1981). Herbert Hoover ran on a law-and-order platform in 1929 and, following his election, appointed the National Commission on Law Observance and Enforcement. The report of this commission (Wickersham Commission) pointed out many defects in the criminal justice system and called for many specific reforms (Cronin, Cronin, and Milovic, 1981). However, it did not lead to the initiation of new legislation because public opinion was insufficient to sustain any serious policy initiatives. As Cronin, Cronin, and Milovic (1981) conclude, "Few of the proposed reforms were put into practice, and during the 1940s, 1950s, and 1960s, the problems identified in the Wickersham report only continued to get worse" (p. 28).

Actually, "getting the problem to government," with respect to crime, had its genesis in the electoral arena. As will be demonstrated, the electoral implications of crime have come to play a major role in crime legislation from the 1960s until the present day. The presidential election of 1964 was pivotal. Crime had not been an issue in the 1960 campaign, but Senator Barry Goldwater, in a press conference just prior to his nomination, stated that it would be an issue in 1964. The senator promised that "the abuse of law and order in this country is going to be an issue — at least I'm going to make it one, because I think responsibility has to start someplace" (Rovere, 1965, p. 84). Richard Kleindienst, then director of field operations for the Goldwater campaign, is credited with shrewdly sensing rising public concern at a point before the widespread urban riots and anti-war demonstrations, combined with growing public upset with street crime, catapulted concern with crime to the top of public opinion polls — in fact, a full year before the Watts riot in Los Angeles (Caplan, 1973).

Contributing to the nascent public unease was not only a growing incidence of street crime — muggings, assaults, robberies — but also a counterreaction to the tactics of the civil rights movement in the early sixties which, while nonviolent, were perceived by many as disruptive (Cronin, Cronin, and Milovic, 1981). In 1964, 74 percent of respondents in a Gallup poll agreed that the demonstrations of the civil rights movement were counterproductive. In addition, the Supreme Court announced a series of highly controversial decisions defining new rights for criminal defendants. In 1964, the *Escobedo* decision was announced, in which a majority of the Surpreme Court justices held that when an investigation begins to focus on an accused suspect, the police must inform him of his right to remain silent and to consult with an attorney before answering any questions. Similar decisions followed and provoked public protests from many in law enforcement and among some attorneys, although other attorneys supported the decisions. FBI director J. Edgar Hoover stated: "Justice is meant for the protection of a society as a whole, not for the protection of a single individual. When you take one individual and permit him, on one pretext or another, to prey upon the public — with occasional periods of restraint — then justice is not being carried out" ("Crime in the United States," 1963, p. 104).

Often, issue creation depends not on policy leaders but on policy entrepreneurs like Goldwater, whose purpose was not to press for immediate congressional action on specific proposals but to raise and frame the issue itself in a national debate. Goldwater, who misgauged the public on numerous issues, nonetheless struck a developing chord in the public mood when he criticized President Johnson for allowing crime to climb "five times faster than the population" and promised that "as the president I am going to do all I can to see that women can go out on the streets of the country without being scared stiff" (Caplan, 1973, p. 586).

A different political conception of the federal role was needed to make possible the initiation of any major policies in crime control, because up to this point, the working assumption on crime control in Washington was that it was a state and local matter, except for the areas carved out for the FBI such as kidnapping and bank robbery. In fact, Johnson at first embraced and announced a federal hands-off position on crime during the campaign and warned against the dangers of a national police force. Later he asserted that his Great Society programs were crime reduction efforts.

Notwithstanding Goldwater's overwhelming defeat, President Johnson clearly perceived the success Goldwater had achieved with the crime issue; Goldwater had formed a new consensus that the president must be involved, must do more, and must be held responsible. Crime had been legitimized as a national issue by the 1964 presidential campaign.

President Johnson was on the horns of a dilemma in developing a response. On the one hand he felt he had to do something; however, he didn't really feel crime control fit with his stress on achieving a Great Society, and many in his political camp and on his staff felt that crime control was a code word for anti–civil rights and was anti-black (Caplan, 1973, p. 589).

In his response, President Johnson tried to nod in the direction of the concerns of crime control, but to also stress his main preoccupation with the Great Society. Four months after the election, on March 8, 1965, President Johnson delivered a special message entitled "Crime, Its Prevalence, and Measures of Prevention" (Johnson, 1965). In the message, Johnson cited the rising crime rates and then called for a "fair and efficient system of law enforcement" which "means giving new priority in the methods and institutions of law enforcement." While stating that our system would not tolerate a national police force, and that protection responsibilities lie primarily with state and local governments, he went on to pronounce: "Yet crime is no longer merely a local problem. Every city, every state is troubled by the same hard statistical and human facts. The extent and seriousness of the problem have made it of great national concern."

Johnson's proposal called for a National Crime Commission to study the causes of crime and suggest solutions, a new aid program for state and local law enforcement, the Law Enforcement Assistance Act, and increased federal law enforcement efforts in areas of federal "special responsibility," such as organized crime and drug control. The Law Enforcement Assistance Act, which sailed through Congress and provided $7 million in the first year, was the precursor to the much enlarged 1968 Safe Streets Act — $63 million the first year.

Riots in the summer of 1965 increased public alarm in the country and political alarm in Washington. On August 3, 1965, President Johnson had given a speech in which he extolled the virtues of "teach-ins, sit-ins, parades, marches, and demonstrations" in the march against the "ancient enemies" of inequality. Then riots broke out in the Watts section of Los Angeles on August 11 and in Chicago on August 12. On August 20, Johnson proclaimed: "We cannot, and must not, in one breath demand laws to protect the rights of all our citizens, and then turn our back, or wink, and in the next breath allow laws to be broken that protect the safety of our citizens." At the same time, Congress enacted into law by big majorities a penalty of up to five years in prison for anyone who destroys or mutilates his draft card. News organizations reported a boom in gun sales nationally — and in Washington, D.C., particularly to women, because crimes against women there were felt to be at a high rate. *U.S. News and World Report* stated that political leaders were predicting in private that a turn in public attitudes was at hand "toward violence in the streets, toward law violation in the name of civil rights, and toward the solicitude shown by many judges toward suspected criminals" ("A Shift in the Wind in Washington," 1965, p. 27).

The President's Crime Commission commissioned the National Opinion Research Center to do a nationwide opinion survey in 1966. When asked to select from a list of major domestic problems, respondents selected crime second, right behind race relations (President's Commission, 1968). *U.S. News and World Report* reported: "The fact that there is a boom on in the U.S. in sales of guns for civilian use also is tending to heighten official concern. In Washington, where crimes against women are at a high rate, many women are said to be buying arms to try to get the protection that law enforcement fails to provide" ("A Shift in the Wind," p. 28). President Johnson attempted to head off the growing public unease, even before his Crime Commission could report, with his second Message on Crime on March 8, 1966.

After declaring that "the safety and security of its citizens is the first duty of government," Johnson called on the Congress and the nation to join a three-stage national attack. Taking them in reverse order, the third stage continued his emphasis on social change and called for support for the "war on poverty" programs and prevention of "social injustice" to "attack crime at the roots." The second stage directed the Attorney General to work with the governors to establish fifty state crime commissions to cooperate with the National Crime Commission. The first stage consisted of making grants to states and localities for law enforcement training, and asking Congress to proceed with a few existing administration legislative proposals, such as gun control and witness immunity. It also called for something new — "the appointment of a commission to conduct a comprehensive review of all the federal criminal laws and to recommend total revision by 1968." By way of declaring "We Must Modernize Our Criminal Laws," the message stated: "A number of our criminal laws are obsolete. Many are inconsistent with our efforts to make the penalty fit the crime. Many which treat essentially the same crimes are scattered in a crazy-quilt patchwork through our criminal code" (Johnson, message to Congress, March 8, 1966).

Before the Congress could begin to act, in June 1966 the Supreme Court in a five-to-four decision announced *Miranda* v. *Arizona,* which held that before interrogation a suspect must be informed of his or her right to remain silent and to have a lawyer present (384 U.S. 436 [1966]). The outcry from law enforcement officials was immediately negative, and the public would come increasingly to believe that the courts were too lenient on criminals. By July 1968, 53 percent of Gallup poll respondents rated the Supreme Court fair or poor, as opposed to 37 percent who rated it excellent or good. In addition, in the summer of 1966, rioting broke out in sixteen cities, including Chicago and New York. These riots exacerbated the public's sense that law and order was breaking down in the country.

During the congressional election campaign of fall 1966, Republicans stressed the law-and-order issue. The Republican Coordinating Committee charged that the Johnson-Humphrey administration had "accomplished nothing of substance to date to promote public safety," and that certain administration officials had "condoned and encouraged disregard for law and order." When Gerald Ford, then House Republican floor leader, was asked to name such officials, he cited Hubert Humphrey's recent statement in New Orleans that if he lived in the degrading slum conditions then existing he "would lead a mighty good revolt" (Cronin, Cronin, and Milovic, 1981, p. 37).

In the midst of the election heat over the crime issue, Congress passed a law establishing the National Commission on Reform of National Criminal Laws on November 8, 1966. This commission effort was not the Johnson administration's major priority in the crime area. Emphasis continued to be placed on downplaying the crime problem, emphasizing poverty as the root cause of crime and urban disorder, and stressing the upcoming President's Crime Commission's approach to social activism which, in part, called for massive federal grants to state and local governments for planning, crime prevention, rehabilitation, and criminal justice system reform. In fact, based on advance copies of the President's Crime Commission Report, President Johnson, in his 1967 State of the Union message, called for massive federal aid to states and localities.

In February 1967, the National Crime Commission issued its report. The report— *The Challenge of Crime in a Free Society* —contained over two hundred recommendations for change which went beyond law enforcement institutions and addressed other institutions, such as the Church and the schools. It clearly took "the crime as symptomatic of larger social problem view." Relatedly, it devoted over twenty recommendations to ensuring that defendants were treated fairly by the police and the courts. In large measure, the commission adopted the Great Society view of national social activism rather than a "get tough" approach to crime control. "Recommendations were often general and less related to crime prevention than to the protection of civil liberties," (Cronin, Cronin, and Milovic, 1981, p. 39). One public reaction was that there was little in the offing for reduction of street crime. This lack of focus, along with the voluminous nature of the report, limited its utility as a blueprint for policy change in the form of a comprehensive legislative package. As Caplan (1973) pointed out later: "At a time when public concern over violence was mounting, when there was increasing polarization within the country, when many people, devoid of racial prejudice, were afraid to walk the streets, to produce a report that did not adopt *some* measures that could be called 'tough' was an indefensible strategy" (p. 602). The report stressed the need for both more planning and more money and envisioned the federal government as providing both (President's Commission . . . , 1968). Several hundred million dollars over the next decade was recommended. In 1968, the beginning of the massive aid program was passed in the Omnibus Safe Streets and Crime Control Act.

Most analysts have come to the conclusion that the President's Commission's report failed in setting a national direction for dealing with crime and defining the federal role. As Cronin, Cronin, and Milovic (1981) observed: "Far from settling questions, the report signaled the opening battle over the nature of the national role — major pulling and hauling over crime control policy would follow. Would the central government lead reform by establishing standards? Would it merely allocate funds? Would it stress broadened powers of prosecution and enforcement, beginning with tougher federal sanctions?" (p. 41). These questions came to dominate the debates over both the Law Enforcement Assistance Administration's aid program and the reform of federal criminal laws. Running through the debates over these questions were basic conflicting positions concerning the direction of federal policy: Was the role of the federal government to "get tough" on crime or to lead the charge for "social justice"?

In a large sense, the creation of a large grant program for state and local governments was the easiest place to start, because it responded to representatives' strong interest in distributing money to their districts. An added benefit of establishing a program is that it does not require Congress to resolve the basic political and philosophical dilemmas about what the federal role should be in order to pass a bill. Congress often launches new policy initiatives by starting a program without settling the question of basic goals. This is because a premium is placed on building a majority that agrees on having a program, with the various members of the coalition expecting that "their goal" is embraced by the program. Being vague about objectives allows more representatives to believe that their goals will be pursued in the context of the program, and this belief facilitates passage. It also often makes it problematic that the program will have any great impact. The fact that the basic divergences over goals and objectives remain unsettled follows the program into its implementation and administrative stages. This is precisely what happened with LEAA (Cronin, Cronin, and Milovic, 1981).

There is not space here to relate the twelve-year rise and decline, in fact the elimination of, the Law Enforcement Assistance Administration and its multi-billion-dollar program that was passed. Over its twelve-year history, the LEAA grants to state and local governments totaled nearly $8 billion, with no perceptible impact on lowering the rate of crime. In the waning days of the Carter administration in mid-December 1980,

Congress appropriated $15 million for administration of existing grants, but nothing for new grants, bringing to an end temporarily the massive-aid approach as the federal role to crime control.

Launching a new grant program fit with the Johnson administration's basic approach to social activism, and it did not require a great expenditure of presidential capital or policy leadership, given that the administration had little definitive information on the nature or extent of the problems to be addressed and declined to define the objective of the federal role very clearly. Johnson's priorities were elsewhere — with Vietnam and the Great Society.

However, Johnson knew that he had to take some initiative on crime because Republicans were beating the Democrats over the head with the issue in the electoral arena. His problem was that launching a new federal aid program in the area of law enforcement raised the issue of federal control in an area that was, and continues to be, overwhelmingly a state and local responsibility. Southern Democrats and Republicans were particularly concerned about this issue.

Johnson knew the Senate, however. He asked Senator John McClellan (D-Ark.), the most respected senator on crime issues, to come and see him. Johnson asked McClellan to sponsor the administration's legislation. He knew that if McClellan agreed, almost all the southern Democrats would be reassured that the bill would be acceptable from a federalism perspective. McClellan asked for a commitment on two points from Johnson. McClellan would include two sections in the bill that were unrelated to financial assistance to local law enforcement — one to broaden the use of federal wiretapping against organized crime, and another to limit the impact of the Supreme Court's *Miranda* decision on the use of a defendant's confession. McClellan wanted Johnson's assurance that he would not veto the bill if McClellan was successful in obtaining these additions in the final bill. Johnson, without even consulting his attorney general, Ramsey Clark, agreed.

The administration then lost control of the LEAA legislation, which was reshaped by a coalition of Republicans and southern Democrats, and Johnson was urged to veto it by several of his advisors (Johnson, 1971). Johnson knew he could not afford the political price of vetoing his own administration's crime initiative, and he signed the bill. Johnson continued to believe that what was really needed was a public will to support the Great Society, and that the public mistakenly suspected that the riots and demonstrations were part of some organized conspiracy. Following his presidency, Johnson wrote: "Until people realized that all the riots and demonstrations were not the product of conspiracy, there was little hope of persuading them to focus on fundamental causes — on poverty, discrimination, inadequate schooling, substandard housing slums and unemployment" (Johnson, 1971, p. 173).

National Commission on Reform
of Federal Criminal Laws

Following President Johnson's message on crime in which he called for a revision of federal criminal laws, bills were quickly introduced in both houses of Congress to accomplish this purpose. This was not the first time Congress would attempt to pass a criminal code, although it had been an infrequent occurrence. There were four previous, at least partial, attempts in the history of the United States to codify the federal criminal law — in 1790, 1877, 1909, and 1948. None of these had produced a comprehensive, logically organized, and internally consistent penal code.

The 1948 revision resulted in the revised title 18 of the U.S. Code. The 1948 effort had been very limited and had not really developed any system of federal criminal laws, but it had placed successive congressional enactments in one place, changed wording, and eliminated overlaps. It was a restatement of existing statutes with no attempt at substantive reform.

In addition, the basic structure of title 18 did not lend itself to easy use and understanding. It arranged subjects alphabetically with little regard to the content of successive chapters. As a result, unrelated offenses exist side by side, while related offenses are separated by several chapters. For example,

"Animals, birds, fish, and plants" is followed by "Arson," whereas crimes related to stealing are divided into four separated chapters: "Embezzlement and theft," "Fraud and false statements," "Mail fraud," and "Stolen property." Title 18 was also simply out of date. Not only had the United States changed since 1948, it had changed markedly in the intervening period since 1909 when much of the substance of federal criminal law—hundreds of statutes—had been enacted as Congress confronted situations on an act-by-act basis. For example, federal laws added one at a time over the years had resulted in a patchwork of statutes dealing with various forms of theft—"larceny," "embezzlement," "fraudulent conversion," and "obtaining by false pretenses." Myriad interpretations of these had accumulated through the individual decisions of thousands of judges represented in federal case law, leaving gaps and ambiguities. This caused wide-ranging penalties to be levied for essentially similar offenses and, at the same time, created loopholes in definitions that accused criminals could exploit.

The American Law Institute had devoted about two decades to developing a model penal code for which it had issued a preliminary report in 1962. Several states had been engaged in drafting state criminal codes based on the institute's work. The American Bar Association had also been working on minimal standards of criminal justice. Thus, the federal effort was proposed against this backdrop of support in the legal community.

The Johnson administration's position, as enunciated by then Deputy Attorney General Ramsey Clark, was that the purpose of the proposed commission was revision of the criminal code—recodification, consolidation, clarification, repeal of obsolete statutes, and an adjustment of the penalty structure of existing criminal laws—in short, a housecleaning and an attempt to make the existing penalties fairer. Several in Congress had something additional in mind. Representative Richard Poff (R-Va.), a member of the House Judiciary Committee, amended the bill to add another function to the commission effort: criminal law reform. He argued that the administration's approach would merely restate the existing law and eliminate disparities, inconsistencies, and inequities, but that what was needed was to improve the entire system of laws, including adding new laws to modernize the system of criminal justice. This was to include review of the criminal case law as it was developing. This last was directed at the Supreme Court's decisions in criminal law and defendants' rights. The administration favored the revision approach because it feared efforts directed at "bashing the Supreme Court," which was moving in the direction of "social justice" that the administration favored.

This emphasis on limiting the charge to the commission is not surprising, given the defeat the administration had experienced in the shaping of the Safe Streets Act. The administration's problem was that while the House Judiciary Committee, under the iron-fisted control of Representative Emanuel Celler (D-N.Y.), had been active in civil rights legislation, it had done very little on crime. Power over crime legislation was slipping away from the committee. A coalition of Republicans and southern Democrats, restive about judiciary's inaction, simply rewrote the Law Enforcement Assistance bill on the floor of the House without Celler's concurrence. Representative Poff, fresh from the LEAA victory and sensing that the majority wanted to do something more that would address the mood of the country, amended the Criminal Code bill to add a reform mission as well. Poff would later become vice-chairman of the commission and would be active in insisting that reform be addressed.

Congress charged the National Commission on the Reform of Federal Criminal Laws with "a full and complete review of the statutory and case law of the United States which constitutes the federal system of criminal justice for the purpose of formulating and recommending to the Congress legislation which would improve the federal system of criminal justice" (Pub.L. No. 89-801, 80 Stat. 1516 [1966]). The reform view triumphed.

The bipartisan commission was chaired by former California governor Edmund G. (Pat) Brown with Representative Poff as vice-chairman. It was also composed of three members of the Senate Judiciary Committee — Senators McClellan (D-Ark.), Hruska (R-Neb.), and Ervin (D-N.C.) — three other members of the House Judiciary Committee — Representatives Kastenmeier (D-Wisc.), Mikva (D-Ill.), and Edwards (D-Calif.)—three federal judges, and three presidential appointees, including Brown. The basic ideological split on the commission was between the Democratic House members, who were some of the House's more noted liberals, and the Senate members, who were known as conservatives on crime. With the other appointees, the majority were on the liberal side. The director of the commission was Louis Schwartz, a law professor who had served as a section chief of the Criminal Division of the Justice Department. John Dean, who later became White House counsel and a prominent Watergate figure, became counsel to the committee. Robert Blakey, who had worked on Representative Poff's Republican Task Force on Crime, was brought in by McClellan as a consultant for the senators.

The commission decided to avoid two approaches in adopting its strategy. The commission would neither reexamine divisive issues, such as wiretapping, that had been debated in the Safe Streets Act, nor would it engage in broad research into the sociological or philosophical bases of crime, which the President's Commission had done. Instead, the commission set out to draft a new substantive federal criminal code. The Model Penal Code developed by the American Law Institute served as a tentative draft (Schwartz, 1977).

The commission was impelled by three sometimes competing goals of its participants. These were to make the federal criminal law: (1) "efficient," (2) "fairer," and (3) "tougher."

The first goal, which enjoyed broad support, was to codify existing law in order to make its application more efficient. The simplest aspect was to organize the federal laws logically, with related offenses being placed together, and to eliminate obsolete offenses, such as seducing female passengers on steamboats. The task became more difficult when it came to revising language to modernize terms and to make different but related statutes conform. Court interpretations had imbued certain terms with advantages to the defense or the prosecution, and redefinition offered the potential for readjusting these to one side or the other. Thus, a fundamental basis for debate was inherent in the process. The second goal, to increase fairness, was related to the first and was also tricky. The main tactic was to provide for a grading of offenses and penalties. For example, penalties for theft would be graduated by the scale of the thievery involved. However, in order to systematize such a penalty scheme, agreement had to be reached on the penalties that would be assigned to each level of offense, opening up the argument about what is an appropriate penalty. The third goal, to make the laws tougher, was of particular concern to Senators McClellan and Hruska. They had recently led the charge to stiffen the Safe Streets Act in the Senate and were convinced that the federal government needed new laws to counter the mounting crime problem and to send a tougher message to deter crime. The conservatives sought to "strengthen" federal law and also to serve as a model for state criminal law reform efforts in order to get tough on street crime.

Divergence between these goals, and thus between the more liberal majority and the more conservative minority on the commission, could have rendered the production of a code impossible. Debates over individual issues, such as the appropriate penalty for a particular crime, went on interminably. Issues such as whether to include the death penalty for any crime provoked sharp splits between the more liberal majority and the conservative minority. McClellan cared deeply about the death penalty, and majority members felt just as strongly that it should be excluded. The possibility that the deliberations could end in stalemate or sharp minority dissent was real. This did not come to pass.

The commission decided to focus its activities by setting a date for a study draft that would provide the basis for obtaining comment from outside groups and would not be binding on the members. The cover of the study draft even contained the disclaimer, "The Study Draft provisions are not to be taken as representing the position of the Commission on any particular issue." In addition, the study draft, at the insistence of the conservative members, included alternative positions favored by the minority members, such as provision for capital punishment for some crimes.

As the commission made its decisions concerning the contents of the final report, Senators McClellan and Hruska became increasingly concerned about being bound by the commission's decisions. They became unsure that they could support the final product. Two factors influenced the momentum of the commission to come to a workable compromise on the final report — the election of 1968, which replaced a liberal Democrat in the White House with a conservative Republican, and the desire of the members to strengthen the momentum for federal criminal code reform following the issue of the commission's report. The majority were aware that the product of their work was going to be submitted not only to Congress but also to a president with different views on crime than the one who had called for the appointment of the commission, and they needed to avoid having the outcome labeled as the former administration's report.

Representative Mikva was an active spokesman for the liberal view, as was Senator McClellan for the conservative view. Before it came to an impasse, Mikva sat down with McClellan's consultant, Robert Blakey, to see if there was a way to devise report langugage that the senators could accept. Mikva was known as a liberal advocate in Congress, but on the commission he became the architect of a compromise. Before coming to Congress, he had served in the Illinois legislature when it had passed a criminal code. Mikva believed in the value of a code and, according to Blakey, took an eminently practical approach. They reached an agreement that was acceptable to both sides and made it possible for Senators McClellan, Hruska, and Ervin not to file a minority report (Blakey, personal interview, 1987).

The compromise was for the commission to issue a unanimous report with alternatives on some issues included (an alternative section with the death penalty was included, for example). The report was also submitted with the declaration, in Chairman Brown's transmittal letter to the president and Congress, characterizing the nature of the report as a "work basis upon which the Congress may undertake the necessary reform of the federal criminal laws." This provided the flexibility for the senators to support the report and then proceed to develop their own proposals further in the legislative process.

Senator McClellan had spent years as chairman of the Senate Government Operations Committee and its Permanent

Investigations Subcommittee, and was also chairman of the Senate Judiciary Committee's Subcommittee on Criminal Laws and Procedure. As chairman of the Investigations Subcommittee, he had led investigations in 1963 of the Cosa Nostra and held hearings in 1964 on illicit traffic in narcotics. He chaired the famous Valachi hearings, in which Joseph Valachi, a former member of the Cosa Nostra and a convicted murderer, revealed the structure and operations of the Mafia for the first time in public. McClellan had authored several bills to combat organized crime, including a bill to outlaw the Mafia by making it a crime to belong to secret organizations "devoted to the violation of laws, to the pursuit of criminal enterprises, and to the protection of the membership of the organization in the commission of unlawful acts." He had also introduced the Safe Streets Act in the Senate and had added title II on wiretapping and removing the federal court's power to review state court rulings that confessions had been freely given.

McClellan had fought hard for the passage of the Safe Streets Act on the floor of the Senate. One McClellan tactic was to place eighteen "crime clocks" in the Senate chamber, each devoted to a different crime — an assault every two minutes, a rape every twenty-one minutes, and so on. Each day for three weeks before the Safe Streets Act was finally passed, McClellan would point to the clocks and ask his Senate colleagues, "Are we going to fiddle while crime destroys America or are we going to stand up like men and vote to do something about it?" ("Crime Time," 1968).

McClellan had protested the Johnson administration's approach of limiting the federal government's role to funds distribution to the states and emphasizing "social justice." He had joined with Republicans to sponsor bills that he felt were sorely needed to stiffen federal laws. He had admonished Attorney General Ramsey Clark, the administration's leading proponent of the social justice approach, in a hearing when Clark had testified for a limited Safe Streets Act: "I would think — I may be wrong, but I would think — that just the two bills you have referred to [the Safe Streets bill and the Federal Corrections Service bill], that you have emphasized in your statement here,

are not alone adequate to deal with the overall crime problem;
that there are other tools and weapons that are needed in this
law enforcement war against crime. . . . I don't think, and I am
sure you do not, that just spending money is the answer to the
crime problem" (McClellan, 1967, p. 153). McClellan had successfully reshaped the Safe Streets Act more in the direction of
the "get tough" approach than the administration had wanted.
He also had an unfinished agenda of strengthening federal criminal laws.

However, between the passage of the bill establishing the
commission and the issuance of the commission's report, the
1968 election would deliver a new president and a new administration — one closer to Senator McClellan's view than to Ramsey
Clark's.

The events outside the Democratic convention in 1968
in Chicago, in which thousands of protestors and police clashed,
served to characterize for many Americans the inability of the
Democrats to address the crime issue. These events capped
several years of urban riots, campus unrest, anti-Vietnam demonstrations, and growing public fear of street crime. Nixon
launched a hard-hitting law-and-order campaign and proclaimed
that, under the Democrats, the country had become a "lawless
society." In speech after speech, he charged that the "peace forces"
had been weakened and that the Johnson administration's emphasis on social concerns was responsible for the increase in lawlessness. Nixon had read the mood of the voters correctly. A
Louis Harris poll before the Democratic convention found that
81 percent of the national sample agreed that law and order had
broken down in the country, and 84 percent felt that a strong
president could make a difference in preserving it (*New York
Times,* Sept. 8, 1968). Further, another Harris poll disclosed
that 54 percent felt personally uneasy on the streets. When asked
which candidate could best preserve law and order, 38 percent
said Nixon, versus 26 percent for Humphrey and 21 percent
for Wallace (*New York Times,* Sept. 13, 1968). By mid-October,
the Gallup poll showed that 25 percent of the people reported
crime as the top problem facing the country, behind only the
Vietnam War with 44 percent.

Nixon attacked Johnson's attorney general, Ramsey Clark, as the symbol of "unprecedented lawlessness" and denounced the Supreme Court for hamstringing law enforcement officials. Nixon won a narrow victory over Humphrey as some Democrats "came home" and Wallace split the opposition vote. Nonetheless, on the "social issue"—crime, race, student disorders—Republicans were perceived as "tougher," which brought Nixon critical votes (Scammon and Wattenberg, 1970).

Thus, from the point of view of the conservative minority on the commission—Senators McClellan and Hruska—the most important thing was to see a report produced that could be used as a basis for legislation. They knew they could reshape the specifics later.

The objectives of the proposed code, as stated in the commission report were: retribution, deterrence, and rehabilitation. These three objectives are not necessarily compatible. Conflicts over what they mean in terms of any particular criminal offense, as well as over which should receive emphasis above the others, are continuing sources of controversy in determining what types of criminal laws we should have. The emphasis has shifted back and forth over the years. In the commission report, as viewed by the director, Louis Schwartz (1977), "Deterrence or, more broadly, prevention is thus the basic policy that underlies the Code" (p. 12). Schwartz almost apologetically defended the inclusion of retribution by stating that, in the commission code, "retribution serves its classic and least objectionable function of setting limits on the state's power to punish" (p. 13). Schwartz may have reflected not only the commission's lack of enthusiasm for the retribution aspect but also its recogniton of the need to bow somewhat to the public will. "In any event, retribution as a goal of the criminal law could not as a practical matter be excluded from a democratically enacted code in this country, where massive popular support for retribution has recently been demonstrated by the surge of capital punishment legislation following the Supreme Court's invalidation of older arbitrary procedures for imposing it" (Schwartz, 1977, p. 13).

The public was becoming increasingly punitive in its attitudes toward criminals. In July of 1966, 42 percent favored capital punishment. By June of 1967, it was 55.7 percent, and it would rise to 67.2 percent by March 1977 (Smith, 1976, p. 261).

The majority on the commission may have opposed inclusion of capital punishment in the code on grounds that they felt it had no deterrent value and could not be applied equitably. Nonetheless, the commission acceded to the demand of the conservatives to heed public opinion, at least to the point of including it as an alternative.

The heart of the code was in its new organization and the changed definitions in federal criminal law. The major components were:

- Defining federal jurisdiction — specifying the criminal acts that would be prosecuted in federal courts as opposed to state courts, where most crimes are tried.
- Defining defenses to prosecution — specifying what is justifiable and excusable behavior. This had never been defined by Congress in federal statutes before, but only by judges on a case-by-case basis.
- Defining a system of criminal offenses.
- Providing a system of penalties with gradations from least to most severe for similar types of offenses.

The critical contribution of the code was the modernized definitions of offenses and the grading of penalties. For example, all the different sections defining crimes like embezzlement and larceny were abolished and replaced by a consolidated section on theft. The penalties were then listed in a graded pattern according to the values of the property stolen and the conditions surrounding the theft — that is, whether the defendant was a public official acting in the course of his official duties or the property was a government file, and so on. This was intended to introduce some consistency into the federal law, so that perpetrators of white-collar or corporate crime would have the same penalties for theft as those who committed burglaries involving property of the same value.

Thus, each offense was divided into several degrees, reserving the most severe penalties for aggravated forms of the offense. The maximum sentence for each grade of offense was reserved for defendants who were dangerous recidivists, professional criminals, mental deviates, or those who employed firearms or bombs in carrying out the offense.

The code also minimized the use of cumulative sentences. For example, no longer would a person be sentenced for five mail fraud offenses for mailing five letters to different people in the same scheme. This would eliminate the inequity that resulted when some judges followed this practice and others did not. The code also included guidelines for judges to use in making sentencing decisions, and gave the federal appellate courts the right to review and modify sentences of lower courts. The commission could not agree on other features of the sentencing review, so it listed options. This was destined to be an area of continuing debate in Congress. The purpose of the sentencing guidelines was to increase equity in sentencing and make sentences fairer. As Schwartz (1977) stated: "Under current law, which provides no guidelines for sentencing and no appeal against arbitrary sentence, two men who have committed identical offenses may find themselves in adjoining federal prison cells serving outrageously different sentences, while a third like offender is granted probation and never goes to prison at all" (p. 4).

The guiding assumption undergirding the goal of deterrence in the commission's code was one of the rational approach—if the criminal law is more organized and consistent, it becomes more understandable and respectable, and thus more observed. An alternate or supplementary approach is to make the law tougher and more feared, and thus more observed. The conservative minority—Senators McClellan and Hruska—were not opposed to logical organization, but they also believed that the law had to be tougher. This was the basis for debate on several issues confronting the commission, and subsequently Congress.

In addition, while it may be easy to get agreement in principle on rationalizing the criminal law, obtaining agreement on the specifics is much more difficult. The criminal code contained in the commission's final report was 317 pages long, which required the harmonization of viewpoints on literally hundreds of issues. This is inherently a process fraught with risk, in that a single issue, such as the death penalty, can start political firefights that could tie up the whole process. The State of California criminal code project was aborted because politicians were fearful of the possible electoral consequences of proposals to decriminalize certain private sexual behavior and the use of marijuana (Schwartz, 1977).

The commission avoided the California code's fate. In part, this was a function of the interest of the majority in obtaining a finished product. In addition, the commission was able to achieve consensus on finishing by characterizing the final report as a "work basis" that could receive further development in Congress.

The commission also was able to deliver a product that could serve to initiate legislative action. Unlike the National Crime Commission Report, the Criminal Code was produced in the form of statutory language with additional explanation and was directed at replacing specific federal statutes, for example, title 18. This facilitated congressional consideration because it eliminated a whole other stage of translating general recommendations into specific legislative proposals.

The Brown Commission completed its work and forwarded its recommendations to the president and Congress on January 7, 1971. Senator McClellan immediately called the first hearings before his Subcommittee on Criminal Laws and Procedures on Februrary 10, 1971, at which Governor Brown, Representative Poff, and Attorney General Mitchell testified. McClellan told the Senate in March, "The Congress must review the work product of the Commission and decide not whether, but how codification, reform, and revision should be undertaken" (*Congressional Record,* Mar. 11, 1971, p. S2962). McClellan called attention to the "alternative formulations" in the report (which he supported) and stated that Congress would now undertake the task of making the necessary choices (p. S2955). Policy initiation was successfully under way. Legislative processing could now begin, if criminal law reform could achieve a high enough priority on the congressional agenda.

Policy Initiation Revisited

As has been demonstrated, the various elements identified at the beginning of this chapter combined to initiate congressional consideration of criminal law reform. Without the widespread growing discontent among the general public over law and order and government's response, it is unlikely that such a large and complex task as criminal law revision and reform would have been undertaken at all. There was no particular set of congressional districts or special-interest groups that saw it in their interest to push such initiatives.

In addition, without political entrepreneurs seeking to define and advance the issue in the electoral arena, the administration, whose priorities were elsewhere, would have had little incentive to put the formulation process in motion. As indicated, formulation of policy responses was not limited to the one approach of criminal code reform. The Safe Streets Act, which focused on funds distribution to state and local law enforcement agencies, proceeded separately. Also, the formulation of policies focusing on federal criminal code reform produced competing alternative proposals on some significant issues in the Brown Commission report. Relatedly, it was explicitly understood in characterizing the report as a "work basis" that the reformulation process would continue over a longer period of time.

Senators McClellan and Hruska lost on having some of their priority reforms included as primary recommendations of the commission—for example, capital punishment—but they knew that there would be other "appeal points" in Congress where they would enjoy more leverage. At this point, supporters of federal criminal law reform had to convince a new administration as well as Congress that reform was worthy of agenda status.

• 4 •

Setting
the Agenda

Even after a specific set of policies has been initiated, it does not necessarily follow that they will be given serious consideration in the legislative process. Congress is confronted with a multitude of problems and proposals at any one time, all clamoring for attention. More accurately, a multitude of interest groups, policy analysts, administrators, and politicians are identifying problems, and as many policy entrepreneurs are pushing various solutions and trying to couple them with different problems and political imperatives. All argue that their problem, solution, and political imperative is the most important. Congressional representatives know that the governmental agenda cannot accommodate even a majority of these at any one time and thus they engage in behavior that helps to narrow it. It is necessary to understand how this agenda-setting process works in the legislative context in order to understand how criminal law reform came to arrive on the governmental agenda.

Getting a Policy on the Agenda

Following Kingdon's conceptualization (1984), the governmental agenda is the list of subjects or problems to which the governmental officials, and people closely associated with those officials, are paying some serious attention at any given time. The governmental agenda should be distinguished from the decision agenda. The decision agenda is a list of subjects that are moving into position for an authoritative decision such as legislative enactment or presidential choice.

It is not necessary to have a specific set of policies already initiated in order to have a set of issues reach the governmental agenda. Sometimes, congressional committees will hold a lengthy set of hearings on issues or on a problem area itself, such as the McClellan Investigations Subcommittee's hearings on organized crime. Specific policies then can come later, as did McClellan's Organized Crime Control Bill. However, having a set of policies already initiated can help place the subject on the governmental agenda, particularly in Congress, because political leaders have the added assurance that at least some relevant serious colleagues have satisfied themselves that there is something government can do other than talk about it.

It would not have been realistic to expect quick passage of a new federal criminal code, particularly not in one session of Congress. Normally, new initiatives do not move onto the governmental agenda, let alone the decision agenda, that fast. They require a gestation period first. A key part of the gestation process is to get those key individuals who are knowledgeable and active in the policy area to consider the proposals seriously. Heclo (1977) describes such individuals as constituting issue networks; Kingdon (1984) labels them policy communities. They consist of specialists in a given issue or policy area who are found throughout the branches of government and also outside it in such places as universities and think tanks. They track, analyze, discuss, and float proposals in the broad range of policy pertaining to some area, such as health, environment, or crime. At any given time, several issues and policy proposals will be in the process of being circulated and considered at once, some more actively than others.

In order to get a proposal seriously considered on the governmental agenda, the objective is to get the relevant policy community involved. This requires going through a softening-up process in which a number of ideas are floated, discussed, dissected, and either knocked down or refined. This process is necessary before a proposal can be taken seriously. Government normally does not act on ideas quickly. They must penetrate the community of policy specialists and last through the softening-up process and reach the decision agenda. Years of effort are often required before they are brought to the point of serious decision making (Kingdon, 1984).

Among those in the policy community who require special attention when it comes to legislation are congressional staff members on the committee, personal, and congressional agency staffs, and also staffs in the departments and agencies in the executive branch. In the latter, top civil servants as well as political appointees require attention. Congressional committees by themselves can seldom generate enough support to pass legislation or move it to the decision agenda. Among the best sources of political support are administrative agencies concerned with the desired legislation; often they constitute the key interest group with respect to a piece of legislation (Woll, 1977).

Another important determinant of the key role of administrators is that legislation requires specialized information before it can be conceptualized, drafted, and implemented (Woll, 1977). The bureaucracy has a much larger staff with greater specialization than Congress, and it also possesses more detailed and intimate knowledge of implementation experience and factors that will influence the feasibility of policy proposals. If the key agencies label the proposal as "blue sky" or "unworkable," Congress has less incentive to move forward, not only because it casts doubt on the solution but also because the agency will be dragging its feet in the legislative process and on into the implementation phase, if the legislation were to pass. As discussed earlier, the bureaucracy will also be advising the president regarding desirable presidential legislative priorities. If the bureaucrats are helpful in getting a favorable presidential priority, the agenda chances in Congress improve as well.

Even if the softening-up process convinces significant segments of the policy community that a refined proposal should move, the proposal is not assured a place on the congressional agenda. The agenda is already crowded with innumerable unavoidable tasks: budgets and appropriations must be passed or parts of the government will be shut down; expiring programs must be reauthorized; presidential appointees must be confirmed or rejected; presidential vetoes must be voted on or accepted;

existing statutes need amendments. These pressing demands
vastly reduce the time or energy for new policy proposals. Walker
(1977) observes that most Senate members do not spend large
amounts of time, resources, or energy on direct efforts to shape
the legislative agenda. The discretionary part of the agenda is
shaped by a minority of activist legislators engaged in promoting proposals for change. These, I have called policy leaders.
Because there is only enough time in a given legislative session
for a few new issues, Walker argues that those possessing certain characteristics are more likely to claim a place on the discretionary agenda — that is, those issues that have broad political appeal, that are addressed to a serious problem, and that
contain an easily understood solution. The problem for many
large-scale policy changes, of which federal criminal law reform
is a prime example, is that while they may possess broad political appeal and be addressed to a serious problem, they often
are complex and do not contain the easily understood solution.

Moving Criminal Law Reform
onto the Congressional Agenda

At the time of the submission of the Brown Commission report,
the political appeal to do something about crime at the federal
level remained widespread. The public was increasingly concerned about street crime and was upset over the campus and
urban antiwar demonstrations and riots. The commission report
boosted the prospects for criminal law legislation to be placed
on the governmental agenda because it delivered a specific set
of proposals, even presented in draft statutory form, that could
be readily considered within the legislative process. This was
in marked contrast to the report of the earlier National Crime
Commission. The Brown Commission also delivered its proposals, for consideration at least, with a unanimous vote of its
members, which included members of Congress on the very
committees — the judiciary committees — that would be considering the legislation. As advantageous as this was, it was not
sufficient to place federal criminal law reform on the government's agenda without some added ingredients.

    Primary among these ingredients were changes in the

political makeup of the federal government. As Kingdon (1984) observes: "Developments in the political sphere are powerful agenda setters. A new administration, for instance, changes agendas all over town as it highlights its conceptions of problems and its proposals, and makes attention to subjects that are not among its high priorities much less likely" (p. 208). As discussed earlier, the Johnson administration felt itself forced into making any crime-related proposals and had its highest priorities elsewhere—in the Great Society programs. It is fairly unlikely that such an administration would have given crime legislation a high priority, especially given its bad experience in losing control of the Safe Streets Act legislation in the previous Congress. However, the 1968 election had produced a new administration with a significantly different set of priorities. "The administration—the president and his appointees—is a particularly powerful agenda setter" (Kingdon, 1984, p. 208).

Shortly after his inauguration, Richard Nixon stated his position on crime: "I recognize . . . that in the long run crime itself also requires much more far-reaching and subtle approaches. But the rapidly mounting urgency of the crime crisis . . . makes immediate, direct anticrime measures as the first priority task" (*Congressional Quarterly*, 1971, p. 27). The new administration sent four major crime bills to Congress in its first thirteen months—the Drug Abuse and Prevention Control Bill, the District of Columbia Crime Control Bill, the amendments to the Safe Streets Act, and the Organized Crime Control Bill. This last bill was built upon Senator McClellan's previous proposals. The Organized Crime bill passed Congress in October 1970. Clearly, the governmental climate for crime legislation had changed.

Other key participants visible in agenda setting are party leaders in Congress, key committee chairs and, as discussed earlier, increasingly subcommittee chairs. Party leaders play a more reactive role and serve more as gatekeepers and emphasizers than as agenda-setting initiators; on occasion, however, they do step out to do this. The movement to committee and subcommittee leadership had already begun at the time of the issuance of the Brown Committee report. Michael Mansfield

(D-Mont.) was the Senate Majority Leader and had far less control of the movement of legislation than Lyndon Johnson had enjoyed. Mansfield's style was that of an accommodating leader. The initiative for setting the agenda on legislation lay elsewhere. It was found primarily in the hands of those who occupied committee chairmanships with great seniority, which conferred power and status on individual senators (Polsby, 1971).

Senator McClellan, who had risen through the ranks and had devoted years to investigating organized crime and other crime issues, was chairman of the Senate Judiciary Committee's Subcommittee on Criminal Laws and Procedures and had served in the Senate since 1943. He was clearly one of the barons of the Senate, even though he voted with his party only about one-third of the time and with the conservative Republican-southern Democrat coalition about two-thirds. He and Senator Hruska, the ranking Republican on the subcommittee, often teamed up to push crime legislation.

The Brown Committee report was issued on January 7, 1971. Senator McClellan began a long and intensive set of subcommittee hearings on February 10, 1971, little more than a month after the report was issued. This timely response was anything but accidental. It is not likely that detailed hearings on something as complex as a new federal criminal code could have been held so soon if preparations had not begun well before issuance of the report. Advance preparations were aided in part by the participation of Senators McClellan and Hruska on the commission. They were in a position to anticipate what would need particular coverage in the hearings. This in itself would have been insufficient, however.

As Kingdon (1984) has pointed out, there is another set of participants—hidden participants—who are key in the agenda-setting process. The actual alternatives, proposals, and solutions are generated by loosely knit communities of specialists. They float their ideas among each other, criticize proposals, hone and revise them, and test for acceptability.

In the case of the Brown Commission, Louis Schwartz, the staff director, was a key architect of the structure of the code. In addition, G. Robert Blakey served in effect as counsel to the

conservatives on the commission and became chief counsel of
the McClellan subcommittee in charge of the code project. Also,
Ronald Gainer, who transferred from the Criminal Division's
appellate section to its legislative section in 1970 became interested in the code project and served as the department's principal liaison with the commission. Subsequently, Gainer became
director of the department's staff unit working on criminal code
revision. A staff member of the Department of Justice criminal
code revision unit was Paul Summit, who became deputy chief
counsel of the McClellan subcommittee in 1973. Blakey was in
a position to anticipate issues that would need to be the focus
of Senate subcommittee hearings and to plan modifications that
would be more acceptable to Senators McClellan and Hruska
once the subcommittee began its work. Gainer was in a similar
position from the executive branch's point of view.

All was not smooth in the relationship between the Justice
Department and the Brown Commission. Attorneys in Justice's
Criminal Division had provided critiques to their superiors of
the commission's staff work and study draft and had been quite
critical. They had had years of experience with the federal criminal case law; as arcane and gap-laden as it was, it was familiar.
They viewed the commission proposals with considerable skep-
ticism, in part because the commission's staff were largely academics researching federal criminal laws rather than professional
prosecutors having in-depth, first-hand expertise. The attorneys
in the department's Internal Security Division were particularly
upset with the commission's treatment of treason, espionage,
and sabotage offenses and were strident in their criticism.

Gainer and some other senior officials reviewed these staff
criticisms and felt that about two-thirds or more were unfounded
and did not appreciate the real structural innovations afforded
by the commission's work. These senior officials saw in the code
an opportunity to streamline federal criminal prosecution and
increase the efficiency with which new assistant U.S. attorneys
could learn and use the criminal law. They felt that this increase
in efficiency could lead to more assured prosecution, because
the prosecutor could more clearly see and establish the basis on
which a successful prosecution would rest. They expected that

more efficient use of law enforcement resources would result, to the point that it would be possible to prosecute 20 percent to 30 percent more cases. Still, in some areas, the existing case law had produced advantages to prosecutors that the professionals were determined to retain. In an effort to improve the commission's final report, Gainer brought in the commission staff and allowed them to review the criticisms. This helped, but it was clear the department would not accept the Brown report as written. Nonetheless, the research and dialogue between Brown Commission academics, Justice Department professionals, and future congressional staffers aided the softening-up process in the criminal law policy community.

During the fall of 1970, as the commission was winding down, Gainer and other Justice Department officials briefed several White House staff members who were keenly interested in criminal justice issues. The administration was fresh from its cooperative successful effort with Congress in passing the Organized Crime bill and was still positive about crime legislation. In effect, this information effort paved the way for administration acceptance. There was the potential that if the report had hit the administration cold, criticisms from the professional prosecutors in the department could have led to a Justice Department position that the approach of the Brown Commission was anti-law enforcement and should be rejected. After all, the commission had been appointed by the Johnson administration and was headed by a former Democratic governor—one who had defeated Richard Nixon in his bitter loss of the election for the governorship of California. Instead, the Nixon administration officials became persuaded that the code approach could provide a basis for reform, but that changes would be necessary. Gainer drafted an acceptance statement for the president that called for a Department of Justice review and generation of alternatives. This became the president's statement.

Because of liaison between the Justice Department and the Brown Commission at the staff level, the Nixon administration was ready with its response and a plan of action when the report was presented to the administration at the White House. The president's statement warmly receiving the report

directed the attorney general to create a staff of Justice Department attorneys to evaluate it, to submit legislation for comprehensive reform of federal criminal laws, and to work with congressional committees and their staffs throughout the process
(Nixon, 1971).

Then, Attorney General Mitchell established a Criminal
Code Revision Unit consisting of eight lawyers within the department's Criminal Division to carry out the review and to provide analysis and recommendations for changes, and also to
recommend "any additional proposals for change in the existing criminal law which may be fairly classified under the head
of code revision or procedural reform" (Mitchell, Feb. 1, 1971).
Gainer became the director of the unit. Mitchell also appointed
a subcommittee of political appointees within the Justice Department to review the recommendations of the code unit to ensure
that views of the policy appointees of the administration would
be included within the department's positions on issues in the
code. William Rhenquist, assistant attorney general at the time,
and later chief justice of the Supreme Court, headed the subcommittee. The department unit worked for two years in reviewing the commission code and, at the same time, worked with the
McClellan subcommittee. In 1973, the Department of Justice
produced its own criminal code bill, which was introduced as
S.1400.

The Brown Commission effort had begun the process, but
now it would be necessary to work over the numerous issues
and proposals included in the vast recommended code and bring
in the participants from all over the legal community. It should
be remembered that as the consideration of the criminal code
was proceeding, Congress was also occupied with considering
amendments to the Safe Streets Act, which meant millions of
dollars to individual districts.

One question that had to be confronted in the softening-
up process was, Why focus energy on revision of federal criminal laws, when most law enforcement is a state and local responsibility in the United States? In fact, the Safe Streets Act was
based on that presumption. At least four reasons were advanced
by proponents who advocated serious consideration. One was

the need for bringing order to the federal criminal law. Many profesionals in criminal law, whether oriented toward prosecution or defense, saw decades of haphazard accretion of individual statutes and case law as having produced a nonsystem of criminal laws— a confusing and antiquated "patchwork" that frustrated participants wherever they practiced in the federal legal system. This "crazy quilt" system, as it was often termed in testimony, speeches, and articles, offended the basic premise of the profession of law: the rule of reason. It was not reasonable for a modern democracy to have to lurch along with this illogical collection of laws when proponents could conceive of simpler and more complete alternatives.

A second reason was that some proponents felt the federal government was not doing its part in attacking the national problem of reducing crime. From their perspective, the federal laws might not just have been neutral in this regard but might actually have been making the problem worse. Obviously, advocates of different approaches saw the nature of the problem differently. Proponents of the social justice school saw the law as arbitrary and inequitable and thus not commanding respect of the people. This attitude bred cynicism about the role of law and thus sneering noncompliance. Proponents of the get-tough school thought that the patchwork left many loopholes, damaging the capabilities of the federal law enforcement forces as they tried to mobilize to strengthen the federal role in the national effort against crime. The law needed updating to aid in confronting modern crime problems of organized crime, drugs, and widespread unrest.

A third reason was that the federal code might serve as a model or, at least, add to the impetus for state action in adopting model criminal codes. The federal effort, as well as several of the state efforts proceeding concurrently with it, was based on the American Law Institute's Model Code. If the issues could be resolved at the federal level, this could give added confidence to state lawmakers. If widespread state reform followed, substantial reform of the nation's criminal laws would be achieved.

A fourth reason, and perhaps the preeminent point of contention, was that federal criminal law served as a symbol of how the country faced the issues of crime and social control. The social justice school thought that the message being sent was that the law was unfair. If it could be reformed, the new message would be that the law was evenhanded and respectful of civil liberites. The get-tough school thought that the federal law had weakened respect for law and order. Through a combination of misguided judicial activism and congressional neglect, according to such proponents, the message that the federal law sent was one of weakness and leniency in the face of a national crisis requiring strong action. President Nixon, for example, had campaigned by promising to strengthen the "peace forces" which had been undermined by recent legal developments. If the law could be reformed and not merely revised, it was argued, the public could be reassured that the federal government would no longer tolerate lawbreaking and that punishment to those challenging the law would be most severe.

The McClellan subcommittee, which included Democratic Senators Ervin (N.C.), Hart (Mich.), Eastland (Miss.), Kennedy (Mass.), and Byrd (W. Va.), and Republican Senators Hruska (Neb.), Scott (Penn.), Thurmond (S.C.), and Cook (Ky.), continued the softening-up process by beginning two years of hearings on the sections of the commission report. In that process, the subcommittee heard in detail from a wide range of the legal community, including representatives of, to mention just a few, the National District Attorneys Association, the NAACP Legal Defense Fund, the Bar of the City of New York, the Federal Bar Association, the American Civil Liberties Union, and Ralph Nader.

Two groups that the commission had not anticipated would be opposed to the code were the National Association of Attorneys General and the National District Attorneys Association. Their early opposition stemmed in part from basic features of the rational approach to constructing a large integrated legislative package like the criminal code — comprehensiveness and clarity. These features would prove to arouse opposition from other groups as well. In particular, the part of the code that provoked the objections from these groups was how it defined the criminal jurisdiction of the federal government. The existing federal statutes, enacted one at a time, combined a definition of the criminal act with a definition of the federal jurisdiction over the act — for example, interstate travel to aid a gambling business (18 U.S.C. 1952), and interstate transportation of wagering paraphernalia (18 U.S.C. 1953). As a result, there were many similar crimes with different definitions of jurisdiction, and in many cases the courts had interpreted these laws in such a way that the prosecutor had to prove the defendant knew he was breaking a federal law rather than a state one.

The code simplified the whole jurisdiction issue by separately defining the crime — for example, illegal gambling business — and then stating in a separate section under what circumstances the federal government could prosecute for such crimes — for example, if the mails were used or interstate travel was involved. The jurisdicion for a particular crime would be indicated by a cross-reference to the particular jurisdiction section. This made it possible to have a simpler set of definitions for crimes and to remove the confusion over jurisdiction. However, it also appeared to, and in some instances did, expand the range of crimes for which the federal government could prosecute. State and local officials, such as state attorneys general, objected to what they perceived as an increased federal intrusion on their authority. The National Association of Attorneys General (1971) adopted a resolution after reviewing the study draft of the Brown Commission report which stated: "If said Study Draft and recommendations were adopted, a centralization of criminal prosecution would take place in the federal courts which would ultimately lead to a consolidation of power, within the Federal government, thus bringing the effect of chartering a national police force" (p. 6). Federalism concerns such as these are not unusual in our system, and state and local officials have become both organized and sophisticated in representing their interests in Congress.

There was some expansion of federal jurisdiction, but not as much as there appeared to be. Because the code brought similar offenses together in greatly simplified form, it was possible to see in stark relief exactly what crimes the federal government was authorized to prosecute. With the existing statutes spread over different sections of the federal statute books, state and local officials had not previously focused on just how much Congress had expanded the reach of the federal government, one law at a time. The American Bar Association's Section of Criminal Law commented on the federalism criticisms: "The growth of federal jurisdiction over the years has apparently gone unnoticed each time a new basis for federal jurisdiction would appear in a discrete statute. Much of the criticism seems to stem from a shock of recognition over what is today the actual scope of federal jurisdiction" (American Bar Association, 1973, p. 5405.) Nonetheless, the subcommittee staff immediately moved to clarify the portions of the code that were based on existing federal law. They also entered into negotiations with groups representing state and local prosecutors to try to minimize conflict with officials who should have been their natural allies in achieving criminal law reform.

As a result of the two years of hearings, the staff of the subcommittee, headed by Robert Blakey, drafted a bill containing their own version of the federal criminal code. The subcommittee bill was based not only on the hearings but also on what Senators McClellan and Hruska, and also Blakey and others, had discussed during the Brown Commision process. The bill was to be introduced with McClellan, Hruska, and Ervin as sponsors — all senators who had served on the Brown Commission. These senators did not necessarily expect the subcommittee bill to be the version of the code that would ultimately pass. Its introduction was a continuation of the agenda-setting process. In Congress, introducing a bill can serve as a means of "getting people to face the issue" (Kingdon, 1984, p. 136) — a part of the softening-up process.

It helps if the sponsor can draw as much attention as possible to the bill to indicate a priority standing for it in the Senate or House. McClellan was one of the old barons of the Senate with great seniority and had accumulated many debts owed to him, and he knew how to legislate. His securing the bill number S.1 for his criminal code bill was testimony to his power and also to the salience of the crime issue. This sent a signal placing criminal law reform squarely on the Senate agenda. To put this priority-sending signal in perspective, S.2 was the bill to require the end of U.S. participation in the Vietnam War at a time when the vast majority of senators, as well as the public, had clearly had enough of Vietnam. S.1 was introduced in January 1973 at the beginning of the 93rd Congress.

McClellan and Hruska wished to keep the momentum going for criminal law reform and were not necessarily wedded to their draft at this point. In introducing the bill, McClellan stated: "We view it only as the preliminary and immediate work product of two years of efforts by the subcommittee. . . . Indeed, there is much room for debate on this bill. I myself have not reached firm judgments on a number of provisions as they are now drafted." Hruska also said that he did not stand behind every line in the bill, but that it was a reasonable vehicle on which to proceed.

When the Department of Justice draft bill was presented, they agreed to introduce that version as well. Senator Ervin declined to do so, however, as at that time he was highly distrustful of the administration. The administration's bill was introduced as S.1400 on March 27, 1973. Senator Hruska said that although there were "a number of differences between S.1 and S.1400 . . . even a cursory comparison between them demonstrates their essential similarity of conception and execution" (Cohen, 1973, p. 541).

One problem in the Brown code that the drafters of S.1 tried to ameliorate was that of federal jurisdiction. Robert Israel, attorney general of Rhode Island and chair of the National Association of Attorneys General's subcommittee to study S.1, stated that S.1 "met the principal source of the objections from the attorneys general," but that he was "not certain" whether it met all the jurisdictional problems raised by the Brown report. Carl Vergari, chair of the counterpart committee of the National District Attorney's Association, however, said he believed S.1 "has met our concern on the jurisdictional issue" (Cohen, 1973, p. 545). Federalism concerns are often a part of the consideration of federal criminal law proposals, and these two associa-

tions are active participants in looking after the interests of state
and local prosecutors. This is inevitable, given the overlapping
jurisdiction in American criminal law.

Both S.1 and S.1400 employed the approach of the Brown
Commission code. The structural reforms were carried through
in all respects. The differences of S.1 and S.1400 with the commission code were more marked than with each other. Chief
differences between S.1 and S.1400 were in the use of termi-
nology where the lawyers in the Justice Department wanted to
preserve the interpretations of existing case law, or where they
thought the use of particular approaches would withstand challenge on constitutional grounds. Ronald Gainer, who had headed
the Justice Department's code unit, credited the subcommittee
with an "outstanding job of extemporaneous drafting" but said
that the subcommittee's problem was that the staff had only one
draftsman (Robert Joost) and one editor (G. Robert Blakey),
who completed their work in six months. In contrast, Gainer
had not only the ten staff attorneys from the Code Unit but he
also called in attorneys from other Justice divisions, as well as
other agencies, such as the Securities and Exchange Commission and the Internal Revenue Service (Cohen, 1973).

The differences between S.1 and the commission code
were more marked. S.1 stated that the code "aims at the articulation of the nation's fundamental system of public values" and
its vindication through punishment. The purposes of the Brown
code, which were dropped in S.1, included "to define the limits
and systematize the exercise of discretion in punishment" and
"to prevent arbitrary or oppressive treatment of persons accused
or convicted of offenses." The Brown code leaned somewhat more
toward the social justice perspective and S.1 more toward the
get-tough approach. The work "leaned" is used because they had
much in common, especially in their basic approaches. There
were, however, differences.

S.1 had longer sentences for violators, permitted cumulative sentences, and deleted the commission's preference for non-
prison alternative sentencing. S.1 provided for stiffer penalties
for drug offenses, including six months of imprisonment for possession of marijuana, where the commission code provided for

a fine. S.1 made participation in a riot a federal crime punishable as a felony, whereas the commission code classified participation as a crime only in federal enclaves. The sections on the circumstances under which disclosure of government information would be a crime also differed, with S.1 providing a broader prohibition on such disclosure.

In some areas, S.1 was more "liberal" than the Brown Commission code. In the area of civil rights, the commission code was somewhat less protective, requiring a conspiracy to deprive of federal rights and limiting protection to citizens, where S.1 penalized individuals as well as groups acting in a conspiracy violating the rights of any "person." Several national security offenses were treated more liberally in S.1. For example, S.1 followed a suggestion of an American Civil Liberties Union report that improper classification of national security information could be a legal defense for those accused of misusing classified information. S.1 also created some new offenses that pertained to business, such as environmental spoliation and unfair commercial practices. With these last two, the sponsors were showing their willingness to get tough with commercial criminals as well as with other types. This was to create a whole new area of controversy and bring a new set of opposing interest groups into the battle.

The Brown Commission was badly split over whether to include capital punishment, so it produced a majority position against it and a minority position for it. Both S.1 and S.1400 provided for capital punishment.

Capital punishment moved up on the governmental agenda because of a dramatic decision of the Supreme Court that was announced in the spring of 1972. In its decision in *Furman* v. *Georgia* (408 U.S. 238 [1972]), the Supreme Court invalidated existing federal and state capital punishment laws. If Congress wished to retain capital punishment, statutory changes would have to be made. This turned out to be a continuing source of controversy in the efforts to reform federal criminal laws. Nothing seemed to symbolize the debate more between those who favored reform from the social justice perspective and those who favored reform from the get-tough approach.

The decision in the *Furman* case was not accompanied by a single majority opinion — each of the nine justices wrote his own opinion, which is highly unusual. Thus, Congress and the people could not be sure what the court was trying to say about the constitutionality of capital punishment. This left plenty of room for debate not only over whether capital punishment was "cruel and unusual" and thus prohibited by the Constitution but also, if it was not prohibited, over what type of statute would survive Court review. Three of the Supreme Court justices based their opinions on objections to statutes that left the decision of imposing the death penalty in a particular case to the discretion of the judge and jury, which the justices believed led to arbitrary and discriminatory imposition of the death sentence. The decision led to a firestorm of public protest and symbolized for many an undermining by permissive courts of respect for law and order in the middle of a crisis of crime. A national survey taken in March 1973 revealed that 60.2 percent of the respondents favored capital punishment (Stinchcombe and others, 1980).

Perhaps nothing joins the debate betwen social justice proponents and get-tough proponents as directly as the capital punishment issue, and contrasts the two approaches to criminal law. There had been a sharp division in the Brown Commission on capital punishment, and chapter thirty-six of the report appeared in two forms. The principal text favored by the majority of the members who supported abolition of capital punishment embodied that view, while a provisional chapter favored by McClellan and Hruska included capital punishment. Governor Brown was a member of the board of advisors of the National Committee to Abolish the Federal Death Penalty, which was formed on May 10, 1967. Senator Philip Hart, a member of the Senate Judiciary Committee, had introduced S.1760 to abolish capital punishment on May 11, 1967. Senators McClellan and Hruska were squarely on the other side of the issue and were determined to see it included in criminal law reform. The conflict over the death penalty would prove to be a constant in the various efforts to pass a comprehensive bill.

While there were differences between S.1 and S.1400, they were felt by the Senate sponsors and the Department of Justice officials to be reconcilable. Senators McClellan and Hruska planned to move quickly to develop a consolidated bill that would reconcile the differences and move to passage as quickly as possible.

The agenda situation was very different in the House. Representatives Kastenmeier (D-Wisc.) and Edwards (D-Calif.) had served on the Brown Commission and were part of its majority. They also served on the House Judiciary Committee's Subcommittee on Criminal Justice, which would be the subcommittee to consider criminal code reform. At that time, the House Judiciary Committee was dominated by liberal representatives, which would continue throughout the seventies and eighties. Emanuel Celler (D-N.Y.), who served as chairman of the House Judiciary Committee from 1949 to 1972, played a central role in the passage of the major civil rights laws of the 1960s, particularly the 1964 Civil Rights Act. The committee was centrally controlled by Celler and had concentrated on constitutional amendments and civil rights legislation. The committee did not even have a subcommittee on crime under Celler.

In 1972, when Peter Rodino (D-N.J.) became chairman, he announced that he was interested in moving into other areas "before other committees move into them for us" (Leventhal, 1972, p. 1759). Rodino cited as instances of lost jurisdiction the establishment and activities of the House Select Committee on Crime and the House Government Operations Committee oversight hearings of the Law Enforcement Assistance Administration. Rodino wanted to regain authority over criminal matters, but not because he wanted necessarily to pass new laws. A House aide at the time commented, "His instincts are every bit as liberal as Celler's" (Leventhal, 1972, p. 1759).

Rodino created a Subcommittee on Crime headed by John Conyers (D-Mich.) and a Subcommittee on Criminal Justice chaired by William Hungate (D-Mo.) in June 1973. As the Ralph Nader Congress Project noted, however: "The subcommittee reforms of June 1973, as will be seen, did not significantly diminish the Chairman's traditional power over the referral of bills. This centralized power in the Judiciary chairman has long been exercised so as to fragment the committee's jurisdiction among its subcommittees in a wholly irrational fashion. . . . During the Ninety-third Congress, this fragmentation has not been significantly reduced; indeed, in the criminal justice area it has been exacerbated, with five subcommittees considering such legislation" (Schuck, 1975, pp. 47–48).

Even though the Brown Commission code was introduced as a bill, H.R.330, the Criminal Justice Subcommittee scheduled no hearings on it. The political context was important in determining this lack of action. The different orientations in the relevant Senate and House subcommittees were striking, with the center of gravity on the Senate subcommittee being conservative, and that on the House subcommittee being liberal.

The divisions on McClellan's subcommittee were philosophical, not partisan. Democrats McClellan, Eastland, Ervin, and Byrd, and Republicans Hruska, Scott, and Thurmond, tended toward a stricter law enforcement approach, while Democrats Kennedy and Hart and Republican Marlow Cook tended toward the social justice approach (Schuck, 1975). The administration was also of a conservative bent. McClellan and Hruska were leading a bipartisan coalition on the subcommittee which worked in harmony with the new administration.

The lack of movement in the House Judiciary Committee was not a result of a lack of appreciation for the Brown code, which leaned more toward the social justice approach. Rather, it was based on estimates of what the likely outcome might be if the bill were moved beyond the committee's control. After all, the Safe Streets Act had been reshaped by a coalition of Republicans and southern Democrats by amending it on the House floor a very few years earlier. The Judiciary Committee Democrats were faced with the question of what would emerge in final form if the Senate produced a conservative bill and the House was debating a Judiciary Committee bill on the floor. As interviews taken during the Nader project's study of the Judiciary Committees revealed, the House liberals' estimates were not misplaced: "Senators often ask McClellan how to vote on criminal issues; they know that he can control thirty to forty votes on such issues, and when these are combined with the fifteen to twenty votes controlled by Senator Hruska, the ranking minority member of the subcommittee, a majority is almost assured" (Schuck, 1975, p. 27). One obviously critical Senate Judiciary staffer explained his view of McClellan's leadership: "McClellan's real power in the criminal area comes when he stands on the floor and waves his hands and gets red in the face, and screams about coddling criminals. . . . Many a liberal senator thinks twice about the headlines at home and voting against him. . . . Of course, the often simplistic structure of public debates and the headlines on law and order are hardly attributable to McClellan's efforts alone. The Nixon Administration is also responsible. But McClellan is able to raise to a fever pitch on the floor his colleagues' fear that they won't be able to adequately explain criminal justice reform to their constituents" (Schuck, 1975, p. 271). Clearly, McClellan's leadership was based not only on his long experience in the criminal law field but also on his ability to tap into what was perceived by numerous senators as majority constituent opinions that could have electoral consequences for them. Anticipation of possible election implications was significant.

Whereas the Senate held hearings on the Brown report as soon as it was issued, Emanuel Celler, as chairman of the House Judiciary Committee, decided not to hold hearings in 1971. According to Kastenmeier, he and Representative Mikva, who had also served on the Brown Commission, had asked Celler to hold hearings. Kastenmeier said later: "We should have hired staff earlier and viewed ourselves in competition with the Senate both institutionally and philosophically. Instead, we have taken a passive role and have permitted the Senate to take the initiative. It's hard to make up for this psychologically; I fear that our committee's version of the bill will be defensive even though it should reflect the views of the Brown Commission more closely than does the Senate bill" (Cohen, 1973, p. 539). As Schwartz (1977) later observed: "There was also a feeling in some quarters that the conservative thrust of the Senate could be most effectively countered by waiting out the battle there between conservatives and liberals, after which the Senate's version could be bottled up or cut up in the House" (p. 11). In Schuck's study (1975), a lobbyist observed that most of the House Judiciary

Committee's efforts were actually expended resisting Senate measures, often on civil libertarian grounds. This strategy would be employed by the House Judiciary leadership over several Congresses in treating crime legislation.

Thus, criminal law reform had been placed on the governmental agenda by virtue of leadership in the Senate and the administration. It would not be ready for the decision agenda, however, until differences between the Senate and the Department of Justice versions could be resolved, and it could somehow be given serious consideration in the House. This latter problem was the more formidable. First, some of the key members who had served on the Brown Commission were no longer in the House. Representative Poff of Virginia retired, and Representative Mikva was defeated. These were significant losses for moving a bill. As a Justice Department official stated at the time: "It is very unfortunate that both Poff and Mikva are no longer in the House. Poff was the intellectual leader of the conservatives and was trusted by the other committee members; Mikva played the same role for the liberals" (Cohen, 1973, p. 545). Key policy leaders on federal criminal law reform were missing in the House.

Instead, William Hungate was the new chairman of the House Subcommittee on Criminal Justice and he had had no connection with the code effort. Hungate stated that the subcommittee would not begin work on the criminal code until it had concluded consideration of changes in the Federal Rules of Evidence (Cohen, 1973). This was to prove to be the least of the barriers to House action.

Agenda Setting Reexamined

The softening-up process necessary to move federal criminal law reform onto Congress's agenda and prepare it for the decision stage had proceeded fairly well. As indicated earlier, key elements of the policy community must begin to focus on the issue and alternative solutions to get a policy on the governmental agenda. The Brown Commission report and subsequent bills drafted within the Justice Department, and the Senate Subcommittee on Criminal Laws and Procedure, had involved significant participation from congressional staffs, political appointees, and civil servants in the executive branch, as well as academics and members of Congress. Serious reformulation of the original commission alternative had been the result.

A significant gain was the endorsement by the president. Instead of rejecting the commission appointed by the previous administration of the other party, the Nixon administration was brought to endorse warmly the general idea. Further, key policy leaders, such as Senators McClellan and Hruska, had managed to secure extensive hearings and engage the Senate Judiciary Committee in the enterprise.

This movement onto the governmental agenda went very well, given the magnitude and complexity of the task and the potentially divisive issues involved. The policy proposal was no doubt aided by the widespread appeal of the opportunity to respond to public disgruntlement about crime control. In addition, the participants had convinced relevant elements of the policy community that the alternatives contained serious solutions.

What remained was to expand efforts to achieve a broad consensus around a single bill and also to get some attention and movement in the House. As will be demonstrated, building a consensus is not a straightforward process.

· 5 ·

Dissensus:
Conflict and
Stalemate

In order to achieve criminal law reform, it was going to be necessary to get a consensus bill in the Senate and to start some action moving in the House. This was derailed not because of any
serious miscues by the policy leaders supporting criminal code
reform, but because of developments in the political environment. These events serve to illustrate that the dynamics of the
legislative process are not contained within the institutions of
government but are intertwined with the larger political process
that proceeds apace and not necessarily coordinate with the legislative process.

Dissensus: Conflict-Producing Tendencies
in the Legislative Process

Once a bill makes it onto the congressional agenda, its handling
is not normally a straight line process from consideration to passage. It is by no means inevitable that a consensus will develop
around the desirability of moving it toward the decision agenda, let alone passing it. Instead, there is normally high potential for numerous false starts, tussles, derailments, and restarts.
Conflict is, thus, an inherent element in the legislative process,
as it is in government generally. Large-scale policy proposals
have even greater potential for conflict. Because of their scope

and complexity, they contain many more issues that embody conflicts.

There are a number of different sources of conflict that are always present in Congress. These include partisanship, ideological differences, regional divisions, interest group loyalties, jurisdictional prerogatives, and personal animosities. Legislators are not isolated in responding to these potential sources of conflict. Pressures both inside and outside Congress can serve to exacerbate or dampen the conflict surrounding any particular policy proposal. Those pressures inside Congress come from party leaders, committee delegations, state delegations, informal clubs and groups, and staff members. Those outside Congress come from the public (mass opinion, the opinion of specialized publics, and the opinion of voters registered in elections), the executive branch (president, presidential staff, and the bureaucracy), interest groups, and state and local officials (Ripley, 1983).

Although certain legislators and other policy leaders are participants in the conflict, they are also managers of it (see Cobb and Elder, 1983, p. 37). They are aided by a norm of reciprocity and accommodation — a general expectation among members of Congress that they will be mutually helpful and accommodate themselves to each other's needs, and will bargain in a way that leaves room for compromise. This serves to reduce extreme partisanship, which could potentially make bargaining and decision making exceedingly difficult (Ripley, 1983).

Reciprocity only goes so far, however, and the skills of policy leaders in reacting to the sources of division — accommodating where possible, and defeating where necessary — is crucial in obtaining the consensus needed to achieve agenda status for a large-scale policy initiative or to move it toward passage. Progress in getting a policy proposal on the congressional agenda does not necessarily mean it will stay there or will move toward the decision agenda. The policy leader cannot count on a favorable political environment, or stability within it, if one happens to exist for a time.

Kingdon (1984) conceptualizes the developments in the political environment as the "political stream," which contains important promoters or inhibitors that determine whether or not policies will achieve high agenda status. Forces in the political stream — changes in national mood, consensus and conflict among organized interest groups, turnover in key personnel in government — can all determine whether the balance of forces favors action or inaction on a policy proposal. These forces are moving in the political stream at all times, but not necessarily in such a way that they change the balance of forces affecting policy in the legislative process. However, a gradual or sudden shift in the political stream can penetrate the legislative process and produce such a change.

Changes in the national mood or climate of the times (Cobb and Elder, 1981) can serve to push some new ideas higher on the governmental agenda while pushing others into relative obscurity. Legislative policymakers also calculate what the balance of forces among organized interests means for action. If the organized interest groups are all pointing in the same direction, this adds to the impetus to move in that direction. If the balance of conflicting forces is tilting against a proposal, it does not mean that the proposal will not receive any consideration, but it does indicate that the price paid for moving it forward will be high. In addition, the turnover of key personnel, either as a result of a new administration, electoral defeat or retirement, or movement to a new post or committee, can have a profound effect on agenda change (Kingdon, 1984).

Opponents of a policy proposal will often try to arouse various elements in the political environment by using symbols that activate latent groups favorable to their position and unfavorable to that of policy proponents. Their efforts will be hampered or aided by developments in the political stream as well. The mass media play an important role in determining the success of this strategy. It is not guaranteed that the media will take an interest in the controversy but, once they focus on an issue, they will often play an important role in reinforcing or altering the prevailing definition of the conflict (Cobb and Elder, 1983).

Defining conflict is not the only effect of the media. The media play an important role in setting the congressional agenda. "Stories and editorials help define problems, link problems and alternatives, and either influence or, perhaps more likely, represent national moods" (Cook, 1989, p. 121). The media can increase awareness of an issue and mobilize opinion, especially for those issues that people do not personally encounter (see Ebring and others, 1980). Coverage by the media can increase the prominence of an issue, and visibility often serves to certify importance (Cook, 1989). On occasion, the media will function as an interest group when media perceive that a policy threatens their own values and interests.

Dissensus Surrounds Criminal Law Reform

As it came to pass, changes in several sectors of the political environment were to have a significant effect on the consideration of criminal law reform. As discussed so far, the national mood had been developing for some time in the direction of a stronger government role in reestablishing law and order, accompanied by a lessening of interest in social justice or the protection of the rights of those suspected of crime. This had not only affected the agenda priority for criminal law reform but had also pushed it in the direction of the get-tough approach. The only organized interests up to this point had been generally supportive of the code efforts, but groups such as the American Bar Association and the National Association of Attorneys General, which were partially supportive, are not large constituency groups that can call on large numbers of people to push legislation. Rather, they are listened to by Congress on the basis of their professional expertise and prestige.

S.1 and S.1400 were likely to draw some attention from more powerful organized constituency groups, such as business and consumer groups, because of the added sections dealing with commercial crime, but these groups were just gearing up for the hearings at this point. As stated earlier, the absence of Representatives Mikva and Poff on the House Judiciary Committee removed two knowledgeable and trusted actors for criminal law reform.

Policy leaders need to choose what kind of strategy to take according to the kind of environment they find — an inside strategy, an outside strategy, or a combination. An inside strategy emphasizes bargaining, accommodation, and compromise. It requires a deemphasis of hard positions, differences, and pressure so that leaders possess enough flexibility to assemble quietly a coalition behind an acceptable bill. It is facilitated by direct communication among members, staffs, and other insiders out of the public spotlight. In contrast, the outside strategy emphasizes issues and their relationship to powerfully held public values. It highlights differences among positions and "who is on the right side." The outside strategy depends on communication through the media and seeks to activate outside publics and groups to pressure congressional representatives. Reagan's television speeches to the country on his budget and tax packages asking citizens to contact their representatives is perhaps one of the most visible and successful examples of the outside strategy.

It is possible to combine the two strategies, but there is an inherent tension between the two. An inside strategy demands pliability and maneuvering room for policy leaders. The outside strategy, because it relies on the media, needs clear-cut positions, which tends to limit flexibility severely (Cook, 1989).

Policy leaders use different strategies depending on the stage of the legislative process and the nature of the political environment. A congressional press secretary stated one option thus: "Before legislative action, you want exposure, you want to generate public attention and public interest. Then you get to actual legislating and putting the pieces of the puzzle together, and you *don't* want it; you've got everything cranked up and then a story in the *Post* can kill you" (Cook, 1989, p. 155). For several years prior to the Brown Commission Report, proponents of federal criminal law reform had pursued an outside strategy to raise the profile of issues involved in criminal law reform. Now McClellan and Hruska needed to build consensus based on accommodation. They needed flexibility and so did their prospective coalition partners. They undertook an inside strategy — one that depended on a continuing stable supportive political environment. They did not get it.

The set of events in the political stream that was to affect profoundly the agenda for criminal law reform can be capsulized in one word—Watergate. The events surrounding the break-in at the Democratic National Headquarters at the Watergate apartments transformed the political stream and course of the legislative process. These events changed the national mood, highlighted different issues in criminal law reform, mobilized different interest groups, diverted the administration, and redirected the attention of congressional representatives and staff— particularly those involved with the Judiciary committees. They also made possible the use of symbols that heightened fear of government repression to block the development of the consensus needed to move a comprehensive bill.

Before Watergate, Senators McClellan and Hruska had succeeded in getting federal criminal law reform on the governmental agenda. However, they could not move it to the decision agenda without developing a consensus around a single bill. They knew that there was a need to develop a compromise between the provisions of S.1 and S.1400, and also the Brown Commission code, if they were going to gain sufficient momentum to obtain Senate passage and to put pressure on the House to act. McClellan had even stated publicly his willingness to be flexible on the content of the bill.

G. Robert Blakey, McClellan's chief counsel on the subcommittee, went to visit Ronald Gainer, head of Justice's code unit, shortly after S.1400 was introduced. He said to Gainer, "I've got no pride of authorship. Let's work together and get a common version." Gainer was not sure that Blakey meant it at the time, but he shortly came to understand that he did mean it. Cooperative activity was facilitated by the movement of some key staff. Blakey, with Gainer's consent, hired Paul Summit, who was working in the Justice code unit, to serve as deputy chief counsel of McClellan's subcommittee. In addition, Hruska hired Paul Lazarus, another Criminal Division attorney, to work on his staff on the code project. Joint drafting sessions were held between the subcommittee staff and the Justice staff in offices on the first floor of the Justice Department.

The efforts to push the criminal reform effort along, however, were soon overtaken by other fast-breaking events. S.1 was introduced at the start of the Congress in January 1973.

On January 17, 1973, the trial of Daniel Elsberg for disclosing the Pentagon Papers got under way. On March 27, 1973, S.1400 was introduced. On April 5, the presiding judge in the grand jury investigation of the Watergate break-in granted immunity to James McCord, who began naming others who were involved. McCord reportedly told the grand jury that he had learned through Gordon Liddy that transcripts of wiretapped conversations from Democratic National Headquarters were hand-delivered to John Mitchell, former attorney general and director of the Committee to ReElect the President. Also in April, in the Daniel Elsberg case, the FBI admitted that Attorney General Mitchell had authorized wiretaps on several government officials and four on newsmen in order to investigate leaks of national security information. The FBI had heard Elsberg on one of these wiretaps in late 1969 and early 1970, long before the Pentagon Papers were published. All during the spring, the Justice Department had fought a running court battle with the *New York Times* to keep the Pentagon Papers from being published, and had finally lost in a split decision before the Supreme Court.

Perhaps the first serious effect of Watergate was that it diverted the attention of Congress in general, and the Judiciary committees in particular, from legislating substantive law to investigating government officials — and ultimately to passing a bill of impeachment on President Nixon forcing his resignation. The proposed law that came to have priority was the special prosecutor law. The priority shifted from expanding the role of government in criminal apprehension to checking the abuse of power by government officials. Robert Blakey, the Senate subcommittee chief counsel, concluded that Watergate would so absorb the energies of the Judiciary committees that moving the criminal code was most unlikely. In September 1973, he left for a position at Cornell University, and the deputy, Paul Summit, became chief counsel.

The McClellan subcommittee did manage to hold hearings on S.1 and S.1400 and the staff continued to work with Justice Department staff to resolve issues in an attempt to arrive at a joint draft. The objective was to produce a bill that would combine features of the original Brown Commission code, S.1, S.1400, and information gained in the hearings into a revised bill that could be introduced into the 94th Congress. However, most of the efforts of even the staff of the McClellan subcommittee went into the Senate Judiciary Committee's activity investigating Watergate. No action was taken in the House, either. The House Judiciary Committee was preoccupied with a very grave task—the impeachment of a president.

On January 15, 1975, a new S.1 was introduced in the Senate with thirteen cosponsors, including Senate Majority Leader Mike Mansfield, Minority Leader Hugh Scott, and Senator Birch Bayh (D-Ind.), one of the most liberal members on the Judiciary Committee. It went beyond the previous S.1 and included procedural law as well as substantive law. Most of this added material was a codification of law existing at the time; a smaller part was new. Nonetheless, it would come to add fuel to the fires of opposition and controversy.

Issues that were neither part of the central core of the code nor central to criminal law reform came to dominate the public debate. This was attributable to both overreaching on the part of the drafters of S.1 and overreacting on the part of certain opposing interest groups. As Schwartz (1977) observed later: "The provocation from the Right was great. The response from the Left was demagogic, deceptive, and probably counterproductive to the struggle to promote liberty and justice" (p. 41). Two interlocking sources of opposition came together to form what became known as the "Stop S.1" campaign. The chief movers among interest groups were the American Civil Liberties Union, the National Lawyers Guild, and the National Committee Against Repressive Legislation (Schwartz, 1977). Their leverage was magnified in the battle by the antagonism of another center of opposition—the media.

While a number of provisions came to be singled out by the liberal opposition groups as "repressive," the section that galvanized the press came to be termed in the media as the "Official Secrets Act." In the Watergate era, the effect of this point of controversy was heavily damaging. Sec. 1124 of S.1 stated: "A person is guilty of an offense, if, being or having been in autho-

rized possession or control of classified information, or having
obtained such information as a result of his being or having been
a federal public servant, he knowingly communicates such information to a person who is not authorized to receive it." In
a tragic example of overreaching, the subcommittee report stated
that prosecution of newsmen for illegally receiving "national
defense information" whether classified or not would be possible under another proposed section which required a person in
unauthorized possession of national defense information to
"deliver it promptly to a federal public servant who is entitled
to receive it" (Staff of the Senate Committee . . . , 1974, Sec.
1123 [a][2][b]). This section carried a maximum penalty of
fifteen years and a $100,000 fine during national emergencies
and wartime, and seven years and $100,000 at other times.

Against the backdrop of the Elsberg case and the suits
against the *New York Times,* and also the Watergate cover-up
attempts, the liberal groups and the media reacted quickly in
opposition not just to the inclusion of this section, but to all of
S.1. The American Civil Liberties Union (ACLU) distributed
300,000 copies of a pamphlet that began: "Among the principal
lessons of Watergate and Vietnam are that secrecy in government is cancerous to our democracy and dissent is healthy. S.1,
a bill now before the Senate, disregards both lessons. The bill's
alleged purpose is to revise and reform the United States criminal
code, but the real purpose of important parts of the bill is to
perpetuate secrecy and stifle protest." The strategy of the opponents was that the bill was a product of the Nixon conspiracy
and that within it were many dangers apparent and hidden so
that the bill was unsalvageable. The *Washington Report,* a publi-
cation of the National Committee Against Repressive Legislation (NCARL), in July 1975 carried a story indicating that the
Senate Judiciary Committee was about to review the bill. It advised that "letters to senators are urgently needed now" and
offered that NCARL's constitutional advisors confirmed that
compromise was impossible. It quoted these advisors, Profes-
sors Vern Countryman and Thomas Emerson, as stating: "The
objective of the draftsman was to incorporate . . . every restric-
tion upon individual liberties, every method and device, that

the Nixon Administration thought necessary or useful in pursuit of its fearful and corrupt policies. As such the bill is permeated with assumptions, points of view and objectives, finding expression in numerous overt or subtle provisions, that run counter to the open and free spirit upon which American liberties are based. This pervasive taint cannot be amended out."

These groups, in all probability, would not have been too effective with such a hyperbolic stance had not a significant number of newspapers and other media outlets picked up the opposition's line. Roger Simon, a *Chicago Sun-Times* reporter, provided an analysis to alert his press colleagues in an article in *The Quill,* the magazine of Sigma Delta Chi, the Society of Professional Journalists. The article was titled "S.1 — a Menace to the Press" and concluded: "If S.1 does get through the Congress, the President and the Supreme Court with its press provisions intact, there is little doubt that American Journalism will undergo the greatest change in its history. Martin Arnold of the *New York Times* wrote that many observers feel this is the most important confrontation between the press and government since John Peter Zenger was acquitted of charges for seditious libel in 1735. The press may not be so lucky this time" (*The Quill,* July-Aug. 1975, p. 21).

A *Wall Street Journal* editorial of September 22, 1975, complained that even if the disclosure of government information section were fixed, the bill would still be unacceptable because it was too long: "Are we really supposed to believe that every Senator and Representative will read all 753 pages and go through the kind of legalistic and philosophical exercises on every point that we have been going through on just a few critical issues? We rather doubt it."

The *Los Angeles Times,* in an editorial of September 15, 1975, titled "Putting Freedom Against the Wall," stated: "Senate Bill 1, a massive and complicated measure 753 pages long, is so pervasively and fatally flawed that it lies beyond the scope of any rational amending process. . . . Whatever this bill is, it is not simply an effort to pull together and rationalize existing federal law. It is, rather, a reflection of an authoritarian view of the way government should function, and a radical departure from the letter and spirit of the Constitution."

These stories had immediate effects in breaking down the attempts to build a bipartisan effort to develop the bill. A letter by Senator Sam Ervin, who gained national fame in chairing the Senate Watergate hearings, appeared in the *Los Angeles Times* on October 5, 1975. It referred to the "Putting Freedom Against the Wall" editorial and stated: "S.1, in its present form, is simply atrocious and would establish what is essentially a police state in which liberties of the American people would exist only by the tolerance of public officials." Birch Bayh, who was campaigning for president at the time, met with lawyers for news organizations and announced that he was withdrawing his cosponsorship of S.1 and would introduce an amendment to narrow substantially the section dealing with release of classified information (Lyons, 1975).

Not all of the Left's complaints were that S.1 was too tough; some were that it was too soft — soft on the wrong kind of people. This charge centered on what became known as the "Nuremberg" or "Ehrlichman defense." In September 1975, the National Committee Against Repressive Legislation issued a pamphlet entitled "Dangerous S.B. 1." Its headline proclaimed: "Senate Bill 1 — a 753 page legislative legacy of the Nixon Administration's fearful and corrupt policies — is moving toward final action by the U.S. Senate. Drafted in major part under Attorneys General Mitchell and Kleindienst and titled the 'Criminal Justice Reform Act of 1975', its enactment would constitute an unparalleled disaster!" Among the objectionable sections were Secs. 542, 544, and 552, which NCARL claimed "would inhibit prosecution of wrongdoing by 'public servants' if illegal conduct is the result of 'belief' that it was 'required or authorized' or based on 'written interpretation issued by the head of a government agency' (e.g., from a President?)."

Also in September 1975, the ACLU distributed nationally a pamphlet entitled "Stop S.1" that proclaimed: "Did you think the President's men were just following orders? S.1 would let them out of jail." In October, a *Washington Post* article entitled "Critics of U.S. Code Hit 'Ehrlichman Defense' " pointed out: "So fundamental are the issues that the debate quickly ranges over some of the most far-reaching legal events of recent history — the rejected 'Nuremberg defense' used by Nazi war criminals who said they acted according to superior's orders, the claims of some Vietnam war resisters of obedience to a higher law, and the argument by former White House aide John D. Ehrlichman and the White house 'plumbers' that the crime of burglary could be legalized by presidential command" (MacKenzie, 1975).

The sections were included in both the Brown Commission code and S.1, because the codes, in order to be comprehensive, sought to list not only criminal offenses but also the principal defenses available under federal criminal law. Schwartz, in a briefing for 100 Senate aides on the Criminal Code, replied to the charges against the defenses involving officials: "That's part of a conspiratorial paranoiac view of what's going on. S.1 wouldn't let them out of jail. . . . Nixon's private instructions to his henchmen that you are to go into houses doesn't come within a million miles. This is just an attempt to frighten people and evoke a knee-jerk reaction" (MacKenzie, 1975).

Later Schwartz explained that the defenses drafted pertaining to officials were in line with the broadly accepted principle in modern law of exculpation for "reasonable mistake." After explaining what led the Brown code drafters to form the defenses, Schwartz (1977) observed: "Against this background we may appraise the opposing positions in the controversy over the 'Ehrlichman defense.' What emerges is that the Left took a strikingly anti-civil liberties position. Trapped by its own volleys of rhetoric against S.1 as a McClellan-Nixon conspiracy, and responding only to yesterday's headlines rather than to the lessons of history, it rushed into a 'law and order' position to the right of Senator McClellan on mistake of law: subordinate public servants and ordinary citizens acting at the request of even high officials were to be convicted of crimes without regard to their good faith belief that they were following society's lawful mandate like model or even heroic citizens" (pp. 45–46).

Perhaps the press controversy that contributed most to the stalling of S.1 was a totally unexpected charge that it showed too much concern for criminals and not enough for citizens. Jack Landau of the Newhouse News Service termed S.1 the "Prowler

Law." Landau (1975), in an article that appeared in newspapers nationwide, claimed: "The bill . . . would negate the widely held belief that a person can shoot a night-time prowler with no questions asked. . . . The American Bar Association (ABA) at its annual meeting last month voted to oppose this provision. The home defense section states that a citizen in his home could be convicted for murdering an intruder unless the citizen had reached the conclusion that 'deadly force' was 'reasonably required to protect' him or his family 'from risk of death or serious bodily injury'."

This article unleashed a storm of protest. Letters, often with the article attached, streamed into congressional offices all over Capitol Hill. Senator Ford (D-Ky.) reported receiving hundreds of letters. One irate citizen wrote, "It seems to me that anyone breaking into my home certainly isn't there for a social visit and I don't plan on discussing my intentions with him" (Schwartz, 1975).

McClellan and his staff tried to explain the inaccuracies in the article, such as the fact that the provision would only apply on federal land and not to private citizens' homes, that the provision was merely a carryover from current law, and that the ABA had not voted as Landau reported. The ABA confirmed that no such vote had occurred. Landau, when later asked about these points, said that he intended to write a clarification explaining that the law applied only to land under federal jurisdiction and that he had inadvertently failed to make that point (Schwartz, 1975).

Newspaper editorials and columns by conservative writers such as William F. Buckley and Paul Harvey, based on a belief that the story was accurate, condemned the bill: "The whole thing is rampant liberalism" (Buckley, 1975). Harvey (1975) stated that S.1 would "make it a federal law that if you shoot a prowler in your home YOU go to jail" and would "supersede any state laws to the contrary." *Louisville Times* editorialist Richard Des Ruisseaux lampooned Washington for aiming to turn a man's castle into a supply depot for criminals. Even *Trial Magazine,* published by the American Trial Lawyers Association, ran a story entitled "A Crime to Shoot Nighttime Prowlers" (1975).

Several congressmen issued news releases condemning the provision without checking the story's accuracy. Others checked and issued clarifying releases. The Justice Department also tried to get clarifications into the media by writing to editors and pointing out errors. For example, Richard Thornburgh, assistant attorney general at the time, wrote a letter on December 13, 1975, to *Trial Magazine* "to correct the false information you have published." He pointed out that the home defense provisions in S.1 would in no way abrogate state laws and would apply only on federal enclaves such as military bases. He went on to state: "Even in a dwelling on a Federal enclave, the proposed provisions do not prohibit the use of deadly force against an intruder or prowler. The use of deadly force is prohibited under S.1 only in a situation where it would be clear to any reasonable man, even in the heat of the moment, that no danger to the life or limb of persons rightfully on the premises was involved, as, for example where the intruder is recognized as an intoxicated neighbor coming in by stumbling through the door." *Trial Magazine* carried a correction to its story and quoted Thornburgh's letter in its February 1976 issue.

Unfortunately, clarifications rarely get the coverage or have the impact of the original charge. In one of the few columns to clarify the bill, Landau, after being asked about the overlooked points, was reported as stating, "My face is red. I didn't realize people would think the bit covered in the story had nationwide implications." In the same column, Des Ruisseaux, who had earlier lampooned the bill, was reported as saying, "Now that I have an accurate picture of the law on defending the home, I'd like to get Landau into my home as an intruder" (Schulman, 1975).

Nonetheless, the damage was done. As Paul Summit, subcommittee chief counsel observed later, "We never recovered from that story. No matter how you tried to explain it, it just went downhill from there" (personal interview, 1986). Even though McClellan's subcommittee unanimously reported out the bill on October 21, 1975, the Senate Judiciary Committee postponed action on it.

The opponents continued to insist that S.1 was unamendable. On November 20, 1975, Representatives Kastenmeier and

Edwards, who had introduced a bill that incorporated the Brown Commission Code in 1973, introduced H.R.10850, which was drafted by the ACLU. Areas of difference with S.1 were the insanity defense, treatment of classified material, marijuana, the sentencing structure, the death sentence, and obscenity. The ACLU did not push for action in the House, preferring to concentrate on stopping S.1.

Two other bills introduced on November 20, however, would serve to change the dynamics of the consideration of criminal reform. These two bills were introduced in the Senate by Senate Judiciary member Edward Kennedy and dealt with sentencing—S.2698, which provided for mandatory minimum sentences for federal crimes, and S.2699, entitled "Sentencing Guidelines Bill."

These bills marked a significant point of departure for Kennedy's entrance into policy leadership on criminal law reform. They did not hew to the standard liberal line of the time, and Kennedy's credentials as a spokesman for liberal issues were well known. Kennedy had become uncomfortable with Republican and Southern Democratic dominance of crime policy and saw a need for a change in approach. In 1975, he hired a new staff member, Kenneth Feinberg, who had been an assistant U.S. attorney in New York. Feinberg reported later that Kennedy told him, "Here's S.1. I can't support it. It's perceived as being anti-civil libertarian. How can we make it workable? What other ideas do you have that we might use to get moving on this?" (personal interview, 1986). The result was the sentencing bills, which brought Kennedy into the field of criminal law reform.

The mandatory minimum sentencing bill, providing for a mandatory two-year sentence for certain types of street crime, appealed to public concern that criminals not get off too easy. The sentencing guidelines bill proposed establishing a Sentencing Commission that would promulgate a fixed sentencing range for similar crimes committed by similar defendants. Thereafter, a court passing sentence on a convicted criminal would be required to impose a sentence within these guidelines. For example, if the commission established in cases of armed bank robbery, in which the defendant was a first offender and no injury resulted, a sentence of between 4.5 and 5.8 years, then the sentencing judge would sentence within that range, unless there were mitigating circumstances. Even then, the bill provided that the reason justifying a variation in sentence outside the guidelines would have to be stated by the judge in writing and would be subject to review by appellate courts.

The departure from the Brown Commission approach could be found in the absence of rehabilitation as a stated purpose or goal of sentencing. In a later article, Kennedy (1976) wrote the reason for the omission: "Has rehabilitation of the offender ceased to be a valid purpose for the imposition of a prison sentence? The answer is yes and for the same reason that indeterminate sentencing is no longer permitted under the bill. The simple fact is prison rehabilitation programs have not been successful — at least in those cases where such programs are compulsory in nature and forced on the prisoner" (p. 15). Kennedy concluded with what had to be considered a surprising declaration for a liberal: "The lingering myths of our criminal justice system — that sentencing is fair and objective, that rehabilitation is a goal of imprisonment and can be forced on the offender, that parole boards and prison officials can 'predict' the offender's future behavior in the community — must yield to a more practical corrections policy" (p. 23). Kennedy's realistic approach to eliminating arbitrariness in sentencing would serve as a basis for moving ahead in the future.

But not right away. The battle to stop S.1 was still on center stage. House Judiciary subcommittee chairman William Hungate made it clear that he would begin hearings on criminal code reform two weeks after the bill passed the Senate, but not before then (Cohen, 1975, p. 1757).

In the late fall of 1975, S.1 was stalled. In fact, in January of 1976, Jerry Friedman, executive vice-president of the American Newspaper Publishers Association, told the association's convention that the bill was dead, "not just because it was ridiculous," but because of the way the American press "got together and convinced members of Congress it was not a good idea" (*Arkansas Gazette,* January 18, 1976).

Governor Brown became concerned that the whole concept of the criminal code might be lost. His letter of January 20, 1976, to the *New York Times* observed: "I have watched with deep concern the efforts of some civil libertarians and representatives of the press to kill S.1. . . . .That bill incorporates a very substantial portion of the recommendations of our commission, and 95 percent of its provisions constitute a major improvement over existing Federal criminal law." He noted that a few sections were objectionable but would be easily amended and stated: "The contention that the whole bill must be defeated because of these few sections is, in my opinion, without a semblance of validity." Brown concluded: "A great deal of misinformation has been spread about S.1. . . .Defeat would be a severe blow to criminal law reform in the country." McClellan and Hruska had continually said that they would consider compromises. On Februrary 14, McClellan again stated: "I have always said nothing is sacrosanct in this bill and some things in there ought to be changed or modified." On the secrecy provisions, he declared: "The government secrecy — I never cared about that part. I'm satisfied with present law so far as that's concerned" (*Washington Post,* February 15, 1976, p. A-5).

At this point, Majority Leader Mike Mansfield and Minority Leader Hugh Scott, both original S.1 cosponsors, took the initiative to get S.1 moving. They wrote a memorandum to Senators McClellan, Hruska, Kennedy, and Hart, members of the Subcommittee on Criminal Laws and Procedure, and the leaders on the opposing sides, asking them to try to reach an accommodation based on dropping both controversial "repressive" and "liberalizing" measures. These would include the sections dealing with espionage and related offenses (official secrets), exercise of public authority, wiretapping, the death sentence, the insanity defense, obscenity, and several other contentious issues (*Congressional Record,* Feb. 16, 1976, S1563). The next day, the *Washington Post* editorialized about the leaders' proposal: "That is probably the best solution under the circumstances and we urge that it be accepted by both sides in this long struggle over how the criminal laws should be reformed" (Feb. 17, 1976, p. A-17).

However, the ACLU saw nothing in accommodation. In a guest editorial article, Charles Morgan, Washington director of the ACLU, listed all the reasons for resisting compromise.

Basically, the ACLU's objections were that it would retain existing law, which in the ACLU's view was too repressive. "Even if Mansfield-Scott had identified all those sections of S.1 which need substantial change, which they have not, their compromise would still be unacceptable" (Morgan, 1976).

In actuality, the staffs of Senators Kennedy and Hart, leaders from the liberal side, and of Senators McClellan and Hruska, leaders from the conservative side, had been negotiating on the various issues for about six months and felt they were getting close to an agreement. On March 8, Senators Mansfield and Scott invited the four senators to a meeting to discuss the prospects for resolving the impasse, and indicated to them that unless agreement could be reached soon, it would be unlikely that Congress would be able to pass a bill that year. This was especially true given that the House was not even going to begin processing the bill until the Senate passed it.

At this point, Senators Kennedy and Hart submitted to Senators McClellan and Hruska a list of amendments to S.1 which they thought would make it acceptable. These included the thirteen proposals from Mansfield and Scott plus twelve others. McClellan and Hruska sat down together with their staffs and went through the proposals and decided jointly what they could accept and what they could not. On March 25, they offered a counterproposal in which they accepted all thirteen of the Mansfield-Scott proposals and rejected only one of the others outright — a Hart-Kennedy proposal to repeal existing federal statutes that prohibited the distribution of obscene material. Of the other eleven, they accepted four completely, agreed to five with modifications, and expressed willingness to negotiate on two. Kennedy and Hart immediately issued a statement terming the response constructive and said they hoped to reach a common understanding on the bill soon. Attorney General Edward Levi issued a statement hailing the attempt at compromise. However, the ACLU's chief lobbyist, Jay Miller, said the compromise did not go far enough and, in regard to the ACLU's concerns, "there are hundreds of parts of the bill" (Mann, 1976).

At this point, outside events intruded. Kennedy was running for reelection to the Senate that year and he did not want to alienate civil liberties groups. His aide, Kenneth Feinberg, met with ACLU officials in Massachusetts and with the Massachusetts Democratic National Committeeman. Going in, he hoped to sell the compromise. However, the ACLU representatives were then concerned with provisions that were not even the subject of the Kennedy-Hart proposals. After the meeting, Feinberg was quoted as saying, "It is a volatile issue and I don't think Kennedy wants to play with it much more" (Wermiel, Apr. 19, 1976). Kennedy and Hart did not reply specifically to the McClellan-Hruska counteroffer, and S.1 never was brought to a vote in the Senate Judiciary Committee. Kennedy, however, was not completely giving up on criminal law reform. He told a reporter in May, "We are going to have to face up to recodification, if not this year then next" (Wermiel, May 8, 1976).

Kennedy's political problem was that if he tried to placate the ACLU and its allies, he would have to depart drastically from the positions he had already taken and embrace positions that were to the left of the Brown Commission majority. The ACLU saw criminal code revision as a once-in-a-lifetime opportunity to reform criminal law from its perspective on civil liberties, and it was not willing to compromise its agenda. The ACLU was not without its critics at the time. Theodore Voorhees, a member of the Brown Commission majority, chronicled the ACLU's activities in an *American Bar Association Journal* article and concluded: "It was amazing that any organization that professed liberal objectives and the protection of civil liberties could seek to strangle legislation that advanced those causes. The ACLU had fallen victim to its own propaganda. All criminal law revision had to be stopped even when all primary objection to S.1 had been satisfied" (Voorhees, 1976, p. 1347).

The Media, Dissensus, and Large-Scale Legislation

The originators of criminal code reform were mindful of the requirements of consensus building, and the Brown Commission itself was part of this strategy. Proponents in the House and Senate tried to approach the legislative process to take advantage of the consensus-building momentum that had developed with the Commission report. However, they harbored no illusions as to what the dangers were. Congressman Poff, the principal leader in the House on establishing the commission, and vice-chairman of the commission, testified at the first McClellan subcommittee hearing on the criminal code: "I think the chief danger this report faces is that it might become victim to the more visible and emotional issues which seem to stand out on its own pages and in the interpretations of those who have read those pages. I hope that won't be the case" (Senate Subcommittee on Criminal Laws and Procedures, Feb. 10, 1971, p. 100). Unfortunately for code proponents, Poff's hope was to be unrealized and for exactly the reason he feared.

The positive side of complex large-scale legislation is difficult to convey through the popular press. While initiatives, such as the criminal code, can have significant system effects, they are longer term, and individualized benefits are difficult to pinpoint. Proponents of code reform could point to the bulk of S.1 as providing an interlocking series of changes that would presumably positively impact the federal law enforcement system. The individual effects that came through within the existing political climate, however, were that the bill would make it illegal for reporters to receive government information and for homeowners to shoot prowlers breaking into their homes. The newsworthiness of a bill is increased if it is less complex, because journalists tend to assume that less comprehensive issues and ones that are more clear-cut will be more understandable and interesting, and also easier to present in a short space. "Clear-cut issues are especially felicitous if they can be dramatized by two (and only two) distinct sides and an easily reported conflict" (Cook, 1989, p. 49).

The direct effect on progress of S.1, or the lack of it, in the Senate may appear surprising. After all, one might expect that because senators are there and in a position to verify the accuracy and significance of a report on a particular provision, they could just ignore an exaggerated or erroneous story or two. However, it must be remembered that the odds are against any given bill. A large-scale policy change runs a greater risk of alienation in that it contains more elements, as Poff stated, "which seem to stand out on its own pages and in the interpretations of those who have read those pages." Thus, opponents have multiple opportunities to single out issues and interpret them pejoratively. If, as in this case, their interpretations resonate with the developments in the external political stream, the political atmosphere surrounding a bill's movement becomes negatively charged and it loses momentum. This can significantly reduce the bill's chances because attention shifts to other bills. Even the congressmen who do not subscribe to the negative interpretations perceive roadblocks that make passage more problematic. The burden of proof is on the bill's proponents to demonstrate to other participants that the roadblocks are being removed and that the dynamics surrounding the bill have sufficiently changed to move it to the decision agenda. Otherwise, attention is drawn to other roles or to bills that are moving.

The media play a role in characterizing a bill's image in terms of developments in the political stream. For many bills, the coverage is slight or nonexistent — as it was for the criminal code before the sudden discovery of the "official secrets act," the "Ehrlichman defense," and the "prowler law." Nevertheless, no matter how selective, media coverage of a bill is one source of information about public reaction for legislative participants. Objection may be raised that news coverage of even fairly long duration is not the same as public opinion with respect to a bill. However, for most bills proceeding through Congress, there are no poll data. If a bill does start to get coverage, its prominence in the media can influence participants' perceptions.

In addition, federal government policymakers intensely follow the media. As Hess's study (1984) of executive branch agencies revealed, news-clipping services operated by agency press offices supply the daily clips, a collection of newspaper and magazine articles, on topics specific to the agency, which constitutes the staple of the officials' news. Members and staff in Congress also subscribe to clipping services, and thus legislative participants in both executive and legislative branches are reading and discussing the same news articles that affect their mutual business. Linsky's survey (1986) found that 57.5 percent of congressional leaders relied on the mass media "very much" for information on their own policy areas (p. 136). Cook (1989) reports from a survey of members of Congress that "while the media lag behind other cues, such as voters, committee leaders, or party colleagues, members themselves estimate the news to be about as influential as presidents and bureaucrats" (p. 122).

These legislative participants, in part, obtain factual information and, in part, use news reactions as surrogates for public reaction. They know that media reaction is not an exact public opinion substitute, but it is taken as a partial indicator and it affects participant perceptions—their sense of the political climate surrounding a bill. "Members of Congress and their staffs are part of the audience for national news; it is the way they discover what the rest of the country is finding out" (Cook, 1989, p. 122).

Linsky's survey of executive branch officials and members of Congress revealed that such officials believe that the media do a lot to set the policy agenda and to influence how an issue is understood by policymakers, interest groups, and the public. In addition to this agenda-setting function, the survey revealed two other prime press impacts—in "framing" the issue and in influencing the speed of the policy-making process. With respect to framing, the interviews revealed that policymakers are often faced with the nearly impossible task of catching up with the first story. Linsky's data show that the press can and does have a great influence on how the issue is characterized. Relatedly, the research showed that negative stories have a substantially bigger impact on policymakers than positive stories. A primary impact is on the speed of the policy-making process: "Negative stories are arresting. They make policymakers pause, although there is no clear consensus about what happens when they do" (Linsky, 1986, p. 142).

It is difficult to predict whether or when a bill will break into the media, and how it will be framed. It depends, in part, on developments in the political stream and, in part, on what else is happening in the world that might seem newsworthy to editors and reporters. Other competing events can crowd out legislative stories even if events in the political stream support them. Further, several issues and bills are often jockeying for attention at the same time. The reporters and editors who produce stories do not necessarily plan or even understand which bills will "make news." Such participants will say that this is governed by the "public's need to know." While acknowledging that such criteria are used as how many citizens are affected and how best to provide comprehensive coverage of events, Bosley (1977) also points out: "Furthermore, the public's need to know is frequently construed to mean merely public curiosity — the public's readiness to be aroused or alerted by the novelty and drama of certain events, whose value is judged in terms of probable audience response. This reinforces the news value of peculiar national happenings" (p. 14). Relatedly, in his survey of congressional correspondents, Blanchard (1974) found that 63 percent were attracted to "new and unusual aspects of subjects" in determining what issues and officials to cover (p. 190). Thus, given the characteristics of the media and the environment, it is not surprising that the "prowler" and "official secrets" provisions came to frame S.1 and bring a pause to the policy-making process involving it.

The media, of course, are not always together and do not always work against a bill. The impact of the media in agenda setting, framing the issues, and affecting the timing of the decision-making process can work for or against a particular bill. When the emphasis in the media was on the "crime problem," as it was increasingly in the late sixties and again in the late seventies and eighties, it helped create a political climate conducive to pro–law enforcement bills, even if the media did not focus on the bills themselves. McClellan and Hruska benefited in achieving passage of the Organized Crime Act of 1970. Even though other senators could not have believed that any sizable group among their constituents would even have known the particulars of the bill, they perceived that they needed to be on the pro–law enforcement side. The prospect that their local media might headline, "Senator Votes Against Organized Crime Control Bill," provided added incentive for several to vote for the bill.

By the same token, the stories surrounding the criminal code must be understood against the backdrop of Watergate.

Those events changed the political climate from pro-law enforcement to concern with law enforcement abuses. In addition,
while much of S.1 incorporated 95 percent of the pro-civil libertarian Brown Commission code (and was characterized by
Brown and Schwartz as 95 percent liberalizing), the "liberal"
groups still portrayed the bill as repressive and unamendable.
This portrayal changed the climate surrounding the bill. The
media were prepared to believe the repression story because of
the changes in the broader political stream.

Why did the media believe the ACLU's characterization
of S.1? First, Watergate resurrected the "credibility issue," raised
during the Vietnam War, and placed the burden of proof on
almost anyone in government. Polls and stories abounded
proclaiming a crisis of confidence in government. The prevailing opinion was that public officals tended to hide the truth and
outsiders were more trustworthy. The Vietnam / Watergate
period represented what Albert Hunt, Washington bureau chief
on the *Wall Street Journal,* called a "'sea change' from healthy skep-
ticism to unhealthy cynicism on the part of the press" (Linsky,
1986, p. 45).

Second, such groups as the ACLU call themselves and
are called by others "public interest" groups. The fact is that
when it comes to legislation, no group has a corner on the public interest — there are numerous interests in play and thus
numerous positions at work. The public has many interests, and
the ACLU is no more capable of objectivity in representing what
are inherently conflicting public wants than is the International
Association of Chiefs of Police or the Washington Legal Foundation — a conservative public interest group. Even when civil
liberties is the focus, numerous perspectives are possible with
considerable room for argument regarding what is *the* civil liberties
position — for example, Schwartz's criticism of the ACLU's "right
wing" stand on the "Ehrlichman defense." While at the time, the
"public interest" lobby was dominated by liberal groups, the conservatives came to understand the political implications for legislation and formed more such groups of their own. The ACLU
was aided by the media's framing of the issue in terms of government repression — the "official secrets act," the "Ehrlichman de-

fense," and so on. "In the process of framing an issue the press can help define which outsiders will be involved" (Cook, 1989, p. 123). Thus, the framing of the issues involved in the code bill as government repression increased the prominence of the ACLU and its allies.

Third, the reporters covering Congress at the time did tend to be more liberal in their personal orientations. Blanchard's survey (1974) of correspondents who covered Congress found that when asked about their political orientation, 43 percent declared themselves liberal and 14 percent Democrats, with only 2 percent conservatives and 4 percent Republicans. This should not be overstressed, however, in that studies attempting to link the personal political views of journalists with the types of stories they produce have been inconclusive, and the relationship is complicated by organizational constraints and journalistic norms.

Finally, exposing attempted cover-ups and secrecy was a journalistic priority raised to a fever pitch at the time. A lively debate still exists in journalism concerning the appropriate approach to the news for a journalist. Woodward and Bernstein's success in investigative reporting and the Vietnam exposés did much to spur new journalistic movements, such as advocacy journalism, counterculture journalism, and alternative journalism. Investigative reporting reached unparalleled success with Woodward and Bernstein's coverage of Watergate, and there is little doubt that numerous Washington reporters saw it as a way to increase their own impact. As Hulteng (1984) points out, some of this was not so careful.

Veterans of legislative battles on Capitol Hill will recognize the dynamic described when the press reaches a consensus of disdain for some bill. It is not confined to criminal code reform. The dynamic can also work the other way when the press decides it likes a bill. This is why legislators often wait to see how it "gets reported" or "plays in the press" before deciding what to do about a bill.

Of course, the press is not monolithic. The question on S.1 could be, Why was there not more diverse coverage of the many parts of a very diverse bill with significant issues throughout? Diverse coverage sometimes occurs, but not often. Blanchard found that certain newspapers influence what others cover. He quotes one congressional correspondent as saying: "Every morning a group of guys comes together and decides what the story of the day is. The *New York Times, Washington Post, Washington Star-News, Baltimore Sun, Los Angeles Times,* and *Boston Globe* lead the pack" (Blanchard, 1974, p. 182; see also Cook, 1989, p. 48). The relied-upon media get their information from a variety of sources, including congressional staff members, members of Congress, and interest group representatives. But once they decide "what the story is," it is very difficult for reporters to go into a series of other aspects of legislation because it will be seen as extraneous to the main story by their editors. With complex large-scale legislation, therefore, the story is likely to center on just a small subset of the issues involved. How they are characterized can substantially influence the speed and degree of difficulty of the bill's processing.

Dissensus — Reprise

Conflict-producing differences among legislators are a constant factor in the legislative process, and they must be managed by policy and political leaders at every stage of the process. Although there are norms present that encourage cooperation, building a consensus is not a naturally occurring constituent in the processing of legislation. Instead, it must be developed and nurtured by policy leaders. This is a matter of concerted political strategy.

As has been discussed, the success of the strategy chosen will depend on the stage of the policy process and the changing nature of the political environment. As will be explored later, the internal dynamics of Congress also play a part. It is often in the interest of those in opposition to emphasize and even create conflicts in order to discourage the building of consensus. Because of the multistage nature of the legislative process, opposition groups have a number of opportunities to decrease the agenda status of a policy proposal and slow its movement.

The access of opponents to important policy processes can

be enhanced or limited by the actions of the media in framing the issues. The media can magnify the importance of certain groups that encompass the values represented as important in the framing of the issues and diminish the importance of other groups. Large-scale policy proposals, because of their complexity, are difficult to portray comprehensively in the media, so only a small subset of issues is likely to be reported. It is inherently a simplifying process in which issues will often be portrayed as clear-cut, and opposing forces defined. Novel or unusual aspects can receive particular emphasis. Opposing forces are advantaged by the difficulty proponents face in portraying the particulars of their comprehensive approach. A supportive political environment becomes even more critical for moving such large-scale initiatives.

Events in the political stream influenced significantly the move to dissensus surrounding criminal law reform — a not uncommon occurrence affecting large-scale legislation. The Watergate cover-up revelations, the Pentagon Papers trials, the revelations of wiretaps on National Security Council staff, and other events created a changed political climate unfavorable to law enforcement. They created new interest groups and strengthened old ones that eventually came together in a "Stop S.1" movement. They galvanized large segments of the press to join the movement. These events altered the national mood to one of suspicion of the federal government. Lastly, they diverted the attention of the primary committees, the Judiciary committees, from legislating in general — and with respect to criminal law reform in particular — to investigation of the events.

The 94th Congress ended with no action on the criminal code bill. The blocking forces had achieved the stalemate they sought. Something different would be required to start movement on the reform of federal criminal laws.

• 6 •

Building
a Consensus

There is nothing inevitable about the achievement of a consensus for a set of legislative proposals. Often, no consensus is achieved. It does not emerge by virtue of some "unseen hand," and it is not an innate positively moving force within the dynamics of the legislative process. If consensus is achieved, it comes about as a result of a deliberate and ultimately integrative effort on the part of policy and political leaders.

The Process of Consensus Building in Congress

The dynamics of consensus building with respect to large-scale policies are not well understood. It is not so much that consensus is arranged for one large-scale alternative versus another — in this instance, reforms that are oriented toward law enforcement rather than civil liberites. Instead, the approach is a synthesis in which diverse parts are combined into a final agreed-upon package. Skills of persuasion, negotiation, and endurance to work through innumerable false starts are required. The would-be consensus builder engages in the process knowing that it may never reach a successful conclusion, but that the ultimate art of the legislator is to beat the odds.

Ostensibly, the activity at the subcommittee and committee stage is intended to inform members and the public about all the aspects of different policies so that members can arrive at an informed judgment. This is true to some extent, but there

151

are more significant stakes involved. "A tremendous amount of prefloor activity, for instance, can be seen essentially as consensus building, an adaptation to the congressmen's use of the consensus mode on the part of those who would want to influence legislative outcomes" (Kingdon, 1973, p. 259).

The reason policy leaders usually engage in building consensus at the very beginning—at the subcommittee and committee level—is not just to get the bill out of committee. It is rather to prepare for the ultimate decision stage when individual members of Congress make up their minds whether or not to vote for the bill on the floor. As Kingdon's study (1973) demonstrates, members normally use a consensus mode to make their decisions, assessing their environment in terms of the degree of consensus they perceive in it. Representatives begin their consideration of a given bill or amendment with one overriding question: is it controversial? If they perceive no controversy in the environment, they will most likely decide to go along with the bill. If there is conflict, the member asks if it exists within his or her field of forces—constituency, party leadership, ideological colleagues, or significant interest groups. If no conflict is perceived in this field, the decision again is most likely to go along with the bill. If one actor in the relevant field is out of line with the rest of the field, then the representative is likely to go against that one actor. However, the more conflict that develops in the field, the more the member is encouraged to avoid the bill or vote against it. It makes sense for members to use the consensus mode much of the time. They need to simplify their decision making in the face of far too many demands and too little time during the session. It is also consistent with avoiding political trouble (Kingdon, 1973).

It is possible that for some issues there will be an absence of conflict, and representatives will naturally come to a consensus. If there is potential or actual conflict, however, policy leaders, preferably with some assistance from congressional leaders, must structure the situation so as to minimize controversy—at least among people who are like-minded—in order to maximize the total vote for their bill. To avoid a situation where the members who are not directly involved in the policy area perceive a significant conflict, policy proponents who have some reasonable prospect of agreement try to come together in order to approximate the consensus mode as closely as possible. Opponents, however, do not need to establish a consensus for their policy positions. They can stimulate controversy in an attempt to convince a majority of those not directly involved that there is significant conflict present.

For the blocking forces, creating a perception of significant conflict is not a sure thing. Representatives do not come to the assessment of conflict as a blank slate. Their policy predispositions and ideologies are important to their assessment of conflict, and members choose ideological colleagues with whom they can consult about voting (Kingdon, 1973). Schneider's research (1979) on congressional voting during the 1971–76 period pointed out that ideological predispositions and the ideological balance of forces are important in congressional voting decisions. If a member who hears that there may be controversy surrounding a bill checks with colleagues and is told that it is only some fringe group upset, then he or she is reassured. Further, representatives' previous votes on similar policies, as well as the degree of unity in their state delegation, can influence their vote. Nonetheless, the central mode of decision is the consensus mode.

There are characteristics of large-scale policies that both inhibit and foster the building of a consensus necessary for passage. The size and complexity can be inhibiting and cause suspicion that only a few insiders really know what the bill will do, raising the danger factor associated with passage. The danger factor is that latent conflicts really do exist that have not yet emerged and which, when they do, will embarrass the representatives. The furor that arose over the graduated payment schedule for catastrophic health insurance for Medicare is one example. There are numerous and diverse components that can serve to alienate various interest groups that combine to form a successful blocking coalition. Alternatively, the numerous and diverse components, if ultimately selected in a politically astute way, can appeal to diverse interests that, on balance, support the package on grounds that there is more in it that they like than dislike. This is often difficult in large-scale complex legislation, however, because the pay-offs are often long-range and not easily identifiable.

The policy leader must look to the requirements of building a winning coalition not only in committees and subcommittees, but also ahead to the Senate or House, and indeed Congress as a whole. The task is one of building and rebuilding a series of consensuses. In doing this, there is a danger at every stage that a consensus reached at one stage will undermine the potential for consensus at a subsequent stage. The policy leader must retain the core of the policy while accommodating enough interests to gain and maintain a majority.

Building a Consensus for Criminal Law Reform

Not much had happened at the end of the 94th Congress to encourage the criminal law reformers to continue their efforts, and many discouraging things had occurred. No bill had been reported out of even one committee. In addition, as the 95th Congress was about to begin in January 1977, some of the members who had played key roles were missing. Senator Hruska, who probably knew more of the details of the code and the issues pertaining to them than any other senator and who had been a major driving force for code reform, had retired. Senator Hart had died. The opposition had been successful in blocking any action on S.1, and there was still no significant identifiable interest group capable of forcing action. The fall election had produced a new president, Jimmy Carter, but law-and-order had not been a major campaign issue and the administration's priorities were elsewhere. Criminal law reform could very well have died right there.

Nonetheless, reform proponents were determined to try again. In actuality, the staff members — Paul Summit for McClellan, Kenneth Feinberg for Kennedy, Michael Mullen for Hart, and Ronald Gainer at the Department of Justice — were already meeting to draft a new bill during the last months of the 94th Congress in order to have it ready for introduction early in the 95th. Continuity of staff in both the Senate and the Justice

Department, and a continuation of their commitment to reform, did much to preserve movement.

The political scene was changed with the beginning of the 95th Congress. The Senate Judiciary Committee was still chaired by James Eastland, but it had eight new members out of seventeen. Five new Democrats—Allen (Ala.), Biden (Del.), Culver (Iowa), Metzenbaum (Ohio), and DeConcini (Ariz.)— were on the committee, along with three Republicans—Laxalt (Nev.), Hatch (Utah), and Wallop (Wyo.). Senator Hruska had retired and Strom Thurmond (R-S.C.) was now the ranking Republican on both the Judiciary Committee and the Subcommittee on Criminal Laws and Procedures.

The new Republicans all came from the most conservative wing of the Republican party; two of the Democrats, Biden and Metzenbaum, were liberal Democrats, while Allen was a conservative Democrat. This could potentially have set the scene for both partisan and ideological warfare, particularly over such volatile issues in the criminal code as espionage, the death penalty, marijuana decriminalization, and obscenity.

Kennedy had been approached by civil liberties groups and lobbied to drop the criminal code. He rejected that idea and instead decided to move further into the leadership of the criminal law reform movement. He and McClellan, who had been on opposing sides on S.1., felt that their efforts to reach a compromise on S.1 had revealed that there was a basis for achieving common ground. Kennedy's entrance into policy leadership on the pro-side of reform rearranged the political landscape surrounding criminal law reform.

Criminal law reform had been a bipartisan pursuit for McClellan and Hruska, but they were both seen as law-and-order conservatives. The primary political cleavage was an ideological one, but it was not a simple liberal-conservative split. As both former Governor Brown and Louis Schwartz had constantly pointed out, the main body of the code was liberalizing, in the sense that it provided clarity and equity for defendants and convicted felons who were similarly situated, and took much of the arbitrary and capricious character out of the system.

However, those groups that wished to achieve a net reduction in federal government law enforcement power did not see it as liberalizing.

Kennedy and McClellan's decision to get together made criminal law reform a bi-ideological effort. As Feinberg pointed out later, "If Senator Kennedy carves out a position and claims that position to be the left of center position, it is hard for somebody to say 'I am going to take a position to the left of Senator Kennedy,' because he has a certain constituency there" (personal interview, 1986). Kennedy knew he was going to take some criticism from the far-left civil liberties groups and moved to shore up his left flank. He recruited Alan Dershowitz, a Harvard Law School professor and a noted liberal spokesman for the criminal defense perspective, as a consultant to advise him on the drafting. As the bill was introduced, Dershowitz announced that it was "a net gain for civil liberties."

The staff group that drafted the new criminal code bill did not start with a blank slate but picked up where S.1 left off. The process was essentially a continuation of the negotiations between the parties involved in S.1. They started by resolving the twenty-two Kennedy-Hart problems. The operating principle was to delete any subject where consensus could not be forged. If anyone objected to a point included in the draft, it would be dropped and current law would be retained. The staff members enjoyed considerable confidence from their senators and would bring them into direct negotiations only on major points that had to be resolved senator-to-senator. It took several months of back-and-forth negotiation before a final bill emerged on which both McClellan and Kennedy could sign off.

In the late fall of 1976 and early 1977, McClellan was seriously ill, dying from congestive heart failure. Although almost totally confined to his home, he remained active in the development of the new bill. His counsel, Paul Summit, traveled to his home every day with materials and news of progress on the development of the bill. McClellan was determined to stay active in legislating, even if he had to do it mostly from home. He was even a little concerned that his colleagues might consider him to be goofing off!

The new draft bill deleted many of the controversial sections, including:

- provisions dealing with disclosure of government information
- making it an offense to impair military effectiveness by making a false statement
- the "official secrets" section regarding disclosure of any "classified information"
- the Smith Act, an existing law that made it unlawful to advocate overthrow of the government by unlawful means
- the "Ehrlichman defense"
- the section redefining the insanity defense
- extension of the death penalty

It also narrowed the riot provisions and the false-statement section.

There were some interesting additions, however. The most significant was a section establishing a National Sentencing Commission to promulgate guidelines for federal sentencing judges. It provided that a judge imposing a sentence outside the guidelines would be required to file reasons for doing so, and such a sentence could be appealed. It also cut back drastically on the possibility of parole. With the introduction of the sentencing commission, Kennedy was putting his stamp on criminal law reform. Also, included for the first time were a provision for an individual or an organization to forfeit criminal proceeds and a provision establishing a federal victims compensation fund. In addition, new provisions defining white-collar crimes were included. These additions showed that the bill was becoming even more a reform vehicle and not simply a recodification.

McClellan agreed to cosponsor a separate sentencing bill of Kennedy's that incorporated the sentencing title of the code, but he let it be known that the only action the subcommittee would take on sentencing would be within the context of passing the code. He felt that sentencing was the area of Kennedy's highest interest and that to retain his interest in code passage, the sentencing provisions could not be allowed to move separately. In fact, this is one of the incentives that comprehensive large-scale legislation has in its favor. By including what others really want and arranging it so that they must push the whole package to achieve their goals, the comprehensive package builds a winning coalition.

Another interesting addition was the redefinition of federal jurisdiction for simple possession of marijuana. Under the new proposal, possession of less than ten grams would no longer qualify as a federal crime. This area was potentially very explosive politically. McClellan did not think that federal law enforcement assets should be involved in pursuing such minor crimes — in fact, few hardly ever were. Federal prosecutors rarely filed charges against people for simple possession of small amounts of marijuana, because their staffs were always overloaded with more serious crimes. However, the issue had tremendous symbolic importance in terms of the message being sent to the public concerning obeying the law as the right saw it, and government intrusion as seen by the left. McClellan hesitated because of concern over the political volatility but finally agreed to the provision restricting federal jurisdiction over possession.

The three-way negotiations involving McClellan, Kennedy, and the Justice Department stretched on into the winter and early spring of 1977. McClellan's health, in part, slowed down the process, but there was a real attempt to seek out views from previously hostile groups to remove as many obstacles as possible, which also took time. Agreement between McClellan and Kennedy was reached and the bill was introduced with both as sponsors on May 2, 1977. A week later would have been too late, as McClellan's condition deteriorated precipitously. Before he became unable to function, he had a long conversation with Strom Thurmond about the future of the code. He asked Thurmond to carry on with the leadership of the law enforcement forces and to preserve the coalition for code reform. McClellan trusted Thurmond and knew many conservative Democrats as well as Republicans would be reassured if Thurmond were part of the partnership with Kennedy.

For introduction this time, the desire of proponents was to obtain an obscure bill number. S.1 had become such a rallying cry for opponents that any priority signified by a repeat of S.1 would be self-defeating. Merely throwing it into the hopper secured the innocuous and forgettable number S.1437.

One source of uncertainty had been what stance the new Carter administration would take. It was possible that the administration would simply write off the code reform effort as a failed attempt by the previous Republican administration. However, Carter appointed Griffin Bell, a federal Circuit Court of Appeals judge, as attorney general. Bell had served as chairman of the Judicial Administration Division of the American Bar Association, so he was already a member of the criminal law policy community and had gained additional familiarity with criminal law issues. At his confirmation hearings in January 1977, Bell told the Senate Judiciary Committee that he favored severing the controversial provisions from the criminal code reform bill so that the committee could move ahead with the bill.

Shortly after moving into the Justice Department, Bell received a briefing from Gainer, who was the acting head of the Office of Policy and Planning at the time. Bell had received a letter from the ACLU stating that there were two holdovers from the previous administration who had taken some nefarious positions on criminal law reform — Roger Pauley, legislative affairs director of the Criminal Division, and Gainer. Bell nonetheless asked Gainer to stay on as deputy in the Office of Policy and Planning and to continue the code reform effort. Bell and Benjamin Civiletti, head of the Criminal Division, received a briefing on the specifics of the draft bill which went section by section and lasted five hours. Bell had previously opposed the sentencing provisions in his ABA work but reconsidered when he focused on the sentencing guidelines approach contained in the draft bill. He saw that providing for appeal of sentence only in those cases in which the sentencing judge went outside the guidelines would apply in extraordinary cases but would not overload the appellate courts, which had been his previous concern. He exclaimed, "This is ingenious, this is ingenious." President Carter then came to endorse the code reform effort in his first State of the Union message.

Bell directed that the Justice Department criminal code reform staff continue to work with the Senate Judiciary Committee on the draft bill. On May 2, 1977, he appeared at the news conference for introduction of the bill in the Senate, along with Senators McClellan and Kennedy and also House Judiciary chairman Rodino and subcommittee chairman James Mann. Bell cited the bill "as fair and workable a code as has yet been devised."

Bell had requested that Rodino introduce the bill in the House, and Rodino had agreed to do it. Bell also lobbied individual senators and representatives on behalf of the bill. In one instance, when the Senate Judiciary Committee was holding a meeting to agree on language for the committee report, Bell was in attendance, but not enough senators had arrived to make a quorum. Bell went to the phone, got the numbers of the absent senators, and called each, saying, "This is important, I'm here. You get down here too." Additional senators arrived and the meeting proceeded. Bell testified on the first day of the hearings on the new bill and endorsed it warmly, calling particular attention to the sentencing provisions: "This system provides an ingenious means of assigning sentences that are not only fair to the individual defendants but fair to the public as well" (Subcommittee on Criminal Laws and Procedures, June 7, 1977). During questioning, he agreed with Kennedy that coercive rehabilitation was impossible and that parole should be abolished: "You exacerbate the disparity through the parole system, because one person will be paroled and another will not be. . . . I do not know how the parole release system rehabilitates anyone" (p. 8596).

Bell added credibility to the criminal law reform effort and demonstrated that the new bill was not merely a holdover from the previous administration. However, the bill was not a major presidential priority, and even if it had been, it might not have benefited very much. Carter made the error of overloading the Congress with proposals in numerous areas at the start of his administration. The congressional leadership complained that it was all too much to process legislatively, and that the administration had confused the Congress as to its priorities. In this environment, the attorney general's endorsement did not have as much impact as it otherwise might have had.

Kennedy attempted to defuse the opposition of liberal groups by accommodating several of their former objections to S.1 and urging them to take a different approach to crime legislation. In a speech before the Center for Democratic Institutions in Chicago, Kennedy urged liberals "to stop confusing social progress with progress in the war against crime." He criticized "well-intentioned people that claimed that crime could be controlled if we would only demolish city slums and end poverty and discrimination," and warned against an attitude of "no crime reform until society is reformed" (Goshko, 1977). The rejection of that part of the social justice approach that claimed crime is caused by poverty had now been announced by the leading Senate liberal.

The reformers attempted to minimize the conflict over the new bill by anticipating objections. Feinberg, Kennedy's aide, circulated a draft of the bill to various liberal groups during March, even before McClellan and Kennedy had made final their agreement over its contents. One such group was the ACLU, and another was NCARL, two leading opponents of S.1. The ACLU was not mollified by the deletions and additions Kennedy had secured. In April, Jay Miller, associate director in ACLU's Washington office, stated that the ACLU could not support the new draft (Wermiel, 1977). This did not exactly surprise code proponents. At an American Bar Association discussion at which the ACLU leader Adrian Neier was expressing the ACLU's many objections, Gainer asked Neier, as so many of the criticisms were directed at provisions found in existing law, what it would take for the ACLU to support the code. Neier replied that the ACLU would never support code reform. He observed that the ACLU could not lose. They would always say that this version is slightly better than the previous version but that it is not good enough (Gainer interview, 1986).

Another active group in the Stop S.1 movement, NCARL, also came out in opposition. Its lobbyist, Esther Herst, said, "We don't see codification in and of itself a desirable enough goal to warrant destruction of civil liberties" ("And Now for Something . . . ," 1977, p. 921). However, the efforts of Senate proponents of criminal law reform to court the liberal opposition did pay some dividends in splitting the opposition. The national Board of the Americans for Democratic Action voted 79 to 3 to endorse the passage of the new bill.

Similarly, the almost shrill media opposition to S.1 became both divided and less perceptible with respect to the new bill. The Reporters Committee for Freedom of the Press, chaired by Jack Landau (of the "prowler bill" story fame), came out strongly opposed. In addition, an ad hoc committee of the American Newspaper Publishers Association (ANPA) released a statement expressing concerns with the bill. However, on May 25, the ANPA committee met with Senate committee staffers, which initiated a series of communications on their concerns. On July 23, the newspaper trade journal *Editor and Publisher* quoted an ANPA statement to the effect that gratifying progress had been made in amending three features of the bill as "a direct result of meetings between representatives of the Senate sponsors of the bill and the ad hoc committee of the ANPA."

When Landau testified before the subcommittee that the new bill was "an official secrets act which would give the government wide-ranging new criminal powers to severely restrict the First Amendment rights of the press to report — and the public to receive — the news," Arthur B. Hansen, ANPA counsel and chairman of the ad hoc committee, wrote to Senator Kennedy blasting Landau's testimony as an "intemperate and unjustified attack." In light of the committee's "good faith, outstanding" efforts to deal with legitimate press objections, Hansen wrote, he found the Landau testimony little short of incredible. News coverage of the press dispute was nowhere evident, which prompted *Washington Star* ombudsman George Beveredge (1977) to write that although the bill's 300-plus pages do not constitute "sexy reading . . . I do argue that the near-total blackout that the whole subject has received from newspapers is an omission of their responsibility to their readers that is wrong."

Liberal columnists were also split. The *New York Times* columnist Anthony Lewis (1977) analyzed the bill and concluded: "The Kennedy-McClellan bill will be an interesting test of liberal attitudes in politics. Perfectionists will no doubt oppose it unless it does such politically impossible things as repeal the obscenity laws. The more practical will consider whether obstruction of reform now is likely to bring a more enlightened code later. I think not. In this case as in so many, perfectionism would be the enemy of progress." The *Village Voice*'s Nat Hentoff talked with Feinberg and observed that Feinberg was enthusiastic about the changes in the bill. In a column titled "Ted Kennedy Presents Son of S.1," Hentoff (1977) wrote that it was not as egregious as S.1, "but it contains a sizeable number of mine fields that could cripple certain kinds of exposure of government misconduct, and that could also endanger the First Amendment rights of those who would demonstrate against the federal government and the courts."

The subcommittee, consisting of Senators McClellan, Eastland, Thurmond, and Hatch, held five days of hearings of S.1437 during June 1977. A few changes were made as a result of the hearings and the continuing negotiations with various parties, such as the American Newspaper Publishers Association. The ANPA approved the revisions, but the Reporters Committee, NCARL, and the ACLU remained opposed. About a week before the subcommittee was to vote to report out the bill to the full committee, Senator Kennedy asked Senator Humphrey (D-Minn.) to become a cosponsor, and Humphrey agreed. In addition, Orrin Hatch (R-Utah), a New Right Republican, became a cosponsor. This signaled to the Senate that a broad agreement had been achieved. The subcommittee approved the bill on August 5, 1977, with only minor changes.

The full Judiciary Committee had more liberals on it than the subcommittee, including Abourezk (D-S.D.), Biden (D-Del.), Bayh (D-Ind.), Culver (D-Iowa), and Metzenbaum (D-Ohio). The potential was present for amendments to be offered that could tear apart the fragile coalition Kennedy and McClellan had put together. This would put Kennedy in an awkward position. He would have either to risk his alliance with McClellan or oppose amendments that he otherwise might be inclined to support. This is often the case in consensus building.

Kennedy let it be known that he would oppose any amendment unless it could also be supported by McClellan. Kennedy could retain the liberals, but McClellan was crucial in bringing along the conservatives and many moderates. Preserving the bi-ideological consensus was going to be a key when and if the bill got to the floor, because it removed a major source of conflict from the perceptual fields of most noninvolved members. As long as the conservatives and liberals were together on Judiciary, most members would look no further.

The consensus almost came unglued in the Judiciary Committee over the emotional issue of marijuana—the very issue that years earlier had killed the California criminal code effort. The compromise in the bill as reported to the committee would have eliminated federal criminal penalties for simple possession of ten grams or less (about seven cigarettes), leaving the states to legislate for possession under this amount. Possession of more than ten grams would be a federal criminal offense.

In the committee markup of October 25, 1977, Senator Bayh, stating that he wanted to send a message to the states, urged that possession of up to one ounce (he estimated about twenty cigarettes) be classified as a federal misdemeanor offense punishable by a fine of $100. He was concerned that young people would acquire a criminal record for possession. Bayh offered an amendment to this effect, which was approved by the full committee 6 to 4, with Kennedy one of the four opposed. The passage of the amendment started an uproar. At the Oct. 26 meeting, Hatch said that Bayh's amendment decriminalized marijuana and sent a message that ought not to be sent. Hatch suggested that he would have to oppose the whole bill if the provision were retained. Laxalt stated that the symbolism of the provision was important, and suggested he would also oppose it. Over the next week, Hatch and Bayh met to try to resolve the differences, but reported to the committee on November 1 that they could not. However, in the meeting, the two senators proceeded to bargain a compromise that resulted in a gradation of penalties for possession of marijuana depending on the amount and whether it was a first, second, or third offense. This passed the committee 11 to 2, with Abourezk and Allen the only nays.

This illustrates the symbolic role of federal law and the importance that is attached to it. Throughout the debate over marijuana, both sides acknowledged that federal law enforcement would not and should not be involved in pursuing simple possession. The debate was over the standard that would be set that the states would be examining in their own legislative efforts, as well as the message sent to the public. The moral and social implications were as important, in terms of the symbolic standard set, as the operational reality for the practice of federal criminal law.

On November 2, the Senate Judiciary Committee voted 12 to 2 to send the bill to the Senate floor, with Abourezk and Allen, ideological opposites, voting no. Chairman Eastland voted McClellan's proxy yes. For the first time, criminal code reform could be debated on the Senate floor. McClellan would never get to take part in the debate, however, because he died on November 27, 1977.

The bill was scheduled for debate before the full Senate in January. Kennedy was the floor manager for the majority and Thurmond for the minority. Both had pledged to fight off amendments not approved by the committee. Kennedy estimated that it would take three weeks to process the bill, and Majority Leader Robert Byrd was prepared to schedule the floor time. The task of processing a complex large-scale bill like this is daunting. Even though the Judiciary Committee members had been intensely engaged in debating it, other senators hardly knew what was in the bill. Many would go along because senators they knew and respected had examined it and had assured them that their interests were accommodated. Others would wait and see what came up in the debate. Throughout the process, dozens of amendments would surface. To avoid a floor fight, it was up to the managers to clear them with the interested senators who might be moved to object. Divisive amendments were opposed by both managers in the interest of preserving the delicate balance of compromise and keeping the bill moving. Above all, the managers had to resist killer amendments that would spell defeat on final passage or provoke a filibuster that could end processing of the bill.

Although the Senate can pass a cloture motion to end a filibuster, it takes a three-fifths vote to do so, and numerous senators will not vote cloture on grounds that they may wish to use the tactic themselves in the future. Other delaying tactics, such as offering scores of amendments, are also available. Thus, the Senate tries to move by unanimous consent on what will be processed. Opponents have delay on their side, but in January, delay is less potent a threat than at the end of a Congress. Further, using delaying tactics is not without its costs. Senate comity exists, to some extent, because undue delay may result in retaliation on subsequent legislation favored by opponents of legislation currently under consideration.

Those senators unhappy at this point were chiefly some conservatives. Kennedy and Thurmond continued to negotiate and identified some amendments that most senators could accept and which would not threaten the bill. These were accepted on a voice vote. Nonetheless, senators are individuals, and some were determined to amend the bill. Dozens of amendments were offered, but most were opposed by the managers and defeated. The coalition held.

One potentially destabilizing amendment was offered by William Scott (R-Va.) to expand the death penalty. McClellan had agreed with Kennedy to keep this out of the code bill and had introduced it as a separate bill, which was pending in the full Judiciary Committee. Scott's amendment was to include McClellan's death penalty bill in the code. Kennedy knew this could kill the bill by provoking a filibuster by Senate liberals, and he objected that the amendment broke his agreement with McClellan. Malcolm Wallop (R-Wyo.), a death penalty supporter and assistant minority floor manager, also urged that the amendment not be considered, but that it proceed as a separate bill. Kennedy promised that the death penalty bill would be processed by the Judiciary Committee, and the Senate would have a chance to vote on it, even though he would vote against it. Kennedy's motion to table Scott's amendment then carried 65 to 24.

The managers did not win them all. Robert Dole (R-Kans.) offered an amendment to provide for judges to have discretion to order preventive detention rather than set bail for dangerous criminals arrested for murder, rape, armed kidnapping, armed robbery, and hostage taking. The committee's bill provided for denial of pretrial release only for aircraft hijacking resulting in death. Here again, the message sent to the public and to the states was the issue, because the proportion of federal crimes to state crimes in these areas is very small.

However, Dole was hitting a central nerve in the crime issue—keeping dangerous criminals off the streets. Kennedy said he opposed the amendment in line with the committee agreement and asked Dole to produce statistics that federal judges were releasing dangerous criminals and not keeping them in jail by setting high bail amounts. Dole replied that he did not want to see such statistics in the future, and the amendment would prevent that. The Senate had previously voted a similar pretrial detention provision in the District of Columbia Bail Reform Act. Kennedy moved to table the amendment but lost 62 to 29.

The adoption of the bail amendment was not enough to kill the bill, however. It had gained momentum and most senators were ready to see the end of the debate. There was no united opposition to the bill on the Senate floor. McClellan, and then Thurmond with Hatch's assistance, for the most part, held the conservatives in line, and Kennedy did the same with the liberals. The liberal organizations' traditional allies were scarce on the Senate floor. According to ACLU Washington director John Shattuck, "The problem in the Senate was that no liberals were willing to take on Kennedy in his deal with McClellan. . . . People were very deferential to Kennedy" (*CQ Almanac,* 1978, p. 166).

Eight days after the debate began, it ended on January 30, 1978, when the Senate voted 72 to 15 to pass S.1437. Criminal code reform passed a house of Congress for the first time, and it passed overwhelmingly. A large majority of both parties supported the bill, prompting Kennedy to claim the measure proved "that law enforcement can be a bipartisan issue, that Democrats and Republicans can work together to improve the quality of criminal justice in America" (Clymer, Jan. 31, 1978). Most of the fifteen no votes came from Republicans such as Dole, who felt that the bill did not go far enough to get tough on criminals because it omitted provisions like the death penalty (*Congressional Record,* Jan. 30, 1978, S.857). In addition, Senators Helms (R-N.C.) and McClure (R-Idaho) had a string of complaints. In particular, they opposed the consumer fraud section because they felt that it unfairly criminalized business conduct (*Congressional Record*, Jan. 30, 1978, S.858). On the liberal side, Senator Cranston objected that the bill expanded federal jurisdiction.

Immediately following passage, Senators Kennedy and Thurmond hosted a luncheon for House Judiciary members, including subcommittee chairman Mann, and arranged for former Governor Brown, who had chaired the Brown Commission, and former Senator Hruska to attend. Both Brown and Hruska, along with the two senators, urged prompt House action. However, Mann indicated that the House subcommittee rated the chances of finishing within the year as a "toss-up," and said, "members of our committee have identified many, many areas where we know we are going to have to go back and work on language" (Clymer, Feb. 5, 1978).

Mann's subcommittee held twenty-three days of hearings and fifty additional hours of meetings between February 21 and April 24. By the halfway point, it was clear the bill had substantial opposition. Mann stated, "Certain members of the Subcommittee and the full Committee have cast doubt whether we have got a bill we can fly with" (Nelson, 1978). Subcommittee member Elizabeth Holtzman (D-N.Y.) complained, "I think it's a colossal waste of time" (Nelson, 1978).

Chairman Mann opened the subcommittee's markup session on the bill on May 12, stating that the criminal law "should not be the subject of trade-offs and compromise in the name of reform" (Berlow, 1978). Members were clearly split on what should be done. The only point of agreement seemed to be that it was not possible for them to agree. Mann denounced the bill as having "too many trade-offs and compromises and special interest influences," and declared that "you just don't compromise or trade-off what is criminal conduct and what is moral conduct" (Clymer, May 13, 1978). Representative Holtzman said, "I don't see how Congress can rationally adopt a code," and Representative Hall stated, "It's too much to be called on to change so much" (Clymer, May 13, 1978).

These members' views of proper legislative process did not go unnoticed. The *New York Times* of May 17, 1978, editorialized: "The subcommittee members—all lawyers by House rule—are making spectacles of themselves and a hash of criminal law reform . . . One wonders what Mr. Mann thinks the criminal code is now, if not a motley of historic political trade-offs. What does he think the legislative process really is, if not the art of political settlements of the kind that were worked out by such divergent Senators as Kennedy and Thurmond?" Nonetheless, subcommittee member Charles Wiggins (R-Calif.) asserted the House's independence when he stated, "It does not follow that there is any format, premise, or formulation set by others that we must accept" (Berlow, 1978).

The subcommittee met for a second day of markup on May 17 and made little headway. It finally decided that it would abandon the code altogether and drafted a much more limited bill, H.R.13959, which deleted some obsolete offenses, established a schedule for fines, and changed some sentences for some crimes. When the bill was reported to the full House Judiciary Committee, the members voted on October 4 not to proceed with it.

The subcommittee issued a report concluding that "it is neither essential nor desirable to enact S.1437 (or a bill similar to it)" (U.S. Congress, 1978, p. 35). The subcommittee found no urgent need for a change in federal criminal law, particularly objected to the omnibus approach, and took a swipe at the Senate, stating: "Federal criminal laws ought not to be the product of extensive horse-trading. The greater the number of substantive changes made by a bill, the more likely it is such trade-offs will occur" (p. 3). The subcommittee rejected the Senate's (indeed, the Brown Commission's) basic premise that the laws should be considered within a comprehensive framework because they are interrelated: "The subcommittee prefers an incremental approach to modernization of Federal criminal laws, not only because S.1437 is flawed, but for more general reasons too. Truly modernizing criminal laws means making substantial changes in them—reforming them to conform them to modern mores and to integrate court interpretations into statutory language. An omnibus reform bill, however, stands little chance of success because constituencies against change multiply in proportion to the number of reforms involved" (U.S. Congress, 1978, p. 3). The fact is that there is a trade-off between comprehensiveness and detailed treatment, and House subcommittees often prefer the details.

With the existing membership of the House Judiciary Subcommittee on Criminal Justice, there was little room for consensus building with the Senate. However, the start of the 96th Congress brought a new lineup. Mann and Wiggins were gone; in fact, seven of the nine members were new to the subcommittee, including the chairman and the ranking minority member. Robert Drinan, a lawyer, a Jesuit priest, and a most liberal Democrat from Massachusetts, became chairman, and Thomas Kindness, a most conservative Republican from Ohio became ranking minority member. Democratic members Hall and Gudger were the only holdovers, with new Democrats Conyers (Mich.), Synar (Okla.), and Carr (Mich.), and Republicans Sawyer (Mich.) and Lungren (Calif.), joining the subcommittee.

Synar, Carr, and Lungren were new to both Congress and the Judiciary Committee. Lungren, as a freshman Republican, had a brother who was a police officer in Los Angeles and had requested membership on Judiciary, even though it is not generally considered a plum assignment. Drinan had vigorously opposed the Senate-passed criminal code bill in the past Congress, as had Conyers. All three Republicans were conservatives on law enforcement matters, as was Hall. Conyers was known as an extreme liberal. Criminal code reform would have seemed an unlikely priority for a subcommittee so ideologically split.

Nonetheless, Kennedy and Drinan discussed the issue, and they agreed to negotiate to remove obstacles to moving the bill. In fact, Drinan decided to make code reform the subcommittee's top priority. At the subcommittee's organizing session, he announced what top priority meant: "I can't promise you a rose garden but I can promise work, more work, and more work. We're going to be here nights, weekends, and holidays" (Sleeper, 1979). Kindness, the ranking Republican, pledged his cooperation in the effort. For the first time, a House subcommittee would start on criminal law reform at the beginning of a session of Congress.

The subcommittee started with four days of hearings to decide upon an approach. The first hearing on February 14 began with former Senator Roman Hruska as the lead-off witness. Drinan said he was leading off with Hruska to show the conservatives that reform is "no pinko conspiracy" (Lyons, 1974). Following the four days of hearings, Drinan's subcommittee reached the opposite conclusion from Mann's: "that revision of the Federal laws could not be accomplished by an 'incremental' piecemeal approach" (U.S. Congress, Sept. 25, 1980, p. 9). They felt that a piecemeal revision would result in an overlap between new provisions and unchanged portions of the old code, and inconsistencies would only be exacerbated. The subcommittee concluded that previous bills had "serious flaws" in increasing federal jurisdiction. Their approach would be confined to redrafting the crimes found in title 18 of the U.S. Code and not dealing with crimes defined elsewhere. The subcommittee agreed to abide by the same mode of operation that had prevailed in the Senate subcommittee. In areas of strong disagreement, existing federal law would merely be recodified. Reform would be limited to areas where a consensus could be forged.

The Drinan subcommittee devoted seventy-four public meetings to drafting a new title 18 between February and the end of July, 1979. These were long working sessions, described by some as "law school seminars," in which numerous points of criminal law were debated. This time, Kennedy held off Senate action in order to allow Drinan to build some momentum. His staff, Feinberg, and also Summit (who was now working for Kennedy) closely monitored the Drinan subcommittee sessions, as did Gainer and Pauley from the Justice Department.

The Senate Judiciary staffers were developing a redraft of the previous year's bill and were negotiating with various groups who had had problems with it. There would be no subcommittee action this time. Instead, Senate staffers representing each of the Judiciary Committee members started with S.1437 and held a series of nine working meetings in May and June to amend it into a new draft.

By August, Drinan's subcommittee had a draft bill. At a news conference, Kennedy, Rodino, and incoming Attorney General Benjamin Civiletti (Bell had resigned) praised the work of Drinan and his subcommittee. Drinan and Kennedy indicated that they planned to introduce their bills after Labor Day. Drinan said later that the news conference had been called to show there was a new consensus on the need for full code revision (Babcock, 1979). Rodino declared, "Finally we are on the last lap of the attempt to bring about a comprehensive reform of our criminal laws" (Membrino, 1979).

In September 1979, both Drinan's subcommittee and Kennedy's committee held hearings. Kennedy, along with Thurmond, Hatch, Simpson, and DeConcini, introduced the new Senate bill (S.1722), and Kennedy also introduced the Drinan subcommittee draft (S.1723) for the hearings. Kennedy's committee held six days of hearings in September and October, and Drinan's subcommittee held ten.

One of the disputed areas, as it had been in the previous year's Senate bill, was the treatment of business crimes. Business groups, such as the Business Roundtable and the U.S. Chamber of Commerce, were fully alerted to the code effort now and were lobbying both the House and the Senate. The House draft did not include several of the provisions affecting business that the Senate bill had contained. Prominent among these was a new crime of "endangerment," which would have made a company criminally liable for subjecting persons to risk of death or severe bodily injury as a result of the company's violations of specified federal environmental, health, and safety statutes.

The ACLU took a somewhat different posture with respect to the Drinan subcommittee's work than they had with the Senate's. In an *Alert*, the ACLU advised members that "with an outstanding civil libertarian, Rep. Robert F. Drinan (D-Mass.), assuming its chair, the House Subcommittee on Criminal Justice will be urged to build on its groundwork of last year in reviewing and unanimously rejecting S.1437." ACLU lobbyists were constantly making suggestions to the subcommittee, several of which made it into the bill, particularly in changing procedures that federal prosecutors would have to follow.

The Justice Department had continually made supporting statements with respect to the overall Drinan effort in order
to encourage House action, but this did not mean that the department supported the particular provisions of the subcommittee bill. As time went on, departmental officials became nervous
that the specifics in the subcommittee bill could introduce impediments to law enforcement that would outweigh any gains
from recodification. Philip Heymann, assistant attorney general
for the Criminal Division during the Carter administration, testified before Drinan's subcommittee: "The generalized benefits
of systematic codification simply pale in comparison with the
importance of adequate tools for detecting and punishing crime.
When I say adequate, I mean adequate and fair. It would be
unwise and unacceptable to trade the patchwork of Federal criminal laws for a systematic and simplified code that made the
investigation and prosecution of crime more difficult" (Subcommittee Hearings, p. 94). Heyman went on to say that the subcommittee's proposed code would seriously undercut the Justice
Department's present ability to fight crime in major enforcement areas.

Following his subcommittee's hearings, Drinan held sixty-
nine additional subcommittee meetings devoted to revising the
draft into a bill. Drinan had promised his members "work and
more work" and he delivered. This was a monumental effort
for a subcommittee, but most members stuck with it, some at
no little political risk. For example, Lungren, the freshman
Republican, was getting pressure from his staff to visit his Long
Beach, California, district more frequently, as is the practice
for most new members who want to get their names established
and get reelected. The subcommittee was meeting most Mondays and Fridays as well as other days—times when most new
members are in their districts politicking. However, Lungren
was engaged and committed and stayed with the code project,
as did several others.

During November 1979, while Drinan's subcommittee
continued to meet to finalize their bill, Kennedy held six days
of Judiciary Committee meetings to mark up S.1722. Even
though the committee had reported out a code bill the previous

year which passed the Senate, this was not a pro forma exercise. New groups were active in lobbying against the bill, and some different as well as some familiar issues were raised. The sponsors attempted to accommodate these to maintain the consensus for passage without endangering the chances on the Senate floor. About 175 amendments were informally adopted by the senators.

The markup sessions were not without controversy. The Business Roundtable (an organization of 191 corporations) was particularly active and negotiated a compromise agreement with members of the Committee on November 20. One concession was to delete the section on consumer fraud and to modify the section on "endangerment." On November 27, Philip Heymann of Justice's Criminal Division phoned Irving Shapiro, chairman of Du Pont, at his office in Wilmington, Delaware. Shapiro represented the Business Roundtable on the code. Heyman told Shapiro that he could not accept the compromise provisions reached days earlier.

The significance of major departmental objections is that when it comes time for the president to decide to sign or veto any bill passed by Congress, it is the departmental officials involved, such as the attorney general with advice from other Justice officials, who will advise him. For this reason, some legislators are reluctant to proceed with legislation that has the tag "veto bait" and look to the departments involved to anticipate such problems.

Shapiro offered to meet with Heymann and within seventy-five minutes, Shapiro was in Heymann's office. They negotiated for seven hours and reached agreement over tougher provisions than in the compromise. The earlier compromise had limited the endangerment provision only to those situations where a person "manifests an extreme indifference to human life," and limited coverage to certain environmental and coal-mine regulations. Shapiro and Heymann agreed to broaden the coverage. The next day Heymann appeared at the markup and discussed the proposed changes. The committee amended the bill so that the "extreme indifference" language would come into play only in determining the severity of the sentence, not in determining culpability for the crime. Heymann and Shapiro agreed to leave the scope of coverage to the committee. Senator Leahy got the committee to extend coverage to regulations relating to occupational safety and health, food and drugs, hazardous substances, medical laboratories, and environmental laws (Mintz, 1979). Senator Metzenbaum, however, was unsuccessful in restoring the consumer fraud section, which lost on a near party-line vote of 7 to 8, with Kennedy the only Democrat voting with the Republicans to preserve the coalition.

The coalition was nearly lost on the fourth day of markup. The issue concerned an earlier Supreme Court decision, and illustrates how the making of laws is very much a process of action and reaction among the branches of government. In 1973, the Supreme Court had ruled that the Hobbes Act, which covers coercive activity in interstate commerce, did not cover extortion during a labor dispute if the objectives of the labor activity were lawful and could have been achieved through collective bargaining (*United States* v. *Emmons,* 410 U.S. 396 [1973]). Republicans were lobbied heavily by business groups to overturn this decision.

At the request of Thurmond and Hatch, Kennedy had hammered out a compromise that continued to exclude labor disputes from Hobbes Act coverage, unless the activity was a serious felony such as murder, kidnapping, rape, or arson. On November 27, Leahy offered an amendment to retain the Supreme Court ruling as is, which passed 9 to 5, with all Democrats except Kennedy and one Republican, Cochran, voting yes. Kennedy voted no with the Republicans. Thurmond and Hatch were angry and threatened to withhold support for the whole bill unless this was changed. Kennedy's inability to hold the Democrats to the agreement on labor extortion threatened to breach the coalition agreement, and reporting the bill on party lines risked a filibuster on the Senate floor.

For five hours on December 4, Kennedy, Thurmond, and Hatch, their staffs, and labor representatives negotiated a new compromise. They agreed to bar federal prosecution for extortion during a labor dispute unless there was "clear proof" that the coercive conduct was a felony that was intended to cause death or severe bodily harm and also was intended to further the aims of the labor dispute. This broke the impasse, and the full committee proceeded to vote 12 to 1 to recommend the bill to the Senate (Cohodas, Dec. 8, 1979). The one nay was Charles Mathias (R-Md.). Minutes later, in accordance with Kennedy's previous promise to allow a separate vote on the death penalty, the committee voted on S.114 to restore the death penalty for treason, espionage, and deaths associated with specified felonies. This death penalty bill passed 7 to 6. The ACLU claimed that the code passed by the Senate Judiciary Committee would have "a disastrous impact on individual rights" and should not be enacted (Pear, Sept. 15, 1980).

The new year came, and Drinan's subcommittee was ready. Drinan and Representative Kindness jointly introduced H.R.6233 on January 7, 1980. The bipartisan and bi-ideological sponsorship of the Senate was now mirrored in the House.

The Justice Department still was not happy with the House bill. Several departmental officials had kept up a running dialogue with the Drinan subcommittee members and staff and had issued numerous memoranda providing legal analyses and the department's position on various proposals. Roger Pauley, legislative director of the Criminal Division, characterized the bill: "They started out writing a bill with all the ACLU ideas in it. It was a catastrophic loss of federal power. But they overestimated our commitment to the project. We don't need a code for the sake of a code" (Ehrenhalt, 1980).

Particularly worrisome were procedural and jurisdictional changes that were in the draft. For example, the draft bill had included language making it harder for the government to prove that a witness had committed perjury under oath. In addition, the bill had tried to spell out federal jurisdiction for various crimes. The Senate bill had included a provision that jurisdictional limitations were guidelines for federal authorities and could not be litigated—that is, raised as a defense. The House bill contained no such disclaimer. Pauley explained the significance of such procedural provisions to law enforcement: "New offenses are nice. They may facilitate prosecuting a few more crimes. But procedure that affects the whole gamut of the system is far more important. If you mess that up, the price for achieving other reforms becomes too high" (personal interview, 1986).

Drinan made some accommodations to the Justice Department's objections. He explained the basis for such accommodations: "If there is a dispute, we tended to go with existing law. A lot of the libertarians are anti-law enforcement. I don't want the feds to have any more power than they have now, but I don't want to take away any. If it takes federal control to get rid of crime, I'm prepared to have that. I'm not a stickler for that sort of thing" (Ehrenhalt, Feb. 24, 1980).

Another of the issues that gave the subcommittee difficulty was the same issue that had troubled the Senate—labor extortion. This issue pitted some of the most highly organized and well-financed lobby groups—AFL-CIO, Teamsters, National Association of Manufacturers, Chamber of Commerce, and Business Roundtable—against each other. Business-labor politics also always carries with it a high potential for partisan warfare, with the unions putting pressure on their traditional allies, the Democrats, and the business groups putting pressure on theirs, the Republicans. Thus, there is definite room for constituency and partisan pressures to escalate, so that one such volatile issue could destroy a carefully nurtured consensus.

Even though the Senate Judiciary Committee had completed its work in December and filed a report on January 17, no Senate floor action had been scheduled. Kennedy's focus had moved from policy-making in the legislative arena to presidential politics in the electoral arena. The New York primary, which was expected to be pivotal in the race, was to be held March 25 and Kennedy spent most of his time campaigning. He did not need a divisive floor fight over emotional issues in the middle of his campaign. Several senators, including Jesse Helms (R-N.C.) planned to offer several amendments, including some dealing with pornography. The loss of Kennedy's policy leadership in the Senate was significant. Without him to push for floor time and hold down the left flank, no movement was possible. Reform proponents had the upper hand, if they could secure policy leadership on the Senate floor.

In addition, the opposing lobby groups did not think they would get any further with the Senate leaders and concentrated on blocking the bill in the House. Charles Carrol, associate director of the Associated General Contractors of America, said, "You can't fight something regardless of the merits when it's given that consensus label. It just makes it 10 times harder" (Cohodas, March 15, 1980, p. 739). On the other side, Charles Fritz, a Teamsters Union spokesman stated, "Right now we'll be focusing on the House, at the full committee. To say we could beat the bill in the Senate, I'd be whistling in the wind" (Cohodas, p. 740).

Drinan's subcommittee, under severe lobbying pressure, attempted to arrive at a formulation that would allow the bill to continue moving. In the fall, the provision on labor extortion had been cited to overturn the Supreme Court decision. The subcommittee reversed this on March 4. This upset the business groups. On March 10, a compromise was adopted that was unclear. The compromise provision stated that it would be a crime to "wrongfully" obtain property from another through a threat of injury or property damage. This was interpreted as leaving the Supreme Court decision intact, in that obtaining higher wages in a labor dispute was a legitimate activity and was not wrongful. However, the provision then stated that it would not be a defense to an extortion if the conduct were "in furtherance of a legitimate objective or activity."

Union representatives were unhappy and confused. Food and Commercial Workers spokesman Mayer attended the mark-up and complained afterward, "In section one, they say 'Thou shalt not prosecute.' And in section two they say 'thou shalt'" (Cohodas, p. 740). This illustrates a time-honored legislative practice known as the "virtue of vagueness." Such a formulation allows each representative to tell his constituents that he obtained language to protect them and allows him to vote for the bill, thus preserving a majority for the bill. Congressmen know that clarity is not always required to pass a bill, but a majority is required. The courts can be left to devise an interpretation of what "congressional intent" was.

The subcommittee made some other changes in the mark-up. The day before the vote, the members agreed to a Conyers' amendment to allow lawyers to be present when their clients are questioned before a grand jury. This was one of those procedural provisions, not in the Senate bill, that was sure to provoke strong oppostion from the Department of Justice. Justice's Criminal Division was concerned that such inclusion would turn grand jury inquiries into adversarial trial-like proceedings, seriously delaying investigations.

On March 11, the Criminal Justice Subcommittee voted 7 to 1 with one abstention to report the bill to the full Judiciary Committee. The one nay was Conyers, and the abstention was Gudger. The Subcommittee bill, like the Senate bill, consolidated a multitude of statutes and grouped crimes into classes depending on the seriousness of each offense, with each crime given a maximum prison term and fine level. The bill differed from the Senate bill in some key respects. In defining crimes, it did not also include the crime of attempting to commit the offense, which was in the Senate bill. It included the Sentencing Commission to establish sentencing guidelines but would only allow the defendant to appeal a sentence outside the guidelines — not the prosecutor. It also retained parole, which the Senate bill abolished. The prison terms for felonies and misdemeanors were also lighter than the Senate bill's. For example, in the House subcommittee bill, a class B felony (certain types of homicides) would have carried a term of up to thirteen and one-third years, whereas in the Senate bill it would have been up to twenty years. There were numerous other differences; there were bound to be in a 447-page bill. The House subcommittee had worked its independent will, but for the first time it had acted.

Drinan's satisfaction with moving the criminal code reform and with his political leverage was short-lived, however. The criminal code bill was about to be deprived of its key policy leader by a completely unexpected source — the Pope. On May 1, the Vatican ordered Father Drinan to cease his secular political role of holding elective office. He would have to choose between his political and religious roles. Drinan appealed, but on May 5, it was announced the appeal was denied. The Vatican was withdrawing the permission needed for Robert Drinan to run for reelection and remain a priest. Drinan would be leaving the House at session's end.

Peter Rodino, chairman of the full Judiciary Committee,

promptly scheduled a full Judiciary Committee mark-up on the bill, but the proceedings soon ran into trouble. Representative James Sensenbrenner (R-Wisc.) became incensed after losing a close vote on an amendment. He had won the vote on the basis of all the members present and voting. However, the chairman had voted the proxies of the absent members against the amendment and thus defeated it. Sensenbrenner objected to this practice. He felt that it was used arbitrarily too often by the chairman when the minority had won over some members of the majority on the merits of debate, and he decided to challenge it. The rules called for a reading of the bill before amendment, a practice usually waived by unanimous consent. Sensenbrenner objected, so consent was not unanimous and the clerk proceeded to read the bill line by line, which soon resulted in adjournment. Sensenbrenner kept this up, which delayed the proceedings several weeks while the majority negotiated with him. Finally, the committee agreed to reconsider later any amendment whose outcome had been determined by proxies, and the mark-up proceeded.

The committee held eighteen mark-up sessions and forty-five hours of debate in considering some 234 amendments that had been filed. These were well-attended, difficult sessions with many tough votes; nearly half of the 234 amendments were debated. This may be as close to a full debate as the nation's criminal laws have ever received at one time. Some of the amendments focused on the heretofore contentious issues, and the votes were very close. On the labor extortion issue, on which members had been heavily lobbied by labor and business groups, Representative Hall tried two compromise amendments, which lost on separate votes, 14 to 16 and 15 to 16. Then Representative Sieberling (D-Ohio) introduced an amendment to reverse the subcommittee's action on labor extortion and exempt labor from federal extortion coverage. This carried 17 to 13, and set up a confrontation with the Senate bill. On sentencing, Representative Lungren (R-Calif.) tried twice to amend the bill to permit government to appeal sentences as well as defendants but lost narrowly both times, 15 to 16.

External political events intervened to change some votes. Former Attorney General Ramsey Clark had traveled to Vietnam to confer with Vietnamese government officials on American policy, which provoked considerable opposition. Representative Hyde (R-Ill.) offered an amendment to restore to the bill an existing little-used statute of great symbolic importance, known as the Logan Act, which prohibits citizens from negotiating with foreign governments in opposition to U.S. policy. Liberal groups such as the ACLU had seen the Logan Act as a primary example of outdated vestiges of an earlier repressive period, which code reform should extinguish. Hyde, however, had argued, "We either have one Secretary of State or 220 million." Hyde's amendment passed 18 to 12.

By voice vote, the committee deleted the provision that allowed lawyers in grand jury sessions. The Justice Department had lobbied hard for the deletion and won. The department had prevailed on Drinan to offer two other amendments that were in the Senate bill. These defined the crimes of solicitation and facilitation, but both lost on voice votes. There were other tough votes on potential killer amendments—to delete definitions of obscene material, to reestablish the death penalty, and to redefine the defense of entrapment. These also lost.

On July 2, the committee was ready for a final vote on the whole bill. Deborah Owen, at the time legislative assistant to Representative Sawyer (R-Mich.), the ranking Republican on the Judiciary Committee, described the scene: "You talk about people having a real sense of public spirit and interest. That criminal code mark-up in the House Judiciary Committee is as close to the spirit I saw in the Senate on the crime package. It almost got to the point where there was almost an academic interest. These guys were feeling like they were back in law school writing the nation's criminal laws. It's really a lawyer's dream. People had tears in their eyes. There was a hush in the room. The only other time I've seen it like that was when they voted out the articles of impeachment [on President Nixon] in the House Judiciary Committee. There was a real feeling that this is an important moment" (personal interview, 1986).

H.R.6915, as amended by the committee, was approved 20 to 12. For the first time, committees in both houses of Congress had approved criminal law reform bills in the same Congress.

All was not rosy for criminal code proponents, however. The Senate had not brought the bill to the floor in the six months since it had been reported by the Judiciary Committee. Kennedy had been engaged in a state-by-state primary battle with President Carter. Although he was behind in the delegate count, he was prepared to challenge the rules at the August Democratic Convention. He was not available to lead the fight once again for criminal law reform on the Senate floor.

In addition, there was no certainty that the House Rules Committee would vote a rule allowing the bill to come to the House floor. Drinan was pushing for a rule that would limit the number of amendments that could be offered on the floor. Code opponents were pushing for an open rule allowing unlimited amendments. An open rule is often, in reality, a death sentence for a bill because opponents can propose hundreds of amendments that force the leadership to pull the bill from the floor so that other legislation can be considered. It is especially damning toward the end of a Congress when the legislative calendar is crowded, and Congress is short on time. The bill's opponents in the House Judiciary Committee called for the bill to be withheld from the floor. Conyers joined Representatives Sieberling and Hughes (D-N.J.) in a dissent to the committee's majority report "to keep this bill off the floor" (Committee on the Judiciary, 1980, p. 671). Conyers also filed a separate dissent enumerating all his particular objections and his opposition to the "omnibus approach" (p. 677). Others also filed "additional views" indicating amendments that would be offered on the floor.

After the July 2 session, Judiciary chairman Rodino indicated he would move slowly on the bill: "I want the bill to go to the floor but the matter is going to take considerable study before we get there" (Cohodas, July 5, 1980, p. 1885). True to his word, the committee did not formally report the bill until September 25.

Several groups were not happy and lobbied to keep the

bill off the floor. John Shattuck, ACLU Washington director, stated that the House bill "contains a number of threats to civil liberties and we are not pleased with the prospects of taking it to the floor or conference with the Senate" (Babcock, 1980). While the Business Roundtable supported the Senate bill, other business groups, like the U.S. Chamber of Commerce, were still opposed. Labor groups were opposed to the Senate bill's labor provisions and were concerned with what might result from a House-Senate conference committee. Drinan continued to push for floor consideration, but with the Senate not moving, there was less impetus for the leadership to schedule floor time for what was sure to be a contentious debate.

In September, just weeks before the October adjournment, Kennedy was back at the Senate following President Carter's renomination at the Democratic Convention. He was in a position to take up leadership on code reform once again, but he faced a problem. Senators McClure and Helms, old foes of the code bill and leaders of a conservative caucus they called the "Senate Steering Committee," had been busy drafting a host of amendments to offer on the Senate floor, dealing with such matters as the death penalty, relaxing federal firearms laws, obscenity, prostitution, and even abortion. They also threatened a filibuster if their amendments were not considered. At least two Democratic senators running for reelection told the leadership that they did not want the criminal code measure brought to the Senate floor before election day, if they would have to vote on such issues (Pear, Sept. 15, 1980). Negotiations with the two senators proved unsuccessful.

The upshot of this was that the leadership in the Senate did not schedule the code reform for floor action. With Senate action unlikely, the House Rules Committee never even formally considered whether the Drinan code bill would be granted a rule at all.

Kennedy's switching of role emphasis from policy leader to electoral leader deprived the code bill of leadership at a critical time. Had the bill passed again in the Senate, pressure would have built on the House to act. In addition, knowledge of Drinan's forced retirement emboldened opponents. If they could simply delay consideration until adjournment, the only policy leader that code reform had in the House would be gone in the next Congress. House leaders had less reason to accede to Drinan's request for floor consideration, because he would no longer be a power in the next term. In Washington, what one can do to someone or for someone is important coin of the political realm, and the Vatican's announcement had deprived Drinan of his political purse.

Consensus Building—An Ongoing Enterprise

As demonstrated, consensus building in Congress means building a series of consensuses that are linked. Early consensus must be achieved with a view toward the ultimate consensus that will normally be necessary to prevail on the floors of the House and the Senate.

Large-scale legislation presents its own problems in consensus building. It is open to the activation of different issues that can spawn new controversies as events unfold, as the political stream shifts, and as new players are aroused and enter the scene. New cleavages are generated and must be confronted. The entry and exit of policy leaders from the process, their level of activity, and the decisions they make also influence the success of efforts toward consensus.

Once a consensus surrounding a policy has begun to be widely recognized, the policy proposal picks up momentum and moves further up on the agenda. However, moving legislation in Congress is a fragmented, multistage process that is, to some extent, time bound. There is only limited time within any one Congress before significant changes in the composition and arrangement of players may take place. Blocking forces are afforded a number of opportunities to delay consideration. Consensus building is an arduous and, at the same time, delicate enterprise, which must be sustained through numerous skirmishes before a policy ultimately reaches the decision agenda.

Consensus building had made headway but was not sufficient to move the criminal code bill to the decision agenda. Nonetheless, progress for law enforcement reform had been achieved in both the Senate and the House. This had demonstrated both bipartisan and, to some extent, bi-ideological support for the effort. To be sure, substantial interests remained opposed. Nonetheless, Drinan became convinced, as a result of negotiations between staff of the Criminal Justice subcommittee and the Senate Judiciary Committee, that compromises between the approaches of the two bodies were possible, and that action could be completed in the next Congress (Drinan and Beier, 1981). It appeared that if the pro-reform forces could be mobilized, the opportunity for passage was there.

• 7 •

Political Change
and Issue
Turbulence

Through the end of the 96th Congress, the proponents of criminal law reform had expended enormous time and effort in developing the components of federal criminal law reform within the framework of the proposed criminal code. In addition, substantial, if not universal, consensus had been achieved for the main ideas of federal criminal law reform. True enough, there were still unhappy groups opposed to some of the particulars, but the votes in the Senate and in the House Judiciary Committee demonstrated significant bipartisan support.

Effects of Political Change on Legislative Issues

Even when a certain degree of consensus is achieved, there is no assurance that a bill will move to the critical decision agenda. A consensus may be fleeting and must be maintained. As Kingdon (1984) has pointed out, developments in the political stream must be coupled with developments in the policy stream at the critical juncture—when the policy window is open—in order to achieve enactment. In terms of influences on the agenda, which Kingdon identifies, two had moved criminal law reform to the point of being ready for floor consideration in both houses of Congress. These were (1) the inexorable march of problems pressing in on the system and (2) the process of gradual accumulation of knowledge and perspectives among specialists in the policy area and the generation of proposals. Crime and the public's reaction to it was worse, not better, and the policy specialists were now well versed on the issues. Relevant changes in the political stream are another important influence on the agenda. These include swings in the national mood, changes in election results, changes of administration, and changes in Congress. Political changes can alter the size and composition of likely policy coalitions. In part, they do this by removing or decreasing the influence of some players and introducing or increasing the influence of others. Political changes can also send new policy signals from the electorate that alter the working assumptions of legislators in regard to desirable policies.

However, political influences do not move as if directed by some unseen hand inexorably pushing a bill to enactment. Some will change to support a bill, and some will change in such a way as to diminish its chances. Even when the influences that are favorable predominate, policy leaders must still capitalize on them. In short, the pro-forces must be mobilized in order to utilize these influences to maximum advantage in overcoming obstacles.

Issue volatility can also be affected by changes in the political stream. A host of new issues may be dumped on Congress, elbowing for room on the agenda and crowding out previously developed issues. New issues buffeting each other as well as old ones create additional uncertainty. This can make for a more contentious legislative climate. Political risk may be heightened. As a result, legislators may seek to deflect as many issues as possible and keep them off the decision agenda. Alternatively, if policy leaders can fashion a policy approach that achieves a significant consensus and seems to satisfy some of the critical political demands, legislators may hop on the bandwagon to remove the source of contention from the agenda and reduce their future potential risk.

Political Change and Criminal Law Reform

By the end of the 1970s, the lack of final action signified the vulnerability of the codification effort to the continual raising of issues by various groups. Many of these were issues raised by groups that were new entrants to the debate who had just discovered the code, such as the U.S. Chamber of Commerce or the Moral Majority. Such groups would state objections to provisions that had been included years earlier but that now had increased salience owing to shifts in the political stream and increased activism by such groups in the legislative arena. In addition, the continuing opponents, such as the ACLU and NCARL, were still active in rallying their allies.

The blocking forces had, so far, had their way in several respects. In the House, even with the indefatigable policy leadership of Robert Drinan and the marathon efforts of his subcommittee, as well as others on the full Judiciary Committee, it took a whole session of Congress to get the bill reported out of committee. The blocking forces were successful in seeing to it that the House leadership did not allow the bill to come to the floor. In the Senate, the presidential election had deprived the bill of vital leadership at critical junctures, which gave opponents the tactical advantage at the end of the session.

The danger for criminal law reform was that having failed to achieve passage in even one house of Congress in the 96th Congress, it might fall off the policy agenda in the 97th. Judiciary committee members in both houses of Congress had expended thousands of hours of effort and had not moved a bill into the main arena. They could hardly have been blamed for turning to pursuits offering more payoff.

The code effort had generated numerous proposals that had been worked over and refined, again and again, by members and staff of the two Judiciary committees and the Department of Justice. Changes in an important agenda influence — political processes — would be required to move criminal law reform further onto the decision agenda. All of these came to have a significant influence on the course of criminal law reform.

The blocking forces opposed to criminal law reform still possessed considerable advantages. One of these was simply that they had been successful in previous rounds in blocking passage, and often past success influences future expectations. Success often breeds success. In addition, as noted, changes in political processes do not all move in one direction, and the 1980 election brought changes both positive and negative for the prospects for criminal law reform.

On November 7, 1980, the national political landscape changed dramatically. Ronald Reagan's stunning and decisive victory over Jimmy Carter not only brought a Republican to the White House but it also brought one with a clear agenda. A. James Richey (1981) identified four major tenets of the Reagan philosophy: supply-side economics (with major budget cuts), decentralization of domestic programs, a strengthened defense, and a return to traditional morality. Even more surprising than the decisiveness of the Reagan victory was the capture of the Senate by the Republicans with a twelve-seat pickup that delivered a majority of fifty-three seats. This was the first time the Republicans had majority control in the Senate since 1952, and the first time a Republican president had his party in control of either chamber since Dwight Eisenhower.

The Senate was a very different place in 1981 than it had been in 1980. Of the eighteen new senators—a large freshman class—sixteen were Republicans. Several of the most prominent long-term Democratic liberals were defeated and replaced by conservatives. Senate Judiciary Democrats Bayh (D-Ind.) and Culver (D-Iowa) were defeated, for example.

The tenor of the Senate Judiciary Committee shifted considerably but did not become either dependably rightist or partisan, as it first appeared it might. The Judiciary chairmanship changed from Edward Kennedy to Strom Thurmond, which at first blush seemed to presage a direction from extreme liberal to extreme conservative. However, Kennedy and Thurmond had worked well together on a number of issues during Kennedy's chairmanship, and Kennedy, faced with independent liberal Democrats, had often had to rely on Thurmond to rally the Republicans to make quorums and to get legislation out of the committee.

Senate Judiciary had a 10 to 8 Republican-Democrat split, but neither the Republicans nor the Democrats could be depended upon to stick with their fellow partisans. New Republicans joining the committee included three members of the "New

Right" who would be interested in moving the social agenda—
Charles Grassley (R-Iowa), Jeremiah Denton (R-Ala.) and John
East (R-N.C.). Moderate Arlen Specter (R-Pa.), former
Philadelphia district attorney, also joined the committee. Second in seniority on the committee was Charles Mathias, Jr.
(R-Md.), a liberal Republican who assumed the chairmanship
of the Criminal Justice Subcommittee. Mathias and Thurmond
often differed, and Thurmond decided not to assign the criminal code bill to the subcommittee but retain it at the full committee level instead. Republicans continuing on the committee
were Senators Dole (R-Kans.), Hatch (R-Utah), Simpson (R-
Wyo.), and Laxalt (R-Nev.). Laxalt was in a unique position as
he was a close friend of President Reagan and able to sit in on
both congressional leadership and White House policy sessions.

On the Democratic side, Kennedy gave up the position
of ranking minority member to Joseph Biden (D-Del.) in order
to serve as Ranking on the Labor Committee, but he stayed
on Judiciary as a member. Biden had assumed the chairmanship of the subcommittee on Criminal Justice and had become
deeply involved in the reform of federal forfeiture laws.

Biden had noticed that statistics on the forfeiture provisions of the Racketeer Influenced Corrupt Organization (RICO)
Act were extremely low. This act allowed federal prosecutors
to ask the courts to forfeit money and assets that convicted defendants had acquired through their illegal organized crime activities. During an approximately ten-year period, the government
had gained only about one million dollars in assets through the
provision. Biden asked the General Accounting Office (GAO),
Congress's investigative arm, to do a study of the situation. The
results revealed gaps in federal law that made forfeiture hard
to accomplish. Biden was convinced that forfeiture was a key
tool in fighting organized drug crime and he developed proposals to strengthen federal forfeiture laws.

Other Democrats on Senate Judiciary included Howard
Metzenbaum (D-Ohio), Patrick Leahy (D-Vt.), Max Baucus
(D-Mont.), Robert Byrd (D-W.Va.), Dennis DeConcini (D-
Ariz.), and Howell Heflin (D-Ala.) DeConcini and Heflin were
regarded as more conservative than the other Democrats. Thus,

the swing votes on the committee would normally be Mathias and Specter for the Republicans and DeConcini and Heflin for the Democrats.

In the House, the Republicans picked up 33 seats, which reduced but did not eliminate the Democratic majority. The Democrats maintained a majority of 243 to 192 but, with at least 30 conservative Democrats, the president and his party had room for significant coalition building.

The House Democratic leadership recognized the peril and used their majority control to shore up their position. Though the ratio of House Democrats to Republicans was about 5 to 4, Speaker O'Neill announced that the committee memberships would maintain a 2 to 1 Democratic majority on the key Rules, Appropriations, and Ways and Means committees.

As for the House Judiciary Committee, with Drinan gone, the chairmanship of the Criminal Justice Subcommittee was assumed by John Conyers, an avowed opponent of the criminal code. William J. Hughes (D-N.J.) took over the Crime Subcommittee from Conyers. In addition, the size of the full committee was reduced from thirty-one to twenty-eight, and Rodino recruited new liberal members to ensure a liberal majority. Patricia Schroeder (D-Colo.), Barney Frank (D-Mass.), and Harold Washington (D-Ill.) all joined the committee. Don Edwards, the liberal chairman of the Civil and Constitutional Rights Subcommittee, observed, "We were very interested in carrying on the Judiciary Committee in the tradition of Peter Rodino and Emanuel Celler and the national Democratic Party, with traditional respect for individual rights and due process" (Cohodas, Feb. 21, 1981). Republicans saw it differently. M. Caldwell Butler (R-Va.) complained, "This is the legislative equivalent of the court-packing plan of Franklin Roosevelt" (Cohodas, Feb. 21, 1981). At the full committee's first meeting, Republican members proposed changing committee rules to place consideration of the criminal code at the full committee level and keep it out of Conyer's subcommittee, but this was defeated on a straight party-line vote.

As for the House leadership, Thomas P. (Tip) O'Neill and James Wright were still in place as Speaker and Majority

Leader respectively, but the Republican leadership experienced wholesale change. Minority Leader John Rhodes (R-Ariz.) had retired and was replaced by Republican whip Robert H. Michel (R-Ill.). The new whip was Trent Lott (R-Miss.), and the chairman of the Republican conference became Jack Kemp (R-N.Y.). Michel made it clear that the Republican leadership would be more active in pushing legislation, particularly the president's program, than the past leadership had been. Michel was well aware of the dissatisfaction expressed by the younger conservative members over their leadership's compromises with Democrats in the 96th Congress. On February 19, Michel said that House Republicans would try to use the expected accomplishments of the Republican-controlled Senate to generate public pressure for similar action by the House Democratic leadership. The ultimate weapon, the Republican leaders agreed, would be to cite the votes of recalcitrant Democrats in the next election campaign. Michel stated, "Those voting records can't be denied. You've got to keep concentrating on them. That's what we're here for, to address the issues, not to duck them" (Arieff, 1981).

The change to a Republican and more conservative Senate was not an unmitigated blessing for criminal law reform, however. As had been demonstrated in previous sessions, support and opposition with respect to the criminal code bill had not divided neatly according to a simple conservative-liberal split. There were, in fact, further ideological fissures within the conservative and liberal camps. These were widened in the 97th Congress. On the conservative side, the "New Right," of which Senators Helms and McClure were charter members, felt it had a claim on the new Senate's agenda, given the defeat of Democratic liberal senators in the election. Senators Helms and East introduced bills to take away the Supreme Court's authority to consider cases dealing with abortion, school desegregation, and school prayer. In all, four court-curbing bills were introduced in the Senate and twenty-three in the House. To the extent these social issues dominated, there would be a highly contentious climate in the Senate.

A major question affecting criminal law reform was what priority it would have on the Senate Judiciary Committee's legislative agenda. The crime issue was in competition with other social issues for space on the agenda, at least as far as the New Right conservatives were concerned. Groups such as the Moral Majority, the National Conservative Political Action Committee, and the Committee for a Free Congress campaigned against most of the Democratic losers, and were determined to push for their agenda items. In addition to the court-curbing bills, they introduced a constitutional amendment to prohibit abortion, a statute to prohibit the use of federal funds to bus school children in desegregating schools, legislation to allow voluntary school prayer, and a constitutional amendment to require a balanced federal budget. These were all potential items for the Senate Judiciary Committee's agenda, and all were highly controversial and unlikely to foster an environment of cooperation.

In addition, Senate Democrats still had all the tools necessary to stop action and tie up the Senate. At his first news conference, new Judiciary chairman Thurmond said that it was likely the criminal code would have to be put over until the next Congress. He altered this later, but it was an indication of how crowded the agenda appeared.

The bigger question was whether Judiciary Committee issues would get on the decision agenda at all. To a large extent, this depended on the president. Thurmond, unlike Kennedy, was not going to move independently of the administration's priorities. Reagan, unlike Nixon and then Carter, had run with his party rather than alongside it throughout the 1980 campaign. Reagan and his campaign staff solicited the advice of Republican congressional candidates, let them participate in the policy formation process, and helped them in their campaigns (Arieff, 1980). Criminal law reform would have to have at least the tacit support of the administration before Senate Republicans would even schedule it for consideration.

The new administration brought a new regime to the Justice Department. Benjamin Civiletti, Carter's second attorney general, had not exercised active legislative leadership and had been hamstrung in his relationship with Congress over his role in the handling of the affair of the president's brother, Billy Carter, in dealing with Libya. Reagan appointed William French

Smith, who had been his personal attorney, as attorney general. Smith's background as partner in the Los Angeles firm of Gibson, Dunn, and Crutcher was in labor law. Even though there was little in Smith's background that would have led anyone to predict it, Smith established his major legislative priorities as pushing law enforcement initiatives.

In organizing the Justice Department's leadership, Smith switched the portfolios of the deputy attorney general and the associate attorney general. Edward Schmults became deputy attorney general and oversaw the civil law functions and the budget, while Rudolph Giuliani became associate attorney general and oversaw the criminal side of the Justice Department. Giuliani had served at Justice during the Ford administration and had been chief deputy to then deputy attorney general Harold Tyler. As an experienced prosecutor in the U.S Attorney's office in the Southern District of New York, Giuliani had personally prosecuted several prominent public corruption and drug cases. Giuliani was familiar with the criminal code from his days assisting Tyler in the Ford administration. For assistant attorney general to head the Criminal Division, D. Lowell Jensen, a Democrat, was chosen. Jensen had spent his entire career as a prosecutor in Alameda County, California, and was elected three times as district attorney. Presidential counselor Edwin Meese had worked for Jensen as a prosecutor and continued his long interest and participation in criminal justice policy through his position at the White House.

When interviewing Giuliani for the associate's job, Smith asked him where the department could make the most impact in the criminal area. Giuliani responded that the average citizen was most concerned about violent crime — street crime that threatened his or her family, particularly as a result of the growing drug epidemic — and he felt the administration should address that. Giuliani explained his perspective in a later news interview, stating that his emphasis on street crime "was to balance what wasn't being done. When I came in here it seemed to me we're doing a great deal — in terms of devotion to time and resources to organized crime. . . . We were doing a lot more in all areas of white collar crime than we did back in the Ford administration. What we really needed—what had really broken down—was how we help state and local law enforcement with some of the serious emergencies they have" (Brownstein and Easton, 1982, p. 384).

As President Reagan was doing, Smith brought in experienced people to staff the legislative relations function. Deputy Attorney General Schmults had served in the Ford administration as deputy White House counsel and had oversight of departmental legislative activities in his portfolio. To run legislative operations and head the Office of Legislative Affairs, Smith hired Robert A. McConnell, who had served as legislative assistant to former House Minority Leader John Rhodes, and who enjoyed a long relationship with current Leader Michel.

Attorney General Smith made violent crime one of his two top priorities (the other being immigration reform) and appointed an eight-member Attorney General's Task Force on Violent Crime. The bipartisan task force was cochaired by former Attorney General Griffin Bell and Illinois Republican Governor James Thompson, a former U.S. attorney himself. It also included several prominent practitioners from the criminal justice field and Harvard scholar James Q. Wilson. Jeffrey Harris, who had served with Giuliani as an assistant U.S. attorney in New York, was appointed task force executive director. The mission of the task force was two-fold: to make recommendations that the Justice Department could immediately implement to combat violent crime without the need for additional legislation or funding, and then to make recommendations that would require additional funding and legislation. The task force had 120 days to report. To a large extent, Bell and Wilson became the leaders of the task force and shaped many of the recommendations. Bell had been involved in the criminal code effort and had been chosen not only for his knowledge and experience with the specifics of criminal law but also for his reputation of weighing policy issues on the merits.

The phase one recommendations emphasized placing a higher priority on drug violations. Also included was a recommendation that the attorney general mandate the establishment of law enforcement coordinating committees by U.S. attorneys in each federal district to work with state and local law enforcement agencies in setting cooperative priorities in fighting crime. The law enforcement coordinating committees were organized and were directed both to establish a plan for local law enforcement priorities and to recommend national priorities that would assist them. In almost every case, the committees recommended that the top priority for the federal role be to fight international and domestic drug traffic, which local law enforcement officials clearly saw as the major cause of violent crime in their communities. The coordinating committee reports consistently called for a stronger federal crime control role to stem the tide of drug crime that washed over jurisdictional borders.

The phase two recommendations also stressed the federal role in narcotics control and called for a foreign policy, a border policy, and a legislative program to combat drug traffic. For the legislative program, the task force pointed out a direct connection between combating illegal drug traffic and criminal law reform: "The seriousness of the drug problem and of the national policy required to combat it must be reflected in the criminal justice system. Many general problems, such as insufficient bail, the suppression of truthful evidence and the imposition of inconsistent and inadequate sentences, are particularly pronounced in drug cases. Accordingly, the recommendations set forth in Chapter Two of this report are especially applicable to narcotics cases so that society will be better able to detect, apprehend, detain for trial, convict, and meaningfully sentence drug traffickers" (Attorney General's Task Force on Violent Crime, 1981, p. 28). The report specifically singled out five reforms in federal criminal procedure that should be achieved through legislation: (1) passage of the sentencing reforms included in the criminal code bill; (2) reform of federal bail laws to allow a judge to consider the dangerousness of the accused in deciding whether or not to release that person on bail; (3) changes in the law so that evidence would not be excluded from a criminal trial if it had been obtained by an officer acting in a reasonable good faith belief that it was in conformity to the Fourth Amendment to the Constitution (modification of the exclusionary rule); (4) modification of the insanity defense by creation of an additional verdict of "guilty but mentally ill" and establishment of a federal commitment procedure for defendants found incompetent to stand trial or not guilty by reason of insanity; and (5) modification of federal habeas corpus rules whereby state prisoners had been appealing to the federal courts for new trials after being convicted in state courts. Even though the task force had approved these recommendations for significant changes in federal law unanimously, the latter three were certain to engender considerable controversy.

Reagan and other administration officials made it clear right after the inauguration that the president would not allow his administration to overload Congress with proposals as Carter had done. The administration's budget and tax proposals were going to receive the priority, and everything else, including the social issues and crime, was going to have to wait. It was questionable whether crime legislation would receive any significant administration or congressional leadership attention at all.

The chances improved with the sudden and dramatic attempt on the president's life on March 30, 1981, when John Hinckley shot and wounded President Reagan and severely injured White House press secretary James Brady outside the Hilton Hotel in Washington. The White House quickly reaffirmed the president's opposition to any new gun control legislation, so that would not serve as a vehicle, but the Hinckley assassination attempt did cause the crime issue to resurface. The administration made it clear that economic policy was still number one, however.

Reagan's stunning victory over the House Democratic leadership on June 26 — when the House passed the president's budget reconciliation package, which had not even gone through the committee process, by a vote of 217 to 211 — went a long way in making the legislative reputation of Reagan and his team. With a dramatic tax reduction package that followed shortly after, the administration quickly gained a reputation for astute legislative acumen.

The Justice Department was initially left to its own devices to put together its own strategy on crime legislation. Senator Thurmond had expressed his hope that the attorney general would support the criminal code revision. Ronald Gainer, who was still in Justice's Office of Legal Policy, gave briefings on the code to the attorney general and other senior administration officials. During his confirmation hearing on January 15, 1981, William French Smith had been asked if he favored recodification of the federal criminal laws. Smith had replied that while he was aware the previous effort had involved a number of controversial issues, he was in favor and thought the controversial issues should be separated out so that the code could go forward (U.S. Congress, Jan. 15, 1981).

There were a number of meetings at the Justice Department in the early months of the Reagan administration, during which Associate Attorney General Giuliani, Deputy Attorney General Schmults, and other political appointees, as well as career officials, debated the approach to take regarding crime legislation. Two schools of thought emerged at these meetings. One group wanted the new administration to offer immediately its own criminal law package devoted to major reforms to strengthen law enforcement. The other group urged supporting passage of the criminal code. Approximately half of the participants at these meetings would argue for the former approach because they thought the code would not make it through the legislative process, given its previous history. However, the Justice Department had had so great a committment to the code for such a long time that Giuliani and the other top Justice officials decided to continue to support it. They also decided that this commitment would be for a limited time; if the code looked as if it would not pass, they would put forth a reform-only package (Giuliani, personal interview, 1990).

Senator Thurmond introduced the criminal code bill (S.1630) on September 17, with hearings held on September 28 and October 1. Attorney General Smith testified in favor of the bill on September 28. The administration, however, was content to follow the lead of the Senate Judiciary Committee, which had developed the code over the years. The Department of Justice legislative liaison effort on the code was carried on through the Office of Legal Policy, but no major political initiatives were launched. The new team at the department was supportive but was putting its own crime initiatives together as well. In addition, the White House was not much involved.

The House Judiciary Committee was going slow on the code. Harold Sawyer (R-Mich.) and Thomas Kindness (R-Ohio) had introduced a criminal code bill (H.R.1647) that was virtually identical to the bill that had been reported by the House Judiciary Committee in the previous Congress. However, Chairman Rodino assigned it to the Criminal Justice Subcommittee, and Chairman Conyers remained opposed to the omnibus approach to criminal justice reform. At a subcommittee meeting on April 8, Conyers announced that the subcommittee would handle the criminal code on a piecemeal basis, issue by issue. Code proponents saw this as a killing tactic.

Meanwhile, the Senate Judiciary Committee decided to process as separate bills some of the controversial provisions of criminal law reform not included in the code, as well as some provisions that were included. On June 12, the Senate Judiciary Committee reported out S.114 to reinstate the death penalty for certain federal crimes and for attempted assassination of the president. The Hinckley assassination attempt was having its effect.

The interest in House Judiciary, meanwhile, was in reviving a scaled-down version of the Law Enforcement Assistance Administration (LEAA) program, which the Cater administration had abolished. One of the reasons that judiciary committee assignments in both houses of Congress were not highly sought after was that very little money was distributed around the country as a result of legislation passing through the committees. Instead, the judiciary committees had handled issues such as abortion, school desegregation, and the Equal Rights Amendment—issues that made few people happy. The new proposal for a Justice Assistance program was, in part, designed to restore some of the largesse lost with the abolition of LEAA, although several proponents undoubtedly believed that federal financial assistance could make a difference to local agencies. Also, the distribution of funds did not raise the ideological issues with outside groups that criminal law reform did. On September 11, William Hughes's House Judiciary Crime Subcommittee reported out H.R.4481, which provided for the creation of an Office of Justice Assistance to distribute block grants to the states for a total of $150 million. The House Judiciary Committee, proving it could move fast when the majority leadership wanted it to, marked the bill up on September 18 and reported it out over the administration's objections on September 22 by a vote of twenty-two to five. All five no votes were Republicans.

The administration had objected to Justice Assistance on grounds of budgetary policy, federalism, and program effectiveness. The administration was opposed to new domestic spending programs; argued that funding state and local law enforcement was a state and local responsibility; and maintained that if the federal government was unable to dent local crime—the crime rate had increased 40 percent between 1970 and 1979—by spending $7.8 billion for LEAA, it would do no better by spending a few million. Proponents argued that LEAA was never intended to reduce crime directly but to provide seed money for innovative programs, and the new Justice Assistance program would provide seed money for innovative programs of proven value. The administration lost five committee Republicans, including the five most senior ones, demonstrating what a powerful motivating force the prospect of the distribution of funds can be.

At the same full committee meeting, Representative Sawyer sought to discharge the Conyers Criminal Justice Subcommittee from handling the criminal code bill in order to allow the full committee to consider it. Chairman Rodino ruled that the motion would have to receive a two-thirds majority to carry. Representatives F. James Sensenbrenner (R-Wis.) and Sawyer appealed the ruling of the chair on the grounds that, according to committee rules, a majority vote was suffiicient. Representative Edwards (D-Calif.) moved to table the appeal of Rodino's ruling, which narrowly carried on a straight party line vote of fourteen to twelve. Rodino had seven proxy votes from absent Democratic members, which he voted in favor of the tabling motion. Sawyer's discharge motion then was voted on and received a majority of 15 to 11—all twelve Republicans plus 3

Democrats — short of the two-thirds needed according to Rodino's ruling.

Still, the desertion of three committee Democrats revealed the deep frustration on both sides of the aisle with Rodino's
and Conyers's stalling on the criminal code reform bill that members had labored over so strenuously. Conyers called the consideration of the motion to discharge his subcommittee "preposterous
in the face of the record that the subcommittee has compiled,"
and stated that "hearings have already commenced on at least
a half-dozen areas of the Code" (House Committee on the Judiciary, Sept. 22, 1981, pp.64–65). Sensenbrenner took exception
to Conyers's remarks and stated that not one hearing had been
called on the comprehensive code revision bill — nor, for that matter, had one bill been marked up by the Conyers subcommittee
on any subject whatsoever. While the House version was more
to the liking of committee liberals than the Senate bill, Rodino
and Conyers could not be assured of retaining control of the
product if it went to the House floor and the Senate had passed
its version. The Republicans and some Democrats were sure to
try to offer floor amendments to make the code more like the
Senate version. The House membership as a whole was not as
supportive of Rodino's views as the majority of Judiciary Democrats were.

Committee Republicans were determined to get the code
bill out of subcommittee. Sawyer, who had participated in the
hundreds of hours of subcommittee and committee markups on
the criminal code in the previous Congress, decided to attempt
to invoke the House's Special Meeting Rule (Rule XI, Clause
2 [c][2]). The rule provides that if a majority of a committee's
members sign a letter to the chairman of the committee stating
that the committee is going to hold a meeting for the purpose
of voting on a particular bill, then the meeting can be held,
whether the chairman wishes it or not. The rule is seldom invoked in that its use is an affront to the leadership. Members
of the chairman's party rarely sign the letter, which prevents
securing the requisite majority.

Several Judiciary Democrats had also spent long hours
on the criminal code in the previous Congress and felt they al-

ready had a good working vehicle that could move to completion. They were so frustrated by the slow pace of the Criminal
Justice Subcommittee that several took the extraordinary step
of signing the letter along with the committee Republicans. However, the House rules provide that before presentation of the
letter, three members must send a letter to the chairman in-
forming him of their intent to present it. Congressmen Sawyer, McClory, and Kindness sent such a letter to Chairman
Rodino. Rodino then approached Sawyer and talked him into
an alternative procedure.

Rodino made the offer that if Sawyer would hold the letter, he would call a meeting of the committee and support a
motion to give the Conyers subcommittee a deadline for reporting the bill. Sawyer went along and Rodino called a meeting
on the bill on October 7. Immediately after the clerk read the
title of the bill, Representative Danielson (D-Calif.) moved "to
refer the bill to the Subcommittee on Criminal Justice, with instructions that it report back to the full Committee on or before
January 31, 1982" (House Committee on the Judiciary, Oct.
7, 1981, p. 4). This passed by voice vote.

The wording of the Danielson motion was crucial. When
the deadline came, Conyers did not report *out* the bill to the
full committee for its consideration. On January 29, Conyers
sent a letter to Chairman Rodino explaining the progress on
the code bill that his subcommittee had made by holding hearings and briefings — that is, he "reported back to" the committee. The Republicans had been snookered. The criminal code
remained bottled up in Conyers's subcommittee.

Meanwhile, the code bill in the Senate was faced with
growing opposition from some New Right senators. Senators
Helms, McClure, East, and Denton, who constituted an informal group called the "Senate Steering Committee," hired a staff
person, Michael Hammond, who worked against the bill along
with other staff members who worked for these senators. Even
though the new Senate code bill had dropped the offense of "endangerment" to which Helms and McClure had objected the
previous year, they were not mollified.

Hammond circulated a document to New Right groups
suggesting that the bill was unduly lenient in the areas of por-

nography, sex offenses, prostitution, and drug trafficking, while being excessively harsh in the areas of business and corporate crime. The document charged that, under the proposed code, penalties for heroin trafficking would be decreased, whereas the bill increased them; that the penalty for rape would be decreased, whereas it would have been increased; and that prohibitions against transporting women across state lines for immoral purposes (the existing Mann Act) would be weakened, whereas the proposed code included provisions to reach major organized crime prostitution activities.

Senate Judiciary staffers, along with Justice Department lawyers, prepared a document rebutting the charges one by one, but the damage was done. The Moral Majority's chief operations officer wrote all members of the Senate and House Judiciary committees expressing outrage that the bill would overturn District of Columbia laws prohibiting sodomy, bestiality, and seduction by a teacher. The bill, in fact, had no effect on D.C. law at all! The Moral Majority lobbied against the code throughout the remainder of the 97th Congress. Ronald Godwin, Moral Majority's vice-president, testified before the House Judiciary Committee that the proposed criminal code "would permit a wide range of obscene materials to be transmitted through the public mails, would inhibit local communities in the prosecution of the dissemination of pornography . . . and would in several other areas alter existing law to lessen the public perception of the seriousness of crimes involving moral turpitude" (*CQ Almanac,* 1982, p. 416).

The Senate Judiciary Committee held meetings to mark up the code bill on November 17 and 18. During the markup, Senators Denton and East offered amendments supported by the Moral Majority. One such amendment offered by Denton would have restored immunity from prosecution for raping a spouse. Denton said he considered sexual abuse of a spouse "a hideous crime," but he did not think it should be labeled rape. He argued, concerning the language in the bill: "What we have done here, gentlemen, is we have tried to pretend that there is no difference between any coercion at all with one's spouse and one who is not one's spouse. When you get married, you kind of expect you're going to get a little sex, right? There is a differ-

ence" (U.S. Congress, Nov. 18, 1981, p. 46). The amendment
was defeated 5 to 3. In addition, Denton offered an amendment
adding the death penalty to the bill. Because this would upset
the agreement that Chairman Thurmond had with Senators
Kennedy and Biden to keep controversial provisions out of the
bill, Thurmond opposed it, and the amendment was defeated,
with Senators East, Grassley, and Denton voting to add the death
penalty. Even though East and Denton had been cosponsors
of the bill, they asked to have their names removed from it.
Nonetheless, the bill was approved by the committee by a vote
of 11 to 5, with Republicans Denton, East, Grassley, and Mathias, and Democrat Heflin, voting no.

The criminal code bill was successfully out of committee
once again. Now the challenge would be to secure time for Senate
floor consideration.

In the meantime, the Senate criminal law reform forces
pursued their dual-track stategy of passing individual crime reform bills at the same time they pushed the criminal code. On
December 8, the Senate Judiciary Committee met to consider
a bill to reform the federal bail system. Attempts at bail reform
stretched back to 1965 during the Johnson administration, when
Senator Sam Ervin had sponsored a bill following a National
Conference on Bail and Criminal Justice. The conference had
concluded that the existing bail system, which relied exclusively
on the accused putting up a money bond set by the indicting
judge, tended to discriminate against the poor, measuring the
right to freedom by a person's financial ability. At the same time,
it gave society too little protection against the truly dangerous.
Nonetheless, Congress had been unable to agree on a bail reform bill during an almost twenty-year period. The Bail Reform
bill considered by the Senate Judiciary Committee was the same
as the corresponding title on bail contained in the criminal code
bill. A major point of controversy was whether there should be
a provision that permitted judges to consider the dangerousness of the accused in deciding whether to grant bail or not.
Cases in which accused defendants had committed crimes while
out on bail pending trial had fueled support for this provision.
In addition, South American drug dealers, particularly those

from Colombia, who were apprehended by federal officers, readily put up million-dollar bonds — in cash — and then disappeared, forfeiting the bonds. Million-dollar bail bonds were an acceptable cost of doing business for such drug dealers.

Justice Department officials strongly supported the dangerousness provision as an essential crime-fighting tool against these drug dealers. The ACLU had vigorously opposed it, claiming that judges would be unable to predict dangerousness reliably, and that such a provision ran counter to the principle of the presumption of innocence. Nonetheless, the Senate Judiciary Committee passed the bail reform bill (S.1554), which included a dangerousness provision, by voice vote.

The criminal code bill was scheduled to be considered by the full Senate on February 4, but Majority Leader Baker learned of a possible filibuster by some conservative senators who considered the bill too permissive, and it was postponed. Shortly thereafter, the House took up the Justice Assistance bill (H.R.4481), which authorized $170 million a year for state and local law enforcement programs, and passed it 289 to 73. No action on the bill had taken place in the Senate.

At a brief meeting of the House Criminal Justice Subcommittee on February 23, Chairman Conyers asked his subcommittee to vote to endorse the letter he had sent to Chairman Rodino in January "reporting" on code bill progress as the official report of the subcommittee. However, the three other members present, all Republicans, voted to reject the letter. Thus, Conyers still had no official report from his subcommittee. Then Sensenbrenner, who tended to be one of the more combative Republicans, offered a criminal code bill that had the basic structure of the already introduced bill but contained several highly controversial changes, such as a death penalty provision, new obscenity provisions, and restoration of spousal immunity for rape. The subcommittee adjourned so that members and staff could review the Sensenbrenner proposal.

On March 16, Conyers's House Criminal Justice Subcommittee finally scheduled a markup on a criminal code reform bill. It was the version that Sensenbrenner had introduced. There were enough votes to report out the bill, with one Democrat prepared to join the three Republicans present. Chairman Conyers refused to call for the vote and insisted that the clerk read the bill line by line. He then adjourned the meeting.

By the end of April, Senate Majority Leader Baker scheduled the criminal code for floor consideration. However, he was unable to get a unanimous consent agreement limiting amendments, or a time agreement. Senators Helms, McClure, and Denton had more than sixty proposed amendments to the bill, dealing with such issues as the death penalty, obscenity, and sexual offenses. They were unwilling to limit debate and began a filibuster. On April 27, a motion of cloture to shut off debate was presented. As a criminal code bill had passed the Senate previously, code proponents were fairly confident that they would prevail. Cloture requires sixty votes to proceed to the vote on the bill itself. The vote on the cloture motion was 45 to 46, short of even a majority. Senators on both the right and left voted against the motion. Thurmond came off the floor and told his staff, "We are going to have to break up the code. Start work on a bill." Thurmond later attributed the defeat to the reluctance of senators to vote on controversial issues in an election year: "Too many members of Congress don't want to face these hot issues this year. That's the bottom line" (*CQ Almanac,* 1982, p. 416).

The almost two-decade long effort to achieve a fully integrated, rational criminal code at the federal level had come to an end. Although there was broad consensus on the need for it, and even for the vast majority of its provisions, there were provisions in the bill to which groups of widely varying political perspectives objected. When combined together, such groups formed an insurmountable blocking force, even though they fundamentally disagreed with each other in their objectives for the criminal law.

Political Change and Issue Turbulence — Observations

Political changes, particularly sweeping ones, can alter the agenda status of policies and issues and introduce a host of new issues into the congressional arena. As has been seen, the whole climate of policy deliberation may change. It may become less conflictual in some respects, but more contentious in others. Some issues previously in contest will be largely settled by a major political stream change, as occurred with the budget package. The House leadership put up a fight but it was largely over before it began, given the Reagan landslide and the Republican gains in the House. However, the climate can also become more contentious as new issues buffet against old ones in the struggle for agenda priority.

Some representatives will see new political opportunities in such issues and will seek to introduce them into policies that have already been on the agenda. This can upset even the most carefully nurtured consensus.

The danger with large-scale complex legislation is that, in an attempt to be complete, the risk is run that too many killer issues may be included. The comprehensiveness and complexity of such efforts make them vulnerable to changing political tides as new priorities spotlight issues previously considered mundane or inconsequential to the overall effort. This is the fate that befell the criminal code.

Thus, in its final debate, the criminal code was accused of being dangerous by the ACLU for being too restrictive, and by the Moral Majority for being too permissive. It was immaterial that the objectives were to a tiny portion of a mammoth piece of legislation, and that they were, in most cases, of symbolic rather than significant operational importance as far as actual federal law enforcement efforts were concerned (spousal rape is not a frequently charged crime by the Justice Department). Symbolism is as important as substance in the dynamics of achieving legislative policy change, and frequently more so. What the criminal code transmitted about the moral makeup and direction of American society was critical to its legislative success and was inevitably bound up in the political changes taking place in the country and Congress.

• 8 •

Mobilizing
a Winning
Coalition

The defeat of one piece of large-scale legislation can mean an end to legislating for a policy, but it does not necessarily have to mean that. Policy leaders must assess the reasons for defeat in order to see if reconstruction of the policy coalition is possible with an altered policy configuration that serves some of the same objectives. They need to determine if they can gain enough adherents and sufficiently energize them to overcome the blocking forces that have to that point frustrated their efforts.

Mobilizing Legislative Forces

As indicated in Chapter Five, a number of potential sources of conflict always exist, including partisan, ideological, regional, or group differences. Policy leaders attempt to manage the construction of policy proposals and their processing in order to achieve consensus. Their efforts to achieve a winning coalition built on such consensus are constrained by pressures both within and outside Congress. To this point, the pressures arising outside as events changed and reverberated within have been demonstrated to have had a significant effect on federal criminal law reform.

Congress exhibits a set of internal dynamics with pressures coming from committee delegations, party leaders, formal clubs and groups, and congressional staff. As discussed in earlier chapters, power and authority in Congress are highly fragmented and disjointed. Particularly in the House, both rules and party dynamics have served to disperse authority widely over the processing of legislation at significant early stages, which has generally strengthened the hands of chairpersons, particularly in delaying or stopping legislation.

As discussed, policy leaders attempt early on to minimize all sources of differences to reduce conflict in order to build a majority coalition for the final vote and, it is hoped, in the stages leading to it. To arrive at the final decision stage, a series of victories in various forums with different players is required. A determined blocking force does not have to win in every forum. It only has to win one—the primary full committee, for example—to bring the processing of the bill, however temporarily, to a halt. It may use such victories to stall out the whole process of consideration or to exact substantial concessions from proponents and transform the legislation to its liking.

The external political stream, including public opinion, may be generally quite supportive of a large-scale policy. Even so, policy leaders cannot assume that this external support, and even internal consensus building, will be sufficient to overcome all internal obstacles. For one thing, one bill has to compete for the attention and efforts of allies who are also preoccupied with many other bills as well as other demands. Tacit support may have been achieved among allies in Congress and the executive branch, but this may be insufficient to overcome obstacles that have developed. Proponents need coordinated active support visible enough for both waverers and opponents to perceive that serious political momentum is building for a policy initiative. They need a surplus of support to continue through the various skirmishes that accompany negotiating the congressional obstacle course—support that can be called forth in a timely fashion to keep the bill moving.

In addition to their efforts on consensus building, such leaders also must mobilize sufficient forces to deter the blocking forces or, if it comes to it, to defeat them. There is a delicate balance involved in such mobilization. On the one hand, the policy leader does not want to damage the aura of consensus he or she has striven so mightily to construct. On the other hand, he or she needs to rally internal and external allies to prepare for and perhaps actually engage in political warfare. Both preparatory activities and actual political attack have the potential to upset the carefully nurtured consensus. Opponents will undoubtedly highlight even preparatory mobilizing activities as proof that the seeming consensus for a bill is a screen behind which proponents are seeking partisan advantage. From another point of view, preparation for political warfare can serve to warn waverers that continuing or joining the opposition may carry with it a significant political price. In short, mobilization requires gathering and coordinating the efforts of allies behind a single legislative vehicle sufficient to sustain its movement.

Mobilizing for Criminal Law Reform

The defeat of the criminal code bill did not mean the end of efforts to reform federal criminal law. The very next week after the defeat of the code, Thurmond's chief counsel for the Judiciary Committee, Vinton D. Lide, held a meeting to regroup. In addition to Thurmond's staff of Lide, Paul Summit, and Eric Hultman, John Nash, Senator Laxalt's chief staffer, and Steven Markman, Senator Hatch's chief staffer, participated along with Assistant Attorney General McConnell and his deputy, Marshall Cain. They put together a tentative list of criminal law reforms, including sentencing, bail, forfeiture, and the death penalty. The idea was not to codify the entire federal criminal law but to reform key aspects of it.

It was clear to Senate criminal law reform proponents that there still remained a broad consensus for several of the proposals contained in the code bill, such as sentencing and bail reform, and potentially for some others that were emerging. Most important, proponents felt that public opinion was with them. A 1982 Gallup Poll showed that 79 percent of the American people believed that the American law enforcement system did not deter people from committing crimes. Gallup also reported that only 51 percent of the American people had a great deal of faith in their legal system, the lowest percentage among

six nations studied. In addition, Gallup found that survey respondents cited court leniency as often as any other factor as
causal to the rise of violent crime. Gallup found only 16 percent worrying that the constitutional rights of the accused were
not being upheld, while 78 percent were more worried that criminals were being let off too easy (Gallup Poll, 1984, p. 165). Finally, Gallup found that 72 percent favored the death penalty
for persons convicted of murder (p. 251).

The Senate criminal law reformers also believed that the
leadership of the House Judiciary Committee was more liberal
toward the rights of the accused than was the public or most
House members. Affirmation of this feeling came the next week.
On May 14, the House Judiciary Subcommittee on Courts,
chaired by Representative Robert Kastenmeier (D-Wis.), took
up a bail reform bill (H.R.4362) that had been drafted by the
Justice Department and sponsored by Representative Harold
Sawyer (R-Mich.). The bill had a strong law enforcement orientation and contained a provision allowing judges to consider the
dangerousness of accused defendants in deciding whether or not
to release them on bail. Kastenmeier has a very strong civil liberties orientation and was not in favor of the bill. As with John
Conyers, the prerogative of a House subcommittee chairman
is to refuse to schedule the markup of a bill that the chairman
opposes, in effect killing it. However, Kastenmeier had become
increasingly sensitive to charges that Judiciary subcommittee
chairmen were bottling up law enforcement bills, and he scheduled the bail bill for markup. This was a most unusual move
for a subcommittee chairman who was not sure he had the votes
to win. Republicans on the subcommittee got help from an unexpected quarter. Representative Barney Frank, considered a
most liberal congressman, voted with the proponents of the bill,
and it carried by one vote. The subcommittee's favorable vote
put Chairman Rodino in a difficult position. He had counted
on the subcommittee chairs to bottle up the bills he did not
like, and now he had the bail reform bill out of the subcommittee with a do-pass recommendation.

During this period, criminal law reform proponents in
both the Senate and the Justice Department were deliberating
over what the final post–criminal code legislative package should

contain. The previous March, the Justice Department had submitted some individual administration legislative proposals in the areas of forfeiture, habeas corpus, and the exclusionary rule, the latter two of which had been recommended by the Attorney General's Task Force on Violent Crime. The political officials at Justice had been supportive of Senate Judiciary Committee leadership efforts on behalf of the criminal code, but they had not been out front publicly on the issue, nor had the White House been engaged. The Office of Legal Policy had run the legislative strategy for the department, but Assistant Attorney General Jonathan Rose was heavily involved in other priorities, such as the legislative proposals to alter the whole federal bankruptcy court system, and left most of the work on the criminal code to Ronald Gainer and officials of the Criminal Division.

The three Republicans on the Senate Judiciary Committee most heavily involved in the preparation of a new crime package were Thurmond, Laxalt, and Hatch. Senator Hatch was considered a New Right conservative, but as much as he might have agreed with some of the amendments that Helms, Denton, and McClure had offered on the criminal code, he knew that they doomed the legislative effort, and thus opposed them. Hatch had labored along with Thurmond on the code bill following McClellan's death and had voted for cloture on the code bill.

The staffs of these senators were not starting from scratch. They remembered the 1968 Omnibus Crime Control and Safe Streets Act and the 1970 Organized Crime Control Act scenario, which had produced multi-title criminal law reform bills. Senators and staff felt that a number of proposals had matured within the several criminal code attempts that could be put together into a new crime package. There had developed substantial consensus in the Senate over the sentencing, bail, forfeiture, money laundering, and drug penalty proposals, along with a scattering of other individual statutory changes.

One question was how much cooperation and sustained support they would get from the ranking Democrat on the committee, Senator Joe Biden. It might have been reasonable to expect little of either. Biden had first been elected to the Senate in 1972 at the age of twenty-nine. His election was an extraordinary feat in that he upset a well-known and much better financed Republican incumbent. His only previous public service had been two years as a member of a county council. Biden had campaigned on a strong anti-Vietnam stance and called for more funds for mass transit and health programs. He seemed destined for the fast track.

A month after Biden was elected, his wife and infant daughter were killed in a traffic accident, and he almost did not take the oath of office. Even though he assumed his seat, he spent the first term, in his own words, "treading water" with little involvement in serious legislating. He admitted later, "I paid more attention to getting my family and me together than I did my job" (Cohodas, Feb. 7, 1987). One resolution he made was never to let his job shut out his family. As a result, he retained his home in Wilmington and commuted home every night. Even though he obtained appointment to the Foreign Relations and Intelligence committees, as well as Judiciary, he accomplished little legislatively. He gained a reputation as being more of an orator and debater than a legislator.

On the Judiciary Committee, although Biden had supported the criminal code revision, he had not been a primary player in the shaping of the code bills. He generally supported Kennedy's approach and particularly his sentencing scheme. In committee, he had argued that his experiences as an attorney had convinced him that discretionary sentencing led to discrimination against poor and minority defendants, who received stiffer sentences than more affluent white defendants for the same offenses. On Judiciary, he seemed to be more active in the debating phase than in the preparation phase. Even though he offered amendments prepared by his staff, Biden was not always fully cognizant of their significance and was fairly often unsuccessful. In one meeting, when he was in the middle of explaining an amendment, a legislative assistant passed him a copy of his proposal, which brought his explanation to a halt. "Obviously, I don't know what the hell I am talking about" he cheerfully admitted (Ehrenhalt, 1983, p. 277). Biden's reputation was that he often thought that making a speech at a hearing was enough of a commitment on an issue (Brownstein, 1986).

Biden's senatorial approach began to change in his second term. He was to observe later, "I view the beginning of my Senate career as the day after my second election" (Cohodas, Feb. 7, 1987, p. 223). Biden became chairman of the Criminal Justice Subcommittee right after his reelection in 1978. As chairman of the subcommittee, he became interested in organized crime and the illegal drug problem.

Some preliminary analysis of the implementation of McClellan's Organized Crime Control Act done by the General Accounting Office, which was brought to Biden's attention by his staff, commanded his interest. The analysis showed that even though the Racketeer Influenced Corrupt Organization (RICO) provisions of the Organized Crime Act (18 U.S.C. 1961–64) and the Continuing Criminal Enterprise statute, part of the 1970 Controlled Substances Act (21 U.S.C. 848), passed under McClellan, had been on the books for ten years, the forfeiture provisions had been little used. These forfeiture provisions permitted the government to petition the court to have illegally gained profits, interest, or property possessed by the corrupt organization forfeited to the government, and were designed to cripple drug organizations economically. Very little in assets had been forfeited, however, and less than $200,000 in fines had been collected, hardly enough to do any significant damage to organized crime.

Biden questioned Philip Heymann, assistant attorney general for the Criminal Division, about the low figures but could not get a satisfactory explanation. One of Heymann's problems was that, through three administrations, no one at the Justice Department had even kept records of the names and numbers of forfeiture actions attempted by the department. Biden asked the GAO to do a report examining instances where forfeiture cases were attempted, and held hearings on forfeiture during July of 1980. During the hearings, Irving Nathan, deputy assistant attorney general, testified that the forfeiture provisions were still "untested" owing to unfamiliarity by departmental attorneys, DEA, and the Judiciary, as well as implementation difficulties in making cases because of unforseen problems with requirements of the act. Among these latter problems were:

finding the illegally obtained assets, establishing a precise nexus between the illegal activity and particular assets (proving that a particular drug deal resulted in the exact cash that the mobster used to buy his mansion), and establishing ownership when the mobster placed the assets in someone else's name. Drug dealers often transferred large amounts of money to relatives or their attorneys as they learned that law enforcement was closing in on them. Even if convicted, they could look forward to getting back a substantial fortune when they were released. Nathan testified that, because of Biden's questioning, the department had revised its RICO manual to give U.S. Attorneys more guidance and instruction in using forfeiture, but he also pointed out changes in statutes where legislation would be needed ("Forfeiture of Narcotics Proceeds," 1980).

Staff from the General Accounting Office and the Justice Department met with Biden's staff during the hearings and shortly after their conclusion in order to draft remedial legislation. Biden then introduced the result of this effort in his forfeiture bill in an attempt to remedy the problems and make forfeiture a major tool in fighting drug crime in 1981. One of the major changes was a substitute-assets section, which covered instances in which the criminal had taken action to place the illegally obtained assets out of reach. In such cases, the prosecutor could locate other assets of equal value owned by the criminal and ask the court to forfeit those to the government. For example, if a drug dealer had made arrangements for the proceeds of a recently executed drug sale for which he was arrested to be deposited in a Swiss bank, the prosecutor would ask that funds of an equal amount which the drug dealer had in U.S. banks be forfeited.

Biden's other pet project got started during development of the forfeiture bill. Edward Stevenson of the GAO team showed Biden's assistant, Mark Gittenstein, some preliminary findings of another GAO study investigating coordination problems in drug enforcement programs, which had historically involved several federal agencies such as Customs, the Coast Guard, and the Justice Department. The GAO team's preliminary conclusions were that there needed to be a national drug strategy that stipulates the roles of the various agencies, and one high-level official appointed to coordinate federal drug programs and policy (General Accounting Office, 1983, p. 54). Biden liked the idea and incorporated it into a "Democratic Crime Package" he was developing. In announcing the package on June 18, 1981, Biden outlined the duties of a cabinet-level director of narcotics operations and policy — who was to become known as the "drug czar." The official was to be responsible for all U.S. policy, resources, and operations relating to the illegal drug problem and the coordination of all related interagency efforts. The drug czar was to have authority over budget priorities and power to resolve conflicts between involved agencies. Biden also included the sentencing and bail provisions from the criminal code, as well as his forfeiture proposals, in the package.

Thus, as Republican leaders were putting together their package, they knew that Biden and other Senate Democrats were already supporting numerous provisions that had been worked over through the years of the criminal code battles, as well as developing some additional reforms, such as forfeiture. The working relationship between Thurmond and Biden was also surprisingly good. It might have been expected that the older, southern conservative Thurmond would be at constant odds with the younger, northern liberal Biden, especially given the social issues, supposedly a part of the Reagan Revolution, that were falling on the Judiciary Committee. This did not happen, however. Thurmond, while articulating his positions forcefully, ran the committee fairly and worked well with Biden to keep the work of the committee moving. Thurmond appreciated Biden's cooperative approach and commented: "He has represented as best he could the thinking of his minority and he has stood up for their rights, but he is not a radical or one who takes positions that are unreasonable. If it was left to him alone, I think we would be even closer in our actions. But he's got members who are more liberal than him" (Brownstein, 1986, p. 441). Staff who saw them interact got the idea that while Thurmond and Biden would always have to be wary as potential party competitiors, a genuine fondness was developing between them. Thus, in terms of both substance and working relationships, the basis for agreement on a bipartisan package appeared very solid.

It did not take the proponents long to get the package together. The new crime package, titled the "Violent Crime and Drug Enforcement Improvements Act" (S.2572, H.R.6497) was introduced simultaneously in the Senate and the House on May 26 with an endorsement by President Reagan. The Senate introduction was a completely bipartisan affair, with Republican sponsors Thurmond, Baker, Laxalt, Dole, Stevens, and Hatch, and Democratic sponsors Biden, Heflin, Nunn, Pell, DeConcini, and Chiles. At a joint news conference with Thurmond, Biden declared, "The fact that we have been able to develop a consensus on this legislation demonstrates that personal security and crime control can and should be a nonpartisan issue" (*Narcotics Control Digest,* May 22, 1982).

It was a little less bipartisan in the House, with all but one Republican member of the Judiciary Committee as cosponsors plus Democrats Sam Hall and Billy Lee Evans. The bill contained provisions covering sentencing, bail reform, drug penalties, forfeiture, protection of federal officials, the insanity defense, witness-victim protection, and miscellaneous criminal justice improvements. In short, it gathered together several criminal law reforms but did not attempt the complete coverage of the federal criminal law that the criminal code had offered.

The Senate Republican leadership had arranged a somewhat unusual procedure for handling the bill. Instead of being assigned to the Judiciary Committee for consideration, the bill was held at the desk of the Senate Clerk. This meant it would be eligible for consideration on the Senate floor as soon as the majority leader could schedule it. This procedure signified both the degree of consensus that had been built for most of the bill's provisions and the leadership exercised by Thurmond and his fellow reformers in mobilizing support.

Before the new package could be considered, an unexpected announcement attracted renewed public attention to the issue of criminal law reform. On June 21, 1982, the jury acquitted John Hinckley with a verdict of "not guilty by reason of insanity" for shooting and wounding President Reagan, presidential press secretary James Brady, Secret Service agent Timothy McCarthy, and policeman Thomas Delahanty. The significance of this verdict went beyond the issue of reforming the insanity defense. The Hinckley acquittal crystallized for many Americans the feeling that the criminal law had gone too far in the direction of protecting the rights of the accused criminal and jeopardizing protection of the public. Legal scholars could argue that the insanity defense involved very few crimes and only a minuscule number of murders and shootings, but the acquittal of an assailant whom citizens had seen on television trying to kill the president was a uniquely powerful symbol. According to an ABC news poll taken the day after the verdict was announced, 83 percent of those polled thought justice was not done in the Hinckley trial.

Based on Federal Court doctirne established by precedent, the judge's instructions to the Hinckley jury had stated: "The burden is on the Government to prove beyond a reasonable doubt either that the defendant was not suffering from a mental disease or defect on March 30, 1981, or else that he nevertheless had substantial capacity on that date both to conform his conduct to the requirements of the law and to appreciate the wrongfulness of his conduct. If the government has not established this to your satisfaction beyond a reasonable doubt, then you shall bring a verdict of not guilty by reason of insanity."

The doctrine governing the insanity defense for the federal system was developed exclusively by the federal courts—that is, Congress had never established it in statute for the federal system. The Supreme Court had not done much about it either, and had generally allowed development of the defense by the Federal Circuit Courts of Appeal. Further, federal law contained no procedure for commitment to mental institutions of persons who are found not guilty by reason of insanity. Under federal law at the time, if Hinckley had shot the president in Maryland, he would not have been committed under federal law to a mental institution, no matter how dangerous he still was. The District of Columbia code has such a provision, and Hinckley was committed pursuant to that.

Many states had statutes governing an insanity defense itself, but there were several variations. Although on a nation-wide basis the number of insanity acquittals was small—less than one-tenth of one percent of the presumed offenders who stood trial—there was evidence that the absolute number of insanity acquittals was increasing. Following New York's enactment of its Insanity Defense Reform Act in 1980, acquittals increased to about one hundred a year from about sixty previously (Caplan, 1987, p. 39).

The Hinckley acquittal resulted in almost immediate hearings by committees in the Senate and House on the insanity defense, and a wide range of reforms were proposed. At one hearing by the Senate Judiciary Subcommittee on Criminal Law held four days after the verdict, five jurors in the Hinckley case appeared, and wide media coverage resulted. All five testified that they believed that Hinckley had some type of mental disability that they could not ignore. Juror Maryland Copelin said, "We had that mental problem to deal with. We just couldn't shut that out." Afterward, Senator Arlen Specter (R-Pa.) stated that he did not think the jurors understood the instructions given them by the judge. Often senators try to capitalize on breaking news events to show their concern and sometimes to focus attention on pending legislation.

Within weeks of Hinckley's acquittal, twenty bills were introduced in Congress to reform the insanity defense. It became a symbol to the public of problems with the criminal justice system, and even though most defendants pleading insanity were in the state courts, the drive in Congress was to set a model that rebalanced the scales of justice. The fact that Hinckley came from a wealthy family that could afford the psychiatrists and expert lawyers needed to cast the requisite doubt in the minds of the jurors exemplified, for many, the condition of the present criminal law—that clever manipulation of a system too solicitous of the rights of the accused could get even the most obvious felon released.

The Department of Justice was on the horns of a dilemma. The Attorney General's Task Force on Violent Crime had recommended a new "guilty but mentally ill" verdict, but the recently introduced crime package included a definition of insanity that sharply restricted its use — the "mens rea" approach. Two days after the Hinckley verdict, Attorney Generl Smith was asked by presidential counselor Meese for Justice's views on ways to modify the defense. Two days later, Smith provided an analysis of proposals that stated, with respect to the guilty but mentally ill verdict, "This approach avoids constitutional problems and offers a jury an attractive alternative to the stark choice between conviction and acquittal." However, the memo recommended that the administration stay with the mens rea approach in the comprehensive bill: "If we were writing on a clean slate, the Department might consider modifying the insanity defense in the manner recommended by the Attorney General's Task Force on Violent Crime. . . . However, at this late date and in light of our commitment to S.2572, we prefer to continue to support S.2572, rather than delay the legislative process by changing our position."

The decision reached was for the administration to support the mens rea approach contained in title IV in S.2572. This approach narrowed the insanity defense so that it would be applicable only to those individuals who were so mentally ill that they could not form the mental state required for the crime. Justice's Criminal Division had recommended this approach.

On July 1, 1982, Attorney General Smith wrote to Majority Leader Howard Baker reiterating the strong support of the administration for the mens rea approach contained in S.2572 as "the most effective, fair, and sound approach to reforming the insanity defense." Although Associate Attorney General Giuliani, in testifying before Representative Conyers's subcommittee on July 21, recommended the mens rea approach, he pointed out that the "guilty but mentally ill" verdict offered the jury an attractive alternative to the stark choice between conviction and acquittal. He observed that the mens rea approach did not eliminate psychiatric testimony on a wide range of issues and could still lead to a battle of experts confusing the jury. In short, the administration was not going to fight to the last for the mens rea approach. Less than a year later, Giuliani's successor, Lowell

Jensen, testified that the Justice Department recognized the consensus that had developed around another approach, which
eliminated the volitional prong of the defense and shifted the
burden of proof to the defendant, and thus the department had
modified its position to favor it.

The insanity defense issue, while affecting few defendants
at the federal or state level, was a most controversial one. It
is complex in both legal and medical terms and goes to the heart
of the moral nature of the law. It poses the question, Whom
shall society hold blameworthy? The answer does not fall on any
simple liberal-conservative axis, as the subsequent debate revealed. Although there was intense interest in placing a reformed
insanity defense in federal statute for the first time, members
of Congress disagreed on the precise approach to take.

While the Judiciary Subcommittee on Criminal Law focused on the insanity defense, the main preoccupation of the
judiciary leaders — Thurmond, Laxalt, Hatch, and Biden — was
to move the whole crime package. They worked with the Senate
leadership and reached a unanimous consent agreement for the
consideration of the crime package. The agreement included
time limits for consideration of specific amendments and, in an
unusual move, specified eight controversial provisions that could
not be included in the bill or offered as amendments — among
them, the death penalty, habeas corpus, and gun control. In
order to achieve the agreement, Chairman Thurmond had to
agree to Senator Heflin's demand that the insanity defense title
be taken out of the bill to allow time for more hearings and additional consideration. Heflin had been a state supreme court
judge in Alabama and had definite ideas about the insanity
defense. He was also well aware of the debate in the legal and
medical communities over it. Thurmond then pulled the insanity
bills out of the Subcommittee on Criminal Law to conduct hearings at the full committee level. He also agreed to keep other
controversial provisions off the package, such as the death
penalty and exclusionary rule reform. One of the institutional
differences between the Senate and the House is that the Senate
often will process bills at the full committee level, while the House
seldom does.

Although the president had endorsed the Senate-developed crime package, the administration had not yet put on a full court press in favor of it. Instead, a two-track strategy was pursued — support for the crime package and, at the same time, support for individual crime reform bills the administration wanted, several of which had come out of the Attorney General's Task Force report and were being developed into draft bills by the Justice Department. The Attorney General's Task Force report had called for legislation to protect vicims of crime and witnesses, for example. The department developed victims' protection and compensation legislation, and the attorney general appointed a Victims of Crime Task Force to prepare further recommendations to assist victims, as the Violent Crime Task Force had recommended.

On August 16, the Senate Judiciary Committee approved S.2420, which would make it a federal offense to intimidate or retaliate against a crime victim or witness and permitted the courts to order restitution to victims. The bill was approved on a voice vote by the Senate on September 14.

The Senate was not only processing bills that would please the administration, however. Also on September 14, the Senate Judiciary Committee reported out S.2411, its version of the Justice Assistance Act, which authorized a grant of $125 million a year for state and local criminal justice improvement programs. Office of Management and Budget (OMB) director Stockman had sent a letter to the committee categorically opposing the bill in any form on budgetary grounds. As in the House, this plea was ignored.

By the second week of September, the crime package had fifty-eight cosponsors in the Senate and thirty in the House. The administration had gone along with the Senate agreement to confine the crime package to the original titles and keep other reforms out, but there was no agreement not to pursue these other reforms separately.

Concurrently, the Justice Department prepared a new crime package with more controversial reforms. The new package would be a presidential initiative. Departments strive to obtain the imprimatur of the president in as bold a form as possible.

A presidential endorsement for a bill is desirable, but not as strong as a bill submitted by the president along with a message to Congress. The president is often a key agenda setter for congressional action in that members of Congress know that, at the end of the process, the president must sign or veto, and that presidential priority will command not only public attention but also support from a considerable number of members of Congress. Nonetheless, presidential submissions are a resource that must be carefully husbanded, lest Congress be overloaded and confused as to the president's priorities, which happened to President Carter.

The new package, titled the "Criminal Justice Reform Act," contained three criminal law reform provisions: (1) insanity defense reform — the same provision as in the original Senate Judiciary bill, that is, the mens rea approach; (2) exclusionary rule reform — providing for a good faith exception; and (3) habeas corpus reform — providing greater deference to full and fair state judicial proceedings and placing a limit on the time within which state convicts could appeal to the federal courts.

On September 13, President Reagan sent the bill and accompanying message to Congress. In his message, Reagan reiterated his administration's strong support for the Senate crime package and stated that together the two bills represented a legislative program to protect U.S. citizens. He quoted from Attorney General Smith's testimony that: "The criminal justice system has tilted too decidedly in favor of the rights of the criminal and against the rights of society." Reagan avowed it was time "to restore the balance — and to make the law work to protect decent, law-abiding citizens" (presidential message, Sept. 13, 1982). This late submission really meant that the second package was more useful for public consumption in the upcoming congressional elections and for preparing for the next session of Congress. Congress likes to deal only with must-pass legislation at the end of a session, and members are anxious to get home to campaign in their districts. Nonetheless, the administration's bill was introduced by Thurmond in the Senate and eleven Republicans in the House.

On September 30, the Senate took up the Senate crime package. About the only opposition on the floor came from Senator Mathias (R-Md.), who still objected to the sentencing provision. Mathias offered an amendemnt to strike that provision but lost on a voice vote. One amendment that did pass was offered by Senators DeConcini and Pell to establish an Office of Director of National and International Drug Operations and Policy (Biden's drug czar). Assistant Attorney Generl McConnell had sent a letter to Senator Thurmond stating the Department of Justice's objections to the proposal, which Thurmond had read on the floor of the Senate as he opposed the amendment. Nonetheless, the drug czar amendment passed.

The Senate passed the amended bill by a vote of 95 to 1, with only Mathias voting no. Once the bill was passed, Thurmond moved to attach the entire crime package as an amendment to a House-passed bill (H.R.3963), which was a small bill dealing with supervision of federal prisoners in release status. The Senate leadership then requested the House leadership to appoint members to a House-Senate conference committee to reconcile the differences between the two forms of the bill as passed by the two houses. This was done to force the House to consider the provisions to the crime package before adjournment.

On November 24, the House, at Chairman Rodino's request, voted to strip the crime package from H.R.3963 and send it back to the Senate as originally passed. Crime bill proponents would not take no for an answer, however, and on December 2 they voted to attach the crime package again to the same bill. The second time, the matter becomes privileged in the House. This was designed to obtain an up-or-down vote on the House floor. This time, the House agreed to go to a conference. Subsequently, on December 9, the Senate also passed its version of Justice Assistance.

Rather than convene a formal conference committee on H.R.3963, the members had their staffs meet to try to work out a compromise in the areas of bail, forfeiture, and sentencing reform. Staff discussions progressed fairly well on the forfeiture provisions, but were stalemated on the other two areas. Then, several members of the House and Senate judiciary committees met on the weekend of December 18 to try to arrive at some resolution. Neither administration representatives from Justice nor from the White House were included or kept apprised of the progress of the weekend discussions. The members had decided that they did not want representatives from what they saw as opposing groups, chiefly Justice and the ACLU, on tap, because then members attuned to these groups would continuously step out of the room to check proposals, and movement on an agreement would bog down. Thus, even though Assistant Attorney General McConnell had offered to be available, neither he nor anyone else from Justice was consulted.

What the members did was essentially to gather together a few bills previously approved by one chamber or the other, along with a few other ideas. Rodino insisted that the House had not had sufficient time to consider the sentencing and bail provisions, but that if they were left out of the bill under consideration, he would see they were considered in the next Congress. This was the one time the commitment of the Senate leaders to the package faltered. Rodino's offer was difficult for criminal law reform proponents. Several of the key elements that applied across the board to federal criminal offenses — for example, sentencing and bail — were left out. Thurmond and Biden decided to salvage what they could and went along with Rodino. They had worked so long on various criminal law issues without obtaining a final product that they wanted to accomplish something.

The result became known as the "mini-crime bill." It included: Justice Assistance, some forfeiture reforms, making product tampering (such as the Tylenol poisoning) a federal crime, the drug czar, and a new federal career-criminal statute. This latter provision, the champion of which was Senator Specter, would have established federal jurisdiction over and a mandatory fifteen-year sentence for the commission of armed robbery or burglary by any person who had previously been convicted of such offenses. This was a change designed to involve the federal government in incarcerating serious repeat offenders facing state and local jurisdictions. Mindful of earlier opposition by state and local officials to expanded federal jurisdiction in the criminal code, the drafters included a provision that a federal prosecutor, before he could begin prosecution under the career-criminal statute, would have to secure the approval of the state or local prosecutor where the third offense had occurred.

Rodino and Judiciary members wasted no time in quickly processing the mini-crime bill, despite the fact that some of its provisions had not been passed by the House Judiciary Committee or its subcommittees. They took it up on the very next day on the floor of the House under suspension of the rules. Representative Hughes, chief sponsor of the House bill, praised it as a useful anticrime package, while Representative Kindness argued that it amounted to "a pitiful dribble of legislation." However, it passed by a vote of 271 to 27 at 5:30 P.M. The Senate took it up immediately thereafter and passed it by voice vote at 2:00 A.M. the next morning. Congress most often works at a glacial pace, but when time is short, and there is substantial agreement among key members, Congress can move legislation with blinding speed. Members know this and often wait until the end of a session when the dissenters are at a disadvantage in even learning about what is happening and are hard put to alert their congressional allies to stop the legislation. The Justice Department got caught in just such a situation.

Officials at the Justice Department were dismayed at the final result. Not only did the bill not include the big-ticket reform items of bail and sentencing, but it included the drug czar and the Justice Assistance program that the administration had opposed. Justice officials also anticipated a possible constitutional problem with the career-criminal provision. The requirement for federal prosecutors to obtain state prosecutor permission before prosecuting was felt to violate the president's, and derivatively the executive branch's, constitutional responsibility to see that the laws are "faithfully executed."

Justice officials signaled almost immediately that they were seriously considering recommending a veto. All bills passed by Congress are prepared for the president's signature by the Legislative Reference Division of OMB, which coordinates a clearance process much like the one for proposed bills. Specifically, OMB asks all departments and agencies with interest and expertise relating to a bill to provide an analysis of it, and a recommendation for signature or veto. This is the formal part of the process. The significant part is the politicking by and among career officials, political appointees of the various agencies, White House staff, and members of Congress for and against the bill.

One of the reasons that departments lobby at every stage of the legislative process is to avoid the situation in which a bill arrives on the president's desk that would be politically difficult or embarrassing for him to veto. The proponents of the mini-crime bill had President Reagan in just such a situation. A veto would make it appear that Reagan was backing off his strong anticrime stance by rejecting a bill that appeared to crack down on crime. The specifics might be hard to explain, with titles like "justice assistance" and "career criminal" in the bill. However, the election had just taken place, and it would be two years until another one—time to pass crime legislation more to the administration's liking. In addition, Attorney General Smith doubted that the public visibility of the mini-crime bill was very high and that a significant negative public reaction would result. He was free to make the decision on the merits, and he felt that the drug czar provision, as it was drafted in the bill, was terrible.

Justice officials were not the only departmental officials involved. The Treasury and Commerce Departments also have law enforcement duties, and the Defense Department had just been given new responsibilities for international drug-trafficking surveillance. The State Department and CIA were also affected because of their international drug traffic control and surveillance activities. Opposition to the drug czar was led by Justice officials but was virtually unanimous within the administration. Among those opposed were Treasury, Defense, State, the CIA, the FBI, the IRS, DEA, Customs, and the Coast Guard. In addition, outside groups such as the International Association of Chiefs of Police and the National Association of Attorneys General stated their opposition.

Senator Thurmond and other Judiciary members met with Deputy Attorney General Schmults and Assistant Attorney General McConnell in order to urge that Justice not recommend a veto. Schmults told the senators that Smith was opposed to the drug czar or to any kind of compromise on it. Smith and other Justice officials, assessing the risks of obtaining what they considered to be stronger criminal law reform legislation in the next Congress, decided they were not going to settle for an inadequate bill.

McConnell sent Justice's recommendation for a veto of the bill to OMB on December 30, 1982. Justice's analysis drew attention to the language in the bill providing that the drug czar would have "responsibility for the coordination and direction of all Federal efforts by the numerous agencies" and would have "broad authority and responsibility for making management, policy, and budgetary decisions with respect to all Federal Agencies involved in attacking this (drug) problem." The analysis concluded: "The creation of such a super-Cabinet official and office, with the power to direct the drug enforcement operations of other Cabinet officers, would alter the very nature of our Cabinet system. It would promote friction and disrupt law enforcement with another bureaucratic layer in the chain of command."

Congressional supporters of a presidential signature requested and obtained a meeting with the president. On February 7, 1983, Senators Thurmond, Biden, and Specter, and Representatives Hughes and Sawyer, met with President Reagan, Attorney General Smith, and Vice-President Bush. Reagan told the members that he had "great doubts" about the wording in the bill that would give the drug czar, who would hold a cabinet-level post, authority over the attorney general and other cabinet officers.

Thurmond suggested that if Reagan would sign the bill, Congress could then pass additional legislation to smooth out the troublesome wording. The president knew that if he signed it, Thurmond would try to make good on his promise to "fix the wording," but this would not bind the other congressmen. The administration would then have lost all leverage, having given them the drug czar and Justice Assistance. McConnell had warned Meese and White House legislative chief Duberstein by citing the example of then President Ford, who had been given assurances in writing that remedial legislation would be passed subsequent to his signing Securities Acts Amendments of 1975, only to see the promise go unfulfilled. The only promise President Reagan made was that he would "soul-search" before making a decision. Senator Biden told reporters afterwards, "If this falls apart, if this thing falls down, I think the ball game is over, and school is out . . . there will be no anticrime legislation in the Reagan Administration" (Hobbs, 1983).

Editorial commentary was split. The *Washington Post* urged approval, but the *New York Times* recommended veto. The Justice Department got some editorial assistance from an unlikely quarter, Representative John Conyers. In a guest editorial in the *Washington Post,* Conyers (1983) charged that, of the seven provisions of the bill, "only one, the Justice Assistance Act, is even remotely related to crime control." Conyers blasted the career-criminal provision and said that the drug czar "adds another bureaucratic layer to an already confused federal drug effort."

The presidential soul-searching resulted in a veto on January 14. In his veto message, Reagan led his statement of reasons with a reiteration of support for the Senate-approved crime package (S.2572), which had passed 95 to 1, and explicitly objected to the mini-crime bill's omission of bail and sentencing reform. The message went on to state the administration's objections to the drug czar and career-criminal provisions. The message concluded by calling for passage of the substantive criminal law reforms in sentencing, bail, exclusionary rule, the insanity defense, and other areas. The administration was going to weather the political heat over the veto and try again in the next Congress.

The heat was not long in coming. Senator Biden attacked the "Justice Department's refusal to seriously consider any compromise on this crime bill" (Maitland, 1981, p. 47). Biden said that the plan was to pass legislation focusing on resources and coordination in the 97th Congress and get on to the more difficult issues of bail and sentencing in the 98th. Biden complained, "The President has destroyed this plan with his veto and perhaps scuttled any chance of meaningful crime legislation in the next two years as a result" (*Law Enforcement News,* Feb. 7, 1983, p. 1). Some of the heat came from the president's own party. Senator Specter complained, "We were telling them head-on that the important issue of the war on crime is riding on our ability to deliver crime legislation" (*Law Enforcement News*). Representative Sawyer criticized the attorney general: "On this crime thing, (Smith) doesn't know what he is talking about" (Hoogterp, 1983). When Attorney General Smith appeared to testify before a Senate Judiciary Committee hearing on organized crime on January 27, Senators Biden and Specter took the opportunity to express their displeasure with the president's veto of the mini-crime bill in no uncertain terms.

Within hours of President Reagan's veto of the mini-crime bill, Justice Department officials were preparing an omnibus crime reform bill that essentially combined the elements of the previous year's Senate-prepared bill (S.2572) and the administration's more controversial Crime Reform Bill (S.2903). The strategy was to lay out the entire agenda for criminal law reform and announce it, while letting the policy leaders in Congress know that the administration was willing to deal on what would be processed. Numerous meetings with other agencies with law enforcement responsibilities, such as Treasury and Commerce, resulted in a finished bill by February 25. Jensen of Justice's Criminal Division and McConnell went to the White House to meet with presidential counselor Edwin Meese to get the final sign-off. Meese liked the bill but not the proposed title, the "Domestic Defense Act." They agreed on the "Comprehensive Crime Control Act." It included what were becoming the consensus items, at least on the Senate side — sentencing, bail, forfeiture, drug penalties, and numerous other smaller changes. It also included the controversial items — the death penalty, the insanity defense, the exclusionary rule, and habeas corpus.

Proposals for reform of aspects of federal criminal law kept coming from outside groups as well. On January 19, the American Psychiatric Association adopted a resolution recommending tightening of the insanity defense to protect the public against the premature release of potentially dangerous individuals, and suggested that psychiatric testimony be limited to the defendant's mental condition and not permit conclusions on whether the defendant was sane at the time of the crime. This was followed on January 27 by the joint recommendation of two American Bar Association committees that the defense be restricted.

Two days before he sent the bill to Congress, President Reagan hosted a meeting in the Cabinet room at the White House for congressional leaders and administration officials. Among those present from the administration, in addition to Reagan, were Vice-President Bush, Meese, Smith, Giuliani, and McConnell. A White House meeting of this type is about the most sought-after introduction for a department bill there is. It is meant to stress presidential priority and, by including members of both parties, is intended to signal a willingness to cooperate if the other participants will. Congressional members from both parties attending were Senators Thurmond, Laxalt, Stevens (R-Alas.), and Specter (R-Pa.), and Representatives Fish (R-N.Y.), Lungren (R-Calif.), Hughes (D-N.J.), and Conyers (D-Mich.).

Following brief introductions by the president and the attorney general concerning the importance they placed upon the bill, Giuliani and McConnell went through the highlights of the bill's contents. Reagan used the soft approach and took pains to point out that while the bill included the catalogue of what the administration desired, he knew that "strategies" were being worked out headed by Justice for processing of the components. This signaled the administration's willingness to compromise to obtain final passage of a bill.

President Reagan sent the bill to Congress on March 16. In his transmittal message, he stressed the bill's heritage — the Senate bill of the previous Congress (S.2572) — and the critical elements the proposed Comprehensive Crime Control Act shared with that bill: sentencing, bail, and forfeiture. Reagan called upon the 98th Congress "to secure, at long last, passage of critically needed substantive criminal law reform." The administration was going for the big-ticket substantive items — not gimmicks.

Senators Thurmond and Laxalt introduced the administration's bill (S.289) in the Senate, and all Republicans on the Judiciary Committee, with the exception of Representative Sawyer, introduced it in the House. However, House Judiciary Chairman Rodino made it known that the committee would not be taking up the bill as a package but would pursue an agenda of individual reforms.

The executive branch was not the only arm of government busy preparing criminal law reform proposals. The judicial branch, represented by the Judicial Conference made up of all federal judges, approved a sentencing reform proposal on the same day the president submitted his package, which also included sentencing reform. While a major thrust of the Senate's and the president's approach to sentencing reform was to reduce disparity in sentencing by reducing the discretion of judges and making sentencing more determinate, the Judicial Conference proposal, unsurprisingly, aimed at retaining as much judicial discretion as possible.

The differences between the approaches were significant. Where the Senate bill provided for presidential appointment with Senate consent of a Sentencing Commission, the Judicial Conference bill provided that it would appoint its own sentencing committee. The Judicial Conference guidelines were to be advisory and applicable at the discretion of the sentencing judge. The ability of the defendant or the prosecutor to challenge sentences outside the guidelines was not included. Parole was retained, but the Senate's scheme for grading offenses was absent. In short, guidance but not determinate sentencing was envisioned by the Judicial Conference proposals.

U.S. Appeals Court Judge Gerald Tjoflat, head of the Judicial Conference's Panel on Sentencing, said that the Judicial Conference wanted judges, or a combination of judges and lay persons with judges in the majority, to write the guidelines. Judge Tjoflat claimed, "A judge could make a substantial contribution to the fashioning of the guidelines, and many times those who have to work on them can have a greater stake in implementing them" (Cohodas, Feb. 12, 1983, p. 339). However, a Senate staffer commented: "If judges could fix the problem, why haven't they? We've known for 12 years we've had a problem. Why haven't they done something? There is a reluctance to have people in the middle of the problem try to solve it" (p. 339).

House Judiciary did not waste any time demonstrating its priorities in taking up Hughes's Justice Assistance bill once again on April 6, which it reported by voice vote.

On March 28, 1983, the staff of Senator Laxalt's Sub-committee on Criminal Law convened a meeting of Senate Judiciary Republican staffers and Department of Justice officials to discuss strategy for processing the administration's crime bill, which had been referred to the subcommittee. It was announced that Laxalt intended to process the bill as one package as soon as possible — September at the latest — to provide a year to put pressure on the House to take an up-or-down vote on the package on the House floor.

On May 4, 1983, Laxalt's subcommittee held hearings on the crime bill. Although Senator Kennedy was not a member of the subcommittee, he took the time to attend. Both Kennedy and Biden expressed support for most of the bill's features but recommended deletion of the "controversial" titles dealing with the death penalty, exclusionary rule reform, and habeas corpus reform. During the month of June, discussions between Senate Judiciary members and their staffs proceeded on how to process the crime bill.

By the end of June, this came to a head in a meeting in Thurmond's office with Thurmond, Biden, Judiciary chief counsel Lide, and Assistant Attorney General McConnell. Biden said that he and Kennedy could go for most of the package if Thurmond would agree to delete the death penalty, habeas corpus, exclusionary rule, and federal officer liability amendments. Thurmond stated that he thought they could work that out. McConnell chimed in that Justice would go along, provided that the deleted portions would be allowed a vote after passage of the core bill. Biden said he thought that would be acceptable and would clear it with Kennedy. Thurmond indicated he would discuss the agreement with Laxalt. Subsequent conversations confirmed they had an agreement.

Harkening back to the days of the McClellan, Hruska, Kennedy, and Hart agreement, Senators Thurmond, Laxalt, Biden, and Kennedy agreed to cosponsor a "core" package taken from the comprehensive bill which included all of its provisions except for four: the death penalty, the exclusionary rule, habeas corpus, and amendments removing personal liability of government officials for constitutional rights violations. Separate bills would be introduced for these four titles.

In exchange for an agreement by Thurmond and Laxalt to move on the core bill (which would allow all senators to record an anticrime vote on the consensus items), Biden and Kennedy agreed to work actively for it. They also agreed to support Thurmond and Laxalt's efforts to have the four "controversial" items considered on the Senate floor as separate bills, even though they would oppose them during debate, and any and all amendments could be offered. This included an agreement to fight against any effort by the bills' opponents to launch a filibuster against the floor consideration of the "controversial" bills. Kennedy and Biden also agreed to urge House Judiciary Chairman Rodino and the House leadership to act on the core crime bill, and indicated they would support efforts to tack the crime bill on to House-passed bills in an effort to force action, if necessary.

Despite this, Rodino demonstrated no increased interest in any crime package bills and his subcommittee chairmen proceeded on their own schedules. Representative Conyers's Criminal Justice Subcommittee finally got around to processing a bill — on insanity defense reform. Although the subcommittee had held hearings in the previous Congress, the 97th, no bill had been reported out. During March and May 1983, the subcommittee once again held hearings on insanity defense reform. This time, Conyers scheduled a markup of a new bill he introduced (H.R.3336), which he offered as an amendment in the nature of a substitute. The Conyers bill, like the Senate provision, eliminated the part of the defense that allowed acquittal if the defendant, as a result of his mental condition, "was unable to conform his conduct to the requirements of the law." It thus eliminated the volitional prong — the claim that the defendant acted in response to an "irresistible impulse." It also shifted the burden of proof to the defendant. However, the standard of proof demanded was different from that of the Senate bill. In the Senate provision, the defendant would have to prove by "clear and convincing evidence" that he was "unable to appreciate the wrongfulness of his conduct." Conyers's bill required the lesser "preponderance of the evidence" standard, making it easier for the defendant to make his case.

In addition, Conyers adopted a different definition of insanity, which had been suggested by the American Psychiatric Association, defining it as "a severely abnormal mental condition that grossly and demonstrably impaired the defendant's perception and understanding of reality." During the markup, George Gekas (R-Pa.) offered an amendment to change the definition of insanity to the one in the Senate bill. Gekas argued that there was no precedent for the new definition and that it would confuse the courts and muddle the case law, particularly since it had not been reviewed by other witnesses or tested in the states before it appeared in Conyers's new bill. Gekas's motion was defeated on a straight party-line vote of 4 to 3. Gekas then moved to amend the standard of evidence to "clear and convincing," but this was also defeated. The bill was then reported out by voice vote.

On July 21, 1983, the Senate Judiciary Committee marked up the new "core" Comprehensive Crime Control Act (S.1762) cosponsored by Thurmond, Laxalt, Kennedy, and Biden—four senators who represented practically the entire partisan and ideological continuum. The four did not exclude all amendments. (They accepted Senator Grassley's amendment to make the theft of certain drugs from a pharmacy a federal crime, for example.) They successfully opposed any amendments that would threaten the bipartisan consensus. During the meeting, Biden explained the reasoning for getting behind the consensus package: "We've learned that the only way to get action is to agree on what we agree on and move on it, and fight over what is left" (Cohodas, July 30, 1983, p. 1559).

One of the close votes was over an amendment proposed by Senator DeConcini to establish a commission to study the need for a drug czar. This risked a replay of the mini-crime bill veto. The four cosponsors asked DeConcini to withdraw the amendment, but he refused. True to the agreement, all four senators opposed it, and the amendment lost 8 to 6. The committee reported the bill to the full Senate by a vote of 15 to 1, with Senator Mathias the sole dissenting vote.

The next Tuesday, on July 26, Senate Judiciary reconvened to consider the three "controversial" bills that had been
carved out of the original bill. The committee voted to report
out all three favorably by substantial votes: Death Penalty
(S.1765) 13 to 4; Habeas Corpus (S.1763) 12 to 5; Exclusionary Rule (S.1764) 10 to 6. The committee also reported out Biden's drug czar bill by a vote of 12 to 5. Biden planned to offer
his drug czar bill on the same day that the core bill was voted
upon.

Department of Justice officials were convinced that they
needed to try to build support around the country for the crime
bill. Top Justice officials decided to undertake a crime bill public information effort to focus attention on crime legislation.
Departmental officials are often called upon to speak before associations of public officials, civic groups, and the like, around
the country, as well as to appear on television and radio shows.
Attorney General Smith and his chief deputies decided to focus
as many of these opportunities as possible on the crime bill. In
addition, Justice's Public Affairs Office was alerted to look for
opportunities where Justice officials could explain the administration's position on the bill. When Justice officials traveled to
major cities or even mid-sized ones, they were interviewed by
local media outlets and met with the editorial boards of local
newspapers. Stories and editorials about the crime bill began
to appear in newspapers around the country.

While federal law prohibits the lobbying of Congress by
executive branch officials, "lobbying" is exceedingly hard to
define, and the law is seldom invoked. As long as officials do
not urge the public to contact their congressmen to vote a certain way, or something similar, they are free to explain in any
way they wish why the administration supports one approach
to legislation rather than another. In reality, members of Congress expect the president and his appointees to explain and argue for their position. For the most part, they are counting on
it, because executive branch support is one of the major resources
behind the successful passage of much legislation. Senator Laxalt
explained the problem as crime package proponents saw it, as
well as their approach for solving it: "Our problems are in the

House of Representatives and our problems are mainly in the subcommittees. When you are confronted by a problem like this, if you can't make them see the light, you've got to make them feel the heat. It's no more complicated than that. . . . And the President is going to be part of this" (St. George, 1983, p. 2577).

The strategy of the crime bill proponents was to pass the core bill quickly and put pressure on the House to act. However, weeks came and went, and Majority Leader Baker did not schedule the bill for Senate floor consideration. Baker's problem was that he wanted a unanimous consent agreement that, in essence, reflected the agreement arrived at by Thurmond, Laxalt, Kennedy, and Biden. However, senators are strong-willed individuals and willing to play hard ball to obtain their individual objectives. Baker knew that one or more senators were going to bring up a death penalty amendment. Often senators will tell the majority leader overtly to put a "hold" on floor consideration of a bill, and he will usually go along for a time — until the political pressure builds to the point where the senator relents, or the majority leader determines he must proceed. However, sometimes a senator will quietly request a hold and only let the majority leader know why. Baker knew that if he scheduled the crime bill and those requesting a hold proposed a death penalty amendment, other senators would drop off the unanimous consent agreement, and the Senate would be embroiled in filibusters.

McConnell urged White House intercession with Baker week after week to schedule the crime bill, but Justice officials were not sure where the problem was. By the first of November, the identity of at least one of the senators refusing to go along with the unanimous consent agreement became clear. Senator DeConcini wanted an agreement that the death penalty would be considered at the same time as the crime bill. Senator Levin had indicated that he would filibuster anything guaranteeing a vote on the death penalty. Thus, the crime bill was deadlocked. However, by the second week in November, Senator DeConcini relented in his insistence that the death penalty be considered in the unanimous consent agreement governing the crime bill.

Meanwhile, the House Judiciary Committee got around to marking up the insanity defense bill that had been reported out the previous June. Gekas again tried to amend the bill to change the definition of insanity to the Senate definition, calling the subcommittee definition too broad and "an adventurous foray into the unknown." Rodino countered that "Congress would never make a change in the law" because to do so would require new court decisions. Gekas's amendment lost 10 to 19. Other Republican amendments met similar fates. House Judiciary reported out the insanity defense bill on November 21, 1983.

Back in the Senate, Majority Leader Baker was unable to achieve a unanimous consent agreement with all senators restricting permissible floor amendments. It was over two and a half months since DeConcini had relented, and Baker decided he had to make a decision. He proceeded to schedule the bill without a unanimous consent agreement, which risked tying up the Senate. The bill finally came to the Senate floor the first week in February 1984. The bill managers knew that a number of floor amendments would be offered, and they needed to keep potentially crippling amendments off the bill. Senator Mathias had tried to amend the sentencing title in the Judiciary Committee but had been unsuccessful. Now he offered those same amendments before the full Senate. He opposed the very concept of the sentencing title that provided for uniform sentencing. In the debate, Mathias called the sentencing provision "ill-conceived, inflexible, and potentially quite costly." He claimed it could be costly because it would add to prison overcrowding. Mathias proposed to delete the sentencing scheme, but he lost 85 to 3. Senator Metzenbaum offered an amendment that would have made it illegal for a federal official to tape-record a telephone conversation to which he was a party without the consent of all the other parties. Senator Goldwater, chairman of the Intelligence Committee, opposed the amendment on the grounds that it would not be acceptable to the intelligence community. Senator Thurmond joined him and read a letter supplied by the Justice Department that stated it would hamper law enforcement efforts. The amendment was defeated 51 to

41. However, while Thurmond and Biden accepted some amendments, there were no killer amendments added to the bill.

On February 2, 1984, the Senate was ready to vote on the crime bill as amended. The final vote tally was 91 to 1, with Senator Mathias, still unhappy with the sentencing provision, the only dissenting vote. The Comprehensive Crime Control Act had passed by an overwhelming bipartisan majority.

The Senate then took up the other "controversial" bills, according to the agreement of the four Judiciary Committee senators. In addition, Biden's drug czar bill would be considered. On February 6, the Habeas Corpus Reform bill (S.1763), which would make it more difficult for state prisoners to challenge their state convictions in federal courts, came to the floor. Senator Baucus (D.-Mont.) offered an amendment to delete the provision requiring federal court deference to state adjudication, but this was defeated easily by a vote of 59 to 17. The vote was then called on the bill, and it passed 67 to 9. The next day, the Exclusionary Rule Reform bill (S.1764) was taken up. It had a little more opposition than Habeas Corpus Reform. Mathias argued that the bill would send a message weakening the Fourth Amendment to the Constitution prohibiting illegal searches and seizures. "We ought to think long and hard before we send that message" (Cohodas, Feb. 11, 1984, p. 282). Thurmond retorted that the exclusionary rule "illustrates much of what is wrong within our present system of criminal justice. Instead of a system of criminal law in which the search for truth, the search for guilt or innocence, is the principal guiding objective, we have seen our system degraded into one in which procedures and details and form are elevated above all else" (p. 282). The exclusionary rule bill also passed handily, 63 to 24, with support coming from Republicans 42 to 6, and Democrats 21 to 18. That same day the drug czar bill passed on a voice vote.

Then came the debate on the death penalty bill (S.1765). The full Senate had not even debated this issue in a decade, even with all the activity by the Supreme Court and that of state legislatures trying to find a formula that would pass constitutional muster before the Court. Even though most capital crimes such as murder are tried in state courts, the significance of the change in federal law was that it might serve in some ways as a model for the states. The debate over the death penalty, although it affects relatively few defendants, is so intense because it strikes at deep moral values embedded in society, and thus makes a strong statement about the very nature of the law itself.

The only federal law on the books that carried a death penalty was homicide committed during an aircraft hijacking. S.1765 proposed to authorize death sentences for treason, espionage, federal crimes that also result in the death of another person, and specific instances in which a person attempts to kill the president. The instances specified were those in which a person seriously injures or comes "dangerously close" to killing the president. The effect of the Hinckley attempt was again being felt in criminal law reform efforts. However, the bill provided that before the death penalty could be imposed, the jury or judge would have to determine if aggravating factors, such as the crime being "especially heinous," outweighed any mitigating factors, such as the young age of a defendant.

The debate went back and forth, and then Senator Levin launched a filibuster against the bill. Senator Thurmond had argued that "society demands the death penalty for the most aggravated murders to send a signal that innocent life is precious indeed and cannot be violated without like consequences to the killer" (Cohodas, Feb. 11, 1984, p. 281). Opponents stressed the imperfect nature of the criminal justice system. Levin argued, "You can't cure your mistake if you put people to death." He also stated, "Many of us have a moral revulsion to the state taking a life" (p. 281). Finally, a cloture motion to choke off debate was offered. It passed 65 to 26, with five votes more than needed, on February 9.

When the Senate returned from the Lincoln and Washington birthdays recess, the death penalty bill went to a final vote. It passed 63 to 32, with Republicans in favor 43 to 11, and Democrats almost tied 20 to 21. A drug coordination bill also passed, but it was not the same as the drug czar in the mini-crime bill. Biden actually had the votes to pass his original drug czar bill again, and officials at the Justice Department knew it. However, in the interest of preserving the coalition behind criminal law reform, Biden had negotiated with the administration and Thurmond, and had substituted a more acceptable Drug Enforcement Policy Board chaired by the attorney general and made up of the Secretaries of Cabinet departments with drug responsibilities. In essence, it codified in statute Reagan's Cabinet Council on Legal Policy and charged it with coming up with a drug strategy and budget proposal for drug enforcement. It was thus acceptable to the administration.

Almost all the so-called controversial bills proved to be not so controversial after all — at least not in the Senate. Senator Thurmond concluded, "It's high time Congress woke up to the fact that the public supports these reforms and others needed to win the war on crime" (Cohodas, Feb. 11, 1984, p. 280). John Shattuck, head of the ACLU's Washington office, appeared to agree that, at least in broad terms, public support was behind his opponents. He lamented after the votes that most senators "have a fear of being soft on crime" (p. 280). The ACLU had fought each bill all the way but, deprived of its allies from the criminal code battles, could not come up with a winning coalition. Shattuck had called the cloture vote on the death penalty "a real blow" and predicted the bill would be hard to stop in the House if it was offered as a floor amendment to another crime bill.

Mobilizing — Another Look

Policy leaders follow a two-track strategy to move legislation. They must build consensus and, at the same time, prepare to attack opponents among the blocking forces. These are not mutually exclusive tasks; if pursued adroitly, they can be combined to minimize the number of members wanting or willing to join the opposition.

The building of consensus for large-scale legislation involves seeking out the right policy configuration that includes sufficient components to attract a mutually supporting legislative coalition. This can involve serious reformulation of particular bills. The attainment of consensus can serve to isolate opponents who, nonetheless, continue to possess significant advantages to block the legislation at key points, such as the subcommittee or committee stage in one house or the other. Policy leaders need to focus the attention of allies on moving the legislation and overcoming the identified sources of determined opposition.

Leaders in Congress can be greatly assisted in both consensus building and mobilizing efforts by the president and officials of the executive branch. Executive branch officials have additional access to external political stream forces as well as allies within Congress who can assist policy leaders in encouraging members to get behind a particular bill. Putting together such a mobilization effort is often necessary to overcome a determined opposing blocking force.

Now that the Senate had passed virtually its entire criminal law reform agenda, the effort shifted to the House, where the core crime bill as well as the other bills were expected to have a considerably tougher time. Following Senate passage of the crime legislation, Representative Hughes pronounced the omnibus package "dead on arrival" in the House (Stone, 1984). Chairman Rodino stated that it was unlikely the House would pass the crime bill, S.1762, as a package because of differences over the sentencing and bail provisions. He also allowed that the habeas corpus and exclusionary rule bills would not come out of his committee (Cohodas, Feb. 11, 1984, p. 282). It would take some astute strategy to force the legislation past Rodino and his allies.

• 9 •

Overcoming
the Opposition:
Pressure and
the Use of
Partisanship

Up to this point, crime bill proponents had mobilized behind a compromise package that had passed overwhelmingly in the Senate. They had also demonstrated that the so-called controversial measures enjoyed widespread support. The bipartisan approach had worked well in the Senate but had produced no movement in the House. The House Judiciary Committee majority leadership had so far blocked consideration of the comprehensive bill.

Pressure and Coalition Building — Striving for Balance

Partisan and/or ideological differences can come to the fore with respect to a given bill in either house of Congress if any significant set of players, such as a committee chair or party leader, makes it such an issue. Such conflicts can readily be used at various points within the legislative process to stop a bill, even when there is substantial consensus in Congress for a particular policy thrust. As demonstrated, the fragmented nature of Congress provides significant advantages to determined minority opponents.

243

Many times, the only way to move legislation through Congress is by molding an agreement between leaders of both parties. The various philosophical strains and regional loyalties that exist in both parties, coupled with the lack of workable methods to enforce party discipline, make it difficult to ensure adherence to party direction as a routine matter. Also, the minority can use delaying tactics to tie up Congress, if sufficiently aroused. Thus, the bipartisan route is often advisable, but it is not always possible. There are issues where those involved perceive and seek to exploit the opportunities for partisan advantage, or use the party apparatus as a shield to protect interests they hold dear. Not infrequently, congressmen profess nonpartisanship but practice partisanship.

When one side uses partisanship, the option for the other is either to condemn the partisan behavior and hope some members of the other party interested in the issue will forsake party discipline, or to mobilize allies to attack the other side as being out of step with the public. This requires an articulation of differences with the blocking forces and statements about how unreasonable their demands are either substantively, procedurally, or both. Whether the consensus needed for final passage is then diminished or strengthened depends on how the positions of opponents come to be perceived. If members of the larger legislative body come to perceive that the involved opponents are blocking legislation that is, on the whole, desirable, and that continued delay may have unpleasant political repercussions for them, potential allies of the blocking forces will become uncomfortable under the pressure and move to join the majority. Alternatively, if the proponents are perceived as arrogant or unreasonable, the blocking forces will gain adherents. It is a continuing struggle for the hearts and minds of uncommitted members. Policy leaders must continue to search for a consensus configuration of policies to include in the package and, at the same time, put pressure on the opposition. Blocking forces seek to stall the processing of legislation or to exact significant concessions to convert the legislation to embrace their positions.

When bipartisanship is ineffective, the skillful use of partisanship is tried as a way to build pressure on the other side to force action. One method is to appeal to the electorate to encourage them to exert direct pressure on their representatives. This is what Reagan did when he appealed to the public to contact their representatives to support his budget and tax reduction policies, and the public responded. A related method is to raise the fear that the electorate will become aroused. Members of Congress often are concerned with anticipating what could crystallize into an election issue, rather than only with issues demonstrably related to vote intentions. They know elections are often won at the margins, and it does not take too much for an issue to cause sufficient vote loss to result in a vulnerable congressman's defeat. Often, congressmen seek to avoid risky votes that an opponent may turn into an election issue later. Bipartisanship had worked in the Senate for crime bill proponents, but not in the House.

Building Pressure for Criminal Law Reform

Criminal law reform proponents had a chance to achieve their goal, but the blocking forces would not be easily overcome. After all, the Senate had passed crime packages before, only to see them languish in the House. Also, Chairman Rodino had expressed his position that the crime package would not be processed as a whole and had not even referred it to subcommittee.

Rodino was in a good position to prevent the processing of crime legislation with which he disagreed. He had further enhanced the liberal philosophical bent of the Democratic majority on House Judiciary by selecting new members at the beginning of 1983. Howard Berman (D-Calif.), one of four newly elected liberal Democrats who joined the committee, recalled that in early 1983, Rodino spent more time than most chairmen lobbying to get new Judiciary members who fit his political specifications (Cohodas, May 12, 1984, p. 1098). In all, between the four freshmen and two others, Rodino signed up six new members who shared his strong advocacy of civil rights and caution in rewriting criminal laws. Of the fourteen committee members who had served in Congress in 1981–82, twelve had scores of 80 or higher on the Americans for Democratic Action liberal voting record ratings, and six had 90 or above. Even more telling were the ratings of the subcommittee chairmen — Edwards (100), Rodino (100), Kastenmeier (95), Conyers (80), Hughes (80), Mazzoli (60), and Hall (5). Representative Hall, the only Democrat with a score below 50, complained, "I am kind of the lone ranger as far as the Democrats are concerned" (Cohodas, p. 1098).

Basic philosophical bent was obviously not the only issue when it came to criminal law reform. After all, every Senate Democrat had voted for the crime package, and the sentencing and bail titles had been passed as separate bills overwhelmingly as well. Kennedy and Biden, in particular, had worked to ensure that the bills were balanced. They felt strongly that the bills had significant liberalizing effects in that they would reduce the disparity of treatment between poor and minority defendants on the one hand, and white and affluent defendants on the other. Kennedy had often declared that Democrats could not ignore the reality of the growing crime problem and the need for the law to respond to it. However, key Democrats on the House Judiciary Committee were not convinced, and they opposed the Senate's sentencing and bail approaches in particular.

The structure of the House Judiciary Committee lent itself to defense against the crime package. Whereas in the Senate crime legislation was processed by one subcommittee, House Judiciary had four subcommittees: Criminal Justice (Conyers, chair), Crime (Hughes, chair), Courts (Kastenmeier, chair), and Civil and Constitutional Rights (Edwards, chair). Of these, the crime subcommittee chaired by Representative William Hughes, who had been a state prosecutor, was likely to process crime legislation, but not necessarily the bills the Senate wanted — or if they were bills Senate leaders supported, not in a form they favored. For example, Hughes introduced his own drug czar bill after the mini-crime bill veto, but it was considerably different from Biden's version. In addition, Hughes introduced his own forfeiture bill, which did not include the substitute assets provision of Biden's bill, and Biden could not budge him on the issue despite repeated efforts to do so. The bicameral structure of Congress assumes that such differences will and sometimes should occur. On the whole, Hughes was actively pushing some crime legislation, which held out the hope to senators that if Hughes was successful in getting even his version of a bill through the House, they could compromise on the final form in conference committee.

Chairman Rodino knew this too, and he was in a position to bury any crime legislation he opposed simply by assigning it to the other three subcommittees. House Republicans were accustomed to calling the House Judiciary Committee the Bermuda Triangle. Veteran Judiciary Republican Henry Hyde observed: "The bottom line is politics, and election-year politics especially. They perceive the politics to maintain the status quo. If they do anything substantial, their constituency and the organizations to whom they respond, like the American Civil Liberties Union, will be unhappy. There's a reluctance on the part of the liberal element that dominates the committee to tighten the criminal code. The giant Bermuda Triangle is as voracious as ever" (Werner, 1984).

Democrats on the House Judiciary Committee often explained the committee's actions in terms of institutional differences. Rodino stated: "The House is as interested in passing criminal justice legislation as the Senate. It becomes a question of doing our thing and doing it responsibly. We have to work on things one at a time, on an incremental basis" (St. George, 1983, p. 2580). The Committee had processed a large package, the criminal code bill, under the leadership of Robert Drinan, just three years earlier. Drinan observed the underlying reason for not moving a package in the 98th Congress: "People are reluctant to pass criminal justice legislation with the Reagan Administration and a Republican-controlled Senate. They don't want to mangle civil liberties. Who knows what would happen in conference with the Administration and the Senate?" (St. George, p. 2580).

This is not to say that there are not institutional differences. With more members and subcommittees, the House is in a position to break up bills into smaller pieces and to give more representatives a piece of the action. Individual provisions can be debated at greater length. As pointed out earlier, however, this allows those who wish to block bills on policy or political grounds greater opportunity to do so. As Hughes observed: "Comprehensive legislation has a very difficult road to travel in the House. It's going to be very difficult to get some things out, like bail reform, and when you try to pass omnibus legislation, it's impossible. You jeopardize the rest of the provisions for the one or two that wouldn't pass. The problem is the structure of the Congress. On our side, it only takes one subcommittee chairman to block comprehensive legislation that has the vast support of the majority of the House" (St. George, 1983, p. 2580).

Chairman Rodino explained his view of the Senate's crime package thus: "The Senate crime package includes much of dubious value in the fight against crime. Some of the provisions should be judged on their merits and not as part of a Leviathan package" (Werner, 1984). Rodino did not, as a matter of course, block or split up all packages. In fact, at the time he was opposing the Comprehensive Crime Control Act, he was in the leadership of an effort with Representative Mazzoli, chairman of the Immigration subcommittee, along with the administration and virtually the entire Senate, to pass a mammoth omnibus Immigration Reform bill.

However, Rodino had become accustomed to burying many of the New Right's social initiatives. Bills containing constitutional amendments on school prayer were not scheduled for votes in Kastenmeier's Courts subcommittee, nor were busing amendments in Edwards's Civil Rights subcommittee. Edwards would not even schedule hearings on abortion amendments. One constitutional amendment for which Rodino not only gave hearings but also took the leadership on the House floor in 1983 was the Equal Rights Amendment (ERA). Rodino got the House leadership to place it on the suspension calendar, a House procedure that allows limited debate and no amendments. Opponents of the ERA were outraged. They lambasted Rodino for an abuse of the suspension procedure, charging that it is intended to be reserved for noncontroversial bills, which the ERA clearly was not. They wanted a full debate and an opportunity to offer amendments. As it turned out, the suspension procedure requires a two-thirds vote for a bill rather than a majority, and

Rodino had miscalculated his voting strength. The ERA lost on the floor by six votes.

Rodino had gained a national reputation for precision and fairness in his handling of the impeachment of Richard Nixon. When it came to processing legislation in the Judiciary Committee, however, Rodino was of the old school where the power of the chairman was to be used, and used strongly. He explained his posture in treating legislation: "I have spoken out and held out, did what I believed was necessary in order to make sure that our present system of government and constitutional guarantees aren't so easily eroded" (Cohodas, May 12, 1984, p. 1097). Constitutional guarantees are open to serious principled debate, and the balance can be struck in a number of different ways, as had been seen in the alternatives pertaining to the insanity defense. The Constitution, in many respects, is a broad document, and competing values come into play in trying to apply its provisions. On most specific issues, the balance between these competing values must be politically determined in large part. Constitutional law is not a monopoly of any one branch of government. As Fisher (1988) demonstrates, "It is a process in which all three branches converge and interact with their separate interpretations" (p. 3). Thus, while Rodino and his allies strove to advance their interpretation of what the Constitution required in legislating crime reform, Senate leaders and the administration worked just as hard to advance their interpretation. Given the momentum behind the crime package in the Senate, Rodino risked having the balance struck in a way unpalatable to him if it got to the House floor, and particularly if it went to conference with the Republican-controlled Senate.

Rodino was credited by many of his constituents with outstanding representation of his district, which includes most of Newark. He had been in the forefront of many legislative civil rights battles, including the Voting Rights Act. He equated civil rights and civil liberties. Representative Conyers, who represented much of Detroit and was one of two blacks on the committee, explained his approach, which in many ways complemented Rodino's: "The progress of black people in this country has turned on enforcement of the Constitution" (Cohodas, May 12, 1984, p. 1099).

There is overlap between the goals of civil rights and civil liberties in law, but it is not total. Members of ethnic and racial minority groups living in central cities are more likely to be victims of crime. Increasingly, leaders of these communities have come to call for stricter control of crime, and particularly drug-related crime. During the summer of 1984, representatives of the National Conference of Black Mayors made an appointment to see Assistant Attorney General McConnell at the Justice Department in order to express their support for the crime package and to learn what they might do to support its passage. They said that they had heard that a chief obstacle to key parts of the package was John Conyers, and they wanted to know what particular problems he had with it. McConnell told them that Conyers had expressed reservations about the effect of the package on civil rights. The representatives of the black mayors voiced their concern about the effect of crime on people in urban centers of the country and said they hoped to be active in supporting strong crime legislation. Later, they presented a resolution to the U.S. Conference of Mayors supporting the crime package they had adopted.

At the beginning of April, Alan Parker, chief counsel of the House Judiciary Committee, told Biden's legislative assistant for crime legislation that Rodino was reluctant to put pressure on Conyers or pull the bills out of his subcommittee. Two years earlier, Conyers had gone to the House floor and had given a scathing speech against Rodino and his willingness to act on the mini-crime package, which was then vetoed by the president. Parker reported that the House Judiciary Committee would wait to see what bills were reported by the subcommittees and then try to develop their own package. Hughes's staff also informed Biden's staff that Conyers was the problem. In addition, they voiced concern that if separate crime legislation were passed, the Senate might then tack on the entire package and also the death penalty and exclusionary rule bills that had passed the Senate.

Rodino and Conyers were not alone in the House in not wanting to see a number of controversial issues coming to the floor of the House. Numerous House members were relieved not to have to vote on controversial matters. Majority Leader James Wright (D-Tex.) claimed at the time: "If a majority of members wanted to bring these matters to the floor we would have done so in the past. The fact that it hasn't done so shows that a majority does not want to be distracted on these issues" (Cohodas, May 12, 1984, p. 1099).

Not all House Judiciary subcommittee chairmen were reluctant to move crime legislation. Representative Hughes was a former assistant prosecutor in Cape May, New Jersey, who had defeated incumbent Republican Charles Sandman, President Nixon's staunchest supporter, in 1974. Hughes, a classic policy entrepreneur, actively pushed legislation as chairman of the crime subcommittee. Republicans and some Democrats complained that he would take their bills and add some twist to them and reintroduce them as his own, a not uncommon practice in the House and one facilitated by the rules that bolster the position of subcommittee chairs. Hughes's forfeiture and drug czar bills were examples. Justice Assistance, however, appeared to originate with Hughes's crime subcommittee, which seemed surprising at the time. The year before he took over the crime subcommittee, Hughes had voted to abolish the Law Enforcement Assistance Administration program — the predecessor to Justice Assistance. Hughes argued, however, that Justice Assistance would be a more modest and targeted program.

Even his critics among law enforcement proponents gave Hughes credit for trying to move crime legislation. Without movement, there are no opportunities for achieving compromise later. The bicameral nature of Congress and the House rules facilitate such policy entrepreneurship and increase the opportunities for different approaches to problems to be offered. One question was whether the crime subcommittee was really addressing the priority issues. Bills on such topics as product tampering following the Tylenol scare, or computer crime following a few highly publicized cases of teenage hackers breaking into computer data banks, while relevant to the issue of respect for the law, would apply to relatively few cases. Issues with widespread impact, such as bail and sentencing, had not been assigned to Hughes's subcommittee.

One of the most active and articulate members on the Republican side when it came to crime legislation was Representative Dan Lungren of California, who had been elected to Congress in 1978. He was a member of the freshman class of Republican representatives who were not comfortable with the traditional opposition role the Republicans had played in previous congresses. That class became particularly critical of Minority Leader John Rhodes and accused Rhodes of being too compliant in his dealings with the majority Democrats. Rhodes retired in 1980 and was succeeded by Robert Michel (R-Ill.), who had been the Republican whip.

These new Republicans, such as Newt Gingrich (R-Ga.), thought that constantly compromising on Democratic bills ensured permanent minority status for the Republicans. Instead, they wanted to push their own agenda and use the House chamber as a forum both to express political opposition and build political support. These members became known as the "Conservative Opportunity Society." They worked together to challenge the majority by pressing for substantive legislation that represented their philosophy and speaking out on issues on the House floor. Crime legislation was one of the issues on their agenda, and Lungren took the lead. He observed later: "We recognized early on that if we just sat back and reacted to things, we would not be voting on things we wanted. We would be voting no all the time. So we had to use some foresight to establish what we considered to be the American Agenda and be pushing for that. We felt crime was one issue that fit within that framework, was really important on its own merits, and was something easily understood by the American public, such that it might be one of the better prospects for action" (personal interview, 1986).

Lungren had asked to be assigned to the Judiciary Committee when he was first elected, and he started out on the Criminal Justice subcommittee. Lungren was a member of the same law firm as former Governor Pat Brown. Brown called Lungren before the congressional session started and told him that he would be traveling to Washington to testify before his subcommittee on the criminal code, and that he considered it very important. Lungren too was quite interested in crime issues and became a most active participant in Representative Drinan's criminal code reform effort.

Normally, freshman representatives spend a large portion of their first term back in their district establishing themselves and building name recognition for reelection. Drinan's subcommittee, however, was holding meetings, hearings, and markups on sections of the bill, often five days a week, making it impossible for Lungren to concentrate on both district and legislating. Much to the growing discomfort of his staff, Lungren stayed in Washington and worked on the criminal code bill to try to make it as strong for law enforcement as possible. Lungren had a personal interest in the issue as well. His brother Brian was a Los Angeles police officer and had spent two years on night patrol in the Watts section of Los Angeles. Brian Lungren had seen at close range what the spread of drugs was doing to the crime problem and realized the difficulties the FBI and Drug Enforcement Administration were having in controlling their part of it. He felt that they did not have the tools required.

Through the dozens of markup sessions in subcommittee and at the full committee level, Lungren developed substantive expertise in a wide range of criminal law reform issues. He worked well with Drinan and tried to strengthen the legislation rather than obstruct it to make political or ideological points. For example, the sentencing title of the code gave the defendant the right to appeal sentences thought to be too strict, but did not give the right to the prosecutor to appeal sentences thought to be too lenient. Lungren offered an amendment, which the Carter Justice Department favored, to give the prosecutor that right. It won in subcommittee, but then narrowly lost in the full Judiciary Committee by 15 to 16.

Lungren became known as a serious conservative who carried a briefcase full of documents and played an active role on most Judiciary issues. In the 1980–82 period, Lungren was a key player in the attempt to pass the massive Immigration Reform bill, but he kept active in crime issues. He was one of the congressmen who advised the White House to veto the mini-

crime bill in 1982. In 1983, he was not even on the Criminal
Justice subcommittee or the Crime subcommittee, but he was
ranking Republican on the Immigration subcommmitee, which
was still trying to achieve passage of the Immigration Reform
bill. Nonetheless, Lungren continued to participate in crime
legislation battles and retained a leadership role through his
chairmanship of the Republican Task Force on Crime.

Through almost half of the 98th Congress, the administration had been following a bipartisan strategy for crime legislation. President Reagan, who by this time had been dubbed
"the Great Communicator," had refrained from blasting the
Democrats on the crime issue. Biden continually told McConnell that senators were grateful for the administration's forbearance. McConnell would tell Biden, "OK, but I am not sure we
can hold this off much longer, unless you can get the House
to move on the crime package." By the end of February, the
administration's forbearance began to wear thin. House Republicans decided that bipartisanship in the House meant something very different than it meant in the Senate — that is, House
Judiciary leaders were using it as a cover for not proceeding
on the crime package. Lungren explained: "Our feeling was that
as long as it was an issue that remained submerged or that no
one had to pay any political consequences from opposing it, that
we couldn't possibly ever hope to have it brought up in real substance. Over fifty-three weeks had passed without significant action. Playing the nonpartisan approach and working within the
committee process was just not working. They had picked up
some small pieces, but were watering those down" (personal interview, 1986).

President Reagan devoted his Saturday radio address to
the nation on February 18, 1984, to the crime package and
described several of its provisions and the reasons for them. He
then gave the House a warning shot: "This issue should never
turn into a prolonged partisan struggle, but it has. The Senate
recently passed overwhelmingly our Comprehensive Crime Control Act. The House has done nothing and continues to wait.
But wait for what? Bottling up long overdue reforms that would
provide you, the people, with greater protection against danger-

ous criminals is a serious mistake you should not tolerate." Following on this, House Republicans launched their part of the public relations effort by making a series of speeches on the House floor focusing on various parts of the crime package and calling for action by the House leadership. Lungren explained the House Republicans' thinking: "We did that without knowledge of when the opportunity would present itself. We did it even with the expectation in fact that we might never have that opportunity (that session), but that we could influence the 1984 elections so that members would be held responsible for their votes and thereby feel some heat at home and maybe change that attitude when it came up in the next Congress, or in the alternative some would be defeated and we would change the population of the House of Representatives itself" (personal interview, 1986).

Attorney General Smith, who did not often indulge in public appeals, also launched a series of speeches in which he described the need for the crime package and chided the House leadership for inaction. Other Justice officials, such as Associate Attorney General Lowell Jensen and Assistant Attorney General Stephen Trott, met with various law enforcement, state and local government, and victims' support groups and briefed them on the crime package and its stalled status in the House.

Some subcommittee chairmen began to react. Conyers took the House floor to state that his subcommittee would hold hearings on all aspects of the Comprehensive Crime Control Act that came within its jurisidiction. Hughes sent a "Dear Colleague" letter saying that his subcommittee on crime would consider all aspects of the bill that came within its jurisdiction. Conyers then proceeded to schedule a hearing on the provisions dealing with assault of federal officials for the end of March, and on foreign evidence and bank crime for the end of April. Hughes scheduled a hearing on the money-laundering title for the beginning of April. Of course, as law enforcement proponents had witnessed so often in the past, a hearing did not necessarily mean action would follow. Also, the House Judiciary leadership continued to refuse to hold a hearing on the Comprehensive Crime Control Act itself, and Rodino would not assign it to a subcommittee.

Proponents of the Comprehensive Crime Control Act decided that if the House leadership would not hold a hearing on the bill, they would hold their own. Under the auspices of the Republican Study Committee, they held a hearing which Lungren chaired on May 7, 1984. Witnesses included Senators Thurmond and Laxalt, Assistant Attorney General Trott, U.S. attorney for the District of Colombia Joseph Digenova, and Rudolph Giuliani, who had moved from the associate attorney general position to be U.S. attorney in New York. Also included were a number of representatives of the growing victims-of-crime movement, such as Roberta Roper, Patti Lineburgh, and Betty Spencer. From police organizations there were Robert Kleismet, president of the Union of Police Associations AFL-CIO, and Richard Boyd, national president of the Fraternal Order of Police. Prominent authors on crime and Roy Cohn, a well-known New York defense attorney, also testified. The purpose of the hearing was not to gain information but to focus attention on the lack of movement in the House on the crime package. Typical of the testimony was that of Roberta Roper of the Stephanie Roper Committee (a victims' organization named for her slain daughter): "I speak for a vastly growing number of victims who will not remain silent and inactive. We have suffered multiple victimizations beginning with criminal offenders and repeated and continued by a judicial system that ignored our needs and rights and deprived us of justice. . . . I urge you to approve House Bill 3997 to demonstrate our Federal Government's commitment to the people and to serve as a model of just sentencing procedures for all our states." Defense attorney Cohn stated: "We cannot allow a handful of bleeding-heart congressmen to thwart the 91 to 1 vote of the Senate, and the increasingly emphatic demands of Americans all over that they be given protection against violent criminals and hard-drug dealers who destroy the very fabric of our society."

While the hearing hardly received what could be called extensive press coverage, it did get some. More important, congressmen on both sides of the aisle started reacting. Non-Judiciary Democrats began nervously asking Judiciary Democrats what this crime bill was that they were being accused of sitting on. Some Judiciary Democrats responded by charging the Republicans with unfair tactics. Representative Hughes responded publicly the day after the hearing: "Unfortunately, the debate over crime in the Congress has taken a decidedly political turn and that really is regrettable, because crime is a bipartisan issue. This is what I fear is the case — they're exploiting it because it's campaign time again; it's the political season, and crime, of course, is a very sexy issue to be talked about" (Rogers, 1984).

Perhaps more important than the discomfort of many House Democrats was the galvanizing effect of the hearing on House Republicans. Members who were not on Judiciary became enthusiastic about speaking on the crime bill on the House floor, and they began volunteering to join in giving one-minute speeches on various aspects of the crime bill. Groups such as the Free Congress Research and Education Foundation, as well as Justice Department staff, drafted a constant flow of speeches on different package components.

The House Judiciary Committee continued to process a few of the pieces of the crime package. During the week of May 21–25, Conyers's subcommittee reported a bill to speed up the collection of fines, and the full committee reported a bill to penalize diversion of legitimate drugs into illicit channels. McConnell reported to White House legislative chief Duberstein: "While this activity heads in the right direction, glaciers move quicker. It would take the House a hundred years to process the President's crime package on this timetable."

On May 25, House Republicans and Justice officials had a strategy session, with Minority Leader Michel, Judiciary ranking member Fish (R-N.Y.), Lungren, Smith, Jensen, and McConnell in attendance. They discussed the fact that the Judiciary leadership's strategy was unfolding to allow a few pieces of legislation to get through, as long as it was on their terms. House Republicans had been told that they had better go along or they would get nothing. Justice Department officials and the House Republicans agreed that they would continue to press for passage of the entire crime package. They agreed, as well, not to accept piecemeal passage of minor crime legislation. In addition, House Republicans would resist efforts to pass what they considered to be weak crime legislation on the suspension calendar. The effort would be to intensify pressure during June to point out House inaction.

Crime bill proponents did not confine their efforts to a pressure campaign aimed at the Judiciary Committee. They also sought to reason with the House leadership. McConnell convinced Attorney General Smith to request a private meeting with House Speaker O'Neill to discuss the Justice Department's top legislative priorities: the Crime bill, Immigration Reform, and Bankruptcy Reform. McConnell doubted that O'Neill had paid very close attention to what was going on in House Judiciary. O'Neill's style was to rely on and support his committee chairmen. As congressional scholar Steven S. Smith observed, following O'Neill's retirement: "O'Neill did not intervene in committee deliberations, except in the most unusual circumstances, unless he was invited to participate. The only committees he monitored regularly were Appropriations, Budget, Rules, and Ways and Means. Like his predecessors, O'Neill avoided the use of party organs to air divisive issues or debate committee legislation, and he seldom challenged the policy recommendations of the standing committees" (Smith, 1987, p. 29).

It was a long shot that O'Neill would do anything, but McConnell convinced Attorney General Smith to give it a try by relating one of O'Neill's favorite stories. When O'Neill first ran for Congress, he went all over his district making speeches to any group that would listen. He was a tireless campaigner. On the day after his victory, coming out of his house he saw his neighbor, an elderly woman, in her front yard and he went over and thanked her for her vote. She told him, "But, I didn't vote for you." O'Neill asked her why not. She replied, "Because you never asked me." O'Neill concluded that in politics if you wanted something from someone, you must not forget to ask. Smith agreed to request the meeting.

Speaker O'Neill agreed to receive the attorney general in his office. McConnell was also in attendance but sat off to the side, while Smith sat next to O'Neill's desk and O'Neill sat behind it. Smith, a rather formal man and an accomplished lawyer, had been a partner in one of the nation's largest law firms. He knew how to make an argument for a position and planned to go right through the reasons that all three legislative priorities—the Crime bill, Immigration Reform, and Bankruptcy Reform—were needed by the country and, thus, deserved O'Neill's attention and support.

Smith brought up the crime legislation first, then the legislation to amend the bankruptcy laws, and then the Immigration Reform bill. With respect to Immigration Reform, he pointed out that it was hard to pass the bill because of the many short-term special interests that overcome the long-term public interest. Smith indicated that the public opinion polls showed overwhelming support for Immigration Reform. O'Neill responded at that point, "I don't deal in polls or public interest here. I deal in politics." Smith was not sure he had heard correctly and began to explain again, but the Speaker cut him off by saying, "Mr. Attorney General, you don't follow me. I deal with votes on the House floor and not these other matters. Floor politics is what I do here." With that, Smith made a few parting remarks and got up to leave. In walking Smith out, O'Neill observed, "Actually, in my view, the president just wanted to see the immigration bill passed so that he could veto it and make points with the Hispanic community." Smith was totally surprised; it was the first time in four years he had heard anyone interject partisan considerations into the immigration debate. After all, on immigration reform the administration was teamed with Rodino and Mazzoli in trying to get the bill through the House. This meeting further convinced crime bill proponents that a bipartisan approach was unlikely to succeed (McConnell, personal interview, 1986; Smith, personal interview, 1990).

The pressure kept building on House Judiciary subcommittees. Sawyer, sponsor of a bail reform bill almost identical to the bail title in the crime package, had been asking Kastenmeier for weeks when he was going to schedule a markup on his bill (H.R.5865). Kastenmeier favored a much milder reform and one that would not allow judges to consider the dangerousness of the accused in making bail decisions. He had twice delayed a vote but scheduled the markup for June 13. The subcommittee was controlled 9 to 5 by Democrats. The day before the markup, members of the Professional Bondsmen of the United States, who were meeting in Washington and who supported bail reform, visited every member of the subcommittee. It is difficult to determine if this changed any minds, but when the vote was called the next day, four Democrats joined all five Republicans in passing the Sawyer bill. This time, in addition to the liberal Barney Frank, Kastenmeier lost the equally liberal Patricia Schroeder, as well as Representatives Glickman (D-Kans.) and Synar (D-Okla.). It was becoming apparent that several Democrats were fearful of being labeled soft on crime in an election year. It remained to be seen if these four would back a strong bail bill at the full committee level, however,

At the same time, Speaker O'Neill was getting concerned as well. Ari Weiss, O'Neill's assistant who monitored the Judiciary Committee, informed Biden's chief counsel Mark Gittenstein that the Speaker was concerned about the political implications of further delay on the crime legislation in the Judiciary Committee. Further, Weiss reported that the Speaker was supportive of anything that could be done by Biden to move the Comprehensive Crime Control Act and that he had told Rodino that.

The House Judiciary leadership were hearing not only from Republicans about moving crime legislation; they were also hearing from Senate Democrats. On June 20, Senator Biden met with Representative Rodino to discuss the lack of action by the House Judiciary Committee on the crime package. Biden had been told that Senator Chiles (D.-Fla.) was prepared to add Biden's forfeiture bill to the Treasury Appropriations bill which was about to be processed in the Senate. Biden had also heard that the Republican National Committee wanted to begin radio ads about the Democrats' lack of action on crime. Biden urged Rodino to step up action.

House Judiciary did begin to move a few of the minor titles of the bill. On June 26, five bills were reported: H.R.5846, which increased fine levels; H.R.5919, which makes it easier to use foreign-kept business records in criminal trials; H.R.5872, to close some loopholes in the banking laws; H.R.5526, to close loopholes in laws covering escape from custody; and H.R.5910, making it a crime to possess contraband in prison. The committee also reported Hughes's computer crime bill creating a new federal crime of computer abuse, which was not a part of the crime package. Of the forty-eight parts of the crime package, twenty-eight had received no action in the House—not even a hearing.

That same week, Representative Brooks (D-Tex.) appeared before the House Rules committee in an attempt to get a rule for the insanity defense bill reported by Judiciary eight months earlier. He was sent away, however, because the House Judiciary leadership had failed to comply with Rules Committee procedures requiring advance notice in the *Congressional Record* of an application for a rule.

On June 23, 1984, President Reagan began to turn up the heat on the House concerning the crime issue. In a major speech on crime, for which he traveled to Hartford, Connecticut, to address the National Sheriff's Association, Reagan accused the "liberal leadership" of the House of "bottling up in committee" for three years the same crime package that had passed the Senate 91 to 1. He told the crowd: "Let them know that you're tired of waiting and that, at a very minimum, the liberal leadership in the House owes the American people a floor debate and vote out in the open on this crime package. Now, if the members of the House feel our package is unwise legislation, let them have the courage to stop hiding behind parliamentary maneuvers and say so publicly. Let them vote against these measures in full view of the people, and let them explain what gives them the right to ignore the will of the people. This they should have the courage to do."

On June 28, the House Criminal Justice subcommittee marked up Conyers's sentencing bill, but it bore no resemblance to the bill that had passed the Senate, and made none of the structural changes in sentencing practices sought by Senator Kennedy and other reform proponents. It did not contain a guidelines scheme and did not restrict judges' discretion. It merely instructed the Judicial Conference to collect, analyze, and disseminate information on the sentencing practices of federal judges. Conyers stated, "It may well be that disparity can be controlled by simply providing federal judges with more information about the practices of their compatriots" (Cohodas, July 21, 1984, p. 1801). Representative Gekas tried to amend the bill by substituting the Senate sentencing title from the crime bill, but he was defeated on a party-line vote. The Conyers bill was then voted out, also on a party-line vote, 4 to 2.

President Reagan hit the House leadership again on the crime issue, on July 6 in a speech before the Texas Bar Association. After reviewing all the initiatives the administration had undertaken to step up federal efforts against drugs and organized crime, Reagan declared: "Our core crime package has already passed the Senate once by a vote of 91 to 1. But in the House of Representatives, the leadership keeps it bottled up in committee. . . . So, I do have some advice this morning for the House leadership: stop kowtowing to the special interests, and start listening to the American people. The American people want this anti-crime legislation; they want it now; and with your help, they can get it."

At a press conference on July 24, Reagan announced that he had met with the House Republican leadership to ask them to try again to bring the crime package to the floor of the House. That same day, frustrated Senate Democrats added fuel to the growing fire. Senators Biden, DeConcini, and Chiles took to the floor of the Senate and amended the House-passed Treasury–Postal Service Appropriations Act by adding on the forfeiture title of the crime package, which the Senate passed and sent back to the House. (Subsequently, the House stripped the forfeiture provision.) In speaking on behalf of the amendment, Biden stated, "Our Democratic colleagues in the House are less than anxious to move this measure, for reasons, quite frankly, that confound me" (*Congressional Record,* July 24, 1984, S.9071). Biden had talked several times with Hughes on the telephone in an attempt to get him to adopt his approach and move the bill. His staff reported, "Biden was angry. You didn't need a telephone to hear him."

The House did act on July 30 on the five smaller bills previously passed by House Judiciary dealing with criminal fines, closing financial institution fraud loopholes, and so on. In addition, House Judiciary took up a major issue — sentencing — on August 8. The majority Democrats, however, did not use the Conyers bill reported by his subcommittee as the vehicle, but instead turned to H.R.6012, sponsored by Representative Frederick Blucher (D-Va.) and supported by Chairman Rodino. The substitute bill did include a sentencing guidelines structure, but it was a different structure from the Senate bill. More important, it provided that the Judicial Conference, the judge's arm, would establish guidelines rather than a presidentially appointed commission. Law enforcement proponents argued that it made sentencing more lenient by: (1) eliminating "just punishment and deterrence" as purposes of sentencing; (2) requiring imposition of the "least severe" sentence; (3) providing for release after completion of 80 percent of sentence imposed, subject to additional reductions to deal with sentencing disparity and prison overcrowding; and (4) making guidelines less binding on the sentencing judge. In addition, few proponents of Kennedy's guidelines structure were enamored of the provision that the Judicial Conference control the process, in that they felt judge's discretion had caused the disparity problem. Gekas offered an amendment to substitute the Senate language; this was defeated, mostly along party lines, 12 to 18. The bill was then reported out 21 to 10.

On August 9, Biden and Kennedy went to the House Speaker's office to meet with O'Neill, Rodino, and Hughes to urge action on crime legislation. Rodino argued that he had to respect the prerogatives of his subcommittee chairmen. Speaker O'Neill agreed to bring some crime legislation to the House floor in September. It would include sentencing, but it would be Rodino's version, and also bail and other items. In exchange, Biden and Kennedy indicated they would refuse unanimous consent to attach the crime package to other House-passed legislation.

The next day, O'Neill and Rodino issued a joint press statement announcing an "ambitious" Democratic crime pro-

gram and listed several bills they would process in the waning
days of the 98th Congress. These included sentencing, bail reform, forfeiture, insanity defense reform, drug enforcement
amendments, and foreign currency transaction amendments.

During the three-day period September 10–12, Rodino
brought five crime bills to the House floor—all on the suspension calendar. The drug penalties bill (H.R.4901) increased
maximum fines for drug violations and also included a forfeiture provision, but one that applied only to drug offenses and
did not include a substitute-assets provision. Biden's forfeiture
bill was much more far-reaching. Lungren protested on the floor
that the suspension procedure once again was being abused. He
had offered a substitute-assets provision in Judiciary that had
lost only 12 to 17, and he wanted a chance to offer it on the
floor. Lungren charged that just because the Judiciary Committee had narrowly defeated a number of law enforcement
amendments did not mean the House as a whole would do likewise. It was difficult to vote against crime bills with titles like
these, however. The bills that passed by voice vote under suspension, in addition to drug penalties, were: Trademark Counterfeiting (H.R.6071), Money Laundering (H.R.6031), and
Drug Czar (H.R.4028).

The drug czar bill had passed Judiciary in 1983, but
Rodino had not formally reported it until the day he brought
it up on the suspension calendar—September 11, 1984. It had
been jointly referred to the House Energy and Commerce Committee, which had not released it until early September. Now
the administration became concerned that this drug czar bill
would be tacked on to a Senate-passed crime bill, and there
would be a repeat of the mini-crime bill confrontation.

One loss for Rodino was the Extradition bill (H.R.3347).
The Justice Department had sought the bill to increase cooperation with other countries in extraditing drug traffickers and
terrorists. The administration's bill streamlined procedures for
extraditing such criminals sought by other countries. The purpose was to encourage other countries to agree, in treaties being negotiated, to simplify procedures for extraditing drug criminals sought by the United States. However, House Judiciary

had narrowly adopted two amendments, one by a vote of 16 to 15 and the other 16 to 14, making it more difficult to extradite people. Hughes managed the floor debate for the Democrats and spoke for the bill. Rodino directed his remarks to the two amendments the committee had added, and explained how he thought they had strengthened the bill. Lungren countered that controversial amendments that pass 16 to 14 should be subjected to debate: "We ought to have the opportunity on the floor of this House to vote these things, instead of bringing them up on the suspension calendar where no amendments are allowed and we have just a short time to debate them" (*Congressional Record,* Sept. 10, 1984, H9245). Republicans and many Democrats went with Lungren. On a recorded vote the bill lost badly, 103 to 307.

On September 18, Chairman Rodino suffered another setback in the Judiciary Committee in the markup of the bail bill. Representatives Glickman and Frank offered a substitute that would have narrowed the types of cases in which a defendant could be denied bail, practically gutting provision for pretrial detention on grounds of dangerousness. The ACLU had relentlessly lobbied against the pretrial detention provision. The substitute was debated vigorously for over an hour. When the vote was taken, five Democrats voted with the eleven Republicans and the substitute was defeated 15 to 16. While in subcommittee, Representatives Frank and Schroeder voted with the winning side; this time they voted with the losing side. Representative Kastenmeier then offered another substitute, which would have allowed judges to "assess" defendant dangerousness in determining the conditions to attach to the defendant's pretrial release, but not to refuse bail. This also was rejected, 13 to 18. The bill (H.R.5865) previously reported by the Courts subcommittee, which allowed pretrial detention, was then voted out by voice vote.

The tide continued to turn against the Judiciary Committee majority. Later that same day, the Judiciary Committee suffered another defeat on the House floor on the insanity defense bill. Conyers, Rodino, and Hughes carried the debate for the Democrats, and Lungren, Gekas, and Dewine for the Republicans. Conyers brought up the bill on the suspension calendar, and defended it by stating, "It restricts the insanity defense to its proper scope." Hughes urged passage and argued, "The bill gives Federal courts the tools necessary to protect the public from truly dangerous persons" (*Congressional Record,* Sept. 18, 1984, H9673). Rodino claimed the bill "will prevent abuses of the insanity defense and protect the public from dangerous persons without abandoning the fundamental principle of our legal system that moral culpability is a prerequisite to criminal responsibility" (*Congressional Record,* Sept. 18, 1984, H9676). Gekas argued that the bill contained an untested new definition of insanity that would confuse juries, and that he needed an opportunity to amend it. Gekas, Dewine, and Lungren all vigorously protested the use of the suspension procedure for so controversial and complex an issue. When it came to a vote, the bill failed to achieve the two-thirds needed by a vote of 225 to 171, which was 39 votes short.

That same day, the House leadership had also scheduled the Judiciary Committee's version of the sentencing bill for the suspension calendar. However, the communication between House minority staff and Justice staff was excellent and Justice was prepared to counter the move.

As Justice officials saw it, the danger was that Judiciary Democrats would succeed in portraying the sentencing bill as a crime-fighting measure, given that under suspension rules, there would only be limited debate. On September 16, McConnell's crack staff counsel on criminal matters, Cary Copeland, prepared a letter detailing the ways in which the bill was deficient from a law enforcement point of view and stated that the bottom line was that it was actually anti–law enforcement. McConnell ordered individual copies of the letter for each member of the House and stayed up far into the night signing them. They were hand-delivered the next day. House Judiciary members began to get inquiries from other members about the sentencing bill and were asked particularly about Justice's objections. Few representatives wanted to risk voting for a bill that could be labeled anti–law enforcement a month and a half before an election. On September 18, when the Judiciary leadership realized that they did not have the votes to pass their sentencing bill, they pulled it from the schedule. The drumbeat of criticism, coupled with anticipation of the coming election, was making many members leery of Judiciary moves on legislation that could be perceived as weak on crime.

The Use of Pressure Reconsidered

As shown, the fragmented and decentralized nature of power in Congress, as well as congressional rules, provides numerous opportunities for determined subcommittee and committee leaders to sidetrack legislation they oppose and move legislation they favor — provided they do not run afoul of the formal leadership in such core legislative areas as the budget or on an issue that has achieved status as a leadership bill.

The formal leadership, under normal circumstances, will defer to such leaders unless and until the political profile of the legislation is raised to a level where members perceive potential political danger. If noninvolved members of the majority begin to feel that they could pay a political price for the recalcitrance of leaders toward seemingly popular legislation, they begin to depart from their normal pattern of tacitly supporting the majority, and start to ask more questions about the legislation and its political consequences. The anticipation, not necessarily the reality, of public reaction through elections plays a key role here.

Proponents of large-scale legislative bills who believe that they have the better public argument cannot allow blocking forces to continue delay on a low-level basis indefinitely. They must raise the profile of the legislation, articulate the policy differences with opponents, build pressure, and isolate the blocking forces from the larger body of members.

The president can potentially play a key role in putting pressure on the blocking forces. If the public is in support of the policy thrust of the legislative package, the president can provide visibility for the legislation by speaking directly to the public in ways that other legislative participants cannot. The president's continuous access to the public through various media provides a skillful president with unique advantages in focusing attention on particular legislative developments out of the multitude of legislative activities. A popular president can raise the profile of a particular bill in ways other legislative actors seldom can. Skillful presidents use this power selectively in favor of bills that have a good legislative fit with their political programs and ones that offer the prospects for a winning coalition. The public provides the fundamental basis for building a winning coalition, and the sensitivity of other legislative actors to public opinion makes the public key to the president's governing coalition (Seligman and Covington, 1989).

By publicly accusing a blocking force of catering to narrow interests for partisan or other special-interest purposes, the president raises the stakes for uncommitted members. They must at least consider the electoral consequences of what will happen on a piece of legislation, if not for themselves individually, then at least for their party. Even though most House seats are considered safe, a major loss at the margin can create substantial power shifts within Congress, as the election of 1980 vividly demonstrated.

If proponents have, along with the president, already demonstrated bipartisanship and built a substantial consensus within Congress for a bill in earlier stages of the legislative process, their charges against the blocking forces gain credibility. Raising fears that avoidable electoral consequences will accrue to noninvolved members, as well as to members of the blocking forces, serves to isolate the blocking forces and diminish the deference they are accorded by other actors in the legislative process.

By the summer of 1984, House Judiciary Committee leaders were feeling the pressure that the president and congressional crime package proponents were putting on them. They attempted to defuse the issues by moving some criminal law legislation that would give other members an opportunity to establish a legislative record on crime. Proponents of the Comprehensive Crime Control Act had stepped up their efforts to articulate the differences between these piecemeal efforts and the larger package. The problem was that they were running out of time as Congress moved toward adjournment. If they could not continue to build the pressure fast enough as the election neared, the crime package would get caught in the end-of-session scheduling logjam.

· 10 ·

Seizing
the Strategic
Opportunity:
A Policy Initiative
Becomes Law

The crime package forces had been somewhat successful, at this point, in putting pressure on the Judiciary leadership and deflecting what they considered to be weak crime legislation. However, they were in a bind in achieving passage of the crime package itself. Congress was scheduled to adjourn October 4, and they were running out of time. As had happened so many times before, it appeared likely that yet another Senate-passed crime package would die upon adjournment in the House. They badly needed a way to circumvent the Judiciary Committee and get the bill to the floor.

Gaining Opportunity for Passage

The internal workings of Congress play a critical role in determining whether or not even a bill that enjoys widespread policy consensus and has political momentum behind it will have the opportunity for final enactment. The flow of legislation to the floors of the two houses of Congress is extremely uneven and far from orderly. Various contending forces involved in processing a bill often delay bargaining and compromise, seeking

269

additional leverage—unless and until pressure builds and they are forced to act.

Pressure can arise from a combination of sources, including demands for action from the political stream, initiatives by the president, initiatives by the formal leadership, and time constraints. With respect to pressures from the political stream, a crystallizing event or coming together of public opinion, such as the Supreme Court's decision invalidating the federal law prohibiting flag burning and the subsequent public reaction, can force a bill to the floor. Presidential initiative is illustrated by President Reagan's request for his budget and tax initiatives to be considered in a reconciliation bill outside the normal budgetary and appropriations process. Initiatives by formal leaders are occasionally the moving force, as illustrated by the actions of James Wright, who, after taking over as Speaker of the House in 1987, pushed highway, water project, trade, and other bills to the floor and obtained highly restrictive rules to contain amending activity and limit floor debate (Bach and Smith, 1988). Time pressures arise from such sources as expiring program authorizations and appropriations, and particularly the approaching end of a Congress, when all activity on bills not passed will be moot and must begin again in the next Congress.

As discussed previously, the formal leadership are primarily engaged in scheduling activities and seek to arrange for legislation that has cleared committees to be considered on the floor in concert with their party's priorities. However, they are normally constrained by the actions of committee chairs, in that they cannot schedule until the bill has been reported. Even when a bill has been reported, leaders must face a host of political problems that can cause delay and tie up floor consideration. The processing of the crime bill in the Senate is a good example of how those not fully satisfied can delay floor consideration by implied threat of warfare on the floor that would disrupt the processing of other legislation.

The minority, such as the Republicans in the House, are in an even more precarious position. If the majority on a committee have not reported out a bill, there is little they can do to force it to the floor without the extraordinary assistance of some significant segment of the majority. This is not impossible, as the minority Republicans demonstrated by teaming up with Southern Democrats to move Reagan's early budget and tax packages, but it is difficult. The majority also control the Rules committee and, in recent years, that committee has become even more of a tool of the majority leadership with which to set and control the floor agenda and to protect bills from unanticipated attacks on the floor (Bach and Smith, 1988).

The complicated rules and procedures of Congress are at once critical to the movement of legislation to the floor and pivotal for the form in which it reaches the floor. Rules govern procedure, but procedure determines the substance that can be considered and how likely a bill is to pass. Thus, even though a policy leader may have succeeded in building an overwhelming consensus for a bill, it will not necessarily arrive on the floor at all, or in a form that will make it possible to be enacted. In 1982, the Senate had passed an Immigration Reform bill which achieved a consensus on House Judiciary, but minority opponents convinced the Rules Committee to issue an open rule permitting unlimited amendments. Once the open rule was granted, opponents introduced eighty-seven amendments and stalled out the bill at the end of the Congress without a final vote. As Ripley (1983) notes, "The rules and procedures in both houses are constructed so that they enhance the influence of those members skilled in parliamentary maneuver" (p. 150). Although the Senate procedures may stress individual rights, and the House procedures may place more stress on majority rule, the manipulation and use of rules in both chambers can make the difference between passage and defeat. As Davidson and Oleszek (1985) point out: "In both chambers . . . members who know the rules and precedents have an advantage over procedural novices in affecting policy outcomes" (p. 285). Skillful tactics in getting the bill to the floor with its central components preserved, and before the body for a final vote, are imperative for policy enactment.

Policy leaders, consequently, seek out the active assistance of formal leaders and skilled floor operatives among their coalition in order to circumvent the obstacles that the blocking forces have erected to meaningful floor consideration. Legislative maneuvering at the floor stage often takes the form of a partnership between policy leaders and formal leaders. Policy substance must be melded with parliamentary maneuvering to secure a strategic opportunity for the legislation to receive a real chance at an up-or-down vote. At this point, if the coalition built upon consensus has been carefully constructed, proponents should be able to hold off last-minute attempts by the blocking forces to derail the package.

The difficulty proponents often face is that their initiative is caught in the legislative logjam that normally characterizes the floor agenda of either house. This is particularly true in the later stages of a Congress when time pressures force committees to make their deals and report their priority legislation, all of which cannot be scheduled for floor consideration. It is almost inevitable that even some consensus legislation will be left behind as one house or the other maneuvers through a gaggle of bills, several of which, such as appropriations bills, must be passed or some segment of the government will shut down. This makes it even tougher for new initiatives, and particularly for those without powerful interest-group support, as the political maneuvering heats up to secure priorities for floor time for legislation before Congress adjourns. Policy leaders must work with formal leaders to try to find or create an opportunity that may never come, and if it does, may only be available for an instant before other actors react and close it off. Choosing the wrong point at which to make the move, or mishandling the opportunity when it appears, can spell irretrievable defeat for painstakingly developed legislation.

Searching for an Opportunity for Criminal Law Reform

On September 20, Justice officials Smith, Jensen, and McConnell met with House Minority Leader Michel, Minority Whip Trent Lott, and Judiciary Republicans Fish, Sawyer, and Lungren to discuss strategy. They decided that they would look for a "must pass" piece of legislation, urge Senators Baker and Thurmond to tack the crime bill onto it in the Senate, and then send it back to the House. This would force a vote on the House floor, bypassing the Judiciary Committee. One possiblity was the debt limit bill. Every so often, Congress must raise the limit authorizing the Treasury to borrow funds or the government will default on its financial obligations. If the crime package were attached to that, the Democrats could not delay; they would have to vote to strip the crime bill or enact it along with the limit. The Republican members also asked Smith to make one more try with Speaker O'Neill. Given their previous meeting, it would have been understandable if Smith refused, but he agreed. The request went to O'Neill, but he declined to meet.

The debt limit bill proved not to be a workable vehicle. Then attention shifted to the Continuing Resolution (CR) that was being put together in both chambers. For a dozen years or so, Congress has been unable to pass all the various appropriations bills that provide funds to the many agencies of government. The new fiscal year started October 1, and Congress had passed only four of the thirteen regular appropriations bills. According to the Anti-Deficiency Act, the government may not spend money before it is appropriated. In 1981, part of the federal government had been shut down because employee salaries are covered by the act as well, and no appropriation had been passed. Congress deals with this situation by passing a resolution stipulating that the covered agencies may continue to spend at the level of the previous fiscal year's appropriation level until the expiration date. If Congress has not passed the appropriations bills by that time, another resolution must be passed.

The same day that the Justice officials met with the House Republicans, September 20, the House Rules Committee took to the House floor a proposed rule for processing the Continuing Resolution that provided that no amendments could be added. In recent years, the House had generally held the line against amendments to continuing resolutions, but the Senate had a terrible time keeping extraneous amendments off. This time, the House Rules Committee's efforts to offer a clean CR were rebuffed when the House voted down the rule, 168 to 225. The chairmen of the Public Works and Foreign Affairs committees, among others, had wanted to attach legislation authorizing spending programs, because legislation passed previously was not being acted on in the Senate. Essentially, this was an argument between the Democratic-controlled House and the Republican-controlled Senate over spending priorities.

The next day, September 21, the Rules Committee reconvened and passed a new rule that allowed eleven amendments, including an $18 billion water projects authorization bill and the entire $11 billion foreign aid authorization package. Rules chairman Claude Pepper (D-Fla.) said the committee decided that the "only fair thing we could do is to let the agency best qualified — the House of Representatives — decide which amendments it wants" (Tate, Sept. 22, 1984). The administration quickly put out word that President Reagan would veto a bill encumbered by costly new programs. Silvio Conte (R-Mass.), ranking Republican on the Appropriations Committee, predicted, "You're going to have the biggest pigpen you've ever seen in your life. It's going to make the Chicago stockyards look anemic" (Tate, Sept. 22, 1984).

The House majority was on a collision course with the president. The effort was to force Reagan to accept spending programs he did not want or to force him to shut down the government in an election year. Administration legislative officials were sending out the word to the House minority leadership to strip the amendments and press for a clean CR.

Lungren and his Conservative Opportunity Society (COS) friends, in discussing the situation decided there might be a chance, though a slight one, to tack on the crime bill or to use it as a lever to force the majority to strip the CR altogether. The idea was to try to open up the rule to allow its further amendment by adding the Comprehensive Crime Control Act. The argument would be, If the Democrats insist on adding expensive pork-barrel projects for special interests, how can they justify leaving out something the public really wants — crime control legislation?

Communication between Lungren's group, Minority Leader Michel, and Justice officials was constant at this point, and Justice officials were also pressing to add the crime package to the CR, as it presented the last chance for passage before adjournment.

On September 24, the day before the Continuing Resolution was to be considered again on the House floor, Hamilton Fish (R-N.Y.), ranking member on Judiciary, held a meeting in his office concerning what to do about the crime package. He was getting nervous about the collision course that the different Republican forces seemed to be on. On the one side, the Justice department, Lungren and COS members, and conservative interest groups were pushing to add the crime package. On the other side, the minority leadership—Michel and Lott—were pushing to keep the CR stripped. Michel could not attend the meeting, so he sent William Pitts, the minority parliamentarian, to represent him. In addition, Lott attended along with Judiciary Republicans Lungren, Hyde, Sawyer, McCollum, Sensenbrenner, Morehead, and Gekas. Justice officials included Smith, Jensen, and McConnell.

Expressing his concern that the CR not be loaded with amendments, Fish asked what other crime package might be put together that might be acceptable to the majority Democrats. If they could reach such an agreement with the Democrats, then the CR could be stripped. Pitts stated the need to keep the CR clean: "We can't send the president a CR loaded with unacceptable amendments. We need to look for another vehicle for the crime bill—not the CR." Lungren interjected, "Now is not the time to cut and run. If they are going to vote down good legislation, they have given us a political issue, and we shouldn't settle for a small piece of crime legislation." Smith argued, "The only thing to look for is a must-pass piece of legislation and the CR is that critical legislation, and we must go for it now. We should not compromise in any way as far as the Comprehensive Crime Control Act is concerned." Pitts observed, "The administration seems to be concerned about keeping the CR clean. The administration position should be clarified." Smith replied, "I am here speaking for the president. If you require affirmation that he wants the crime bill on the CR, then I will call him right now." With that, Smith reached for the phone, but before he could place the call, several said that "would not be necessary." Smith's record with the president was such that few doubted that he would not only be put through to the president but would also receive his support. The meeting broke up with the understanding that they would go for attaching the crime bill to the CR (Lungren, personal interview, 1986).

The next day, the CR was again brought to the floor of the House. Representative Long (D-La.) introduced the rule on behalf of the Rules Committee that would allow consideration of the eleven amendments, with thirty minutes to debate each one. The key vote would come when Long moved the previous question, shutting off further debate or action other than that on the eleven amendments. Minority Whip Lott described all the amendments, which included not only new spending authorizations but also changes in law, such as enacting a District of Columbia reorganization plan. Lott argued, "In short, the Rules Committee has completely capitulated to the perceived will of the House in wanting to make this continuing resolution a pick-up train for all the loose cars that might otherwise be left in the rail yards in this 98th Congress" (*Congressional Record,* Sept. 25, 1984, H10026). However, Republicans were somewhat split. Judiciary Republicans Fish, McCollum, and Lungren, and also Lott and Appropriations member Conte, argued to defeat the previous question so that the crime bill could be added, whereas Appropriations Committee Republicans Quillan (R-Tenn.) and Myers (R-Ind.) supported its passage so that Congress could move to adjournment.

Lungren argued that the crime bill had passed the Senate 91 to 1 but the House had never had a chance to vote on it. He observed that when the leadership wanted to bring things to the floor quickly, they had done so, as had been done with the ERA. "The point is when the leadership wants certain bills to get to the floor, we have an opportunity to vote on them. There is no other opportunity, evidently, in this House for us to go on the record on bail reform, on sentencing reform, on insanity defense, all those things that are contained in the President's comprehensive crime control package bill that passed the Senate overwhelmingly" (*Congressional Record,* Sept. 25, 1984, H10027).

Hughes accused Judiciary Republicans of partisanship and "not representing the facts correctly." "We have passed or will have passed some twenty-four crime bills in this Congress. That is probably the most productive effort on crime in the entire five terms I have been here ten years" (*Congressional Record,* Sept. 25, 1984, H10029). Rodino echoed Hughes's arguments about all the bills passed, such as Justice Assistance, and castigated Republicans who had complained about his use of the suspension procedure. "Here some of the same members support an entire omnibus crime package which in part attempts to undo legislation already passed by the House without any opportunity to carefully review and perfect the myriad segments of the bill" (*Congressional Record,* Sept. 25, 1984, H10030). (Rodino did not mention that he had not assigned the package to subcommittee.) Both Hughes and Rodino argued that the crime package should not be added.

The basic argument that Judiciary Democrats constantly made was that they had passed crime legislation. They played a numbers game by citing the numbers of bills passed. The Republicans countered that while these bills were desirable, they were not those of greatest importance to crime control. Judiciary Republicans did not disagree that bills dealing with trademark counterfeiting and credit card fraud or even Justice Assistance were needed. They disagreed that these were the priority crime reform measures. However, on the vote on the rule, the Republicans had a problem. The vote to defeat the previous question is a procedural motion, and members usually vote with their party leaders on such motions. The majority leadership could just advise their members, "Vote with us, this is just a procedural motion, not on the crime bill itself." When the vote came, the previous question motion passed 218 to 174. The Comprehensive Crime Control Act was apparently going the way of the criminal code.

The House then went on to approve the rule making the eleven amendments in order, 257 to 135. At this point, Lungren left the floor to go back to the conference committee, which was trying to resolve the differences between the two versions of the Immigration Reform bill. Minority Leader Michel was talking with minority parliamentarian Pitts about what to do next. Suddenly, it occurred to Michel they might have one more chance at enacting the crime bill. Michel said to Pitts, "If all this stuff is added it no longer is an appropriations bill, is it? That is, if the amendments are adopted, what is the germaneness situation?" Michel was referring to House rules that state that nonfinancial amendments offered to an appropriations bill can be ruled out of order on a point of order because they are not germane to the bill. However, if the House added items like authorization measures and D.C. government provisions, the CR was no longer strictly an appropriations bill, and substantive legislation such as the crime bill could not be ruled out of order on germaneness.

Pitts went to his office and looked up the House precedents on the subject of germaneness. He found that Michel's idea could work and returned to the floor and told him so. Michel told Pitts, "Keep this under your hat until later in the game." At the right moment, Pitts was to approach the House parliamentarian and get an unofficial ruling that a substantive amendment would not be ruled out of order. Michel then instructed Pitts to get Lungren and the others together for a meeting to decide what to do. Lungren was called out of the Immigration conference to attend the meeting. Some of his COS friends, Newt Gingrich and Robert Walker, who had joined in giving speeches on the crime bill, were there, as were Hamilton Fish and others from Judiciary. McConnell from Justice and Tom Donally from the White House Office of Congressional Relations came in while the meeting was in progress.

One problem was how to get the floor to make a motion. Pitts said there would be one opportunity to try. On appropriations bills, after all the votes on amendments are taken, the Appropriations Committee chairman takes the floor and makes a short speech thanking the members of Appropriations, including the minority, for all their work on the bill. He then yields the floor to the ranking Republican — in this case, Silvio Conte — so that he can make a similar short speech. If at that point, Conte should make the motion or yield the floor to a Republican on House Judiciary, the requisite motion to recommit the bill could be made. Such a motion allowed only five minutes of debate on each side by House rules. Although there was no rule against yielding floor at this point in the proceedings, to do so would be considered a severe breach of protocol by some members, particularly Appropriations Committee members. There was a risk that they would lose for violating protocol.

There was no guarantee that Conte would go along. Gingrich and Walker were not sure it was worth the effort. The argument was, "We already got them on the vote going into the election. Let's not put another vote up that lets them off the hook." Lungren argued, "Wait a second. Here we had a vote on defeating the previous question on the rule so that the rule could be opened up to allow us to add an amendment for the Comprehensive Crime Control Act so it could be considered. That's going to be easily explained at home? You and I know what happened, but that's not going to do it." After some more discussion, Michel said, "I don't understand. You guys want me to be tough around here. Now when I want to be tough, some of you guys are heading for the hills." Lungren spoke up, "Look, Bob, I'm willing to do it. You want me to do it. This is what I want to do. I think we ought to do it." Michel said, "I think we ought to do it," and it was agreed to proceed. Michel said that he would talk to Conte to see if he would go along. When it came to the discussion of who would make the argument, Fish, who had seniority as ranking member and could make a claim to do it, nonetheless said, "It should be Lungren. He's done the work on this." Michel went to Conte and he agreed that Lungren, but no one else, could make the motion. (Lungren, personal interview, 1986).

In the meantime, Republican National Congressionl Committee staff had been making calls to their constituent organizations around the country telling them of the votes against the crime bill by particular congressmen. These organizations called radio and television stations, and by mid-afternoon telephones in some congressmen's offices began to ring with questions about why they had voted against an anticrime bill. Such questions one month before an election are political dynamite.

At this point, Congress was meeting into the night. About eight in the evening, the House was almost finished amending the Continuing Resolution. Sponsors of the amendments had proceeded through them one by one. The $18 billion water projects package authorized construction of 300 projects, including dams, harbors, levees, and locks, and was agreed to by a vote of 336 to 64. The foreign aid authorization package was adopted by voice vote, as were several other amendments, including an amendment affecting D.C. home rule and child-care facility staff training. All eleven Democratic amendments had been added to the CR.

Michel indicated to Pitts it was time, and he went over to the House parliamentarian and asked his question to clarify the germaneness issue. The parliamentarian agreed that the scope of the bill had been expanded, which Pitts reported to Michel. When Conte got the floor, he yielded it to Lungren. Immediately, the floor erupted. This was out of the ordinary, and members on both sides of the aisle were surprised and knew something significant was going to happen. Lungren moved to recommit the CR to the Committee on Appropriations with instructions to report it back to the House forthwith with the amendment of the entire Comprehensive Crime Control Act as it had passed the Senate. Such a motion gives the Appropriations Committee no discretion whatsoever. A vote to recommit is a vote to pass the crime bill, because if the motion carries,the amended bill will be back on the floor in a matter of minutes containing the crime package and will be subject to a vote for final passage. In addition, such a motion allowed debate of only five minutes on each side, which meant essentially one speech on each side.

Many of the members had not been on the floor, nor had Speaker O'Neill, but word went out quickly that a major vote was about to take place and members came streaming in. Speaker O'Neill came rushing onto the floor, glared at Lungren, and walked right over to the House parliamentarian, who told him there was nothing he could do. He then came down to the rostrum with a grimace on his face and looked over at the minority side.

Lungren was to give the sole speech for the Republicans. The Democrats selected Hughes to give the opposing speech. Of the Judiciary Democrats, it was felt that Hughes had the most credibility on the crime issue, and it was to the leadership's advantage to use that credibility.

Lungren knew that with only five minutes he did not have time to be fancy. He would have to make as simple and straightforward an argument as he could. His argument would be evaluated against a year and a half of proposing the bill. He recounted the history of the consideraiton of the bill and the fact that it had passed the Senate 91 to 1, with the one being a Republican. He pointed out that proponents had been trying to get an up-and-down vote for almost two years. Lungren concluded: "This is that single vote that you will have a chance to cast. It is not procedural; it is substantive. It has every single element of the package here. If we have an opportunity, as we did today, to attach the foreign aid bill and the public works bill, we should do no less than attach this bill since the American people have shown in the latest poll this is the No. 1 issue facing them. You cannot dodge it; this is your chance to do it. I would hope we would have an overwhelming yes vote on behalf of the American people in favor of the Comprehensive Crime Control Act of 1984" (*Congressional Record,* Sept. 25, 1984, H10129).

Hughes said he had not intended to speak but there had been too much misinformation about the crime package. He criticized the president for vetoing the mini-crime bill and the attorney general for recommending it. He recounted the bills his subcommittee had passed which had been passed by the House and sent to the Senate. He said the Judiciary Committee was then seeking a rule on bail and sentencing reform. He concluded by stating: "So, yes we have not passed everything that is in the 42 provisions but I would say half of the provisions in that 42 provision bill are housekeeping provisions that Hal Sawyer and I, when it was referred to our subcommittee, decided not to take up because we had other priorities that would make a wider impact on the criminal justice system. I say to my colleagues, This is no way to legislate" (*Congressional Record,* Sept. 25, 1984 H10130). Hearing his name invoked by Hughes, Sawyer, ranking Republican on Hughes's subcommittee, asked him to yield the floor, which Hughes did. Sawyer stated, "I have no objection to what the gentleman says is true about our sub-

committee, but that was 10 bills out of 42, and the others are
all sitting in John Conyers's subcommittee, and they will sit there
until doomsday" (*Congressional Record*, H10130).

Confusion was rampant on the floor. Democratic members were coming up to Lungren and asking, "What is this?"
"What is this crime bill?" Lungren told them: "This is the crime
bill that passed the Senate 91-1. Every Democrat voted for it.
It includes Kennedy's sentencing bill and he voted for it."

As the voting started, with the votes being registered on
the electronic tally board, Lungren was not at all convinced he
would prevail. At one point, the vote tally registered a tie with
100 on each side, and a colleague tugged at Lungren's sleeve
and said, "Dan, look at that. We're tied." Lungren observed,
"We better savor the moment because this is the closest we are
going to get to passing this bill." The vote for the bill did drop
behind in the count but then tied again at 115. Then it dropped
again, but retied at 125.

In the meantime, Democratic members were going up
to Speaker O'Neill and telling him that he had to release them
to vote their own way. They could not vote against this major
crime bill, not with the election coming up. O'Neill told them
to "go ahead" if they felt they needed to make a public stand
against crime to boost their reelection prospects. (Tate, Sept.
29, 1984). The vote for the package edged ahead, and then there
was a discernible surge in its favor. The final vote tally was ayes
243, nays 166, not voting 23. A majority of Judiciary Democrats
joined Hughes and Rodino in voting against the bill, but the
defections by 89 Democrats who joined with 154 Republicans
(only 3 voted no) proved law enforcement proponents' claim that
if they could get to the floor, the crime package would pass.

Crime bill proponents were jubilant and were slapping
each other on the back and hugging each other. In the middle
of the celebration, Lungren stopped and said, "What do we do
now?" They had not expected to win, and while the crime bill
was attached to the CR, so were several other provisions that
the president could not accept and could very well veto. President Reagan had vetoed a Continuing Resolution in 1981, which
had shut down part of the government. The risk was that the

Senate would either accept too many of the House's amendments, and the president would be put in the embarrassing position of vetoing the CR that contained much of his own crime bill, or that the Senate would strip all amendments in the interest of sending the president a clean CR. In the latter event, the Republican-controlled Senate would be embarrassed by stripping the crime bill.

Lungren went over to the Senate floor to see Strom Thurmond, explained what had happened, and said, "We can't allow this to fall apart." Thurmond said, "No, we can't. We have got to win this. I didn't think we were going to pass it over there, and we have to make sure we don't lose this now." Lungren also talked to Laxalt, who was in constant contact with White House strategists. The White House legislative staff did not have clear signals at this point, as they were discussing internally going for a clean CR.

When the Senate took up the CR, the amendment problem became even more complex. In addition to the House amendments, some senators were adding their own. Senators voted 51 to 48, for example, in favor of debating Senator Byrd's amendment attaching a major civil rights bill designed to overturn the Supreme Court's decision in *Grove City College* v. *Bell*. The Appropriations Committee had also attached a raft of foreign aid amendments, and still other amendments were in the offing. On September 27, Senate Majority Leader Baker said that the Continuing Resolution attracted the members' favorite proposals "on the theory that the president will not veto." However, he urged senators not to discount a veto. Baker said he had "a terrible feeling of déjà vu" about the continuing resolution. "I am afraid that I am going to see 18 years of legislative combat reel before me in the next few days" (Tate, Sept. 29, 1984).

Meanwhile, back in the House, the Judiciary leadership scrambled to recover from their loss on the crime bill amendment to the CR. They hurriedly put together an Anti-Crime Act of 1984 (H.R.5690), the chief sponsor of which was Hughes. It consisted of twenty-four titles which were a collection of bills, some of which had passed the Senate, and some of which had passed the House, and others that had not even been acted on in committee. Hughes got the leadership to schedule it on the suspension calendar for October 2. Copies of the over 200-page bill were not available to members until the morning of October 2, and only four copies were distributed. Although a week earlier he had argued that voting on a large package was "no way to legislate," Hughes's "Dear Colleague" letter explaining the move to members stated, "We need to have a single legislative vehicle available to move these items, most of which are consensus items, to enactment." It also advised, "The Crime provisions in the Continuing Resolution (S.1762) many of which are similar to our package are not likely to be signed into law." The sentencing, forfeiture, and insanity titles in the new bill were far from "consensus items," and some law enforcement proponents wanted to oppose the bill on grounds that it was weaker than the one the House had just passed. However, while this bill would give those Democrats who voted no on the Comprehensive Crime Control Act a chance to record a yes vote on a crime package, it posed a problem for Republicans. House Republican leaders decided that they would not oppose this bill, but would simply point out to their members that the bill did not really matter. Republicans discussed the deficiencies in the various titles, particularly sentencing and the insanity defense, and then suggested it be passed so that, in the event the Senate took it up, it could be amended and strengthened. The bill passed the House 406 to 16. Meanwhile, the Senate had no intention of taking up this later bill and concentrated on the Continuing Resolution.

While awaiting final Senate action on the Continuing Resolution, Congress approved an interim funding resolution on October 1 to fund the government until October 4. For several days, the Senate was embroiled in a far-flung fight over Senator Byrd's civil rights amendment to the CR, which had involved complex parliamentary maneuvering involving the addition of gun control, anti-abortion, and school busing amendments with cloture votes, tabling motions, and so on. Baker's worst nightmare was coming true. On October 2, Senator Packwood, one of the chief sponsors of the civil rights amendment, called it off, saying the procedural tangle was about to result in the Senate's violating and raping Senate procedures.

Agreement on the CR had still not been reached on October 4, and President Reagan ordered the shutdown of eight cabinet-level departments and several independent agencies at noon. Five hundred thousand "nonessential" workers were sent home at midday. Reagan, referring to the "loaded CR," said, "You can lay this right on the majority party of the House of Representatives." Speaker O'Neill retorted, "We passed a continuing resolution September 25. That continuing resolution has been sitting in the Senate ever since, roadblocked by the President's far-out allies." Representative Hoyer (D-Md.) had introduced legislation that would keep offices open during a funding gap, unless Congress took positive action to close them. His bill never advanced, he said, "because the leadership knows the only thing that gets this institution moving is a crisis. If you remove the crisis, you remove the incentive for action" (Tate, Felton, and Tovell, 1984, p. 2420). On October 5, Congress approved another interim measure to expire on October 9.

During this period, the Senate was meeting around the clock in an attempt to settle the issues, pass the CR, and adjourn to go home to campaign. They had already missed the October 4 deadline, and many members had their luggage packed and in their offices, ready to bolt for the airport upon adjournment. Groggy senators were wandering in and out of the chamber between naps in the cloakroom. At 4:30 A.M., in the midst of one debate on the CR, one senator said that some of his colleagues "don't know where they are. They think we are on the farm bill" (Granat, 1984).

The Senate was working its way through amendment after amendment on the CR around the clock, with Senator Hatfield, chairman of the Appropriations Committee, desperately trying to fend off measures from federal funding for abortion to foreign aid to Turkey. Senator DeConcini's amendment to waive antitrust laws so that exclusive beer distribution arrangements would be allowed was defeated on a germaneness vote of 28 to 67. Senator Bradley's amendment to add an additional $6 billion for the Superfund hazardous waste clean-up program similarly went down, 38 to 59. Senator Inouye's amendment to bar aid to the Nicaraguan contras was rejected, 42 to 57. Some smaller funding amendments were accepted, but then came the $18 billion water projects amendment, which had been passed by the House. This was also rejected, 36 to 60. However, the Senate did accept a smaller $82 million for twenty-six water projects, which still could provoke a veto.

Senator Thurmond initially had thought the preferred tactic for crime bill proponents was to urge defeat of the Appropriations Committee's motion to delete the Comprehensive Crime Control Act from the CR. Senator Hatfield and the other Appropriations Committee members were not opposed to the crime bill but were following a strategy that essentially said to senators, "You can't have your amendment, because nobody else is allowed to keep theirs and tie up the CR." Assistant Attorney General McConnell suggested to Thurmond's staff that a better tactic would be not to vote against Hatfield's motion to delete but to offer a motion to table it. A motion to table is a privileged motion and not subject to debate. Thurmond agreed to go with the motion to table.

Thurmond had been up all night waiting for any attempt to strip the crime package from the CR. His aides had even seen Representative Hughes on the Senate floor sitting next to and conferring with Senator Mathias. It is highly unusual for a member of one house to actually be on the floor, even counseling over pending legislation. Even though he was eighty-two years old, Thurmond was not going to go home to bed until the crime bill was safely contained in the CR. Hatfield had an Appropriations Committee motion on the floor to sever several amendments. This was divided to allow one separate vote on several of them, which would then leave the motion to delete the crime package from the CR.

In the middle of this, Senator Mathias requested a division of the crime package itself into its twelve sections. His motion was out of order at that point, but now Thurmond and his staff knew what Mathias intended to do. If Mathias were successful in dividing the crime package, it would be dead. There was no time for a prolonged debate, and the leadership would have pulled down the crime bill. Thurmond's chief judiciary counsel, Vinton D. Lide, and his chief legislative assistant on crime legislation, Deborah Owen, were on the floor with Thurmond and advised him that the planned motion to table would cut Mathias off. Lide advised Thurmond to make sure he made the motion before yielding the floor. After the votes were completed to delete the other amendments, Thurmond sprang to his feet, as did Mathias. As Thurmond was president pro tempore, he was recognized first, and he made a motion to table the motion to delete the crime package from the CR. If this passed, Mathias's motion to divide would be out of order. Mathias demanded a division, section by section, but the presiding officer ruled with Thurmond that while a tabling motion is pending, a division of the underlying matter is not in order. The vote had to be called immediately, and Mathias must have been taken by surprise, because even he voted for Thurmond's motion, which passed 97 to 0. The Comprehensive Crime Control Act remained attached to the CR, and the Senate had refrained from accepting the veto-bait amendments in the House bill.

Crime package proponents were not out of the woods yet, however. Mathias was a seasoned veteran of Senate floor battles and could elect to try other parliamentary maneuvers to delay consideration. A filibuster at this point could kill the crime package. Thurmond got a recess to enable negotiations with Mathias to take place. Baker gave them until 2:00 P.M. to complete negotiations.

At 8:00 A.M. Senators Thurmond, Laxalt, Biden, Kennedy, and Mathias convened in Thurmond's president pro tempore office to try to work out an agreement. One of Mathias's main concerns was his long-standing opposition to Kennedy's sentencing scheme. At this point, Mathias still had the leverage because there was no more time. However, while Mathias could be tenacious, he also was a politician who knew the process was one of give and take. His goal became to modify the sentencing title to bring it more in line with the Judicial Conference proposals. He asked for more judges to be appointed to the Sentencing Commission, and their membership was increased from two to three of seven voting members. He also got a direction to the Sentencing Commission to construct the guidelines to minimize prison overcrowding. In addition, Mathias got some additions to the bill, including a Trademark Counterfeiting title and a doubling of fees paid to defense attorneys representing the indigent in criminal cases.

By 2:00 P.M. they had an agreement and went back to the floor. The amendments agreed to were made and accepted. Senate action on the CR was then completed. Now the CR was ready for a Conference Committee made up of Senate and House Members to resolve the differences between the bills passed by the two houses.

The concessions to Senator Mathias illustrate the power one senator can exert under the time pressures that often exist in Congress. The effect of the changes in the sentencing title came to be visibly significant in the work of the Sentencing Commission itself.

In addition, at the time, Mathias's amendments changed the nature of the crime package title, which was Title II of the Continuing Resolution. Had that title been unchanged there would have been no differences to resolve between the House and Senate versions of the crime package title of the CR. Both houses would have passed exactly the same language for that title. Technically, the House Judiciary leadership could have tried to argue that because the two overall versions of the CR were not identical (for example, the Senate's version did not include the $18 billion water projects authorization), they then should be allowed to make changes in the crime title. They would then have had to convince the leaders of the Conference Committee to place in contention something to which both houses had agreed—a highly unlikely prospect.

Because a continuing resolution is managed by the Appropriations committees, the conferees named by the leadership of the two houses came from these committees. Members of the Judiciary committees were told that they would not be participating in the conference. Senator Warren Rudman (R-N.H.) and Representative Neil Smith (D-Fla.) were the Appropriations Committee conferees designated to work out the few differences in the crime title. Senate Judiciary members who had been up for forty-eight hours or more were exhausted and went home. Biden took the train to Delaware; Kennedy and Laxalt went to their Washington area homes. Over on the House side, several members were attending Representative Sawyer's retirement party. The final act of the Congress would be to vote on the Conference Committee report resolving the differences between the two bills, and that was scheduled for the next morning.

In the early evening, however, Rudman and Smith notified the Judiciary committees that they could meet in an advisory capacity to them to resolve the few differences in the crime title. In effect, an informal Judiciary conference would occur. The initial decision was to try to have the staffs meet to work it out. Deborah Owen, Thurmond's assistant for crime legislation, was in her office and received a frantic call from Thurmond's office telling her a staff conference was about to convene in a hearing room in the Capitol. She rushed over to the Capitol and was one of the first staff members there, but others representing virtually every member of both Judiciary committees soon came in, with the House staffers congregating on the left side and the Senate staffers on the right.

The looks on their faces showed that this was going to be a confrontational session. Jaws were clearly set. Elaine Melke, House Judiciary counsel representing Representative Rodino, started off with the demand that the vehicle for discussion should be Representative Hughes's Democratic crime package (H.R. 5690), which had passed only the House after the CR had passed. House Democratic staffers wanted the negotiations to proceed line by line over that bill. Owen replied that the separate House bill was outside the scope of the conference, as it was the Comprehensive Crime Control Act that both houses had passed on the CR. The talk then got very contentious. Melke and the House Judiciary Democratic staffers said there was nothing to discuss unless the group started with the Hughes bill. Owen said absolutely not, that they did not understand that the separate House bill was outside the scope of the conference. The argument went back and forth, with the House Democratic staffers insisting that the House bill be used as the vehicle. Charlene Vanlier, minority crime subcommittee counsel, urged the Senate staffers to hold firm. Finally, Owen said, "Look, I am not authorized to go outside the scope of the conference. If we are going to go into any discussions that are outside the scope of the conference, I have to go back and get permission from Senator Thurmond." House staffers said, "Fine, you do that."

At this point, Owen went back over to the Senate side and found Senator Thurmond, who responded, "I don't have time for this. Get the members." The members who could be located convened in Thurmond's Senate pro tempore office. Rodino, Hughes, and Sawyer were there from House Judiciary, and Thurmond, Specter, and DeConcini, who also served on Appropriations, were there from the Senate. Rudman and Smith came in as well. Thurmond was at somewhat of a disadvantage in that several of the sponsors of key parts of the crime title — Kennedy, Biden, Laxalt, and Lungren — were not there.

This was like no other conference committee the members had ever attended. It really was not a formal conference committee — ostensibly, the Judiciary members were there as advisors to Rudman and Smith. In reality, the participants were there to negotiate the bill. Nonetheless, the negotiations were unlike any that members had seen before. In the first place, the issues addressed were largely determined by who was in the room rather than the few differences between the two bills. For example, Rodino, supported by Hughes, wanted to take the sentencing portions out of the bill even though they were identical in both versions. Rather than an agenda with votes, it was more of a free-for-all. They took no votes but simply proceeded by consensus. If someone raised something he or she wanted changed and someone else objected, they often had staff representing them go off to the side to negotiate a compromise while the principals continued to debate other sections. At other times, Rudman would say to one, "What's your argument?" and then, "What's Yours"? and then, "O.K. We'll take this and that." Then they would move on to another issue. Several senators not in the room participated as best they could over the phone through their staff. Rudman and Smith partially refereed the tangle of discussion.

The discussion started out going back and forth over what the approach should be. Rodino and Hughes were arguing for fundamental changes in what had been passed, and Thurmond was resisting. Finally, Rudman told them, "We either all work this out tonight or Smith and I will settle it." The CR was going to be voted on the next day as far as the Appropriations Committee members were concerned.

Rodino kept maintaining that the House could not accept the sentencing and bail titles. Hughes wanted to change the forfeiture section and particularly delete the substitute-assets provision. He also wanted to change the Justice Assistance provisions to make them more like his bill. Several discussions were going on simultaneously. Senate staffers representing their absent bosses were calling them at home to post them on developments and get them into the debates. As Rodino was pushing on sentencing, Carolyn Oscelenik reached Kennedy at home and put him on with Rodino and then Thurmond. Sentencing remained unchanged.

McConnell and two of his staff, Marshall Cain and Cary Copeland, were outside in the hall. Sawyer's assistant, Charlene Vanlier, would come out and post them on developments and get additional information to bolster Sawyer and Thurmond. Lungren was participating in a Catholic Mass being given in his home for several couples who met regularly for services. Even so, several times McConnell called Lungren at home and got his position on an issue in contention and had that conveyed into the room, or Sawyer or Vanlier would get on the phone with him.

Thurmond was doing the best he could, but he was not an expert on every provision, and Rodino and Hughes were pushing hard. Thurmond would argue that if they wanted to change the crime title significantly, he had a few additions that the Senate had passed overwhelmingly, including the death penalty, exclusionary rule reform, and habeas corpus reform. However, Thurmond needed some help in the room to respond to several proposals, and Lide went out and asked McConnell if Lungren could get there. McConnell called Lungren at home and told him, "Dan, I know what you are doing and I wouldn't ask if it wasn't critical, but you have got to get down here." Lungren agreed and drove down to the Capitol, arriving at about 10:00 P.M. Lungren was more familiar with the forfei-

The Dynamics of Legislation

ture provisions and countered Hughes on some of the changes he wanted. However, by the time he got there, Hughes had practically succeeded in convincing the others not to oppose taking substitute assets out of the forfeiture title. With neither Lungren nor Biden in the room, there was no one there to counter him on the specifics.

Biden received his first call of the evening as he entered his home in Wilmington. Lungren got on the phone with Biden and told him, "Joe, they're doing some things down here I don't think you'd like being done." Biden said, "Yes, this really upsets me. They told me no one would be allowed in there, and I went home." Lungren asked if there was any way he could get down there, but at that hour no planes or trains would get Biden there in time. Biden had to do the best he could over the phone.

The negotiations did not just focus on changing what was in the bill. Some members pushed to add other items. Hughes insisted that his computer crime bill be added because it had passed the House. The Senate had not held hearings on the bill and Senator Laxalt had some objections to it, which John Nash, Laxalt's counsel raised. To resolve the impasse, Nash and Edward O'Connel, Hughes's crime subcommittee counsel, went around the corner and negotiated. They agreed to take the provisions that applied to federal government computers but to delete those sections that dealt with private-sector and other computers. Lungren, Thurmond, and the other crime package proponents held firm on keeping the main body of the package intact as the Senate had passed it, with the exception of substitute assets. Instead, they agreed to some demands to add some items, which became essentially Chapters 13–20 of the bill. They also took the opportunity to make an addition or two of their own, such as Chapter 17, which increased the salaries of U.S. attorneys. Senator Specter also got his modified armed career-criminal bill included as Chapter 18.

All the issues were not contentious in that they were supported by the administration and most members of the committees in the House and Senate. For example, the administration had only recently developed two anti-terrorism bills covering hostage taking and aircraft sabotage, which members readily agreed to add as Chapter 20.

The session finished in the early hours of the morning on October 5. The congressmen and senators went home to sleep. The staff stayed for the remainder of the night to draft into statutory language the agreed changes. They finished at 6:00 A.M. The Appropriations mini-conference on the crime bill was ready to report.

As it turned out, the mini-conference on the crime package finished on time, but the other groups meeting on other amendments did not. A major obstacle remaining was reaching agreement on the $18 billion worth of pork-barrel water projects that were in the House bill. Water project conferees recessed on October 5 and did not meet again until October 9. Other unresolved issues included what to do about aid to the Contra rebels fighting in Nicaragua, and funding for the MX missile. Another short-term funding resolution was passed to expire on October 9. On October 9, Senator Rudman lamented, "We're essentially in a state of gridlock. We've run aground" (Tate, Oct. 13, 1984, p. 2617). The stalemate forced Congress to approve yet another short-term Continuing Resolution (HJ Res. 5663), which lasted until midnight on October 11.

Crime package proponents could only watch in frustration from the sidelines. If amendments unacceptable to the president stayed on the CR and he vetoed it, the crime package might not become law after all. Not infrequently, the fortunes of one piece of legislation are tied up with other, completely unrelated, legislation. That was the situation for the crime package.

Conferees finally resolved the differences over the Contra aid issue by providing enough funding to carry them through until the following March, when the whole issue would be revisited again. However, the water projects remained a stumbling block. Conferees backed off the $18 billion figure but sought to salvage $78 million for such projects. OMB director David Stockman sent a letter to Capitol Hill threatening a Reagan veto of the CR if any water project money was included. Crime bill proponents were sitting on pins and needles, worrying that the largest change in federal criminal law in decades might be lost over a few million dollars for water projects.

During the evening of October 10, water project proponents caved in and deleted water projects from the CR. Silvio

Conte, ranking Republican on House Appropriations, whose observations about congressional pork-barrel legislation were well known, chortled, "It wasn't easy catching all those little piglets, but we caught them all and sent them back to the farm" (Tate, Oct. 13, 1984, p. 2617).

This broke the impasse. The night of October 10, the House agreed to the amended bill as reported by the conference committee, 252 to 60. The next day, the Senate approved it, 78 to 11. Of the 565-page bill, 112 pages dealt with appropriations; the other 453 consisted of the Comprehensive Crime Control Act.

A pasted-together copy of the amended bill was rushed to Andrews Air Force Base the next morning to accompany President Reagan, who was flying on Air Force One to the West Coast. Justice Department officials received word that the Comprehensive Crime Control Act officially became law somewhere over Kansas.

Strategic Opportunities Revisited

In considering legislation on the floors of the two houses of Congress, there is both order and disorder at the same time. The rules of the two houses are quite different, but they provide a rough framework within which legislative maneuvering and warfare takes place. As demonstrated in this chapter, time pressures, rules and procedures, actions of the leadership, and actions and reactions of the various contending forces all play a role in determining which items are going to have a chance for final enactment. Mastery of the rules, astute strategy, and skillful tactics are all crucial to ultimate legislative success. The successful effort is a partnership of members of the legislative coalition, each of whom brings different skills to the process. Policy leaders combine efforts with party leaders and skilled floor operatives in a final contest with the opposing coalition to present the bill to the membership for a final vote.

The procedures of the two houses are complex and often nonmajoritarian in nature. Yet, over time, a majority for a major policy supported by the public can ultimately find a way through the labyrinth to give the representatives a chance to enact it into law, if the leaders of the coalition persevere and are skillful legislators.

Large-scale legislation displays both advantages and disadvantages in the modern Congress. On the one hand, by including numerous policy components, it risks confusing the noninvolved with its complexity and risks preventing the construction of a consensus by the accumulation of opponents concerned about different parts. On the other hand, it facilitates coalition building by including at least something that a majority wants. Given the scarce opportunities for only a minority of bills to be considered on the floor, when the omnibus bill representing the overall policy priority does arrive, those who have their components included must support the whole package to achieve their individual policy goal. Also, in that the package represents a policy, at least in broad terms, that a majority among the public desire, other noninvolved legislators are encouraged to vote for it in anticipation of public reaction in ensuing elections.

As demonstrated in the consideration of federal criminal law reform, there is nothing preordained in the legislative process. Rules and procedures, partisan lineups, and ideological predispositions all influence the consideration of legislation, but none is determinative. The achievement of final passage and enactment into law requires skillful political maneuvering and astute policy leadership to manage even the most widely supported policies according to the dynamics of legislation.

• 11 •

Aftermath:
The Effect
of the Policy
Breakthrough

The enactment of a law in one sense marks the conclusion of the legislative process. Congress has worked its will and made a new policy pronouncement. In a larger sense, however, such passage marks one point on the policy process continuum that constitutes a given policy field.

In part, upon enactment of a new statute, the policy process undergoes a shift in focus to the administrative and judicial policy arenas, within which further remaking of the policy occurs. In the administrative and judicial processes, further modification or even invalidation of the decisions made in the legislative process are commonplace.

In addition, the passage of a bill in a given policy area does not necessarily end legislating in that area. Passage may constitute a temporary aberration in the longer-term policy trend, and its force may be minimized or nullified by subsequent legislative action. For example, the passage of catastrophic health insurance for the elderly in the 100th Congress was succeeded by repeal in the 101st Congress.

Alternatively, the passage of a major piece of legislation may constitute a breakthrough affecting the pace and/or direction of policy for a considerable period. Kingdon (1984) points out that normally within a given policy area, policy changes occur incrementally in small, nearly invisible steps. There are times, however, with the passage of landmark legislation, that a new principle is established. When that occurs, public policy in that area is never quite the same again. The first success creates powerful spillover effects. Policy entrepreneurs are encouraged to rush to the next available issue in the area, coalitions are transferred, and arguments from analogy take hold (Kingdon, 1984). Once a new precedent is established, it can be used to further changes in areas similar to the first. Passage of the Comprehensive Crime Control Act constituted such a breakthrough in the federal approach to crime legislation. As will be seen, it set the pattern for subsequent crime legislation that, while balanced, moved federal criminal law further in the direction of the get-tough approach.

Implementation — Policy Making Continues

Following passage of the crime package, the interpretation of what had happened and the implementation of the law began. Attorney General William French Smith called the Comprehensive Crime Control Act "the most far-reaching and substantial reform of the criminal justice system in our history." Representative William Hughes called it "the most comprehensive crime bill Congress has ever passed" (Taylor, Oct. 15, 1984). U.S. Attorney for New York Rudolph Giuliani concluded, "In each area of the bill, there is a slight shift in favor of the Government and away from the criminal defendant" (Stengel, 1984).

Not everyone was happy, of course. Ira Glaser, executive director of the ACLU, stated, "It is fraudulent to claim that these measures which undermine fundamental constitutional liberties will reduce violent crime or make this a safer society" (Taylor, Oct. 15, 1984). Jerry Berman, ACLU chief legislative counsel, was particularly critical of the computer crime provision, saying that it was so broad it amounted to a "government secrecy" law (Cohodas, October 20, 1984). In a statement that must have been galling to House Judiciary Democrats, ACLU lobbyist David Landau blamed House Judiciary for the defeat, claiming, "Had they moved sooner to develop their own positions on bail and sentencing, you might have had a much better version" (Riley, Oct. 24, 1984, p. 3).

Some time later, however, even some ACLU officials had a different view of the events. After all, Biden and Kennedy had only agreed to go along with the package if the provisions most troubling to liberals, like the death penalty and exclusionary rule reform, were stripped from the bill. A year and a half later, the ACLU's Berman concluded, "My overall sense is that Biden's strategy was the correct one" (Brownstein, 1986).

The passage of the act had come so late in the session and was such a surprise that the Justice Department had to put together a crash program to implement it. The vast majority of its provisions had no delayed effective date and became law the moment the president signed it on Friday, October 12. Associate Attorney General Lowell Jensen's office sent out a photocopied "cut and paste" version of the act taken from the *Congressional Record* and the legislative history over the weekend to the offices of U.S. Attorneys', who prosecute the vast majority of cases.

Because few statutes become law in fact until they are tested in court, Jensen and Criminal Division Assistant Attorney General Stephen Trott took special steps with the new bail provision. They advised the U.S. Attorneys to expect constitutional challenges and to institute procedures to ensure that cases presenting consitutional issues involved fact situations where there was no doubt as to the defendant's dangerousness. Justice officials knew there was risk that what had just been won in Congress could be lost in court, because opponents would ask the federal courts to invalidate the law on grounds that it violated constitutional guarantees. The explicit objective was to avoid situations where bad cases make bad law (Trott, 1985). The U.S. Attorneys were to review personally all motions for pretrial detention based on dangerousness and to consult with the Criminal Division in all cases, unless there was clear evidence of dangerousness, such as threats of violence directed toward victims or witnesses. Such preparedness paid off and resulted in victory for the Justice Department in a key appellate court case that upheld the constitutionality of the law (*United States* v. *Powell*

No. 84-2430 [8th Cir. 1985]). The bail provision had an immediate impact on federal criminal prosecutions. By August 23, 1985, 1,100 out of 1,331 pretrial detention requests had been granted, and 504 of these were drug cases (U.S. Department of Justice, 1985).

The asset forfeiture provisions have also yielded increasing dividends for law enforcement. The total amount of illegal proceeds forfeited to the government had increased from $27.2 million in 1985 to $460.3 million in 1990. Much of this was in confiscated cash. The provision drafted at the last minute that made cooperating state and local agencies eligible to share in the illegal proceeds has resulted in distributions to them of $543.8 million through fiscal year 1990. Of this figure, $474.3 million was in cash and $69.5 million was in tangible property such as automobiles. Federal prison construction has also received funds with $115 million distributed in fiscal year 1990 (U.S. Department of Justice, Office of Asset Forteiture). While such sums are still insufficient to cripple multibillion-dollar drug cartels, they are increasing at a substantial pace. As federal prosecutors become more familiar with forfeiture techniques, crime organizations will experience increasingly significant economic damage. In addition, state governments have been following the federal example and have been enacting their own forfeiture laws.

The U.S. Sentencing Commission created in the sentencing title began its work in 1985 and submitted its sentencing guidelines to Congress, which took effect on March 1, 1987. The guidelines require the sentencing judge to assign numerical weight to aggravating and mitigating factors relating to the conduct attending the offense committed and the defendant's criminal history. The calculation relating to offense conduct generates a total sum called a "total offense level." The calculation for a defendant's past criminal activities results in a numerical "criminal history category." These two numerical results, intersecting on a sentencing table, determine a sentencing range that specifies a maximum and a minimum number of months of imprisonment. It is still too early to determine the impacts the sentencing scheme will have on the federal criminal justice system. The Supreme Court decided it was constitutional in 1989 (*Mistretta* v. *United States* 109 S. Ct. 649 [1989]). During the first year of guidelines implementation and before the Supreme Court decision, 15 percent of the cases nationally were sentenced under the guidelines. After the Supreme Court upheld the constitutionality of the Sentencing Commission on January 18, 1989, statistics for 1989 show that 54.4 percent were sentenced pursuant to the act. In 1989, almost half of the defendants sentenced under the guidelines were convicted of drug offenses (U.S. Sentencing Commission, 1990). One of the key unanswered questions is whether the reduction in sentencing disparity sought by the congressional sponsors will be attained. However, one of the major concerns expressed in the debates over the sentencing guidelines was that they would lead to prison terms for more convicted defendants and would unduly increase the federal prison population. Early data indicate that this is not happening to any great extent as yet. Congress has subsequently made other changes in minimum sentences for drug-related offenses which will have independent effects from those caused by the guidelines. Nonetheless, early data show that whereas in May 1985 the proportion of convicted offenders sentenced to prison was 50 percent, in May 1989 it was 60.7 percent — an increase but not an explosion (U.S. Sentencing Commission, 1990). As a result of guideline amendments effective November 1, 1989, average time served for all offenses rose from 26.9 to 28.7 months, an increase of 6.7 percent compared with past practice (U.S. Sentencing Commission, 1990).

Another concern in the debates over the guidelines was whether there would be fewer guilty pleas and more trials, resulting in greater expense because of less flexibility to bargain over sentences. Data from November 1987 to the beginning of 1990 reveal the national rate of 88.1 percent for 1989 to be essentially unchanged and indistinguishable from the average plea rate of 89 percent for the period from 1984 to 1987 (U.S. Sentencing Commission, 1990). There is still much debate over whether the guidelines will reduce sentencing disparity, but there can be little doubt that the get-tough approach is being mirrored in the federal approach to sentencing as a result of the cumulative effect of criminal law changes in recent years.

There will be a continuing debate over the cost/benefit contribution of the sentencing guidelines in reducing crime. Congress will no doubt be in and out of the issue. The effect of the sentencing guidelines and their attempt to "rationalize" federal sentencing practices will not be to replace political debate but most likely to give it a different focus. While the courts cannot be hauled before congressional committees and asked about the effects of federal criminal laws and their implementation, the Sentencing Commission can. Whether, in sum total, the system will produce better justice in terms of a more understandable system, reduced unwarranted disparity in sentences, and reduction in crime remains to be seen.

The Comprehensive Crime Control Act did not end the movement to reform the federal criminal laws. In a larger sense, it was merely a beginning. It was a breakthrough in two respects. It showed Congress taking action after a long stalemate, and it set a new pattern of crime legislation that was more favorable to the law enforcement side of the accused criminal–law enforcement balance.

Subsequent Criminal Reform Legislation

Many expected that there would be a long hiatus before Congress acted again. However, not two years after the passage of the Comprehensive Crime Control Act, the drug-related death on June 19, 1986, of basketball star Len Bias seemed to crystalize the illegal drug problem in the national consciousness, and Congress was once again sent into a frenzy of criminal law reform activity.

In the 99th Congress, the scenario was different, but key dynamics were the same. The House majority leadership clearly learned from the crime package experience. Following Bias's death, which was revealed by autopsy to be cocaine induced, Speaker O'Neill, on July 23, announced that several House committees — not just Judiciary — would develop an antidrug bill

before Congress adjourned in the fall. He directed House Majority Leader Wright to have a bill ready for the Rules Committee by September 9.

Wright took the lead and adopted a bipartisan approach,
working with Minority Leader Michel in overseeing the development of the bill. House Republicans put Wright and O'Neill
to a stern test of the commitment to bipartisanship by demanding an opportunity to offer amendments on the House floor.
Among these were the death penalty for murders related to continuing criminal enterprise, and relaxation of the exclusionary
rule. Wright worked with House Minority Leader Michel to
craft a rule (H. Res. 541) that permitted thirty-one separate
amendments, eighteen of which would be offered by Republicans. Judiciary Chairman Rodino met with Speaker O'Neill and
Wright and vigorously opposed their allowing the death penalty
and exclusionary rule amendments in particular. According to
Wright, O'Neill told Rodino, "You're wrong. They've got to be
allowed" (Calmes, 1986, p. 2361). Wright said later that O'Neill
"wasn't in favor of all of the amendments. I wasn't for some of
them either. But, if you're going to have a bipartisan bill, then
you must give both sides a right to offer their amendments" (p.
2361). Both amendments passed the House by large margins,
and the House bill passed on September 11.

President Reagan unveiled his "Drug-Free America Act"
and the Senate introduced its own package, incorporating many
of the administration's proposals. Reminiscent of final action
on the Comprehensive Crime Control Act, a compromise version was passed in another series of marathon sessions in the
final rush to adjournment to allow the members to go home and
campaign. The leadership were determined to pass an anticrime
drug bill, and both movement and compromise were again facilitated by election-year pressure. Neither house of Congress
wanted to adjourn and be accused of failing to respond to the
drug crime issue. Anticrime legislation had become must-pass
legislation.

One of the final compromises was again arranged after
Senator Mathias, along with Senator Levin, threatened a filibuster in the waning hours of a marathon session unless the death

penalty and exclusionary rule provisions were deleted. The final bill was cleared by both houses on October 17, barely three weeks before Election Day.

The media attention and much of the maneuvering surrounding the 1986 act was over the funding for state and local drug enforcement and treatment programs as well as federal enforcement efforts. As in the battle over Justice Assistance within the Comprehensive Crime Control Act, the House originally authorized more money—$6.2 billion—than the Senate, and the final outcome was $1.7 billion. However, substantive criminal law changes were abundant as well. The act provided new fines for simple drug possession, defined new money-laundering crimes, modified the Freedom of Information Act to protect sensitive law enforcement information, established new penalties for drug crimes, and made a host of other criminal law changes. Again, the omnibus approach was successful.

In the 100th Congress, law enforcement proponents were back at it again, and finally cleared the Anti-Drug Abuse Act of 1988 in the wee hours of the morning on the final day of the session on October 22. Again, the exclusionary rule and death penalty were issues, and while the exclusionary rule provisions were dropped, this time the bill included a death penalty provision for anyone who intentionally kills or causes the killing of someone in a drug-related crime. The money authorized in the act was $2.8 billion, of which $1.5 billion was for drug treatment, prevention, and education. It included other substantive criminal law changes as well, affecting federal firearms laws, child pornography and obscenity, mail fraud, money laundering, increased penalties for drug users, and chemical diversion and trafficking, to mention a few of the titles. Senator Biden also finally got his drug czar included in the bill.

The 101st Congress once again considered anticrime bills. The political dynamics in Congress had somewhat changed. President Bush had made significant political points in his presidential campaign by labeling Michael Dukakis, his Democratic opponent, as soft on crime. His television commercials highlighted Willie Horton, a convicted murderer who had raped a woman while out on furlough from a Massachusetts prison.

This tactic changed the atmosphere in the Senate; Senate Democrats became determined to keep control of crime legislation in order to show that their party was not soft on crime. While there was clearly majority support for increased use of the death penalty, habeas corpus reform, and a narrowing of the exclusionary rule, determined minorities in the Senate and the House were opposed to these.

Perhaps the single biggest change in the political dynamics was the introduction of gun control proposals to ban semiautomatic weapons. The killing of school children in Stockton, California, by a man with a semiautomatic rifle gave new impetus to gun control proponents. The gun control issue has the pivotal effect of dividing pro–law enforcement proponents. Most police groups favor banning such weapons, but sizeable numbers of rank-and-file police officers do not. In Congress, many see gun control as restricting the liberty of individual citizens and preventing people in dangerous areas from arming themselves to protect their homes. Others see the growing arsenal of weapons in private hands as a serious law enforcement problem. The National Rifle Association, a vaunted lobby which can deliver hundreds of thousands of letters against a bill in a matter of weeks, vehemently opposes weapons bans and heavily lobbied members during the 101st Congress.

President Bush announced a comprehensive crime plan on May 15, 1989. Much of the plan was incorporated into a bill (S.1225) that Senator Thurmond introduced. Bush's plan asked Congress to broaden the applicability of the death penalty to a number of offenses, create an exception to the exclusionary rule, set a one-year filing deadline for federal habeas corpus claims, authorize new federal law enforcement agents and prosecutors, and appropriate $1 billion for new prison construction. It also included two provisions on semiautomatic weapons. One provision called for doubling to ten years the current mandatory minimum sentence for use of a semiautomatic weapon in a violent crime or drug-related felony. The other called for a permanent ban on imports of foreign-made semiautomatic weapons found to be unsuitable for sporting purposes.

In a preview of the trouble gun control would cause for

the 1990 crime bill, some members of Congress criticized Bush's assault weapons plan as going too far while others said it did not go far enough. Senator Metzenbaum, unhappy that only foreign assault rifles were included, complained, "I have yet to hear any police officer say that domestic assault weapons are somehow less dangerous than imported ones" (Biskupic, May 20, 1989, p. 1196). Senator McClure (R-Id.) warned that the crime bill could get bogged down "in the same old, tired arguments about gun control" (Biskupic, May 20, 1989, p. 1196).

Senator Thurmond introduced a separate death penalty bill (S.32), which would have authorized the death penalty for a number of federal crimes and spelled out procedures for its imposition. However, Senator Biden would not schedule action on the bill in the Senate Judiciary Committee, and Thurmond and other Republicans held up other unrelated legislation by trying to tack on its provisions as an amendment. On July 20, a unanimous consent agreement was reached that ordered the Judiciary Committee to act on S.32. If the committee did not act, the bill would come directly to the Senate floor. A hearing was held on the bill on October 2, during which Senator Kennedy indicated he would propose an amendment containing the provisions of a bill he had introduced (S.1696) that barred a death sentence if a defendant can prove with statistics or other evidence that his race or that of the victim played a role in the sentencing decision. The prosecutor would then have to show by clear and convincing evidence that the racial disparities are not the result of discrimination, and if he could not, the death sentence would be vacated.

On October 17, the Senate Judiciary Committee acted on S.32. As expected, Senator Kennedy offered his amendment to bar the death penalty if it furthers a "racially discriminatory pattern." Senator Thurmond called it a killer amendment and threatened to read the entire Supreme Court opinion from *McCleskey* v. *Kemp* in which the court said that the introduction of statistics to show race-related disparities in the imposition of the death penalty are not enough to have death penalty laws declared unconstitutional. Senator Thurmond argued, "Race should play no role whatsoever, but this would allow vicious

killers to get off by talking about the race of the defendant"
(Biskupic, Oct. 21, 1989). Senator Kennedy countered that the
provision would not undermine the death penalty, but would
assure it was not imposed in a racist manner. The committee
approved the amendment 7 to 6 with Senator Specter the lone
Republican supporting it. The committee turned down a Biden amendment 6 to 6 that would have required court appointed
lawyers in capital cases to meet certain requirements of court-
room and felony trial experience, but it approved a Biden
amendment 8 to 5 that increased the mitigating factors a jury
would have to consider in imposing a death penalty. The committee also approved on a voice vote a Biden amendment to
bar execution of mentally retarded defendants convicted of capital crimes. The committee then split 7 to 7 on a vote to report
the bill to the full Senate with a favorable recommendation —
not enough to send it to the floor. Under the unanimous consent agreement, this meant the unamended bill would have been
taken up on the Senate floor. The committee voted again on
a motion to send the bill to the Senate floor without a recommendation, and this passed on a voice vote.

The Senate Judiciary Committee had taken up two semiautomatic weapons bills that went further than Bush's proposals. Senator Metzenbaum's S.386, would have banned twice as
many weapons as the other, S.747, which was introduced by
Senator DeConcini. On July 27, 1989 the Judiciary Committee had narrowly approved sending the DeConcini bill to the
full Senate by a vote of 7 to 6. The majority consisted of all
the Democratic senators (Biden, DeConcini, Metzenbaum,
Kennedy, Kohl, Leahy, and Simon), except Senator Heflin, who
joined Republicans Thurmond, Grassley, Hatch, Humphrey,
and Simpson in opposition. If Senator Specter had voted with
the minority the vote would have been tied and the bill would
not have been reported out, but Specter said he was not ready
to decide (Biskupic, July 22, 1989).

The majority leadership was not anxious to bring up the
crime bill, in that it was certain to cause hours of acrimonious
debate. The focus in this Congress was on money for antidrug
programs and a major battle shaped up over whether to ap-

propriate more money for drug treatment and education than the administration had requested. This largely partisan fight prevented the Senate from passing the regular appropriations bills before the new fiscal year began on October 1. Just a few days before the deadline, a unanimous consent agreement was finally reached to pass a continuing resolution that would keep the government going past October 1 and to adopt an $8.8 billion compromise package for drug programs for 1990. The concession to Republicans was to agree that before the Senate adjourned, the crime proposals including death penalty, exclusionary rule, and habeas corpus rights would be considered.

Death penalty advocates scored a victory when the Senate passed a death penalty bill (S.1798) on October 26, 1989, with a vote of 79 to 20. The bill would subject terrorists who murder U.S. citizens abroad to the death penalty.

On November 21, Senator Biden introduced a bill, S.1970, that covered six items in the unanimous consent agreement. It included authorization of the death penalty for thirty federal offenses primarily involving murder, espionage, and treason; the exclusionary rule modification, which permitted the use of evidence seized in a search with a deficient warrant if the search and seizure were carried out in a good faith belief that the warrant was valid; additional money laundering investigative powers; and a proposal to reorganize the Justice Department's crime and dangerous drug divisions. It also included the provisions of the DeConcini bill that prohibited future sales of five types of foreign and four types of domestic semiautomatic weapons.

The Biden bill also contained habeas corpus reform. It required prisoners on death row to file federal appeals within one year after they exhausted state appeals and required that adequate legal counsel be provided to such prisoners for the appeals. Defendants convicted of capital crimes in state courts regularly ask federal courts to issue writs of habeas corpus to challenge the state court; this proceeds in conjunction with other appeals in their attempt to reverse their sentences and to delay their executions.

Pursuant to the requirement for a study of the issue under the provision of the 1988 Anti-Drug Abuse Act, a panel chaired by former Supreme Court Justice Lewis Powell had is-

sued a report showing that the average time between conviction and execuion in death penalty cases was more than eight
years, with the delay coming from the multiple appeals of death
sentences at both state and federal levels. The panel recommended that those sentenced to the death penalty in state courts
be given a six-month period in which to file a writ of habeas
corpus requesting a federal court review of the state trial after
exhausting their state appeals. In addition, only one round of
federal appeals would be permitted, rather than the multiple
appeals state defendants often used. The panel recommended
that the provisions only apply to cases from states that guaranteed prisoners adequate legal help to prepare their appeals. Chief
Justice Rhenquist sent the panel's recommendations to the House
and Senate. The federal judiciary was not united on the issue,
however. On October 4, 1989, fourteen members of the Judicial Conference sent a letter to L. Ralph Mecham, the Conference secretary, requesting that he ask the judiciary committees
to hold hearings "so that the recommendations of the Judicial
Conference which will be adopted at the next meeting will be
considered" (Biskupic, October 14, 1989, p. 2718).

    S.1970 came to the Senate floor during the week of May
21, 1990, and faced dozens of amendments from all sides. The
ban on semiautomatic weapons had produced fierce lobbying
by the National Rifle Association (NRA) against it and by
numerous law enforcement groups for it. On May 22, the Senate
voted 82 to 17 to table a Metzenbaum amendment to perma-
nently ban an additional twelve types of semiautomatic weapons
and limit ammunition magazines to fifteen rounds. The next
day, however, Senator Hatch offered an amendment to delete
the weapons ban, but it failed 48 to 52. The administration
had threatened to veto a bill with a weapons ban, and the NRA
promised to defeat the whole bill if it remained.

    The provision to require prosecutors to show that racial
disparities in sentencing were not due to racial discrimination
was vigorously debated. Senator Kennedy argued that the 1987
Supreme Court decision, *McClesky* v. *Kemp,* which rejected
challenges to capital punishment based on statistics showing racial disparities was wrongly decided. Senator Robert Graham

(D-Fla.) stated that Kennedy's provision would destroy a state's capital punishment procedures. Graham argued that the criminal justice process does not lend itself to statistical analysis and that a jury should be left to assess the specific acts of a defendant. Graham moved to strike the racial statistics provision and won 58 to 38 with a majority of Republicans and just under half of the Democrats supporting the motion.

On May 23, Senators Thurmond and Specter offered an amendment designed to tighten restrictions on the use of habeas corpus petitions by state prisoners. Among the modifications were to remove the requirement of exhaustion of state remedies and to shorten the time for filing to sixty days after the appointment of counsel and resolution of the appeal in the state's highest court. The amendment failed 47 to 50. Specter voted against it when he saw it was losing in order to preserve his right to move for reconsideration of the vote. The very next day, Specter and Thurmond tried again, and the motion to reconsider was adopted 52 to 46. Their amendment was then adopted on a voice vote.

At the time of the Memorial Day recess, whether the bill had a future was unclear because 87 Democratic amendments and 184 Republican amendments were still pending. The Senate leadership feared a filibuster as well, and both Majority Leader Mitchell and Minority Leader Dole doubted there were the required 60 votes to invoke cloture and shut off debate (Biskupic, May 26, 1990). When the Senate reconvened after the recess, gun control opponents did filibuster and votes to invoke cloture fell short of the required 60 votes: 54 to 37 on June 5 and 57 to 37 on June 7. Majority Leader Mitchell indicated he did not want to devote any more Senate floor time to the crime bill, but was persuaded by Senators Biden and Thurmond to allow them to try to reach a compromise.

Once again, the effect of election-year pressure came into play, as neither side wished to be viewed as killing an anticrime bill a few months before an election. Biden and Thurmond agreed to each give up a pet provision in the bill. Biden gave up the provision to reorganize the Justice Department's crime and dangerous drug divisions, which the administration opposed, and Thurmond agreed to give up the exclusionary rule modifications. On June 28, agreement was reached on how amendments would be presented. As part of the agreement, senators would refrain from reopening the contentious crime issues for the remainder of the year.

Senator Phil Graham tried once again to delete the semiautomatic weapons ban in favor of an amendment to mandate minimum sentences for firearms violations. His amendment narrowly lost, however, 50 to 48. Senator Hatfield (R-Oreg.) tried an amendment to substitute mandatory life imprisonment for the death penalty, but this, too, failed, 25 to 73. An amendment by Senator D'Amato to authorize the death penalty for defendants convicted of being leaders of continuing criminal enterprises was adopted 66 to 32. Senator Biden offered an amendment to add 1000 FBI agents, 1000 Drug Enforcement Administration agents, 500 border patrol officers, and 480 prosecutors, which passed 96 to 2.

After being amended, the Omnibus Crime Bill was approved on July 11, 1990, by a vote of 94 to 6. The Senate bill included, besides the firearms and habeas corpus provisions, provisions to expand to thirty-four the number of federal crimes that could receive the death penalty including kidnapping, the taking of a hostage, killing a foreign official, and murdering for money. As in past years, the pressure shifted to the House in the waning days of the Congress.

In the more than a year since President Bush had announced his anticrime package, the House Judiciary Committee had not reported out a crime bill comparable to the one passed by the Senate. House Judiciary Chairman Jack Brooks (D-Tex.) had stated in April, "All of us have voted for crime bills almost every year for the last few years. We have got almost as many crime bills passed as they have crimes committed" (Biskupic, July 21, 1990, p. 2321). The House Republicans took to the House floor to repeatedly make speeches calling for action on the crime package. Reminiscent of the maneuver that led to successful House floor consideration of the Comprehensive Crime Control Act in 1984, Robert Walker (R-Pa.) tried a procedural move to instruct the Rules Committee to allow

a floor amendment that would attach the crime provisions to
an unrelated bill before the House. This did not work, but it
served to indicate that crime bill proponents were going to keep
up the pressure into the final election season. The House leadership was put on notice that they risked a repeat of the 1984 defeat
just before the coming election.

The House Judiciary Committee took up HR.5269 the
week of July 17. The death penalty provisions provoked significant conflict. The House bill extended the death penalty from
the existing two offenses to ten, including killing the president
or vice president or injuring them trying. Representative George
Gekas (R-Pa.) tried to amend the bill to cover the murders
of other federal officials, saying that all homicides of federal
officials should be covered, but the committee rejected his
amendment 12 to 22. Representative Bill McCollum (R-Fla.)
offered an amendment to allow someone who is convicted of
running a major drug-trafficking empire to receive the death
penalty, but his amendment was defeated 14 to 22. The committee's bill did contain a provision like the one that Senator
Kennedy had offered in the Senate that would allow a defendant to use statistical evidence to establish a prima facie case
that either his or her race or that of the victim was the reason
the death penalty was assigned.

The habeas corpus issue also received attention. Representative Hughes (D-N.J.) and Representative Kastenmeier (D-
Wis.) offered an amendment that required such defendants to
file the petitions within one year of losing direct appeals of their
death sentences. It also required states that wanted to impose
the time limit to provide lawyers to the inmates for their appeals and set standards of experience that the lawyers would
have to meet.

The House bill did not have a provision comparable to
the Senate bill that banned nine semiautomatic assault weapons.
The House Judiciary Committee defeated an amendment by
Representative Campbell to ban semiautomatic pistols 15 to 21
and an amendment by Representative Smith (D-Fla.) to outlaw the manufacture or import of cheap handguns by a vote
of 15 to 21. The Committee did approve by a vote of 19 to 15

an amendment by Representative Glickman (D-Kan.) to increase from five to ten years the mandatory prison sentence for using a sawed-off shotgun or rifle in drug crimes and to impose a thirty-year sentence for using a bomb or grenade in a drug crime. The committee also adopted an amendment by Representative Sangmeister (D-Ill.) to establish mandatory sentences of ten years to life imprisonment for certain officers of savings and loan associations convicted of fraud. House Judiciary approved HR.5269 as amended on July 23, 1990, by a vote of 19 to 17.

The House leadership brought the crime bill to the floor at the beginning of October, and the death penalty was prominent in the three days of debate. Once again, the majority of House members turned out to be more pro-law enforcement than was a majority of the Judiciary Committee. Representative Gekas tried again to expand the list of crimes for which the death penalty could be levied to thirty, and the full House agreed to his amendment by a vote of 271 to 159. Gekas's amendment also provided that a judge or jury would be required to sentence a defendant to death if the judge or jury found that one aggravating factor, such as torture, existed, and that factor outweighed any mitigation factors. Representative McCollum offered his amendment to extend the death penalty to those who run large-scale drug operations or through "reckless disregard" cause a drug-related death, which also passed 295 to 133. Representative Hughes offered an amendment similar to the one that Gekas had offered, but it did not include the procedural changes. It lost 108 to 319.

On habeas corpus appeals of death sentences to federal courts, Representative Hyde (R-Ill.) offered an amendment that would keep the requirement that states provide lawyers for death row appeals, but did not set standards for experience as the Judiciary Committee's bill had done. It also made it more difficult for defendants to challenge their convictions based on court rulings in cases announced after their convictions. Representative Hughes offered an amendment to allow more exceptions for additional appeals, but the full House rejected it 189 to 239. Hyde's amendment passed 285 to 146. Hughes did have one success on the House floor with a racial statistics amendment. He offered it to head off a Republican challenge to the Judiciary Committee's provision that allowed defendants to challenge their death sentences on grounds of racial discrimination. Hughes's amendment would have required a court to examine the validity of the statistics and decide whether they provided a basis for finding a significant pattern of discrimination. His amendment passed 218 to 186. Opponents of the statistics provision argued that because statistics are misleading, prosecutors would have to bring forth statistics to prove that race was not a factor, and the uncertainty over the use of such statistics would effectively end the states' ability to impose capital punishment (Biskupic, Oct. 6, 1990, p. 3225). Representative Sensenbrenner (R-Wis.) offered an amendment to eliminate the racial statistics provision that narrowly lost, 204 to 216. This vote ultimately meant the end for several major provisions of the bill.

The full House adopted the amended crime bill on October 5, 1990, by a vote of 368 to 55. The impending election clearly affected the building of majority support for provisions that stiffened punishments and were more oriented toward the concerns of law enforcement authorities. Representative Hughes acknowledged as much when he stated, "I hope we never, ever bring up a crime bill again a month before an election" (Biskupic, Oct. 6, 1990, p. 3223).

However, the more liberal members of the House Judiciary Committee were not beaten yet. There were substantial differences between the House and Senate bills. The Bush administration had said that the president would veto the bill if the section allowing defendants to use statistics to prove racial discrimination were included. A conference committee was not appointed until October 25, 1990, three days before adjournment. The Democratic members, all from House Judiciary, were Brooks, Kastenmeier, Edwards, Conyers, Hughes, and Schumer. The Republicans were McCollum, Gekas, Hyde, and Dewine. Representative McCollum, wishing to safeguard the floor victories over the Judiciary Democrats, introduced a motion on the House floor to instruct the House conferees to insist on the House provisions on the death penalty, habeas corpus, and the exclusionary rule.

This passed 291 to 123 with every Democrat on the conference committee except Brooks voting against it (*Congressional Record*, Oct. 25, 1990, H11740).

The conference committee met on October 26. House Committee chairman Brooks proposed taking out the death penalty provisions altogether, but Senator Thurmond resisted, arguing "what would the bill amount to if we take out capital punishment?" (Biskupic, October 27, 1990, p. 3615). Representative McCollum proposed a deal that would have removed from the bill all provisions relating to placing limits on habeas corpus petitions and the use of statistics to demonstrate racial discrimination, but it failed among House conferees, 4 to 6. Democrats on the committee generally wanted to adopt the Senate provisions barring assault-type weapons, and the Republicans opposed this. With time almost gone, the conferees agreed on October 26, just two days before adjournment, to strip out all the death penalty, habeas corpus, exclusionary rule, and gun control provisions. Provisions that were left included increased penalties for child abuse, prison alternatives such as house arrest, new penalties for bank fraud and certain drug offenses, and more funding for local law enforcement.

The next day on the House floor, Republicans were castigating the Democrats for stripping out the provisions for which the House had voted three weeks before. Representative Brooks said that it was impossible to reach agreement on major issues contained in both bills. "The differences were simply too great to bridge at this late hour in the session" (*Congressional Record*, Oct. 27, 1990, H13288). Representative McCollum termed the final product a "mini-crime bill" (*Congressional Record*, Oct. 27, 1990, H13291). Representative Hughes objected to McCollum's characterization and called the remainder "strong anti-crime measures" (*Congressional Record*, Oct. 27, 1990, H13292). Representative Hyde stated, "now, the laws are not only written in conference, they are shredded in conference" (*Congressional Record*, Oct. 27, 1990, H13292). Representative Shumer, noting that many of the complaints which had been made concerned what the bill "is not," argued, "well, with that argument we could vote against every piece of legislation that ever came up" (*Congressional Record*, Oct. 27, 1990, H13296). Representative McCollum concluded for the Republicans, "Pass the bill tonight, but remember our work is not done. We have to come back and produce a truly anticrime bill in the next Congress" (*Congressional Record*, Oct. 27, 1990, H13296). The bill passed the House 313 to 1 with 118 not voting (*Congressional Record*, Oct. 27, 1990, H13296). The Senate passed the bill the same day on a voice vote, one day before adjournment.

The defeat of such long-standing items on the criminal law legislative agenda, such as the death penalty, habeas corpus reform, and exclusionary rule modification in the 101st Congress came because the majority Democrat House conferees would not give up on the racial statistics provision which the Senate had rejected, and the majority Democrat Senate conferees would not give up on banning automatic weapons. With too few days left, the majorities existing in both houses of Congress for provisions such as the death penalty, habeas corpus, and exclusionary rule modification could not take action to save them. It is unlikely that this defeat will be the end of those issues, however. Given the public's continuing concern with crime, and the prevalence of criminal law issues such as the death penalty in recent elections, it is more likely that these issues will be rejoined again in Congress, and the outcome will again be determined near the end of the session and just before the election.

A Need for a Comprehensive Federal Criminal Code?

It is clear that all of the goals of federal criminal law reformers have not been achieved. A major outstanding question is, Should the United States have a Federal Criminal Code? Proponents argue that Title 18 of the U.S. Code should be revised to accomplish this aim. Their overarching objective is to simplify the federal criminal law.

As criminal code proponents aver, a criminal code implies "systematic arrangement" of laws with revisions to "harmonize conflicts, supply omissions, and generally clarify and make complete the body of laws" involved. Robert Joost, a code proponent, states: "Title 18 is not arranged 'scientifically' nor is its arrangement 'systematic'. Its provisions do not 'harmonize conflicts, supply omissions' or 'clarify ambiguities'; rather they do quite the reverse" (Joost, 1986, p. 8).

What the recent criminal law legislation has done is add provisions and modify a few existing statutes. The amended statutes do not constitute a major overhaul of the federal criminal law or even of Title 18. They have not set forth a comprehensive, integrated statement of federal criminal law. Many major federal crimes are still described in other titles of the U.S. Code, and many others are still described only in case decisions of the federal courts. For some criminal law provisions, a prosecutor, defense attorney, or citizen is left to discern what the law is by comparing the number of federal courts of appeal that support interpretation A with the number that support interpretation B. Other provisions are determined by reference to the position that a 5 to 4 Supreme Court majority took on an issue of interpretation in a case years ago. Code proponents argue, "In these circumstances, the Administration and Congress should determine policy positions on the basis of experience, rationality, cost-benefit analysis, and the purposes of criminal law, rather than on the basis of existing law" (Joost, 1986, p. 8).

Criminal code proponents have thought that now that many of the more controversial criminal law changes have been made, it may be time to take up code revision and provide a truly comprehensive statement of federal criminal law. In fact, right after passage of the Comprehensive Crime Control Act, Senate Judiciary leaders considered such an undertaking. On November 19, 1984, Senator Thurmond wrote to the attorney general expressing an interest in returning to the subject of criminal code revision. Lowell Jensen, associate attorney general and the highest-ranking policy official who handled criminal affairs for the Justice Department, replied that the department was inclined "to postpone a renewed criminal code initiative." He also stated, "Moreover, obtaining sentencing reform legislation via the Comprehensive Crime Control Act removed much of the impetus for an omnibus criminal code revision bill, although we recognize that much needs to be done in this area" (Jensen to Thurmond, letter of Dec. 13, 1984).

Criminal code proponents argue that a truly comprehensive statement of federal criminal law is still needed, and a greater level of understanding by judges, jurors, and attorneys would result in efficiency gains that would allow federal courts and law enforcement agencies to do more with existing resources than they can do today. Thirty-five states have criminal codes, and proponents argue that there is no reason for the federal government to remain a laggard.

Code reformers' political argument is that now that successive recent substantive criminal law changes have removed many of the old controversies, Congress should be able to tidy up the whole structure. Reformers acknowledge that for this to happen, the president would have to state that code reform is a major administration goal, a single bill would have to be negotiated that could be introduced in both houses of Congress, and the bill could not contain controversial substantive changes (Joost, 1986).

Doubters question that the attention of Congress and the administration can be engaged without substantive provisions that attract the public and are therefore controversial. A major political question is whether simplicity, efficiency, and understandability have enough of a constituency to encourage legislators who remember the old battles to embark on the expedition once again. Even code proponents acknowledge that a certain amount of "filling the gaps" is necessary. The question is, Will such gap filling reignite old wars and start new ones as groups again focus on what is already on the books in light of current political disputes? Alternatively, are the players wary of the dangers and committed to resolving disputes, by resort to existing law if necessary, in order to achieve a code?

At the current time, most attention has shifted from the area of law reform to the question of how to finance increased enforcement. Congress and state legislatures have increasingly responded to majority sentiments to get tough. The costs are increasing rapidly. H.R.3015 (P.L. 101-164) brought total federal antidrug spending for fiscal 1990 to $8.8 billion, up from $5.7 billion the year before. Congress may decide that some efficiency gains that could be achieved through code reform may help control costs, but this approach has little electoral appeal. The focus is shifting to distributional politics — that is, how federal money can be distributed for prevention, treatment, and enforcement to state and local levels.

Conclusion: Evaluating How Well the Legislative Process Works

A major question addressed in this book is that of the potential for passage of large-scale public interest legislation. Accompanying the debate over various federal crime reform bills was a parallel debate over whether to take an incremental or a comprehensive approach. Such a debate is a central issue in policy-making in the United States. Charles Lindblom's classic statement (1959) comparing the incremental and rational-comprehensive approaches to policy-making found real world significance in the debate over the reform of the federal criminal laws. Lindblom (1979) predicts that a truly comprehensive approach to policy problems (a synoptic approach) is impossible because inevitably too many contentious issues will be raised that ignite opposing interests which form a successful blocking coalition. A proposal too comprehensive is its own worst enemy because it inflames interests that otherwise would have nothing in common. Such a blocking coalition is advantaged in the U.S. system because of the numerous veto points that exist in the system. This is exactly what happened when liberal groups combined with conservative ones to defeat the last criminal code bill in 1983. The administration and congressional leaders finally concluded that the synoptic criminal code approach would inevitably confront a repeat of the same blocking phenomenon. Lindblom postulates, however, that the United States may not be relegated to policy-making by small incremental bits either. He claims that policy is improved by the guiding ideal of strategic analysis, one form of which is to focus on pivotal issues critical to policy choices.

It appears that the Comprehensive Crime Control Act was clearly not comprehensive in the synoptic sense. It was not as comprehensive as any of the criminal code bills. However, the case could be made that it was comprehensive in Lindblom's strategic sense. That is, by focusing on a major bundle of substantive reforms, it set the pattern for a period of reform that was more oriented toward protecting society and less oriented toward criminal defendants. In this case, the key policy leaders kept the focus on pivotal issues of sentencing and bail, which were central to the new policy thrust. The omnibus approach hinged on the pivotal issues but, over time, numerous other issues had gained consensus and were included in the package. The final product was the result of innumerable bargains and compromises that achieved widespread support. It had something in it for most interests, and legislators were put on notice that "if you want your thing, the price is you have to support the entire package." In this way, a blocking coalition large enough to kill the bill is prevented from forming. Since the passage of the Comprehensive Crime Control Act, crime bill proponents have used the same approach to pass other multi-title crime bills.

Although there can be little doubt that the Comprehensive Crime Control Act had some significant effects on federal criminal law, it would be hard to claim that in itself, or combined with subsequent statutory changes, it will dramatically reduce street crime in the near future. Critics have charged all along that since crime control is primarily a state and local responsibility, that is where most of the emphasis must be placed. However, the same criticism can be made of federal funding assistance efforts to state and local law enforcement agencies. The federal funds (even several billion dollars) will always be a small portion of state and local law enforcement efforts. Whether changes in federal criminal law or the provision of federal crime funds stimulate state anticrime policies and actions will continue to be an area of sharp debate in federal crime legislation.

The conceptual separation of state and local efforts relating to street crime and federal efforts relating to something else is too facile and fundamentally inaccurate. In an age when criminal enterprises are formally or informally both vertically and horizontally integrated, law enforcement cannot be treated as a set of discrete operations. Local law enforcement officials have repeatedly called for the federal government to do more about the international drug enterprises, and there is a national consensus that this is a key federal responsibility that directly affects street crime.

In addition, the significance of federal criminal law will always extend beyond the direct impact of federal law enforcement operations. As Representative Lungren stated upon the passage of the Comprehensive Crime Control Act, "The states take their cues from the Federal Government. This is an example for them to follow" (Stengel, 1984). Actually, the federal government and the states take their cues from each other in a continuing dialogue over appropriate criminal laws. The Minnesota sentencing guidelines law and other state determinate sentencing laws influenced the federal law, and in turn the federal approach to sentencing influenced the states. The federal government, however, is the singularly largest speaker in the dialogue of national policy, and major policy changes at the federal level very often reverberate substantively and symbolically throughout the system.

Even counting its value as an example for the states, the Comprehensive Crime Control Act and its progeny do not constitute the comprehensive answer to street crime in America. There will continue to be a wide-ranging debate about the effect of criminal law on crime. Crime reform proponents never claimed that such legislation would end street crime. Even the most enthusiastic law enforcement proponents believe that the criminal laws as a social institution can only play part, along with such other social institutions as the family, schools, neighborhoods, and churches, in affecting attitudes toward crime. Law enforcement, however, is a central responsibility of government. Law enforcement proponents argue that government must play its part, not only in catching and punishing criminals to reduce the overall level of criminal activity but also in encouraging the other institutions to realize that there is a chance to reduce crime if all institutions are committed. As those involved in the original Brown Commission understood, the instrumental value of criminal law is only part of the issue. What criminal laws communicate about moral values and justice to other institutions in the society is also important. By this standard, the Comprehensive Crime Control Act and its progeny have signaled a strategic commitment to punish wrongdoers as a means of reducing crime.

The System Works — If Not Reliably and Dependably

As discussed at the beginning of this book, there have been serious questions raised about the capacity of the system to produce large-scale policies that serve the public interest. Divided party government, interest group control, institutional fragmentation of power have been identified as causes of governmental paralysis. One case does not resolve the issue, but it is important to observe that these do not appear to be insurmountable barriers. Of course, both supporters and opponents of the "deadlocked-government" thesis can find ammunition in the saga of crime legislation to support their positions.

Supporters of the deadlocked-government thesis can point to the failure to achieve a comprehensive criminal code, which was picked apart by numerous interest groups. They can also point to the long period of time it took to achieve any meaningful legislative action, even though the crime problem continued to worsen and the public had long since decided that a basic change in policy direction was necessary. They can direct attention to the effects of the division between the House and Senate and how a single committee chairman and subcommittee chairman could bottle up legislation that clearly commanded majority support. They can also argue that legislation passed in a last-minute rush at the end of a congressional session is unlikely to be understood, let alone supported on its merits, by a majority of the people's representatives.

Supporters of the "government works" thesis can point to the Comprehensive Crime Control Act as having achieved massive changes in federal law. They can mention its effect in redirecting the policy stream so that subsequent changes in criminal law came rapidly in the next three congresses. They can also observe that although there were numerous fits and starts, the process served to smooth off the rough edges of criminal law reform proposals and to bring about a result that the overwhelming proportion of legislators of both law enforcement and civil liberties orientations could support. Government-works proponents must concede that a minority of representatives understand even a significant part of an omnibus bill at final passage. However, they can argue that the winnowing process that occurs in earlier stages makes it rare that some affected interest will not be alerted and mobilize opposition somewhere in the system. It will be remembered that even a single senator can make the whole process pause at the end of a session to ensure that a provision is reconsidered.

While there is ammunition for both sides, on balance, the government-works supporters get the better of the argument. It is not that the deadlocked-government proponents have posited nonexistent obstacles to the passage of large-scale public interest legislation. The obstacles are real all right, and they have significant effects. However, they are not insurmountable. What the deadlocked-government proponents leave out are the dynamics of the legislative process that can serve to overcome the obstacles. That is, there are countervailing factors in the legislative process that can serve to foster passage of such legislation, and actors in the legislative process have reacted to the obstacles to achieve significant legislative results.

One of the important factors is policy leadership. To reiterate, policy leadership is a multifaceted phenomenon exercised by several participants in both legislative and executive branches of government who place their priority on policy change, and who play either single or multiple roles according to their resources, and according to the dynamics of the particular legislative process involved in a given legislative effort. This is the factor that energizes the process. It is important to understand the structure and processes of legislation. It is equally important to understand the dynamics of legislation and what moves legislators to make the decisions they do within the extant framework.

As has been demonstrated, policy leadership is not necessarily a function of position, although some participants' potential to exercise it are enhanced by their formal position. Chief among these is the president. Divided government does not necessarily mean policy stalemate. The president's potential to exercise policy leadership is not merely a function of his party's controlling both houses or even one house of Congress, although he is significantly aided by such an eventuality. Since 1952, divided party government has been the norm rather than the exception, and major policy changes have been enacted within this period. In addition, during the periods when the White House and Congress were in the hands of the same party, the country did not necessarily see policy leadership on behalf of the president. The Carter administration is the most recent case in point.

There is more to it than party control. American legislation is driven more by policy than it is by ideology or party. Despite this fact, partisanship can still work for the president, especially in those instances when he correctly discerns the disposition of the public and the other party is playing a partisan strategy but has misgauged public opinion. At other times, the president's leadership is more effective when it rises above partisanship, and sympathetic legislators in the other party, perceiving the president to be correct on substance, decide it is both bad politics and bad policy to follow the president's opponents in their own party. The president is the one actor in the legislative process who starts out with the premise of a national constituency, can speak directly to a national audience, and can speak with one voice. Further, the president's position at the end, in signing or vetoing a bill, gives him leverage all through the process. These advantages do not automatically produce presidential policy leadership, however.

The president requires the assistance of his aides and the agencies to produce specific policies aligned with his political program that will command congressional support, and he and his appointees must possess and exercise the legislative skills to pursue policy positions once they become identified as administration positions. The president's potential for exercising policy leadership is inextricably intertwined with his political power position at any given time. Congressmen in both parties constantly make calculations of the advantages and disadvantages of supporting or opposing the president in both legislative and electoral terms.

Policy leadership does not end with the president. In fact, it does not necessarily start there. Important parts of the Comprehensive Crime Control Act were developed before Ronald Reagan came to office. Key provisions were developed by members of the opposing political party. However, it was Reagan who pushed the whole package to conclusion by making it electorally untenable to publicly oppose it.

Nonetheless, policy leaders in both houses in Congress had moved the package to the point where final action was either possible or feasible. They were responsible for moving it onto the decision agenda. Some were committee and subcommittee chairs or ranking members. Over several Congresses, Senators McClellan, Hruska, Kennedy, Biden, and Thurmond, and Representatives Poff and Drinan, used their positions on behalf of comprehensive criminal law packages. However, key roles were played at the end by members who were neither chairpersons nor ranking members, but who had built up credibility over time on both the substance and politics of the policy. Senator Kennedy and Representative Lungren were in the minority in their respective houses of Congress, and they were not the ranking members of their party on the Judiciary committees. Nonetheless, their policy leadership was important to the passage of the legislation.

These members of Congress brought to the legislative enterprise different capabilities. What they shared was a willingness to invest in a large-scale public interest policy package under conditions where they could not know when, if ever, the payoff would occur.

Political appointees and staff members also played important roles. Attorneys General Bell and Smith invested heavily in the effort. Smith's associate attorneys general, Giuliani and Jensen, and his assistant attorney general, McConnell, worked with both the media and Congress to articulate the law enforcement priorities and keep them visible. Staff members in both branches, including Ronald Gainer, Roger Pauley, and Cary Copeland in Justice, and Paul Summit, Deborah Owen, and Kenneth Feinberg on Senate Judiciary, worked for years to develop the specific proposals and to keep the issue alive. Others outside government working on special groups had an impact, including Governor Brown, Louis Schwartz, and Robert Blakey of the Brown Commission effort, and Governor Thompson and James Q. Wilson of the Attorney General's Task Force on Violent Crime. Numerous other staff members at Justice on the Judiciary committees and subcommittees all invested heavily in policy change.

The electoral factor has been blamed by some observers for leading members of Congress to concentrate more of their efforts on district and constituency service. Yet, the anticipation of electoral consequences can be an important dynamic in the passage of large-scale public interest legislation. Such a factor can overcome determined opposition by the blocking forces who use powerful structural impediments to their advantage. True, there is no assurance that the public's view will find effective expression through electoral anticipation. Issue salience and the skill of policy leaders in positioning their legislation in terms of the issues, along with the timing of the electoral cycle, can have important consequences for legislative success.

None of this is to say that interest groups are not important in large-scale public interest legislation. They can be crucially important to both proponents and blocking forces. The interest groups in the Stop S.1 movement and conservative groups such as the Moral Majority ultimately defeated the criminal code approach to criminal law reform. Eventually, the rise of victims' organizations helped shift the moral ground of criminal law reform. Such groups as the American Bar Association, the National Association of Attorneys General, the National District Attorneys Association, and the American Psychological As-

sociation had important impacts on the substance of federal jurisdiction and the insanity defense in the final crime package, for
example.

Such organizations and numerous others articulate interests that legislators attempt to accommodate in large-scale
public interest packages. No one member of Congress can articulate them all. Rather, through a process of bargaining and
accommodation, the winning coalition of interests can be assembled. Such a process may not be rationally integrated on
a logical basis, but if it achieves the minimum coalition, it will
be integrated on a political basis. The coalition reaches the critical number when wavering members are convinced that the
train is leaving the station and the price of a ticket is to support
the whole package if their interests are to be accommodated.

It becomes much more difficult to assemble an effective
blocking force under such a circumstance because the coalition's
supporters are effectively in a position to adapt, change, or circumvent the very rules that give the blocking forces their advantage. In 1986, Chairman Rodino did not want certain amendments considered on the House floor, but a special rule placed
them there anyway, and they passed. The system is much more
fluid than it at first might appear, and the political dynamics
have more to say about legislative outcome than might be predicted based on the structural obstacle course.

Other Cases of Large-Scale Public Interest Legislation

It may be argued that criminal law legislation is unique and
somehow different in its public interest component from other
types of large-scale public interest legislation. Deadlocked-government proponents argue that the federal budget deficit, for
example, is a symptom of the problem of divided government.
However, as discussed in an earlier chapter, the example of immigration reform was often cited as a similar example of system failure.

Immigration reform was the other omnibus bill Congress
was considering at the same time as the Comprehensive Crime

Control Act. Immigration reform bill sponsors such as Senator Alan Simpson (R-Wyo.) and Representative Romano Mazzoli (D-Ky.), in partnership with the administration and the leadership of the Judiciary committees, tried for three Congresses to pass the bill. It failed in the 98th Congress after passing the Senate but not the House. It failed in the 99th Congress after passing both houses in different forms but with no conference agreement. In the waning days of the 100th Congress, after it again passed both bodies, the conference committee on the bill once again appeared to be deadlocked. Each time, the bill had hung up over objections by interests such as farmers and ranchers, certain Hispanic organizations, and state and local governments who wanted to be guaranteed federal money to pay for their costs as a result of legalization. Key policy leaders refused to give up and, after a six-hour negotiating session, reached a compromise conference report on S.1200, which passed October 15, 1986, in the House and October 17 in the Senate. After the conference had concluded, several members who had been members of the 1984 negotiations concluded that the previous fights over the immigration bill had helped make the 1986 round more conciliatory. Senator Simpson stated, "Every one of us gave up something painful as hell, but we stayed at the table" (Cohodas, 1986, p. 2596). The near misses had the effect of raising the public profile of the problem. Representative Charles Schumer, one of the negotiators, observed that "the problem of immigration had reached the American consciousness. . . . Everybody wanted a bill" (Cohodas, 1986).

Five years later, at the end of the 101st Congress, the second large-scale change in immigration was achieved. In the waning hours of the Congress, conferees agreed to a bill that would both open the nation each year to new immigrants who are skilled workers and managers and completely overhaul the number and classes of people who would be granted entry. It ended many political and medical restrictions that had their roots in the 1950s' anti-communism crusade of Joseph McCarthy. Compromise was once again the order of the day, with conservatives accepting the removal of political ideology or association as a reason for exclusion and liberals accepting a provision that permits the secretary of state to prevent the entry of certain persons into the United States for political reasons "under exceptional circumstances."

The proposed Tax Reform Act of 1986 clearly pitted the wealthiest and most powerful special interests represented in Washington against the populist notion of tax equity. It was widely recognized as providing a benefit to the undifferentiated mass of people who could not take advantage of special-interest deductions, exclusions, and tax credits by lowering the overall tax rate. However, it was known to be highly damaging to those who benefited by the breaks and to whom Congress in general and the tax-writing committees in particular had been continually responsive in passing tax bills for fifty years.

The first brought out an army of the highest-paid lobbyists in Washington. Two weeks before it happened, all of them were betting the bill would fail. The approach was thought to be too bold, too great a change. It spread the benefits over the largely voiceless mass of the public but concentrated the costs on the very interests who were best represented in Washington and who had given millions in campaign contributions.

The lobbyists pulled out all the stops in one of the biggest money fights in history, but they failed. The interests never put together an effective blocking coalition. They grew fearful of being seen as opponents of reform, a position with which members of Congress could not afford to be aligned. The electoral anticipation factor was too strong. As Birnbaum and Murray (1987) observe: "The lobbyists' failure also reflected the difficulty interest groups face in combatting 'populist' legislation. Even though they had made enormous campaign contributions and had much-vaunted access to important legislators, the anti-reform lobbyists remained outsiders throughout the tax reform debate. They could find few allies in the highest councils of power. At each step President Reagan threatened to label lobbyists' friends in Congress as toadies to the special interests and enemies of rate cuts for the people, and that was a threat that could not be taken lightly" (p. 287). This was no small defeat for the well-organized and heavily financed special interests. To quote Birnbaum and Murray's chronicle once again: "The bill closed loopholes worth roughly $300 billion over five years and replaced them with lower tax rates. It also raised corporate taxes by $120 billion over five years, the largest corporate tax increase in history. Congress was acting in response to larger, broader forces, which, in the end prevailed" (p. 288).

Another example of large-scale public interest legislation is the Clean Air Act Amendments, which was taken up again in the 101st Congress. Environmental legislation is an area where seemingly divided party control and the fragmentation of power in Congress have combined to prevent added air pollution control legislation from emerging. Supporters of more stringent air pollution control had tried for over a decade to amend the Clean Air Act, which was passed in 1970 and last amended in 1977. While the act has served to reduce some pollutants, it has failed to reduce others such as ozone, air toxics, and sulphur dioxide; the latter produces acid rain. These issues are not only extremely difficult for Congress to resolve because of their technological and economic complexity and uncertainty, but also because of their political divisiveness. These issues pit region against region, urban areas against rural areas, industry group against industry group, labor group against labor group, and so on. The Clean Air Act Amendments had been stalled in continuing struggle between representatives from high-sulphur coal-burning states against low-sulphur coal-burning districts, automobile producing districts versus high urban smog districts, agricultural districts versus urban districts, and west coast off-shore oil districts versus gulf districts. For ten years the administration has not been a major player in support of legislation.

President Bush had run for president with a promise of support for stronger environmental protection. With the announcement of his administration's multifaceted Clean Air bill on June 12, 1989, he stated, "We've seen enough of this stalemate" (Hager, June 17, 1989, p. 1460). Fred Krup, executive director of the Environmental Defense Fund, attested to the effect of Bush's leadership move: "The logjam has been broken. We are now a hundred miles downstream" (Hager, June 17, 1989, p. 1460). The move prompted long-term congressional opponents such as John Dingell (D-Mich.), chairman of the House

Energy and Commerce Committee, and Henry Waxman (D-Calif.), chairman of that committee's Subcommittee on Health and Environment, to begin serious negotiations that signaled to all participants that this time real movement was likely. While the process stretched into 1990, in the House a bill was put together through intensive negotiations among Energy and Commerce committee members. Long-term rivals Dingell and Waxman, and ranking Republican Norman Lent (R-N.Y.) were key participants in the negotiations and kept them moving. Agreement after agreement was reached; when the bill passed the House and Senate in different forms, leaders of the House conferees were bound to many of those agreements unless they could agree on a compromise in the conference committee.

The bill's fate came down to a final marathon negotiating session during the week of October 15, 1990, over perhaps the most contentious issue of all — acid rain. Congress had been unable to agree for over a decade because any legislation would have to meet the needs of both the "clean states," those in the northeast that have received acid rain and have utilities that burn low-sulphur coal, and the "dirty states," those primarily in the midwest that have coal mining industries to protect and utilities that burn high-sulphur coal. Bush's proposal was to devise a system of market-based pollution allowances that could be granted to utilities that limit sulphur dioxide emissions. This proposal would give plants flexibility to clean up in the most cost-effective manner for them. Utilities that had been high users of high-sulphur coal could sell valuable allowance credits and recover their costs for installing less polluting plants and equipment. Cleaner utilities that wanted to expand their operations could buy the allowances to gain room under the new caps on emissions. Conferees wrangled in the final days of the 101st Congress over a requirement that two-phase emissions limits be imposed in 1995 and 2000, which midwestern representatives opposed as being too costly. Compromise was reached at approximately 5:00 A.M. on October 22, 1990, when conferees agreed to grant plants in Ohio, Illinois, and Indiana 200,000 extra allowances a year from 1991 to 1995 (Pytte, Oct. 27, 1990).

The conference committee report was adopted by the

House on October 26, 1990, by a vote of 401 to 25, and by the Senate on October 27 by a vote of 89 to 10, clearing the bill for the president one day before adjournment. These overwhelming votes did not mean that everyone was exceedingly pleased with the outcome. Environmentalists were pleased that the final bill went beyond what the administration had originally proposed, but were unhappy that it included delayed compliance deadlines. Representatives of industry said the result would be higher prices for fuel, electricity, and automobiles, but were satisfied that industry would have time to adjust to the new requirements.

The 101st Congress was probably the most publicly scorned Congress in recent years, because of the conflict surrounding the budget and tax package. A Wall Street Journal/NBC News poll showed that 70 percent of those polled rated the 101st Congress as average or below average, and one in five said it was "one of the worst" ("Washington Wire," Oct. 26, 1990).

Although the public was upset over the atmospherics and the long months of the budget summit negotiations and disapproved of the first budget-tax package put forth by the president and the House and Senate leadership, the fact is the administration and a majority of each house of Congress were able to conclude a deal and prevent the automatic across-the-board spending cuts that would have taken effect under the Gramm-Rudman-Hollings budget control law. The package of tax increases and spending cuts totaled $42.5 billion for fiscal 1991 and $496.2 billion over a five-year period. These far exceeded the two-year $75 billion package agreed to in 1987 or the $121 billion three-year package of tax increases and spending cuts in 1984.

The 101st Congress also produced a number of other large-scale bills of significance. As part of the budget-tax package, Congress broke a long-standing stalemate and approved a new child care program, which provided $18.3 billion in tax credits and $4.25 billion for a new grant program over five years. It also passed the Americans with Disabilities Act, which prohibits discrimination on the basis of disability in employment, public service, and public accommodations. The 101st Congress also passed the first overhaul of federal housing programs since 1974, which continued current housing programs and created a number of new ones. It also overhauled the vocational education programs. Together with the Clean Air Act Amendments and the Immigration overhaul, this output hardly indicates a do-nothing deadlocked government.

The point is that while criminal law legislation may be a good example of the dynamics surrounding the passage of large-scale public interest legislation, it is by no means isolated. The United States has seen important legislative changes made in this fashion in a number of diverse areas. The fact is that Congress is increasingly passing omnibus bills as a key method of legislating. A striking decline in the number of bills enacted, combined with a significant increase in the average page length of those enacted, is indicative of this thrust. In the 84th Congress (1955–56), there were 1,028 bills enacted, with an average of 1.8 pages per statute. The comparable numbers for recent Congresses were: 97th (1981–82) 413 bills, 8.1 average pages; 98th (1983–84) 623 bills, 7.8 average pages; 99th (1985–86) 664 bills, 10.8 average pages; 100th (1987–88) 713 bills, 6.8 average pages (Ornstein, Peabody, and Rohde, 1989). From his analysis of congressional workload, Davidson (1989a) finds: "In the late 1960s, more than two-thirds of all public laws took up a single page or less; in the 1980s less than half of all laws are that brief. And the proportion of truly long enactments — 21 pages or more — grew threefold during the same period. Legalistic verbosity is partly to blame; legislative packaging is also at work" (pp. 8–9).

Passing omnibus legislation places a premium on effective policy leadership. Legislators must be able to assemble large coalitions of somewhat diverse interests behind a bill and draft the legislation in such a way that it commands the loyalty of fellow legislators by including their provisions without alienating fundamental interests of others. It is a complex substantive and political balancing act and one that can be aided significantly by electoral incentives. All members of the supporting coalition are unlikely to give enthusiastic support for all the provisions, but they are more likely to continue their support for the package if they anticipate that they might pay an electoral price for opposing it, and if it contains their own provisions. Whether or not the legislators have a factual basis for feeling that their constituents could vote against them for an opposing vote is immaterial. It is the anticipation that they just might that is significant.

Much bargaining and accommodating must be done to assemble the winning coalition. Much of it is done behind the scenes in the drafting and amending stages at the committee level, although on occasion it will continue to the floor stage. The process for large-scale public interest legislation is likely to proceed over a number of congressional sessions. It will involve numerous interactions with and among interest groups, concerned agencies, and officials of the executive branch.

There are likely to be numerous fits and starts, provisions dropped and others added, as the leaders react to events that introduce new issues and highlight old ones. As a collective enterprise, it is likely that no one legislator will be intimately familiar with all the provisions of the bill. The protagonists involved with a particular provision will be conversant with that provision, but not even all the members of the relevant committee will know all the ins and outs of the bill.

Democratic-theory scholars may object that a true system of representative government requires that representatives both know what a bill contains and support it on the basis that their constituents support its provisions (or would if they had all the information that their legislators possess on the matter). Both American society and the American Congress are too complex and too fluid for the legislation to function that way. The branches of government are engaged in a joint legislative enterprise in a myriad of cross-cutting policy areas simultaneously. The complex subjects involved require very different types of expertise and are subject to their own politics.

At the beginning of this volume, two primary governmental concerns were discussed: whether the system furthers representative government, and whether it delivers quality public policy. Two criteria were given: whether it preserves popular control and its essential freedoms, and whether it produces public policies that are responsive to public needs. Admittedly, a complete answer to these questions must be based on performance over time and across numerous areas of policy, but a partial answer may be derived from the analysis here.

The debate surrounding federal criminal law was in part devoted to the specific policy disputes. In a very real sense, however, it was and is a debate about how to make the hard trade-offs between responding to public demands for tougher policies that represent popular control and, at the same time, preserving the rights of the accused and the guilty as essential American freedoms. Through the long consideration, with hundreds of meetings and thousands of debates, congressional representatives struggled with the trade-offs involving issue after issue. Compromises and amendments were made at countless stages of the process. Whether the proper balance was found and is still being sought is somewhat a matter of opinion. Overall, I believe the evidence shows that these critical considerations were fairly represented within the legislative process. It is not necessary to show that a majority would have approved every trade-off as it was made. In the end, the legislation passed in the direction the voters wanted, and with significant safeguards included for the accused. The anticipation of the evaluation of the legislative outcomes through the electoral process played a large role in the legislative dynamics. Thus, responding to public needs was a key consideration in what the legislators actually did and, it seems to me, furthered popular control of government.

With respect to the quality of public policy, I expect some time will be needed to assess the effects of what has been passed. As discussed, it takes some time for laws even to be implemented on anything like a widespread basis. The debates over what is and what is not reducing crime are certain to continue. At this time, with regard to the two public policy criteria outlined earlier—whether it represents a significant level of public spirit in the system, and demonstrates the capacity to produce policy that validates the choices citizens believe they made through the political process—I believe that the system delivered. The changes in federal law and the resources devoted to federal efforts at crime control are substantial. More resources are being devoted to investigation, prosecution, and corrections, stronger tools have been made available to law enforcement officers, and more criminals are being punished. The federal government is getting tougher on crime. The deliberations have been largely concerned with where the public good lies in dozens of issues. In short, policymakers, regardless of their stands on specific issues, have validated the public's basic concern with crime control, and done so in a way that many major public interest issues have been considered, debated, and voted upon at some important stage in the legislative process. This would seem to demonstrate that a significant level of public spirit does exist in the system.

Representative-government theorists may remain unsatisfied, in that it would not be possible to show that a majority of congressional representatives deliberated upon and considered their constituents' desires in terms of each issue. By that criterion, it is unlikely any modern legislative body could qualify as representative. There are too many issues in too many areas of public policy. Congress must proceed in a segmented way but must still integrate the diverse views of the various publics of which the United States consists.

The committee system is only the beginning of the division of labor that addresses the dilemma, but it is also part of the problem. Policy issues are not discrete and, as both the complexity and significance of issues and the power of subcommittees have increased, multiple referrals of bills have become more common. The legislative gauntlet has become more daunting and crowded.

Members of Congress have had to develop other coping mechanisms to move legislation, and omnibus legislation is one of them. Such legislation requires skillful policy leadership. Members need to rely on colleagues who are conversant with the particulars of complex legislation or who are in the network of conversant members, and this will differ by subject and shift according to the politics of the time. Members learn over time who the policy leaders involved with major legislation are and come to trust their judgment. Policy leaders evaluate legislative proposals not only in terms of their own position but also in terms of what is required to bring the winning coalition with them in support of the overall package. In this way, Congress has come to cope with very large and complex legislative matters.

The dynamics of the legislative process may not be obvious to onlookers or simple for legislative participants to understand in order to achieve their goals. I would not argue against the need for changes in statutes or regulations to improve understanding and facilitate majority rule. Proposals to reform the campaign finance laws for congressional races could potentially help. However, the antecedents of the context for the congressional process as it has evolved must be understood when evaluating any reform proposals. These are multiple and not easily susceptible to change. Thurber (1990) points to six root causes: (1) constitutional ambiguities that mandate both divided and shared legislative powers between the president and Congress; (2) the difference between the constituencies represented—the president's being national in scope and the senators' and representatives' more local; (3) different terms of office of the president, senators, and representatives; (4) weak and decentralized political parties; (5) the potential for divided party government; and (6) power between the president and Congress being constantly in flux. These factors are not easily manipulable by policy changes, but would only be altered by wholesale constitutional change.

A basic alteration of the constitutional structure is not only extremely unlikely, it is also unwarranted. The framers intentionally designed the system so that power was not easily gathered behind any particular ideological or policy movement in a short period of time. They were willing to give up fast and efficient action for greater deliberation and protection of liberty for groups and individuals variously situated in the polity. In the 1980s the Supreme Court articulated again the priorities of governance in the United States when it stated, "Convenience and efficiency are not the primary objectives—or the hallmarks—of democratic government" (*INS.* v. *Chada et al.* 462 US 919), and also, "That this system of division and separation of powers produces conflicts, confusion, and discordance at times is inherent, but it was deliberately so structured to assure full, vigorous, and open debate on the great issues affecting the people and to provide avenues for the operation of checks on the exercise of governmental power" (*Bowsher* v. *Synar, et al.* 478 US 714). Even configured as the system is, significant public policy legislation is still possible within it.

References

"A Crime to Shoot Nighttime Prowlers." *Trial Magazine,* Nov. 1975, p. 58.

Adams, B. "The Limitations of Muddling Through." *Public Administration Review,* 1979, *39,* 545–552.

Alston, C. "Mazzoli Redux: Who Needs PACS?" *Congressional Quarterly,* June 30, 1990, p. 2026.

American Bar Association, Section of Criminal Law. "Information Report of Committee on Reform of Federal Criminal Laws." Hearings Before the Subcommittee on Criminal Law and Procedures of the Committee on the Judiciary, U.S. Senate, 93rd Cong., 1st sess., *Reform of the Federal Criminal Laws,* May 2, 1973, part IV, pp. 5403–5425.

"And Now for Something Completely Different: S.1437." *ABA Journal,* 1977, 907, 921–922.

Anderson, J. E. *Public Policymaking.* Boston: Houghton Mifflin, 1990.

Arieff, I. B. "Congressional Factions Seek Power Balance." *Congressional Quarterly,* Nov. 15, 1980, pp. 3362–3366.

Arieff, I. B. "House GOP Still a Minority Seeks Peace with Democrats; Senate Parties Reverse Roles." *Congressional Quarterly,* Feb. 28, 1981, p. 379.

Arnold, R. D. "The Local Roots of Domestic Policy." In T. Mann and N. Ornstein (eds.), *The New Congress.* Washington, D.C.: American Enterprise Institute, 1981.

Attorney General's Task Force on Violent Crime. *Final Report.* U.S. Department of Justice, Aug. 17, 1981.

Babcock, C. R. "Criminal Code Revisers Are Praised for Their Efforts." *Washington Post,* Aug. 2, 1979, p. A-4.

Babcock, C. R. "Hill Unit Clears Criminal Code Overhaul." *Washington Post,* July 3, 1980, p. A-2.

Bach, S., and Smith, S. S. *Managing Uncertainty in the House of Representatives.* Washington, D.C.: Brookings, 1988.

Bartlett, J. W., and Jones, D. N., "Managing a Cabinet Agency." *Public Administration Review,* 1974, *34,* 62–70.

Berlow, A. "House Wariness of Senate Package Dims Outlook for Criminal Code Reform." *Congressional Quarterly,* May 20, 1978, p. 1284.

Berry, J. M. "Subgovernments, Issue Networks, and Political Conflict." In R. Harris and S. Milkis (eds.), *Remaking American Politics.* Boulder, Colo.: Westview Press, 1988.

Beveredge, G. "An Issue the Press Isn't Covering." *Washington Star,* Aug. 22, 1977, p. A-11.

Bibby, J. F., Mann, T. E., and Ornstein, N.J. *Vital Statistics on Congress, 1980.* Washington, D.C.: American Enterprise Institute, 1980.

Birnbaum, J., and Murray, A. S. *Showdown at Gucci Gulch.* New York: Random House, 1987.

Biskupic, J. "Critics on Both Sides Take Aim at Bush's Anti-Crime Plan." *Congressional Quarterly,* May 20, 1989, pp. 1196–1197.

Biskupic, J. "Ban on Some Assault Weapons OK'd by Senate Committee." *Congressional Quarterly,* July 22, 1989, p. 1873.

Biskupic, J. "Death Penalty and Appeals Move Front and Center." *Congressional Quarterly,* Oct. 14, 1989, p. 2718.

Biskupic, J. "Death Penalty Expansion Bill Is Moved to Senate Floor." *Congressional Quarterly,* Oct. 21, 1989, pp. 2805–2806.

Biskupic, J. "Anticrime Package Falters After Gun Ban Retained." *Congressional Quarterly,* May 26, 1990, pp. 1654–1656.

Biskupic, J. "Judiciary Panel Presses On in Drafting Crime Bill." *Congressional Quarterly,* July 21, 1990, pp. 2321–2323.

Biskupic, J. "Taking Tough Stance on Crime, House Boosts Death Penalty." *Congressional Quarterly,* Oct. 6, 1990, pp. 3223–3225.

Biskupic, J. "Death Penalty, Other Hot Issues Dumped from Crime Bill." *Congressional Quarterly,* Oct. 27, 1990, p. 3615.

Blanchard, R. O. "The Correspondents Describe Their Work." In R. O. Blanchard, *Congress and the News Media.* New York: Hastings House, 1974.

Block, M., and Rhodes, W. "The Impact of the Federal Sentencing Guidelines." National Institute of Justice, September 1987.

Bonner, A. "Kennedy Strongly Defends His Criminal Code Revision." *Washington Post,* Dec. 8, 1978, p. A-3.

Bosley, C. E. "Senate Communications with the Public." In *Senate Communications with the Public,* prepared for the Commission on the Operation of the Senate, Committee Print, 94th Cong., 2nd sess., 1977, pp. 3–23.

Brownstein, R. "The Politics of Passion." *National Journal,* Feb. 22, 1986, pp. 436–442.

Brownstein, R., and Easton, N. *Reagan's Ruling Class.* Washington, D.C.: Presidential Accountability Group, 1982.

Buckley, W. F. "Reforms That Handcuff You When You Surprise a Burglar." *Washington Star,* Oct. 23, 1975, p. 23.

Bureau of Justice Statistics. *Report to the Nation on Crime and Justice: The Data.* Washington, D.C.: U.S. Department of Justice, 1983.

Burnham, J. "Some Administrators' Unkindly View of Congress." In R. T. Golembiewski and others (eds.), *Public Administration.* (2nd ed.) Chicago: Rand McNally, 1972.

Burns, J. M. *The Deadlock of Democracy.* Englewood Cliffs, N.J.: Prentice-Hall, 1963.

Burns, J. M. "U.S., Model for Eastern Europe?" *New York Times,* Feb. 18, 1990, p. A-28.

Calmes, J. " House Leadership Power Shift Is Under Way," *Congressional Quarterly,* Oct. 4, 1986, pp. 2360–2364.

Caplan, G. "Reflections on the Nationalization of Crime, 1964–1968." *Law and the Social Order,* 1973, pp. 583–635.

Caplan, L. *The Insanity Defense and the Trial of John Hinckley, Jr.* New York: Dell, 1987.

"Carter's Harried Businessmen." *Business Week,* May 29, 1978, pp. 80–84.

Chamberlain, L. H. *President, Congress, and Legislation.* New York: AMS Press, 1946.

Chubb, J. *Interest Groups and the Bureaucracy.* Stanford, Calif.: Stanford University Press, 1983.

Clymer, A. "Bell Asks Fast Criminal Code Action." *New York Times,* May 3, 1977, p. 2.

Clymer, A. "Revision of Federal Crime Code Is Adopted by the Senate, 72 to 15." *New York Times,* Jan. 31, 1978, p. 1.

Clymer, A. "New Criminal Code Is Due for Still More Decoding." *New York Times,* Feb. 5, 1978, p. 1.

Clymer, A. "Criminal Law Change Meets Snag." *New York Times,* May 13, 1978, p. 2.

Clymer, A. "Kennedy Gives Priority to Antitrust Policy and Criminal Code." *New York Times,* Jan. 5, 1979, p. 24.

Cobb, R. W., and Elder, C. D. "Communications and Public Policy." In D. Nimmo and K. Sanders (eds.), *Handbook of Political Communication.* Newbury Park, Calif.: Sage, 1981.

Cobb, R. W., and Elder, C. D. *Participation in American Politics.* (2nd ed.) Baltimore: Johns Hopkins University Press, 1983.

Cohen, R. "Justice Report/Legislation for White Collar Crime Reform May Evoke Controversy at Code Hearings." *National Journal,* Apr. 14, 1973, pp. 535–545.

Cohen, R. "Justice Report/Criminal Code Revision Picking Up Steam in Congress." *National Journal,* Dec. 27, 1975, pp. 1755–1757.

Cohen, R. "A Report Card for Congress — An F for Frustration." *National Journal,* Aug. 11, 1979.

Cohen, R. "On the Run with Richard Gephardt: A Day in the Life of a House Member." *National Journal,* Oct. 10, 1983, pp. 2059–2063.

Cohen, R. "Foley's Honeymoon." *National Journal,* July 15, 1989, pp. 1799–1803.

Cohodas, N. "Senate Judiciary Passes Criminal Code Bill." *Congressional Quarterly,* Dec. 8, 1979, p. 2792.

Cohodas, N. "Labor, Business Seek to Kill Criminal Code Bill." *Congressional Quarterly,* Mar. 15, 1980, pp. 739–740.

Cohodas, N. "House Judiciary Approves Criminal Code." *Congressional Quarterly,* July 5, 1980, pp. 1885–1887.

Cohodas, N. "House Judiciary Liberals Work to Retain Influence Amid Conservative Gains." *Congressional Quarterly,* Feb. 21, 1981, p. 347.

Cohodas, N. "Sentencing Reform Measures Seek to Reduce Disparities." *Congressional Quarterly,* Feb. 12, 1983, pp. 337–340.

Cohodas, N. "Senate Panel Again Approves Package of Anti-Crime Bills." *Congressional Quarterly,* July 30, 1983, pp. 1559–1560.

Cohodas, N. "Senate Votes Major Changes in Federal Criminal Statutes." *Congressional Quarterly,* Feb. 11, 1984, pp. 280–284.

Cohodas, N. "Peter Rodino Turns Judiciary into a Legislative Graveyard." *Congressional Quarterly,* May 12, 1984, pp. 1097–1102.

Cohodas, N. "Changes in Sentencing Process Approved by Judiciary Panel." *Congressional Quarterly,* July 21, 1984, p. 1801.

Cohodas, N. "Enactment of Crime Package Culmination of 11-Year Effort." *Congressional Quarterly,* Oct. 20, 1984, pp. 2752–2758.

Cohodas, N. "Congress Clears Overhaul of Immigration Law." *Congressional Quarterly,* Oct. 18, 1986, pp. 2595–2596.

Cohodas, N. "Joe Biden's Record Depends on Who Plays It." *Congressional Quarterly,* Feb. 7, 1987, pp. 222–227.

Committee on the Constitutional System. "A Statement of the Problem." In D. L. Robinson (ed.), *Reforming American Government.* Boulder, Colo.: Westview Press, 1985.

Congressional Directory, 1960–1976.

Congressional Quarterly. *Crime and the Law.* Washington, D.C.: Congressional Quarterly Press, 1971.

Converse, P. E. "Public Opinion in the Political Process." *Public Opinion Quarterly,* 1987, *51,* 512–524.

Conyers, J. "A Political Move to Look Tough." *Washington Post,* Jan. 12, 1983, p. A-16.

Cook, R. "Popularity, Savvy Use of Veto Leave Bush with 12–0 Record." *Congressional Quarterly,* June 23, 1990, pp. 1934–1935.

Cook, T. E. *Making Laws and Making News.* Washington, D.C.: Brookings, 1989.

Cooper, J., and West, W. "The Congressional Career in the 1970's." In L. Dodd and B. Oppenheimer, *Congress Reconsidered.* (2nd ed.) Washington, D.C.: Congressional Quarterly Press, 1981.

CQ Almanac. Washington, D.C.: Congressional Quarterly Press, published yearly.

"Crime in the U.S. — Is It Getting Out of Hand?" *U.S. News and World Report,* Aug. 1963, p. 104.

"Crime Time." *Newsweek,* June 3, 1968, p. 36.

"Criminal Code Revision Dies." *Congressional Quarterly Almanac,* 1982, pp. 415–417.

Cronin, T. *The State of the Presidency.* Boston: Little, Brown, 1975.

Cronin, T. E., Cronin, T. Z., and Milovic, M. *U.S. v. Crime in the Streets.* Bloomington: Indiana University Press, 1981.

Cutler, L. N. "Party Government Under the Constitution." In D. L. Robinson (ed.), *Reforming American Government.* Boulder, Colo.: Westview Press, 1985.

Cutler, L. N. "The Cost of Divided Government." *New York Times,* Nov. 22, 1987, p. A-26.

Davidson, R. H. "Subcommittee Government: New Channels for Policy Making." In T. Mann and N. Ornstein (eds.), *The New Congress.* Washington, D.C.: American Enterprise Institute, 1981.

Davidson, R. H. "Senate Leaders: Janitors for an Untidy Chamber." In L. Dodd and B. Oppenheimer (eds.), *Congress Reconsidered.* (3rd ed.) Washington, D.C.: Congressional Quarterly Press, 1985.

Davidson, R. H. *The Presidency and the Three Eras of the Modern Congress.* Working Paper 89-2. Washington, D.C.: Center for Presidential and Congressional Studies, School of Public Affairs, American University, 1989a.

Davidson, R. H. "The Senate: If Everybody Leads, Who Follows?" In L. Dodd and B. Oppenheimer (eds.), *Congress Reconsidered.* (4th ed.) Washington, D.C.: Congressional Quarterly Press, 1989b.

Davidson, R. H., and Oleszek, W. J. *Congress and Its Members.* (2nd ed.) Washington, D.C.: Congressional Quarterly Press, 1985.

Deering, C., and Smith, S. S. "Subcommittees in Congress." In L. Dodd and B. Oppenheimer (eds.), *Congress Reconsidered.* (3rd ed.) Washington, D.C.: Congressional Quarterly Press, 1985.

Dillon, C. D. "The Challenge of Modern Governance (1982)."

In D. L. Robinson (ed.), *Reforming American Government.* Boulder, Colo.: Westview Press, 1985.

Dodd, L. C., and Oppenheimer, B. I. "Consolidating Power in the House." In L. Dodd and B. Oppenheimer (eds.), *Congress Reconsidered.* (4th ed.) Washington, D.C.: Congressional Quarterly Press, 1989.

Dowd, M. "Lost for Words: George Bush's Communication Breakdown on the Budget," *New York Times,* Oct. 21, 1990, p. E-1.

Drinan, R., and Beier, D. "The Federal Criminal Code: The Houses Are Divided." *American Criminal Law Review,* 1981, *18,* 501–531.

Dror, Y. "Muddling Through — Science or Inertion." In A. Etzioni (ed.), *Readings on Modern Organization.* Englewood Cliffs, N.J.: Prentice-Hall, 1969.

Ebring, L., Goldenberg, E. N., and Miller, A. H. "Front-Page News and Real World Cues: A New Look at Agenda Setting by the Mass Media." *American Journal of Political Science,* Feb. 1980, pp. 16–49.

Edwards, G. C., III., and Wayne, S. J. *Presidential Leadership.* New York: St. Martin's, 1985.

Ehrenhalt, A. "New Criminal Code Faces Fight in Congress." *Washington Star,* Feb. 24, 1980, p. A-8.

Ehrenhalt, A. "In the Senate of the 80's, Team Spirit Has Given Way to the Rule of Individuals." *Congressional Quarterly Weekly Report,* Sept. 4, 1982.

Ehrenhalt, A. *Politics in America 1984.* Washington, D.C.: Congressional Quarterly Press, 1983.

Ehrenhalt, A. "Media, Power Shifts Dominate O'Neill's House." *Congressional Quarterly,* Sept. 13, 1986a, pp. 2131–2138.

Ehrenhalt, A. "Speaker O'Neill's Stature Is on the Ascendancy." *Congressional Quarterly,* Sept. 13, 1986b, p. 2133.

Etzioni, A. "Mixed Scanning Revisited." *Public Administration Review,* 1986, *46,* 8–14.

Eyestone, R. *From Social Issues to Public Policy.* New York: Wiley, 1978.

Fenno, R. *Homestyle.* Boston: Little, Brown, 1978.

Finletter, T. K. *Can Representative Government Do the Job?* New York: Reynal & Hitchcock, 1945.

Fiorna, M. P. *Congress: Keystone of the Washington Establishment.* New Haven, Conn.: Yale University Press, 1977.

Fisher, L. *The Politics of Shared Power.* Washington, D.C.: Congressional Quarterly Press, 1987.

Fisher, L. *Constitutional Dialogues: Interpretation As Political Process.* Princeton, N.J.: Princeton University Press, 1988.

"Forfeiture of Narcotics Proceeds." Hearings Before the Subcommittee on Criminal Justice, Committee on the Judiciary, U.S. Senate, 96th Cong., 2d sess., July 23–24, 1980.

Froman, L. A., Jr. *The Congressional Process.* Boston: Little, Brown, 1967.

Gallup, G. H. *The Gallup Poll 1983.* Wilmington, Del.: Scholarly Resources, 1984.

General Accounting Office. "Federal Drug Interdiction Efforts Need Strong Central Oversight." GGD-83-52, June 13, 1983.

Gettinger, S. "Bush Success on House Votes Heads for a Record Low." *Congressional Quarterly,* October 13, 1990, p. 3387.

Goshko, J. M. "Sen. Kennedy Urges Liberals to Help Change Criminal Code." *Washington Post,* Apr. 3, 1977, p. A-8.

Granat, D. "Congress Struggles to Quit, But Does Not Finish." *Congressional Quarterly,* Oct. 6, 1984, pp. 2415–2416.

Hager, G. "Bush Sets Clean-Air Debate in Motion with New Plan." *Congressional Quarterly,* June 17, 1989, pp. 1460–1464.

Hall, R. "Committee Decision Making in the Post Reform Congress." In L. Dodd and B. Oppenheimer (eds.), *Congress Reconsidered.* (4th ed.) Washington, D.C.: Congressional Quarterly Press, 1989.

Hammond, S. W. "Congressional Change and Reform: Staffing the Congress." In L. Rieselbach (ed.), *Legislative Reform.* Lexington, Mass.: Heath, 1978.

Hammond, S. W. "Committee and Informal Leaders in the U.S. House of Representatives." In J. J. Kornacki (ed.), *Leading Congress.* Washington, D.C.: Congressional Quarterly Press, 1990.

Hargrove, E. C., and Nelson, M. *Presidents, Politics, and Policy.* Baltimore, Md.: Johns Hopkins University Press, 1984.

Harvey, P. "Protest Prowlers?" *Oakland Tribune,* Dec. 10, 1975, p. 22.

Heclo, H. "Issue Networks and the Executive Establishment." In A. King (ed.), *The New Political System.* Washington, D.C.:

American Enterprise Institute for Public Policy Research, 1977.

Heffner, R. D. (ed.). *Alexis de Tocqueville: Democracy in America.* New York: Mentor, 1956.

Hentoff, N. "Ted Kennedy Presents Son of S.1." *Village Voice,* May 2, 1977, pp. 2-3.

Herzberg, R. "Blocking Coalitions and Policy Change." In G. C. Wright, L. Rieselbach, and L. C. Dodd, (eds.) *Congress and Policy Change.* New York: Atherton Press, 1986.

Hess, S. *The Government/Press Connection.* Washington, D.C.: Brookings, 1984.

Hobbs, M. A. "Crime Bill Authors Meet Reagan in Bid to Avert Veto." *Philadelphia Inquirer,* Jan. 8, 1983, p. 5-A.

Hoogterp, E. "Sawyer Blames Reagan Aides for Crime Bill's Veto." *Grand Rapids Press,* Jan. 21, 1983, p. 3.

Hook, J. "Bush's Congressional Lobbyists Have Experience in the Capital." *Congressional Quarterly,* Jan. 14, 1989, p. 90.

Hook, J. "The Turmoil and Transition: Stage Set for New Speaker." *Congressional Quarterly,* May 27, 1989, pp. 1225-1226.

Hook, J. "House's New Leadership Brings Next Generation to Power." *Congressional Quarterly,* June 10, 1989, pp. 1376-1377.

Hook, J. "Mitchell Learns Inside Game: Is Cautious As Party Voice." *Congressional Quarterly,* Sept. 9, 1989, pp. 2293-2296.

Hook, J. "Rout of Democratic Leaders Reflects Fractured Party." *Congressional Quarterly,* Sept. 30, 1989, pp. 2529-2531.

Hook, J. "Big Win for Majority Leader Marks His Rite of Passage." *Congressional Quarterly,* Apr. 7, 1990, pp. 1045-1047.

Hook, J., and Congressional Quarterly Staff. "Stalemates of Last Decade Haunt Agenda for 1990." *Congressional Quarterly,* Jan. 6, 1990, pp. 9-12.

"Hopes for New Crime Bill Dimmed by Reagan Veto." *Law Enforcement News,* Feb. 7, 1983, p. 1.

House Committee on the Judiciary. Transcript, Markup Session, H.R.4481 — Justice Assistance Act of 1981, Sept. 22, 1981.

House Committee on the Judiciary. Transcript, Committee Session, Oct. 7, 1981.

Hulteng, J. L. *The Messenger's Motive: Ethical Problems of the News Media.* Englewood Cliffs, N.J.: Prentice-Hall, 1984.

Hunt, A. R. "Special Interest Money Increasingly Influences What Congress Enacts." *Wall Street Journal,* July 26, 1982, pp. 1, 13.

Hyneman, C. S. *Popular Government in America.* New York: Atherton, 1968.

Iyengar, S., and Kinder, D. R. *News That Matters: Television and American Opinion.* Chicago: University of Chicago Press, 1987.

Johnson, L. B. *Crime, Its Prevalence, and Measures of Prevention.* H.R. Doc. no. 103, 89th Cong., 1st sess., 1965.

Johnson, L. B. *The Vantage Point.* New York: Holt, Rinehart, and Winston, 1971.

Jones, C. O. "House Leadership in the Age of Reform." In H. Mackaman, *Understanding Congressional Leadership.* Washington, D.C.: Congressional Quarterly Press, 1981.

Jones. C. O. *The United States Congress.* Homewood, Ill.: Dorsey Press, 1982.

Jones, C. O. *An Introduction to the Study of Public Policy.* (3rd ed.) Monterey, Calif.: Brooks/Cole, 1984a.

Jones, C. O. "A New President, A Different Congress, A Maturing Agenda." In L. A. Salamon and M. Lund (eds.), *The Reagan Presidency and the Governing of America.* Washington, D.C.: Urban Institute Press, 1984b.

Joost, R. H. "Simplifying Federal Criminal Laws." *Pepperdine Law Review,* 1986, *14* (1), 1-38.

Kaufman, H. *The Administrative Behavior of Federal Bureau Chiefs.* Washington, D.C.: Brookings, 1981.

Kelman, S. *Making Public Policy.* New York: Basic Books, 1987.

Kennedy, E. M. "Making Time Fit the Crime." *Trial Magazine,* March 1976, pp. 14-15, 23.

Kenworthy, T. "Looking for Some Reins to Chafe Under." *Washington Post National Weekly Edition,* June 18-24, 1990, p. 14.

King, G., and Ragsdale, L. *The Elusive Executive.* Washington, D.C.: Congressional Quarterly Press, 1988.

Kingdon, J. W. *Congressmen's Voting Decisions.* New York: Harper & Row, 1973.

Kingdon, J. W. *Agendas, Alternatives, and Public Policies.* Boston: Little, Brown, 1984.

Koenig, L. W. *The Chief Executive.* (2nd ed.) New York: Harcourt Brace Jovanovich, 1968.

Landau, J. C. "Congress to Debate Prowler Law." *Atlanta Constitution,* Sept. 4, 1975, p. 4.

Leventhal, P. "Outlook 73: Turnover in Key Committee Chairmanship Foreshadows Policy Changes in 93rd Congress." *National Journal,* Nov. 11, 1972, pp. 1750–1761.

Lewis, A. "A Victory for Reform." *New York Times,* Mar. 14, 1977, p. 29.

Light, P. *The President's Agenda.* Baltimore, Md.: Johns Hopkins University Press, 1982.

Lindblom, C. E. "The Science of Muddling Through." *Public Administration Review,* 1959, *19,* 79–88.

Lindblom, C. E. "Still Muddling, Not Yet Through." *Public Administration Review,* 1979, *39,* 517–526.

Linsky, M. *Impact: How the Press Affects Policymaking.* New York: Norton, 1986.

Lipset, S., and Schneider, W. *The Confidence Gap.* (Rev. ed.) Baltimore, Md.: Johns Hopkins University Press, 1987.

Loomis, B. "The 'Me' Decade and the Changing Context of House Leadership." In F. Mackaman (ed.), *Understanding Congressional Leadership.* Washington, D.C.: CQ Press, 1981.

Loomis, B. A. "The 'New Style' House Member and Legislative Policy-Making." Paper presented at American Political Science Association meeting, Chicago, Sept. 1, 1985.

Luttbeg, N. *Public Opinion and Public Policy.* (3rd ed.) Itasca, Ill.: Peacock, 1981.

Lyons, R. L. "On Capitol Hill." *Washington Post,* Feb. 14, 1974, p. A-4.

Lyons, R. L. "Bayh Cancels Support of Bill to Codify U.S. Criminal Laws." *Washington Post,* Aug. 20, 1975, p. A-3.

Maass, A. *Congress and the Common Good.* New York: Basic Books, 1983.

McClellan, J. L. *Hearings: Controlling Crime Through More Effective Law Enforcement.* Subcommittee on Criminal Laws and Procedures of the Committee on the Judiciary, U.S. Senate, March 7, 1967.

"McClellan Considers Compromise on S.1." *Washington Post,* Feb. 15, 1976, p. A-5.

McCombs, M. E., and Weaver, D. H. *Public Opinion* (forthcoming).

Mackaman, F. H. *Understanding Congressional Leadership.* Washington, D.C.: Congressional Quarterly Press, 1981.

MacKenzie, J. P. "Critics of New U.S. Code Hit 'Ehrlichman Defense'." *Washington Post,* Oct. 5, 1975, p. A-4.

Maitland, L. "President Vetoes Crime Bill Calling for Drug Czar." *New York Times,* Jan. 15, 1981, p. 47.

Malbin, M. J. "Delegation, Deliberation, and the New Role of Congressional Staff." In T. Mann and N. Ornstein (eds.), *The New Congress.* Washington, D.C.: American Enterprise Institute, 1981.

Mann, J. "Compromise Sought on Bill to Rewrite Criminal Laws." *Baltimore Sun,* Apr. 7, 1976, p. A-4.

Mann, T. E. *Unsafe at Any Margin.* Washington, D.C.: American Enterprise Institute, 1978.

Mann, T. E. "Elections and Change in Congress." In T. Mann and N. Ornstein (eds.), *The New Congress.* Washington, D.C.: American Enterprise Institute, 1981.

Mayhew, D. *The Electoral Connection.* New Haven, Conn.: Yale University Press, 1974.

Membrino, J. O. "U.S. Criminal Code Plan Gets a Big Push." *Boston Globe,* Aug. 2, 1979, p. 3.

Mezey, M. *Congress, the President and Public Policy.* Boulder, Colo.: Westview Press, 1989a.

Mezey, M. *Congress Within the United States Presidential System.* Working Paper 89-1. Washington, D.C.: Center for Presidential and Congressional Studies, School of Public Affairs, American University, 1989b.

Mintz, M. "Swift Action Points Up Interest in Criminal Code." *Washington Post,* Dec. 1, 1979, p. C-8.

Mitchell, J. W. "Memorandum: Departmental Review of Proposed Revisions in United States Criminal Code." U.S. Department of Justice, Feb. 1, 1971.

Mitchell, J. W. "Memorandum: Departmental Review of Proposed Revisions in the United States Criminal Code." Hearings Before the Subcommittee on Criminal Law and Procedures of the Committee on the Judiciary, U.S. Senate, 92d Cong., 1st sess., *Reform of the Federal Criminal Laws,* May 24, 1971, part I, p. 84.

Moe, R. C., and Teel, S. C. "Congress As Policy Maker: A Necessary Reappraisal." *Political Science Quarterly, 85,* 1970.

Morgan, C., Jr. "A Compromise That Lynches the Constitution." *Washington Star,* Feb. 29, 1976, p. 26.

Narcotics Control Digest, May 22, 1982.

Nathan, R. P. *The Plot That Failed: Nixon and the Administrative Presidency.* New York: Wiley, 1975.

National Association of Attorneys General. "Disapproval of Study Draft of Proposed New Federal Criminal Code." Hearings Before the Subcommittee on Criminal Laws and Procedures of the Committee on the Judiciary, U.S. Senate, 92d Cong., 1st sess., *Reform of the Federal Criminal Laws,* part I, 1971, p. 6.

National Commission on Reform of Federal Criminal Laws. *Final Report.* Washington, D.C.: U.S. Government Printing Office, 1971.

Nelson, W. D. "U.S. Crime Code Overhaul Faces Opposition in House." *Washington Star,* Mar. 26, 1978, p. A-9.

Neustadt, R. E. *Presidential Power.* New York: Wiley, 1980.

Newland, C. A. "Executive Office Policy Apparatus: Enforcing the Reagan Agenda." In L. A. Salamon and M. Lund (eds.), *The Reagan Presidency and the Governing of America.* Washington, D.C.: Urban Institute Press, 1984.

Niemi, R. G., Mueller, J., and Smith, T. W. *Trends in Public Opinion.* New York: Greenwood Press, 1989.

Nixon, R. "Statement After Receipt of the Report of the National Commission on Reform of Federal Criminal Laws." Hearings Before the Subcommittee on Criminal Laws and Procedures of the Committee on the Judiciary. U.S. Senate, 92nd Cong., 1st sess., Feb. 10, 1971, p. 5.

Olezsek, W. J. *Congressional Policymaking in the 80s: Some Forms and Some Conditions.* Working Paper 89-3. Washington, D.C.: Center for Presidential and Congressional Studies, School of Public Affairs, American University, 1989.

Ornstein, N. "Can Congress Be Led?" In J. J. Kornacki (ed.), *Leading Congress.* Washington, D.C.: Congressional Quarterly Press, 1990, pp. 13–25.

Ornstein, N. J., Mann, T., and Malbin, M. J. *Vital Statistics on*

Congress, 1984–90. Washington, D.C.: Congressional Quarterly Press, 1990.

Ornstein, N., Peabody, R., and Rohde, D. "Change in the Senate: Toward the 1990s." In L. Dodd and B. Oppenheimer, *Congress Reconsidered.* (4th ed.) Washington, D.C.: Congressional Quarterly Press, 1989, pp. 1–12.

Ostrom, V., and Ostrom, E. "Public Goods and Public Choices." In E. S. Savas, *Alternatives for Delivering Public Services.* Boulder, Colo.: Westview Press, 1977.

"PAC Receipts for Senators." *Congressional Quarterly,* Apr. 28, 1990, p. 1293.

Parker, G. R., and Davidson, R. H. "Why Do Americans Love Their Congressmen So Much More Than Their Congress?" *Legislative Studies Quarterly,* 1979, *4,* 63–78.

Peabody, R. L. *Leadership in Congress.* Boston: Little, Brown, 1976.

Peabody, R. L. "Senate Party Leadership: From the 1950's to the 1980's." In F. H. Mackaman (ed.), *Understanding Congressional Leadership.* Washington, D.C.: Congressional Quarterly Press, 1981.

Peabody, R. L. "Leadership in Legislatures." *Legislative Studies Quarterly, 9,* 1984, 441–473.

Pear, R. "Congressional Action Is Near on Thirteen-Year Effort to Revise Criminal Code." *New York Times,* Dec. 12, 1974, p. 22.

Pear, R. "Crime Bill Challenged by Conservative Republicans." *New York Times,* Sept. 15, 1980, p. A-17.

Peters, R. *The American Speakership: The Office in Historical Perspective.* Baltimore, Md.: Johns Hopkins University Press, 1990.

Pfiffner, J. P. *The Strategic Presidency.* Monterey, Calif.: Brooks/Cole, 1988.

Pfiffner, J. P. *Divided Government and the Problem of Governance.* Working Paper 89-4. Washington, D.C.: Center for Presidential and Congressional Studies, School of Public Affairs, American University, 1989.

Polsby, N. W. "Policy Analysis and Congress." *Public Policy, 18,* 1969.

Polsby, N. W. *Congress and the Presidency.* Englewood Cliffs, N.J.: Prentice-Hall, 1971.

Polsby, N. *Political Innovation in America.* New Haven, Conn.: Yale University Press, 1984.

President's Commission on Law Enforcement and Administration of Justice. *The Challenge of Crime in a Free Society.* Washington, D.C.: U.S. Government Printing Office, 1968.

Price, D. E. "Congressional Committees in the Policy Process." In L. Dodd and B. Oppenheimer (eds.), *Congress Reconsidered.* (3rd ed.) Washington, D.C.: Congressional Quarterly Press, 1985.

"Putting Freedom Against the Wall." *Los Angeles Times,* Sept. 15, 1975, part II, p. 4.

Pytte, A. "A Decade's Acrimony Lifted in the Glow of Clean Air." *Congressional Quarterly,* Oct. 27, 1990, pp. 3587–3592.

Richey, A. J. "A Change in Direction." In J. A. Pechman (ed.), *Setting National Priorities: The 1982 Budget.* Washington, D.C.: Brookings, 1981.

Rieselbach, L. "Congress and Policy Change." In G. C. Wright, L. Rieselbach, and L. C. Dodd (eds.), *Congress and Policy Change.* New York: Agathon, 1986.

Riggs, F. W. "The Survival of Presidentialism in America: Para-Constitutional Practices." *International Political Science Review,* 1988, *9,* 247–278.

Riley, J. "U.S. Changes the Rules on Crime." *National Law Journal,* Oct. 29, 1984, p. 3.

Ripley, R. B. *Congress: Process and Policy.* (3rd ed.) New York: Norton, 1983.

Ripley, R. B., and Franklin, G. A., *Congress, the Bureaucracy, and Public Policy.* (3rd ed.) Homewood, Ill.: Dorsey Press, 1984.

Ripley, R. B., and Franklin, G. A. *Congress, the Bureaucracy, and Public Policy.* (4th ed.) Homewood, Ill.: Dorsey Press, 1987.

Robinson, M. J. "Three Faces of Congressional Media." In T. Mann and N. Ornstein (eds.), *The New Congress.* Washington, D.C.: American Enterprise Institute, 1981.

Rogers, E. "Crime Bill Is Termed Object of Politicking." *Washington Times,* May 9, 1984, p. 1.

Rovere, R. *The Goldwater Caper.* New York: Harcourt Brace Jovanovich, 1965.

St. George, D. "Criminal Law Bill Again Caught Up in Political and Jurisdictional Wars." *National Journal,* Dec. 10, 1983, pp. 2577–2580.

Scammon, R., and Wattenberg, B. *The Real Majority.* New York: Coward, McCann & Geoghegan, 1970.

Schick, A. "Congress and the 'Details' of Administration." In F. S. Lane (ed.), *Current Issues in Public Administration.* New York: St. Martin's, 1978.

Schlozman, K. L., and Tierney, J. *Organized Interests and American Democracy.* New York: Harper & Row, 1986.

Schneider, J. *Ideological Coalitions in Congress.* Westport, Conn.: Greenwood Press, 1979.

Schuck, P. *The Judiciary Committees.* Report sponsored by the Ralph Nader Congress Project. New York: Grossman, 1975.

Schulman, B. "In All Fairness—It Wasn't a Dinky Story to Concerned Homeowners." *Louisville Times,* Oct. 6, 1975, p. 16.

Schulman, P. R. *Large-Scale Policy Making.* New York: Elsevier, 1980.

Schwartz, B. "Misunderstood Home-Defense Bill Draws Heavy Fire." *Louisville Times,* Sept. 25, 1975, p. A-4.

Schwartz, L. B. "Reform of the Federal Criminal Laws." *Law and Contemporary Problems,* 1977, *4* (1), 1–64.

Seidman, H., and Gilmour, R. *Politics, Position, and Power.* (4th ed.) New York: Oxford, 1986.

Seligman, L. G., and Covington, C. R. *The Coalitional Presidency.* Chicago: Irwin, 1989.

"Senate 1." *Wall Street Journal,* Aug. 8, 1975, p. 8.

"A Shift in the Wind in Washington." *U.S. News and World Report,* *59,* 1965, pp. 27–28.

Simon, R. "S.1, a Menace to the Press." *Quill,* July–Aug. 1975, pp. 19–21.

Sinclair, B. "Majority Party Leadership Strategies for Coping with the U.S. House." In F. H. Mackaman (ed.), *Understanding Congressional Leadership.* Washington, D.C.: Congressional Quarterly Press, 1981.

Sinclair, B. "Senate Styles and Senate Decision Making." *Journal of Politics,* 1986, *48,* 877–908.

Sinclair, B. "House Majority Leadership in the Late 1980s." In L. Dodd and B. Oppenheimer (eds.), *Congress Reconsidered.* (4th ed.) Washington, D.C.: Congressional Quarterly Press, 1989.

Sinclair, B. "Congressional Leadership: A Review Essay and a Research Agenda." In J. J. Kornacki (ed.), *Leading Congress*. Washington, D.C.: Congressional Quarterly Press, 1990.

Sleeper, P. "Revising Criminal Code Top Priority for Drinan." *Lowell Sun*, Feb. 14, 1979, p. 2.

Smith, H. *The Power Game*. New York: Random House, 1988.

Smith, S. S. "O'Neill's Legacy for the House." *The Brookings Review*, Winter 1987, pp. 28–36.

Smith, S. S. "Taking It to the Floor." In L. Dodd and B. Oppenheimer (eds.), *Congress Reconsidered*. (4th ed.) Washington, D.C.: Congressional Quarterly Press, 1989, pp. 331–350.

Smith, S. S. "Informal Leadership in the Senate: Opportunities, Resources, and Motivations." In J. J. Kornacki (ed.), *Leading Congress*. Washington, D.C.: Congressional Quarterly Press, 1990.

Smith, T. W. "A Trend Analysis of Attitudes Toward Capital Punishment." In J. A. Davis (ed.), *Studies of Social Change Since 1948*. National Opinion Research Center Report 127B. Chicago: National Opinion Research Center, 1976.

Spitzer, R. J. *The Presidency and Public Policy*. University, Alabama: University of Alabama Press, 1983.

Staff of the Senate Committee on the Judiciary, U.S. Senate, 94th Cong., 2d sess. *Report on Criminal Justice Reform Act of 1975*. Committee print, 1974.

Stanga, J. E., Jr., and Farnsworth, D. N. "Seniority and Democratic Reforms in the House of Representatives: Committees and Subcommittees." In L. Rieselbach (ed.), *Legislative Reform*. Lexington, Mass.: Heath, 1978.

Starkie, D. "Policy Changes, Configurations, and Catastrophes." *Policy and Politics*, 1984, *12*, 71–84.

Stengel, R. "More Muscle for Crime Fighters." *Time*, Oct. 29, 1984, p. 4.

Stinchcombe, A. L., and others. *Crime and Punishment—Changing Attitudes in America*. San Francisco: Jossey-Bass, 1980.

Stone, M. "Why Dead on Arrival." *U.S. News and World Report*, Mar. 12, 1984, p. 84.

Sundquist, J. L. *The Decline and Resurgence of Congress*. Washington, D.C.: Brookings, 1981.

Sundquist, J. L. *Constitutional Reform and Effective Government.* Washington, D.C.: Brookings, 1986.

Sundquist, J. L. "Needed: A New Theory for the New Era of Coalition Government in the United States." *Political Science Quarterly,* Winter 1988–89, pp. 613–635.

Tate, D. "House Panel Opens Door to Massive Stopgap Measure." *Congressional Quarterly,* Sept. 22, 1984, p. 2293.

Tate, D. "Congress Loads Up Emergency Funding Bill." *Congressional Quarterly,* Sept. 29, 1984, p. 2357.

Tate, D. "Politics Prods Congress to Clear Money Bill." *Congressional Quarterly,* Oct. 13, 1984, pp. 2616–2619.

Tate, D., Felton, J., and Tovell, P. "Last Minute Appropriations Bill Tripped Up." *Congressional Quarterly,* Oct. 6, 1984, pp. 2417–2421.

Taylor, S. "Senate Approves an Anti-Crime Bill." *New York Times,* Feb. 3, 1984, p. 1.

Taylor, S. "New Crime Act a Vast Change Experts Assert." *New York Times,* Oct. 15, 1984, pp. A-1, B-6.

Thurber, J. A. "Introduction: The Roots of Divided Democracy." In J. A. Thurber (ed.), *Divided Democracy.* Washington, D.C.: Congressional Quarterly Press, 1990, pp. 1–8.

Trott, S. "Implementing Criminal Justice Reform." *Public Administration Review,* Nov. 1985, pp. 795–800.

Tucker, R. *Politics as Leadership.* Columbia: University of Missouri Press, 1981.

United Nations. *Demographic Yearbook 1985.* New York: United Nations, 1987.

U.S. Congress. House. Subcommittee on Criminal Justice, Committee on the Judiciary. *Report on the Recodification of Federal Criminal Law.* 95th Cong., 2nd sess., 1978.

U.S. Congress. House. Committee on the Judiciary. *Report on Criminal Code Revision Act of 1979,* 96th Cong., 2nd sess. Sept. 25, 1980.

U.S. Congress. Senate. Subcommittee on Criminal Laws and Procedures. Committee on the Judiciary. 92nd Cong., 1st sess., Feb. 10, 1971.

U.S. Congress. Senate. Committee on the Judiciary. "Confirmation Hearing on William French Smith, Nominee to Be Attorney General." 97th Cong., 1st sess., Jan. 15, 1981.

U.S. Congress. Senate. Committee on the Judiciary. Transcript, Markup Session, S.1630—Criminal Code Reform Act of 1981, Nov. 18, 1981.

U.S. Department of Justice, *Crime Control Act Bulletin.* Sept. 1985, p. 1.

U.S. Sentencing Commission. *Annual Report.* Washington, D.C., 1990.

Uslaner, E. "Policy Entrepreneurs and Amateur Democrats in the House of Representatives." In L. Rieselbach (ed.), *Legislative Reform.* Lexington, Mass.: Lexington Books, 1978.

Voorhees, T. "Pursuit of a Cause: Lobbying for S.1." *American Bar Association Journal,* Oct. 1976, pp. 1346–1347.

Walker, J. L. "Setting the Agenda in the U.S. Senate: A Theory of Problem Selection." *British Journal of Political Science,* 1977, *7,* 423–445.

"Washington Wire." *Wall Street Journal,* Oct. 26, 1990, p. 1.

Wayne, S. J. *The Legislative Presidency.* New York: Harper & Row, 1978.

Weaver, D. H., Graber, D. A., McCombs, M. E., and Eyal, C. *Media Agenda-Setting in a Presidential Election: Issues, Images, and Interest.* New York: Praeger, 1981.

Weaver, D. H. "Media Agenda-Setting and Public Opinion: Is There a Link?" In R. N. Bostrom (ed.), *Communication Yearbook 8.* Newbury Park, Calif.: Sage, 1984.

Wermiel, S. "Kennedy Pulling Back on Crime Code Bill." *Boston Globe,* Apr. 19, 1976, p. 5.

Wermiel, S. "Kennedy Pushing Criminal Code Plan." *Boston Globe,* May 8, 1976, p. 2.

Wermiel, S. "Persistence Paying Off for Kennedy." *Boston Globe,* Apr. 10, 1977, p. 2.

Werner, L. M. "Of Crime and the Bermuda Triangle." *New York Times,* June 14, 1984, p. 10.

Wilson, J. Q. "The Politics of Regulation." In J. Q. Wilson (ed.), *The Politics of Regulation.* New York: Basic Books, 1980.

Woll, P. *American Bureaucracy.* (2nd ed.) New York: Norton, 1977.

Wooton, G. *Interest Groups: Politics and Policy in America.* Englewood Cliffs, N.J.: Prentice-Hall, 1985.

Wright, G., Rieselbach, L., and Dodd, L. C. (eds.) *Congress and Policy Change.* New York: Agathon, 1986.

Name Index

Subject Index

A

Agenda, congressional, 102–123
American Bar Association, 114, 325
American Bar Association Journal,
161
American Civil Liberties Union,
112, 132, 172, 188, 207, 241;
and bail reform, 205; and Comprehensive Crime Control Act,
297–298; and H.R.10850, 138;
and S.1, 131, 134, 140–142,
147–148, 161
American Newspaper Publishers Association (ANPA), 162
Anti-Crime Act, 283–284
Anti-drug legislation, 3, 76, 303. *See
also* Drug czar
Apprenticeship, 39
Assassination attempt, 197; jury verdict on, 217–220
Attorney General's Task Force on
Violent Crime, 195, 219–220;
recommendations of, 195–197

B

Bail reform, 204–205, 211
Bar of the City of New York, 112
Bowsher v. *Synar et al.,* 336
Brown Commission, 100, 101; and
congressional agenda, 105–123
Bureau of Justice Statistics, 79, 80

C

Cabinet, and legislative process,
60–64
*Can Representative Government Do the
Job?* (Finletter), 6
Capital punishment, Brown Commission on, 117–118. *See also*
Death penalty
Clean Air Act, 56–57; amendments
to, 329–331
Committee system, and legislative
process, 33–35
Committee on the Constitutional
System, 16
Comprehensive Crime Control Act,
230–231, 239; approval of, 294;
effects of, 319–321, 323; and
House, 254–267; implementation
of, 297–301; opportunity for passage of, 274–294. *See also* Criminal law reform
Congress: building consensus in,
151–154; committee system in,
33–35; doubts about, 1–3; election preoccupation in, 41–44; and
interest groups, 46–50; and media, 44–46; norms in, 37–41;
party leadership in, 24–33; policy
leadership in, 64–71; staff role in,
35–37; and strategic opportunity,
269–272, 294–295
Congressional Directory, 45
Congressional Quarterly, 47, 106

365